T0355601

The Middle East

THE MIDDLE EAST

A political history from 395 to the present

Jean-Pierre Filiu

Translated by Andrew Brown

polity

Originally published as *Le Milieu des mondes. Une histoire laïque du Moyen-Orient de 395 à nos jours* © Éditions du Seuil, 2021 and 2022 for the new conclusion

This English edition © Polity Press, 2023

Polity Press
65 Bridge Street
Cambridge CB2 1UR, UK

Polity Press
111 River Street
Hoboken, NJ 07030, USA

ISBN-13: 978-1-5095-5600-7- hardback

A catalogue record for this book is available from the British Library.

Library of Congress Control Number: 2023930960

Typeset in 11.5 on 14 Adobe Garamond
by Fakenham Prepress Solutions, Fakenham, Norfolk NR21 8NL
Printed and bound in Great Britain by CPI Group (UK) Ltd, Croydon

The publisher has used its best endeavours to ensure that the URLs for external websites referred to in this book are correct and active at the time of going to press. However, the publisher has no responsibility for the websites and can make no guarantee that a site will remain live or that the content is or will remain appropriate.

Every effort has been made to trace all copyright holders, but if any have been overlooked the publisher will be pleased to include any necessary credits in any subsequent reprint or edition.

For further information on Polity, visit our website:
politybooks.com

3

Thanks to Diego Filiu for his attentive reading and his sharp gaze.

Tyranny is a land of oblivion. A general imposition of secrecy.
This is also why rebelling against it means emerging from anonymity and moving towards the possibility of a society of memory. It means getting out of jail. It means returning from exile.

Yassin Al-Haj Saleh, 'Syria, land of oblivion', written in hiding in Damascus in January 2013.

No minority will be protected in the future if it is not part of a secular political project.
The non-separation of religious affiliation and the exercise of power is a calamity.
It de facto compromises the notion of citizenship, social cohesion, the coexistence of differences, and the building of a state.

Dominique Eddé, *Le Monde*, 2 April 2021.

Contents

List of maps · viii

Introduction: A secular history · 1

1 Byzantines, Sassanids, and Arabs (395–661) · 11

2 From the Umayyads to the Abbasids (661–945) · 46

3 The era of the two caliphates (945–1193) · 81

4 Sultans and invaders (1193–1501) · 115

5 Ottomans and Safavids (1501–1798) · 147

6 Colonial expansion (1798–1912) · 180

7 Reforms, renaissance, and revolutions (1798–1914) · 207

8 The time of mandates (1914–1949) · 236

9 The Cold War and the Arab–Israeli conflict (1949–1990) · 270

10 The life and death of the American Middle East (1990–2020) · 309

Conclusion: The cradle of crises · 349

Index · 357

List of maps

1.1 The Middle East between Byzantines and Sassanids (395–630)
1.2 The spread of Islam in the Arabian Peninsula (612–632)
2.1 The Umayyad Middle East (661–750)
2.2 Abbasid Iraq (749–945)
3.1 The Middle East of the two caliphates (969–1095)
3.2 The first two Crusades (1095–1149)
4.1 The Middle East from the Ayyubids to the Mamluks (1193–1260)
4.2 The invasion of Timur the Lame (1387–1404)
5.1 The Middle East from 1501 to 1555
5.2 The 1639 border between Ottomans and Safavids
6.1 The Middle East from 1798 to 1810
6.2 The United States at war in Libya (1801–1805)
7.1 The Middle East in 1882
7.2 From the 'Armenian crisis' to genocide (1894–1916)
8.1 The Middle East in 1923
8.2 The formation of Saudi Arabia (1902–1932)
9.1 The Middle East from 1949 to 1971
9.2 The 'Six-Day War' in 1967
10.1 The Middle East in 1990–1991
10.2 The Syrian crisis (2011–2021)

To every chapter there correspond two maps, the one a general map of the Middle East, the other focusing on a specific region and/or conflict.

Cartography: Frédéric Miotto, Légendes cartographie

Introduction
A secular history

Historical reflection does not spontaneously describe its method by stating that it will be adopting a secular approach. But the Middle Eastern terrain is too undermined by theological controversies involving both exclusion and reconciliation for secularism not to be a highly effective practical guideline in this domain. If we reduce this part of the world to its role as merely the cradle of the three monotheisms, we are already ignoring whole swathes of its heritage. This is especially the case since, in the Middle East, 'sacred histories' – what are euphemistically called 'grand narratives' – are not all religious: far from it. There is indeed a 'sacred history' of colonization, a 'sacred history' of Zionism, a 'sacred history' of Arab nationalism and a 'sacred history' of eternal Persia. The symbolic saturation of the Middle Eastern domain makes it important, here even more than elsewhere, to guard against such inclinations to sanctification. Moreover, resorting to narratives that are thus rendered sacred, even when indulged in by well-meaning practitioners, generally leads to disillusioned considerations on the inexpiable nature of the conflicts in the Middle East and on the irreducible alterity of its religious mosaic. It is as if this region and its people were inevitably doomed to war, in all its absurdity.

The rejection of such intellectual abdication has nourished the conception and writing of this book. There is indeed a strong expectation that a study of this area will adopt a *longue durée* perspective to interpret present-day Middle Eastern news that arouses so much interest and passion – but also disquiet and even anxiety. This expresses a genuine demand for meaning which, from the point of view of the historical discipline, calls for the overcoming of the chronological boundaries that exist between specialists of different periods. While adopting a contemporary stance, I have been compelled to stick to this approach, starting with my *Apocalypse in Islam*,[1] inspired by

[1] Jean-Pierre Filiu, *Apocalypse in Islam* (Berkeley: University of California Press, 2011).

1

my appointment as a director of research, up to my *Gaza, a history* and *Le Miroir de Damas* (*The mirror of Damascus*).[2] At Sciences Po (the Paris Institute of Political Studies), from 2017 to 2020, I gave a masters course on the history of the Middle East from 395 onwards. The educational dimension of this teaching was adapted from year to year to meet students' expectations and questions. It is in the same didactic spirit that each of the ten chapters of this work is followed by a summary chronology and bibliographical suggestions for further reading, all inevitably incomplete.[3] A section of twenty maps presents, for each of the chapters, an overview of the Middle East at the beginning of the period concerned, together with a map dedicated to one dimension of regional history, different each time. I have transcribed Arabic names in a way that faithfully reflects their origins while also making the reality of the Middle East accessible to readers.[4]

The choice of 395 as the opening year of this book corresponds to the founding of the Eastern Roman Empire. At this point, the Middle East emerged as a specific entity, freed from external domination, while a Christianity of the East asserted itself, turned towards Byzantium rather than towards Rome. This choice expresses my desire to follow a strictly Middle Eastern dynamic, and not the simple projection onto this region of rivalries between external powers, even if these latter will have their due place, especially in contemporary times. The milestone of 395 also makes it possible to position the Middle East as a pole of state stability and institution-building in the face of a 'West' that was then subject to barbarian invasions and the successive sacks of Rome. It is useful to underline this reversal of perspective in regard to those ages when Christianity in the East, operating outside the clerical hierarchy and sometimes against it, invented the cult of the saints and the monastic vocation that were destined to shape so decisively the 'Christian West'. Moreover, 395, as the year in which a political

[2] Jean-Pierre Filiu, *Gaza, a history* (New York: Oxford University Press, 2014) and *Le Miroir de Damas* (Paris: La Découverte, 2017).
[3] Reference books are mentioned only once, at the end of the chapter to which they appear most relevant, even if they cover a broader period or issue.
[4] I have endeavoured to do the same for English-speaking readers, adopting a pragmatic approach to nomenclature. (Translator's note.)

body was established, is free from the burden attached to the founding dates of the monotheistic calendars, namely 0 and 622. It thus offers a surer opportunity to emancipate ourselves from the symbolic influence of those two year zeros, while acknowledging the importance of one vanished monotheism: Zoroastrianism, the state religion of Sassanid Persia.

In general, the periodization followed in the way the ten chapters are divided up is deliberately counter-intuitive. The first chapter covers the period from 395 to 661, when the first dynasty of Islam was established. Going beyond the lightning speed at which the Qur'anic message spread, it raises another question, just as fruitful: why did the Eastern Roman Empire, even in Anatolia, resist the onslaught of jihad, while Sassanid Persia, everywhere on the offensive at the beginning of the seventh century, was overwhelmed a few decades later? Another example of this deliberate chronological split: the two centuries in which the Crusades took place are not seen as lying at the heart of a continuous development, but are treated in two different chapters, with the rivalry between the caliphates of Baghdad and Cairo dominating one chapter, and the Turco-Mongol invasions dominating the other. One last example: rather than 1453 and the Ottoman capture of Constantinople, so often chosen as the date marking a new era, it is the year 1501 that is highlighted, because this founding year of the Safavid monarchy opens the sequence in which the Persian challenge drove the Ottomans to conquer most of the region.

The Black Sea, the foothills of the Caucasus, and the Caspian Sea define the contours of the Middle East to the north, which, to the south, extends to Upper Egypt and includes the Arabian Peninsula. It is the Sahara and its Libyan desert which represent its (necessarily imprecise) African limits. The region stretches east to Khorasan, the Levant of Persia, whose borders fluctuate over the centuries, sometimes incorporating parts of present-day Afghanistan and Turkmenistan. Such geographical shifts will lead me to mention the western and eastern peripheries of the Middle East as and when needed, even if they cannot occupy the heart of this historical reflection. The Middle East, straddling Asia and Africa, stands out as a crossroads between these two continents, as well as between Asia and Europe. It lies at the nerve centre of two land routes destined to mark their eras: the 'Silk Road' to Central Asia and China;

and the 'Road to India'.[5] It covers just over 7 million square kilometres, including the great deserts of Arabia and Egypt, and represents around 5% of the earth's land surface.

In 395, the Middle East had around 40 million inhabitants, representing between a fifth and a quarter of humanity at the time, while Europe comprised a sixth. Its population was overwhelmingly rural and its two metropolises, each with hundreds of thousands of inhabitants, were the imperial capitals of Constantinople and Ctesiphon. The plague pandemic in the middle of the sixth century, as well as the ravages of the wars between Byzantines and Persians, caused the Middle Eastern population to fall at the beginning of the seventh century to around 30 million people. It stabilized around this level during the next six centuries, before dropping to around 20 million in the middle of the thirteenth century. It hovered around this low-water mark – due, among other things, to the Mongol invasions and the Great Plague – until the division of the region between the Ottoman and Safavid Empires at the beginning of the sixteenth century. The Middle East then regained its population of around 30 million inhabitants, and retained it until the middle of the nineteenth century. But this represented only about 3% of humanity and a sixth of the population of Europe. The demographic explosion of the twentieth century enabled the Middle East to make up for some of this gap. More than 400 million people live in the Middle East today – some 5.5% of humanity, and slightly less than the population of the European Union. The region has two megacities with more than 10 million inhabitants (Cairo and Istanbul), and five agglomerations with more than 5 million (Tehran, Alexandria, Baghdad, Riyadh, and Ankara).

The Middle East was historically organized around the three poles of Egypt, Syria, and Iraq. Since the third millennium BCE, autocratic systems have managed the primordial resource of water: to the west, in the Nile Valley and, to the east, in the Mesopotamia of the Tigris

---

[5] The Middle East formed a barrier to the two Mongol invasions at the end of the Middle Ages, preventing the first invasion from reaching Africa and the second from reaching Europe. As for the 'Mongol peace', it favoured the spread of the plague in the middle of the fourteenth century. The pandemic ravaged the Middle East, then spread to Europe and Africa.

and Euphrates rivers. The power thus centralized around these two hydrographic basins has relied on the human and economic resources of the irrigated areas to resist the threats emanating from the vast desert. On the other hand, the Syria of the geographers, the central territory of the Middle East, comes in a complex variety of environments (coastal plains, the mountain ranges overlooking them, inland valleys, intermediate plateaus, and networks of oasis cities) which nurture a formidable diversity of population and organization. The Syrian space has long been, from the Pharaohs to the Parthians, the stake of the rivalry between the powers established on the present-day territories of Egypt and Iraq. The Eastern Roman Empire controlled Syria and Egypt from Constantinople, but Iraq came under Sassanid Persia, which had also established its capital there, in Ctesiphon. This balance of power gradually gave way under the pressure of the Sassanids, who seized Syria and Egypt at the beginning of the seventh century. It was only briefly restored by the Eastern Roman Empire before being swept away by an unprecedented invasion springing from central Arabia, which until then had remained outside the field of geopolitical struggle in the Middle East.

This was to be the one and only time that the region would be extensively reorganized from the Arabian Peninsula.[6] Islamic power soon left an Arabia traumatized by the civil war between the first caliphs. The dynasty founded by the Umayyads, in Damascus, slipped into the Byzantine mould in order to subjugate Iraq and Egypt, which themselves acted as stepping stones for spectacular expansion. For nearly a millennium, from 661 to 1516, Islamic power was organized around these three poles. The Syria of the Umayyads was supplanted by the Iraq of the Abbasids in 750, before being itself challenged by a competing caliphate, that of the Fatimids, which came from Tunisia to conquer Egypt and consolidate its power there. While Damascus, like Aleppo, is one of the oldest cities in history, Baghdad and Cairo were state capitals founded by triumphant dynasties: the Abbasids founded Baghdad in 762; the Fatimids founded Cairo in 969. The rivalry between these

---

[6] The 'Arab revolt', which started in the Hejaz in 1916, in fact failed to consolidate its 'Arab kingdom' in Damascus. As for Saudi Arabia, despite its fabulous wealth, it has so far proved incapable of occupying a dominant role in the Middle East.

two caliphates favoured Byzantine incursions into Syria, followed by Crusader expeditions. The very laborious process of mobilizing against the Crusades ultimately proved fatal to the Fatimids, with the emergence in 1171 of a Syrian–Egyptian sultanate.

This sultanate, formally subject to Abbasid Iraq under the Ayyubids, emancipated itself from this tutelage under the Mamluks after the devastation of Baghdad by the Mongols in 1258. There followed two and a half centuries of Egyptian hegemony, to which the Ottoman Empire, long turned more towards Europe than towards Asia, put an end. The Middle East again found itself being managed from Constantinople, as under the Eastern Roman Empire. The Ottomans, however, were in a much better position against the Persians than the Byzantines had been, since the border drawn up in 1639 placed Iraq firmly in their domain.[7] It was under the Ottoman Empire that the rivalries between European powers became formalized in a competition for privileges described as 'capitulations', with the opening of consulates in the different *échelles* (commercial stations) *du Levant*. The Italian city states, active on the Mediterranean coast, and Portugal, which was busy in the Persian Gulf, gradually gave way to France and Great Britain. In the nineteenth century, the 'Eastern question' was the great diplomatic affair of a 'concert of nations' which believed, after the Napoleonic adventures, that it had settled the fate of Europe.

London and Paris relied respectively on Constantinople and Cairo before Great Britain supplanted France in Egypt, which it occupied by force of arms in 1882. These two countries agreed to divide up the post-Ottoman Empire: as the so-called 'Sykes–Picot' agreements of 1916 were never applied, it was the international conference in San Remo in 1920 that established the 'mandates' of France and Great Britain in the Middle East. This Franco-British collusion was part of the dynamics of a Middle East where, over and above its own challenges, vocations of power on a global scale were being forged. Conversely, it was at Suez in 1956 – a military victory and a political rout – that the French and the British witnessed the definitive end of their imperial status. This internationalization of the Middle East took

---

[7] This border largely corresponded to that which still separates Iraq from Iran, and which the terrible war of 1980–1988 did not affect.

on a new dimension with the Cold War between the United States and the USSR. The founders of Israel managed to mobilize Eastern and Western support for the Zionist project before unreservedly siding with the Americans in 1967. Conversely, Arab leaders suffered repeated defeats, despite the support of a Soviet power that itself was left at a loss by the antagonisms between its partners. What had comprised the triangle of a regional balance between Egypt, Syria, and Iraq began a slow process of decomposition, against the backdrop of the continuing 'Palestinian question'. It was after enlisting Syria and Egypt into a coalition dedicated to driving Iraq out of Kuwait that, in 1991, the United States laid the post-Soviet foundations of its 'new world order' in the Middle East in 1991.

It would, however, be wrong to see the contemporary history of the Middle East simply as the result of the conflicts that, either directly or by proxy, have led to various external participants confronting one another there. Israeli governments and the Assad regime have proved the ability of local 'clients' to manipulate to their own advantage the great powers mobilized on their side. The Islamic revolution that triumphed in Tehran in 1979 aimed to promote a 'third way' between Washington and Moscow, before reviving, a generation later, the expansionist tendencies of Sassanid Persia. Above all, the local populations have demonstrated that their exclusion from decision-making can lead to uprisings,[8] as in the West Bank and Gaza in 1987 and in 2000, in Iraq in 1991 and in 2004, and in Egypt, Syria, and Yemen in 2011. The crushing of these uprisings has left many 'questions' open: the Palestinian question, the Kurdish question (which cannot be reduced to the 'Iraqi question'), and, more recently, and for a long time to come, the Syrian question. These questions will tragically remain unanswered as long as the myth of a Middle East 'manageable' from the outside prevails, whether this outside takes the form of foreign powers or regimes that have run out of steam because they are cut off from their societies. A century after the division of the region between France and Great Britain, the past three decades of US domination are now, as we watch, coming to an end in a disengagement that involves both confusion and humiliation. The time of foreign hegemons is well

---

[8] '*Intifada*', the Arabic word for 'uprising', has passed into common parlance.

and truly over, despite the desires of dictatorships that wager every-thing on distant protectors in order to deny the aspirations of their peoples.

My decision to write a political history, even in the religious field, means that I have given priority to the processes whereby powers and their areas of domination have been established. This is why I will frequently be referring to borders and battles, not out of any mere fascination with military developments, but because there is always conflict in the Middle East, even today. The significance of war has, moreover, transformed the region into terrible 'bloodlands' at least four times: during the two waves of Mongol invasions in 1256–1261 and 1393–1404; during the First World War; since the Arab Spring of 2011; and indeed since the invasion of Iraq in 2003. The approach thus favoured does not allow for any comprehensive reflection on the societies concerned. As for the actors mentioned, they are practically all male, and women are only mentioned in their roles as wives, with the exception of the Sufi Rabia of Basra, the Sultana Shajar al-Durr and the Nahda, or 'Arab Renaissance' feminists. There is no doubt that a long-term historical reflection carried out from the angle of societies or gender would be fascinating. But that is not the purpose of this book.

The Middle East is literally at the centre of the continental whole made up of Asia, Africa, and Europe. This middle of the world, in many respects the cradle of humanity, is a land of intermixtures and exchanges, both in war and in peace. This geographical centrality nourishes a form of political centrality that in 395 was structured around two of the most powerful empires of the time. It was from the Middle East that the forces radiated which extended their influence in neighbouring areas, an evolution that led to the Islamic expansion of the seventh and eighth centuries. The Byzantine Empire itself drew from Anatolia some of the resources which enabled it to control the Balkans until the eleventh century. This trend was only partially reversed during the two centuries of the cycle of the Crusades, contained along the Levantine coast, while Constantinople again became Byzantine in 1261, half a century after its conquest by the 'Latins'. The two waves of Mongol invasions of 1256–1261 and 1393–1404 meant that the Middle East fell prey to the terror of a destructive set of incursions, but Egypt was untouched. Moreover, once these invaders had departed, the region was left largely to its own devices,[9] with the consolidation of the Ottoman and then Safavid Empires. Islamized Constantinople was for a long time the capital of a power that looked towards Europe rather than Asia, where its presence was mainly designed to block the way to Persian ambitions.

In 1798, the French expedition to Egypt marked the beginning of the era in which colonial powers started to nibble away at the Middle East of Middle Easterners. But it was not until the beginning of the twentieth century that an American admiral conceptualized the 'Middle East' as such as a major factor in world hegemony. Indeed, with the disappearance of the Ottoman Empire, the middle of the world succumbed to the competing ambitions of France and Great Britain. It has now been a century since they divided the region between them, in complete disregard of the aspirations of the peoples concerned – a century of an imperialist diktat that weighs on the destiny of the region not so much because of the imposition of artificial borders as because of the persistent denial of the right to self-determination, a right which was formerly crushed by colonial powers, and is now rejected by ruthless dictatorships. Such regimes can wage war against their own peoples, whether openly or surreptitiously, only with the support, direct or indirect, of foreign powers. This is how the internationalization of Middle Eastern crises often turns into a nightmare for the millions of civilians trapped in these situations. The current decomposition of American domination is leading to an escalation of new forms of interference and thus a proliferation of conflicts: local populations are always the main victims.

The reader will search this book in vain for the leitmotif of any imagined 'clash of civilizations'. The frequent, violent, and sometimes terrible wars in the Middle East have very rarely been between two coherent blocs, in terms of religious or ethnic affiliation. Even the internal polarization of Islam between Sunnis and Shiites took many generations to consolidate, and assumed its modern dimension only in the context of the confrontation between the Ottoman Empire and Safavid Persia. This does not mean, however, that harmony and tolerance

[9] The Mongol dynasty that reigned over Iran and Iraq from 1260 to 1353 marked its integration into the Middle East by converting to Islam in 1295.

were the rule in the Middle East; far from it. But its contradictions are found in more complex forms than the community structures that are today presented as if they can be taken for granted. The construction and evolution of such contradictions will be studied throughout this book, whose chronological ambition requires a rigorous selection of the events and sequences discussed. This secular history is therefore inevitably unfinished, at a time when the women and men of the Middle East are continuing to struggle to win back the right to finally define their own destiny by telling their own stories.

ONE

Byzantines, Sassanids, and Arabs (395–661)

The two centuries during which Byzantine Constantinople and Persian Ctesiphon shared the Middle East between them, from 395 to 602, are too often overlooked. However, they represent a very long period of real and then relative peace from which the entire region benefited, for its greater prosperity. It was in Europe, and not in Asia, that the Eastern Romans fought the 'barbarians', whether they were Lombards, Ostrogoths, or Avars. The Middle East, whose advanced civilization contrasted with the contemporary 'barbarism' of the West, was structured around the coexistence of two imperial theocracies, one Christian and the other Mazdean. They both chose to restrain their aspiration to universality in order to focus on repressing internal dissent. In Late Antiquity, neither Egypt, nor Syria, nor Mesopotamia had any independent existence; Egypt and Syria were absorbed into the Byzantine domain, and Mesopotamia into Persian territory. It was from an area located on the margins of the two dominant empires, and outside their direct influence, that a new power would emerge in Arabia at the beginning of the seventh century; it was destined to reshape the whole of the Middle East.

A political construction

In 325, Constantine, the first of the Christian emperors of Rome, convened and presided over a council with a universal remit, a council that was called 'ecumenical' because of its ambitious scope.[1] This assembly, meeting in Nicaea (the current İznik in Turkey), concluded with the proclamation of Jesus as 'very God of very God, begotten, not made, consubstantial with the Father'. The following year, Helena, mother of Constantine, conveniently discovered various sacred relics in Jerusalem, including a piece of the True Cross. In 330, the emperor set up

[1] *Oikoumené* means 'inhabited land' in Greek.

his capital on the site of ancient Byzantium and baptized it 'New Rome', though the name 'Constantinople', the 'city of Constantine', ultimately prevailed. He thus brought the heart of the empire closer to two of its most prosperous provinces, Syria and Egypt. Constantine thereby rooted his power in the face of the twofold threat of 'barbarian invasions' (on the Danube) and of Sassanid Persia (on the Euphrates). Later references to the 'Christian West' generally forget that this first sovereign of Christianity established the seat of his power astride Europe and Asia, and actually more in the East than in the West.

It was not until 380 and the reign of Theodosius I that Christianity became the empire's official doctrine. It was as much a matter of fighting against paganism as of imposing the Nicene dogma on dissidents who rejected the Trinity. This first schism, referred to as 'Arianism', spread widely among the Goths and Vandals. During his lifetime, Theodosius I paved the way for the joint management of the empire by his two sons, Honorius and Arcadius. But on his death in 395, this theoretical sharing of power quickly led to an actual division between the west and the east of the empire, managed respectively from Ravenna and Constantinople. To the north of the Mediterranean, the dividing line between the two entities would pass between today's Bosnia and Serbia. To the south, it divided the territory of present-day Libya, in the Gulf of Sirte, with Tripolitania to the west and Cyrenaica to the east. So there was nothing 'natural' about the border between the two empires; it was decreed that the Asian territories would belong to the East, but so would some of the European and African imperial domains. The date of 395 was no less crucial in that it constituted, in the literal sense, an autonomous power in the east of the Mediterranean, a power whose prosperity would soon contrast with the decline of the Italian peninsula.

This Eastern Empire was a political rather than a religious construction, since it shared state Christianity with its Western twin brother. Although this empire was described as Byzantine (from the ancient name of Constantinople), it sought to be 'Roman', and its claim to universality was reinforced by its 'Catholic' mission.[2] Latin was its official language, but Greek was the most commonly spoken tongue, while Syriac/Aramaic in Syria and Coptic in Egypt remained so popular that they

---

[2] *Katholikos* means 'universal' in Greek.

achieved liturgical status. Antioch and Alexandria were historically the two main cities, with some 200,000 inhabitants, a population figure that Constantinople soon surpassed after the enlargement of its walls in 413. The Eastern Roman Empire was a pole of stability – especially so after Rome had been sacked by the Visigoths in 410, then by the Vandals in 455, before being besieged and pillaged in the civil war of 472. Indeed, in 476 the imperial insignia were sent from Rome to Constantinople, now the seat of the one and only Roman Empire, that of the East. It is worth recalling this transfer of imperial legitimacy from the West to the East, given the common plaint nowadays that the supposedly incurable crises of the Middle East are an unbearable burden to the West.

The borders of the empire of Constantinople, drawn by decree in the west, were guaranteed in the east on the basis of a lasting balance of forces with Persia. The Sassanids, who had ruled Persia since 224, set up their capital at Ctesiphon on the course of the Tigris, about 30 kilometres south of present-day Baghdad. The Euphrates constituted the western limit of effective control of the Sassanid territory, which a no man's land – namely the desert – separated from the first Roman garrisons. Arab leaders patrolled these intermediate zones, selling their services to the highest bidder and maintaining hostilities at the quite tolerable level of occasional raids. Farther north, the kingdom of Armenia was converted to Christianity at the beginning of the fourth century. Around 387, it was split between a 'Minor Armenia' (one-fifth of its territory), incorporated into the Roman Empire, and a province managed by vassals of the Sassanids, and then annexed by Persia in 428. The division between the Western and Eastern Roman Empires was political; so was this border between the two other empires, the Byzantine and the Persian, each of which prided itself on a state religion. I will discuss the origins of Sassanid theocracy below.

It should be emphasized at this point that the main axis of the Eastern Roman Empire was the road linking Constantinople to Antioch, which continued, via Beroia/Aleppo, towards Palmyra and Damascus. The Levantine coast and Egypt traded more easily with the capital by sea, while Gaza was the outlet for the Arabian caravan routes. Administrative management was centralized in an 'Eastern Praetorium', with a thousand employees in Constantinople. The prefect at the head of this praetorium wielded authority in the Middle East over the provinces of the East

(Antioch), Egypt (Alexandria), Asia (Ephesus), and Pontus (İzmit).[3] In order to avoid the constitution of fiefdoms, the provincial representatives of the various departments obeyed their hierarchy in the capital rather than the local governor. The development of trade was encouraged by monetary stability, itself guaranteed by the corporation of money changers: the solidus of 4.51 grams of almost pure gold[4] would maintain its value and weight for nearly six centuries. There was a major gold mine in central Egypt, halfway between Thebes and the Red Sea. Other goldworking sites were active in Nubia and the Balkans.

The emperor and his Church

The emperor inherited from Rome the rites of access to the throne, namely proclamation by the army, acclamation by the people, and ratification by the Senate. He embodied all of this, but also much more, as God's lieutenant on Earth. His legitimacy as autocrat was directly derived from that of Christ Pantocrator.[5] This was why the dynastic transmission of power, although the most common process, took a long time to impose its strict rules of succession. The imperial liturgy employed, among other things, the colour purple, reserved for the chosen one of God. Given these conditions, the clerical hierarchy were inevitably subject to the emperor. It was for him to convene and preside over the councils: that of Nicaea, which in 325 recognized the three patriarchates of Rome, Antioch, and Alexandria, and that of Chalcedon in 451, which promoted Constantinople and Jerusalem to the rank of patriarchates. It was the emperor who alone appointed the patriarch of Constantinople, admittedly chosen from a list put forward by the synod. Leo I was the first emperor to receive the blessing of the patriarch of Constantinople after his coronation in 457.

The patriarch of the imperial capital more and more openly harboured an ecumenical ambition, one which contradicted the claims of the pope

---

[3] The other three provinces were Thrace, Dacia, and Macedonia, managed from Constantinople, Sofia, and Salonika respectively.

[4] A 'pound' of gold (actually 325 g) was the equivalent of 72 solidi.

[5] *Pantokrator*, 'master of everything' in Greek, has the same root as *autokrator*/ 'autocrat', the master without rival or superior.

in Rome to exercise a universal magisterium. From the Eastern point of view, the pre-eminence of the man who was considered the 'patriarch of Rome' was at best symbolic, while Antioch and Alexandria, even more than Jerusalem, contested the rise to power of Constantinople. According to the so-called principle of 'accommodation', the ecclesiastical hierarchy reproduced the categories of the administrative hierarchy: the cities, basic units of the Roman structure, became the seats of dioceses in charge of this territorial subdivision; their bishops were described as 'suffragans' because they played a part in electing a metropolitan bishop, also called 'metropolitan', who was responsible for a province. The emperor could redraw the map of bishoprics as he wished. He nevertheless respected the inalienable nature of the property of the Church, which had become the second landowner in the empire after the Crown.

Christianity had gained the support of the urban elites, who saw it as the only bulwark of Greco-Roman civilization against the barbarian peril. In 415, Theodosius II banished pagans from the army and the adminis-tration; twenty years later, he ordered the destruction of their temples. Even if such an order was far from being unanimously followed, the Christianization of the populations of the Eastern Empire was profound and conclusive. In the cities it was based on a network of relatively close churches, without any formal attachment to a parish. The celebrations of Sunday Mass and the feasts of saints were preceded by a prayer vigil, which was sometimes accompanied by a procession. The countryside, on the other hand, only very gradually came under the power of the clerical hierarchy. This lack of religious supervision was compensated for by lay people whose level of education, even if elementary, made it possible to perform the weekly office. The faithful also turned to 'holy men' who had chosen to withdraw from the world, alone or in communities. Local pilgrimages developed to their places of seclusion and, after their deaths, to their tombs. The Church chose to acknowledge the 'saints' thus venerated in order to better appropriate their charisma.

Monasticism, or the desire to be one[6] with Christ, emerged in fourth-century Egypt. Its pioneer was the future Saint Anthony, who gave away land and goods to devote himself to an ascetic life in the desert. This demand for piety aroused such enthusiasm that, if only to escape

[6] In Greek *monos*.

it, he subjected himself to ever more demanding ordeals and severe isolation. He is said to have died in 356, over a hundred years old, not far from Thebes. The patriarch of Alexandria published shortly after, in Greek, a hagiography whose immense success and translations into Latin, Syriac, and Coptic fuelled the vocations of many hermits.[7] The temptations that Anthony resisted in the desert, in imitation of Christ, would inspire centuries of Christian art. One of his Egyptian disciples, Pachomius, was less rigorous, preferring to organize retreats in a form of 'common life', the etymology of 'cenobites'. Solitary hermits and monasteries of cenobites, generally for men but also for women, thus structured the monastic field. It was indeed the East that acted as the crucible for these forms of Christian spirituality that were destined to spread far and wide.

In 386, Jerome, one of the Fathers of the Church, established a double monastery in Bethlehem whose female division was managed by Paula, a widow of the Roman nobility. There, in 405, he completed a Latin translation of the Bible from Hebrew, which for a millennium would be referred to as the Vulgate and in 1455 would provide the material for the first printed book. Jerome was also the author of a popular hagiography of Hilarion (291–371), the founder, near his native city of Gaza, of a monastic community. The complex built around the tomb of this saint attracted ever more vocations and pilgrims. A complex of comparable size was then created northwest of Antioch, where Simeon lived until 459 at the top of a column. The transfer of the remains of this 'holy man' to Antioch, then to Constantinople, did not affect the popularity of the pilgrimage to 'Saint Simeon's', as the site of these austerities was called. Finally, at the beginning of the sixth century, a community in the Judean desert attempted a synthesis between hermits and cenobites. This was the *lavra*, with retreats during the week, a shared life on Saturdays and collective celebrations on Sundays. These different ascetics were reference points and models for all of Christianity, extending far beyond the East. Their prestige was commensurate with their distance from the everyday world, but also from the court and its intrigues.

---

[7] This term is derived from the Greek *érémos* ('desert').

Christological controversies

The Church of the East, by the very fact of its multifaceted vitality, was riven by bitter quarrels, which its structural subjection to the Roman Empire only exacerbated. Nestorius, appointed archbishop of Constantinople by Theodosius II in 428, believed that the sovereign's favour allowed him to challenge Cyril, the powerful patriarch of Alexandria. Nestorius refused to accept that Mary was not just the mother of Christ, but also the 'mother of God'; embroiled in the manoeuvrings of the courtly elite, he had failed to gauge the profound popularity of a growing Marian cult. He stuck to his positions at the Council of Ephesus in 431, which stripped him of his titles and repudiated his theses. Nestorius ended his days in exile, in an oasis in Upper Egypt. The 'Nestorian' heresy, relatively confined to the Eastern Empire, flourished in Sassanid Persia, which even encouraged its missionary ambitions to distant China. This was the first time that Christians driven out of the Christian domain by a Christian monarch had found refuge in a part of the Middle East whose ruler was not himself a Christian. This precedent would be followed by a host of others.

Indeed, the disputes over the nature of Christ were far from being settled by the Council of Ephesus: Cyril and his supporters in Alexandria pushed their dogmatic advantage for all it was worth. The Emperor Marcian, who came to the throne in 450, endeavoured the following year to work for appeasement through the Council of Chalcedon. The compromise formula then proposed, and validated by Rome,[8] supported the view that Jesus was both God and man in 'one person and two natures'. But Constantinople, determined to neutralize or even supplant Rome, underestimated the virulence of Eastern sensitivities. A 'Miaphysite' (for 'one nature')[9] resistance mobilized against the new dogma and against the imperial power intent on imposing it. The monks and the faithful of Jerusalem, united in their rejection of Chalcedon, appointed dissident bishops who held the Holy City for twenty months,

---

[8] The 343 bishops gathered in Chalcedon were Eastern, with the exception of two legates from Rome and two 'African' (in fact Tunisian) bishops.

[9] The term 'Monophysite' (for 'a single nature') is now considered too simplistic, and has been abandoned by scholars in favour of 'Miaphysite'.

until the intervention of the imperial army. These Christological controversies were also anchored in the self-assertion of a linguistic identity of a proto-national type, based on the Coptic and Syriac languages.

The Coptic language was so identified with Egypt that its own name came from that country.[10] Its liturgical status contributed to consolidating the individual tendencies of the patriarchate of Alexandria, which raised the standard of revolt under Dioscorus, Cyril's successor. Deposed by the Council of Chalcedon, he was immediately confirmed by the Coptic faithful on the 'seat of Saint Mark', as the patriarchate of Alexandria was called, in reference to the evangelist who stayed there in the first years of the Christian era. Only the fierce repression of the rioting populace allowed a clergy loyal to Constantinople to continue to officiate in Egypt. But this clergy was relatively powerless against the Coptic Church, which was organized in an autocephalous way, i.e. under its own authority. The Coptic patriarch even reactivated the obsolete title of 'pope' for himself, in open provocation against the capitals of the two Roman Empires. In 506, a comparable process led to the establishment of a Church of Armenia, also autocephalous, on the basis of a rejection of the dogma of Chalcedon. Thus, one century after the consolidation of the Christian East into an empire, three Churches – the Nestorian, the Coptic, and the Armenian – had already been formed in opposition to Constantinople.

The break was less brutal in the Levant, even if the spread of Syriac as a liturgical language there fuelled a muted hostility to official doctrine, especially in the countryside. An overt Miaphysite, Severus, managed to accede to the patriarchate of Antioch in 512, but he was driven out six years later by a wave of imperial repression of Christian dissidents. Constantinople was, however, forced to deal with the Arab tribes who protected the borders of the empire against the Persians. It was the intercession of the most powerful of these Arab leaders, who went over to Miaphysitism, that in 542 allowed the appointment of two Miaphysite bishops, one in Bosra, southeast of Damascus, the other in Edessa, the current city of Urfa/Şanlıurfa in Turkey. Jacob Baradaeus became bishop of Edessa, and travelled throughout the region for thirty years to organize the Miaphysite Church of the Syriac rite. It is in his memory that

---

[10] Via the Greek *aiguptios*.

this so-called 'Syriac-Orthodox' Church is sometimes called 'Jacobite'. Autocephalous like the first three schismatic Churches, it is nowadays directed from Syria by a 'patriarch of Antioch and of all the East', a title which four other Christian dignitaries contest.

In order not to get lost in this efflorescence of the Churches of the East, one often ignored fact must be underlined: the overwhelming majority of the faithful of the various Churches were unaware of the substance and the details of the theological controversies which formed the base of each creed or its specific form. It was mainly local solidarity and close ties that, especially in rural areas, underpinned the sense of belonging transmitted from generation to generation of each different group. All those involved naturally decked themselves out in the lustre of orthodoxy to cast out their adversaries and co-religionists into the darkness of heresy. The intervention of the masses, often whipped up by fanatical preachers, inevitably inflamed these quarrels to the point where they sought to eliminate the Other, at least symbolically. Added to this was the determination of the bishops and patriarchs to keep their titles in their respective Churches, despite the fact they had the authority to promote a dogmatic compromise. Over the course of these reshapings of Christianity, Egypt, Syria, and Mesopotamia followed divergent courses: the first with the consolidation of a Coptic national Church; the second with a diversity of Churches which survived both repression, on the one hand, and proselytism, on the other; and the third with a 'Church of Persia', also called the 'Church of the East', Nestorian in inspiration, which relied on the protection of the Sassanids. We will now turn to this Persian side of the Middle East.

The Persians in Mesopotamia

The Sassanid dynasty, which succeeded the Parthians in Persia in 224, established its capital at Ctesiphon. Located on the left bank of the Tigris, connected by canals with the Euphrates, this city faced Seleucia, where the Seleucid monarchs had reigned from 305 to 240 BCE before moving the seat of their power to Antioch. The exceptionally long reign of Shapur II, from 309 to 379, was marked by the intense centralization of Sassanid power. The sovereign took the title of 'king-of-kings' (*shah-an-shah*), which allowed him to generously distribute to his vassals, especially in the border regions, the title of 'king' (*shah*) – a title without much substance. But most of the empire was organized into provinces, each managed by a governor (*marzban*) chosen from among the senior nobility. The state's coffers were filled from the land tax (based on the fertility of the land), the poll tax (from which soldiers, priests and civil servants were exempted), income from the imperial domains and customs duties. This *Eranshahr*, or empire of the Aryans/Iranians, had Pahlavi – also called 'Middle Persian' – as its language of administration and communication.

The cult of Ahura Mazda, the 'Lord of Wisdom', gradually established itself as the state religion. This Mazdaism was also called Zoroastrianism, in that it was thought to link back to the teachings given in ancient Persia by Zoroaster/Zarathustra, a millennium before our era. Its sacred book, the Avesta, was made up of two liturgical sections, one connected to a solemn sacrifice, the other broken down into different ceremonies. The both hereditary and initiatory nature of clerical functions, as well as the current preservation of just part of the Avesta, limit our grasp of this highly ritualized religion. Its interpreters note the way it combines a monotheistic tendency, with the exclusive veneration of Ahura Mazda/ Ormazd, on the one hand, and a dualistic confrontation between the cosmogonic principles of Good and Evil, on the other. The creation of the world by the divine Light of Mazda, itself a manifestation of his Wisdom, led to the maintenance of a sacred fire in dedicated temples by priests called, in Persian, 'magi' or 'masters of the fire'. The religious hierarchs, designated under the name of *mowbed*, were led by a '*mowbed-of-mowbeds*' (*mowbedan-mowbed*), a 'high-priest-of-high-priests', with a title modelled on that of the king-of-kings in power.[11]

The cycle of recurrent wars between Persians and Romans subsided in 387, with the partition of Armenia, in an outcome that was very favourable to the Sassanids. The peace that was formally concluded between Arcadius, the first emperor of the East, and Yazdegerd, who ascended to the Persian throne in 399, proved to be lasting and solid. This peace entrusted Yazdegerd with symbolic guardianship of the son

[11] It was only in the fifth century that this religious hierarchy was formalized in an authentic national religion. The Avesta was not written down until the following century, in a canonical text, under the aegis of the Sassanid rulers.

of Arcadius, the future emperor Theodosius II, to whom the Sassanid sovereign sent one of his closest advisers. A significant web of inter-communications developed between the two empires, with Upper Mesopotamia as the hub. Two neighbouring places, Roman Dara and Persian Nisibis/Nusaybin, shared the same Syriac language. The Christian population in Persia, hitherto perceived, and often treated, as a fifth column of the Romans, could not fail to benefit from this peace between the empires. A regional council met at Ctesiphon in 410, placed under the formal authority of the king-of-kings. The Nestorian schism, which took the form of a definitive break in 431, found refuge in Sassanid land, far from the wrath of the Eastern patriarchates. The same happened for the theological school of Edessa, whose members fled after their condemnation by Constantinople in 489 and joined Nisibis. The Church of Persia was organized in an autocephalous mode, with at its head a 'catholicos', i.e. one who had a universal remit. The Sassanid administration rewarded the loyalty of the Nestorians by opening up the roads of Central Asia to their preaching.

Ctesiphon was one of the densest metropolises of its time; like Constantinople, it had several hundred thousand inhabitants. It now extended over both banks of the Tigris, with commercial districts where the crops from surrounding Mesopotamia and the goods transported by caravans were traded. Canals and dykes were carefully maintained to contain the unruly river. The Sassanid capital was profoundly diverse; Syriac was the most widely spoken language there, and the Mazdean elite, despite its undisputed domination, was less numerous than the Christian and Jewish notables. The imperial palace, richly decorated with brightly painted marble and stucco, included private apartments, a religious complex, and a huge audience hall.[12] The Sassanid sovereign spent every winter in Ctesiphon, but liked to summer in Hamadan, 500 kilometres to the northeast, both to escape the intense Mesopotamian summer heat and to be closer to the heart of his Persian domain. Only the first circle of advisers accompanied the king-of-kings in this migration, while the imperial bureaucracy continued to manage the state from the capital.

Apart from an outbreak of violence in 421–422, peace prevailed between Romans and Persians throughout the fifth century. An elaborate protocol

---

[12] The arch of this hall, called Tāq Kasrā and standing 37 metres high, still exists.

governed relations between the two courts; each had a body specialized in the language and culture of the other. The two emperors tacitly agreed to share the world, or what they perceived as such, without denying the incompatible nature of their two state religions. Thus secured on their western border, the Sassanids were able to develop a maritime power in the Persian Gulf, and from there to the Indian Ocean. Their silver *direm* (drachma)[13] was as well accepted as the gold solidus minted by Constantinople, and it bore, on one side, the portrait of the king-of-kings and, on the other, a Mazdean altar dedicated to the sacred fire. The Romans sometimes agreed to contribute to the Sassanid fortifications in the Caucasus, in order to stem the barbarian incursions that posed a threat for both empires. It was the refusal to make this contribution in 502 that led to the opening of hostilities by the Persians. The conflict with Constantinople ended in 506 with a return to the status quo for fifteen years.

Justinian and Chosroes

The destiny of the two empires changed with the accession of Justinian to the throne of Constantinople in 527, followed four years later by that of Chosroes/Khosrow I as ruler in Ctesiphon. The two men's long decades in power profoundly transformed the Middle East. Justinian inherited from his predecessor a situation of conflict with the Sassanids. He was victorious at Dara in 530, but his forces were defeated the following year at Callinicum, present-day Raqqa. The Persians, however, decided not to exploit their advantage and the general trend was towards appeasement. The accession to the throne of Khosrow I allowed Justinian to seal with him, in 532, an 'eternal peace', based on Roman financing of the Persian defences in the Caucasus. This peace came at a time when a popular insurrection had shaken Constantinople before being bloodily suppressed. Once order was restored in the capital, Justinian launched a formidable campaign westwards to restore the unity of Roman Christianity based on his own person. The term 'Byzantine', which historians would not use for another millennium to designate the Eastern Roman Empire, now appeared all the more relevant as Greek gradually supplanted Latin as the language of administration.

---

[13] Its weight then fluctuated between 3.65 g and 3.94 g.

Within about twenty years, from 533 to 554, Justinian managed to conquer 'Africa' (current Tunisia and Algeria), Illyria, Italy, and southern Spain. The Byzantine Empire thus controlled two-thirds of the circumference of the western Mediterranean. But this expansion came at the cost of the devastation of Italy, and it was an exorbitant drain on imperial finances. Khosrow I, meanwhile, took advantage of the 'eternal peace' with his western neighbour to reorganize his tax system and his military institutions. He permanently enlisted penniless nobles in an increasingly professionalized cavalry. He allocated land in border zones in return for a commitment to mobilize in their defence. He divided his empire into four military regions, each being under a general (*spahbad*) placed under his supreme command. The palace of Ctesiphon, at the pinnacle of the Sassanid hierarchy, was itself located in this region of Lower Mesopotamia, the most prosperous of the Persian provinces.

In 540, Khosrow I realized that Justinian was too absorbed in the Mediterranean to oppose an attack on Antioch. The 'City of God', the *Theopolis* of Byzantine rhetoric, with its walls weakened by a recent earthquake, resisted the Persian siege machines for only a few days. Not only was Antioch pillaged and burned, but thousands of its craftsmen were deported to Ctesiphon. They were assigned to the construction of a new city to the glory of the conqueror, called *Weh-Antiok-Khusro*, the 'Best Antioch of Khosrow', built on the plan of the devastated city. The king-of-kings, however, failed to seize Edessa in 544. Hostilities continued, interspersed with truces and tribute payments, and mainly affected the territory of present-day Georgia. The Christian communities of the Sassanid Empire were regularly the victims of this sometimes open and always festering conflict. A peace, theoretically meant to last for fifty years, was finally concluded in 561.

As for Justinian, he simultaneously pursued his campaign in the west and a considerable activity as legislator and builder. The code and the collections of laws that bear his name profoundly restructured administration, justice, and trade in the Eastern Empire. In 537, with great pomp, Justinian inaugurated the new basilica of Hagia Sophia[14]

---

[14] Hagia Sophia means 'Divine Wisdom' and not 'Saint Sophia', hence the preservation of the name Ayasofya during its Islamization (see below, p. 137, note 19).

in Constantinople, five years after the original building of Constantine had been burned down in a riot. The emperor, whose glory was exalted by the monument's unprecedented proportions and the gleaming gold of its mosaics, proclaimed on this occasion that he had 'surpassed' Solomon. Moreover, his code systematized discrimination against the Jewish community; in particular it banned the establishment of new synagogues. Justinian ordered the construction of eight monasteries in Jerusalem, two of which were dedicated to pilgrims from the Transcaucasia, where he was waging war against the Sassanids. In his treaties with the Persians, he included clauses guaranteeing the freedom of worship of local churches. He also built a fortified monastery at the foot of Mount Sinai, at the site associated with the Burning Bush.[15] But his demolition of the pagan sanctuary of Philae, the most important in Egypt, was not enough to win the Coptic Church over to him. He also failed, despite deploying gestures of tolerance interspersed with crackdowns on dogmatic dissidents, to gain the support of the Syriac-Orthodox Church.

The name of Justinian is associated with the plague that raged in the Middle East from 541 to 544. The pandemic broke out in Egypt, where sources of the time claimed it had originated in Ethiopia, a provenance still much debated today. It is certain, on the other hand, that this 'Plague of Justinian' spread through the Eastern Roman Empire long before it was reported in the Persian domains. The Sassanid troops, victorious in Antioch, are said to have accelerated their withdrawal from Byzantine territory to escape the contagion. Constantinople probably lost half of its population, with dead bodies being piled up in mass graves that were filled with terrifying speed. Justinian himself was not spared the plague, though he ended up surviving it. The splendour that we now associate with the magnificence of Hagia Sophia was thus, for contemporaries, tarnished twice over: a few years earlier by the bloody suppression of the insurrection in the capital and, a few years later, by the carnage of the epidemic. The plague also fed into an apocalyptic mindset that combined the ravages of the plague and the destruction of Antioch. The main wave of the Plague of Justinian would be followed,

---

[15] This monastery took the name of Saint Catherine in the ninth century.

for two long centuries, by recurrent epidemics every ten or twenty years.[16]

The death of Justinian in 565 left Khosrow I with a free hand at the strategic crossroads between the Red Sea and the Indian Ocean. Yemen had passed into the orbit of Byzantium since the seizure of power in Sanaa, around 535, by an ambitious general, Abraha, who until then had been a vassal of Ethiopia. During his three decades of reign, Abraha, a faithful ally of Justinian, fostered the Christian pilgrimage to Sanaa and embarked on several campaigns in the rest of Arabia. The quarrels over the succession of Abraha's son that started in around 570 now favoured the intervention of the Sassanids. Not far from the current port of Aden, their fleet landed a contingent summoned by an Arab pretender to the throne. A tributary power of Persia was established for the first time in Sanaa. Yemen's desire for independence was crushed at the end of the sixth century, with the South Arabian territory becoming incorporated as a Sassanid province. Thus, it was in this peripheral theatre of operations that a new balance of power started to emerge in the Middle East.

The ebbs and flows of Persian power

The grandiose edifice bequeathed by Justinian did not take long to crumble shortly after his death, in particular due to the reconquest of Italy by the Lombards. The resumption of hostilities by Constantinople against the Persians, in 572, in a fraught context in Armenia, did not result in any lasting advantage for either side, except for the Sassanid conquest of the stronghold of Dara. Khosrow I died in 579 without having restored peace, and the conflict dragged on, to the great misfortune of the border populations. General Maurice, commander of the Byzantine armies against the Persians, himself became emperor in 582. The military stalemate had an ever greater impact on Sassanid politics, where it also increased the power of the generals. The rebellion of the commander of the Armenian front led to a palace revolution in Ctesiphon in 590, when

---

[16] The Middle East was hit hard between 627, with a huge death toll in Ctesiphon, and 639, the year of the 'Plague of Imwas' (Emmaus), which decimated the Muslim conquerors of Syria. The last wave, also very deadly, lasted from 740 to 750.

the successor of Khosrow I was assassinated and his son, the grandson of Khosrow I, was proclaimed king-of-kings under the name of Khosrow II.

The young Sassanid monarch was soon obliged to flee his capital, which was occupied by the rebels. He took refuge in the Byzantine garrison of Circesium, near present-day Deir ez-Zor, on the middle course of the Euphrates. Khosrow II offered to restore Dara to Maurice and release him from any form of tribute in return for his support against the rebels. But the leader of the Persian insurgents was simultaneously tempting Maurice with even more attractive proposals. The Byzantine sovereign waited several months before deciding, in 591, in favour of dynastic legitimacy on the Sassanid throne. He thereupon placed part of his army, as well as various Armenian protégés, at the service of Khosrow II, who was soon restored to power in Ctesiphon, even though his authority was only gradually restored throughout the Persian territory. The lavishly celebrated peace between the two empires did not erase the debt that Khosrow II felt he had contracted to Maurice during his exile. The king-of-kings thus treated his Christian subjects with greater respect, while opening his court to Greek thinkers and artists. This improvement in relations between Persians and Byzantines lasted for only a few years, however, due to various power struggles, this time in Constantinople.

In 602, General Phocas, head of the Balkan army, mutinied against Maurice, who was assassinated with his five sons, and proclaimed himself emperor. Khosrow II, shocked by the murder of his saviour, condemned this coup and threw the ambassador sent by Phocas into prison. The war resumed with Persian victories at Edessa and Dara in 604. The Sassanid assaults sowed disorder within the Byzantine general staff. A rebellion from Carthage seized Egypt in 609, soon overthrew Phocas, who was summarily executed, and installed General Heraclius in his place. The overtures of peace from the new emperor[17] were swept aside by Khosrow II, whose expansion into Byzantine territory seemed irresistible: he seized Antioch in 611, Damascus in 613, and Jerusalem the following year. The relics exhumed in 326 by Saint Helena, the mother of the Emperor Constantine, including the True Cross, were transported in triumph from the Holy City to Ctesiphon. Khosrow II gave himself a few years to absorb these territorial gains before returning to the offensive. The

[17] Heraclius took the Greek title of *basileus* ('king'), instead of the Roman *augustus*.

capture of Gaza in 618 opened the way to Egypt, the breadbasket of the Byzantine Empire. With the fall of Alexandria in 619, the Sassanids could pose as the heirs of the Achaemenid conquerors, the only Persians to have advanced so far into Africa, a millennium earlier.

The apogee of Khosrow II was, however, of much shorter duration than that of his ancient predecessors. Heraclius, at the head of the Byzantine armies, showed an impressive fighting spirit in Armenia and Anatolia. In 623, he broke the Persian defences in Azerbaijan and destroyed the most venerated of the Mazdean sanctuaries there, at Takht-e Soleyman.[18] The desecration of the sacred fire was revenge for the Sassanid capture of the True Cross in Jerusalem. Khosrow II reacted to the sacrilege by deciding to strike at the Byzantines in their very capital. But even though the siege of Constantinople by the Sassanids in the summer of 626 was coordinated with a barbarian advance, that of the Avars, from Europe, the Byzantine navy repelled the attackers, inflicting heavy losses on them. Heraclius then forged his own reverse alliance, much more formidable than that between the Persians and the Avars: in 627, the Turco-Mongol hordes encamped north of the Caucasus broke through the Sassanid fortifications and joined the Byzantine army in Georgia. Heraclius won a resounding victory over the Persians at Nineveh, present-day Mosul. He moved towards Ctesiphon, where Khosrow II, like his father before him, was assassinated by a military conspiracy which brought his own son to the throne.

The peace that was concluded in 628 forced the Sassanids to return all the conquered territories to the Byzantines, as well as to pay them tribute. As Persia descended into factional strife and civil war, the True Cross was solemnly exalted in Hagia Sophia in Constantinople in 629, before returning in great splendour to Jerusalem the following year. This symbolic restoration was accompanied by a revival of the persecutions carried out in the name of Byzantine 'orthodoxy' against the Copts in Egypt and the Miaphysites in the Levant, followed by the decision to impose baptism on all the Jews of the empire. So Heraclius could as legitimately believe in the solidity of his triumph as Khosrow II had believed

---

[18] The sanctuary, called the 'Fire of the Stallion' (*Adur Gushnasp*), was associated with the Mazdean caste of warriors, and therefore with its supreme representative, the king-of-kings.

in his own, a decade earlier, during the Persian occupation of Egypt. The reality was that the two empires that had divided the Middle East since 395 were exhausted by a quarter-century of devastating conflict. The standoff between Byzantines and Sassanids, which swung in favour first of the latter, then of the former, ended with the illusion of a return to the status quo. The two imperial structures, however, were at the end of their tether and they would prove incapable of containing the rise of a profoundly original power, emerging from central Arabia to impose itself throughout the region.

The pre-Islamic Arab kingdoms

In the second century CE, the geographer Ptolemy distinguished between three very distinct 'Arab' spaces: from north to south, they were 'Arabia Petraea', which corresponded to the Roman province of Arabia, established in 106 with its capital Bosra, in the south of present-day Syria (the adjective 'Petraea' was derived from Petra, the historic home of the Nabataean kingdom, long flourishing and independent but by now absorbed into the imperial domains); 'Arabia Deserta', an immense territory with a very small population, where the domestication of the dromedary made caravan exchanges possible but also facilitated raids by nomadic tribes (two of the main cities in the region of the Hejaz, the coast of the Red Sea, were Yathrib/Medina and Mecca); and 'Arabia Felix', associated since Antiquity with the fabulous kingdoms of Yemen and unified, at the end of the third century, under the authority of the Himyarites, who themselves converted to Judaism a century later. (It was by the camel route that crossed the Hejaz to Gaza, as well as through the Red Sea ports, that spices and other rare products from Yemen were transported to the Mediterranean.)

This classic description of the three Arabias (Petraea, Deserta, and Felix) needs to be fleshed out with the gradual emergence, farther east, of an Arab kingdom, a vassal of the Sassanid Empire. The capital of this kingdom was located on the right bank of the Euphrates, at Al-Hirah, less than 200 kilometres south of Ctesiphon. Here, the Arab family of the Lakhmids[19] organized the transmission of power in a hereditary

---

[19] They are also known as the Nasrids.

mode. Imru al-Qays, who died in 332 after a long reign, was described in the posthumous inscription on his tomb, written in archaic Arabic, as 'king [*malik*] of all the Arabs'. This claim naturally involved only 'all the Arabs' subject to Persian power. It nevertheless revealed a substantial authority, one that the Lakhmids would even mobilize during the power struggles in Ctesiphon, imposing their favourite on the Sassanid throne in 420. At its stage of greatest expansion, the Lakhmid domain extended over much of the southern shore of the Persian Gulf. The prosperous city of Al-Hirah hosted a large Christian community, attached to the Nestorian rite of the Church of Persia. However, the Lakhmid rulers did not convert to Christianity until much later, in 580.

The Eastern Roman Empire did not initially have, in its *limes* (defensive frontier) in the Syrian desert, a support as solid as that which the Lakhmid dynasty represented for Persia. It was not until the beginning of the sixth century that an alliance was forged between Constantinople and the powerful Arab family of the Ghassanids,[20] who, though Christian, were committed to the Miaphysite sect. For Justinian to carry out his expansion projects in the Mediterranean, he absolutely needed peace to be guaranteed on the eastern borders of the empire. For this purpose, in 529, he decided to promote the Ghassanid chief Al-Harith/Arethas to the rank of phylarch, or 'commander of the tribes'. A Ghassanid sovereign subject to Constantinople could now be set up to counter the Lakhmid king dependent on Ctesiphon. Harith led a devastating offensive on Persian territory in 541, in retaliation for the Byzantine humiliation in Antioch. Harith was powerful enough to successfully plead the Miaphysite cause in Constantinople and obtain the ordination of two Miaphysite bishops. Harith even obtained from Justinian, in 563, the privilege of organizing his own succession, effective upon his death in 569, so that the crown would pass to his son Mondhir/Alamoundaros.

However, relations between Mondhir and Justin II, in power in Constantinople from 565 to 578, deteriorated very quickly, against a backdrop of accusations of treason and Christological quarrels. The Ghassanids withdrew from the Byzantine alliance in 572, leaving the Sassanids and Lakhmids to operate without resistance in this strategic

---

[20] They are also known as the Jafnids.

area. The reconciliation between Byzantines and Ghassanids was not sealed until three years later, with oaths exchanged at the tomb of Saint Sergius, at Resafa, on the middle course of the Euphrates. Mondhir gave pledges of his loyalty by attacking the capital of the Lakhmid capital, Al-Hirah, whose wealth he plundered, sparing only its churches. This meant that he was treated with all the more respect in Constantinople, where, in 580, he received a royal crown from the hands of the Emperor Tiberius. This consecration remained short-lived because the death of Tiberius in 582 revived the disputes between supporters of Byzantine orthodoxy and the Miaphysite Arabs. Mondhir was exiled to Sicily, where he was soon joined by his son, who had in vain raised the Arab tribes in an attempt to free him. Unlike the Lakhmids, a firm pillar of Sassanid power for three centuries, the Ghassanids exercised a similar function for the Byzantines for only a few decades.

The Ghassanid court, located at the foot of the Golan Heights, would not have the brilliance or splendour of the court of Al-Hirah either, even though the arts were honoured in both Arab dynasties. Literary compositions thrived in this privileged environment and spread to the Hejaz via the caravan routes. They here encountered the enthusiasm of the Bedouin populations for oratorical contests, where confrontations between champions sometimes replaced armed duels. Arab poets were especially respected the more they were associated with the heroes whose exploits and loves they celebrated. Their works, transmitted and enriched by word of mouth, are known only through anthologies published in the eighth century, whose richness testifies to the sophistication of this largely oral culture. Thus, the myth of a language emerging fully armed with the revelation of the Qur'an is belied by the refined reality of an Arabic poetry forged over the centuries. In the same spirit, the saga of the early days of Islam has too often overshadowed the heritage of the Arab kingdoms which were located for so long on the Syrian–Iraqi borders, without being the mere auxiliaries of the two great empires of the time.

Pagan Mecca

Far from the opulence of the capitals of Mesopotamia, Yemen, and Syria, all linked to a strong power, the caravan cities of the Hejaz experienced only a very relative prosperity, most often safeguarded by vigilant autonomy. They represented veritable islets in the ocean of the Arabian Desert, where the hostile environment imposed its law on inhabitants whose very survival was regularly threatened. Individuals could not exist outside the group that defined and defended them. Families were attached to different clans whose coalition constituted a tribe claiming to descend from an eponymous ancestor. The leader, respectfully called 'sheikh',[21] was often voted into power by the group, which could decide to replace him if he failed in his mission to promote the general interest. Each life was so precious that the clan had to commit to requesting blood money in the event of the death or injury of one of its members. The deterrent nature of this threat of vendetta helped to curb the violence of a stateless society. The temptation for nomads to steal from the peasants was also curbed by the agreements to promote the 'fraternity' (in real terms protection) concluded between the Bedouins and the sedentary populace. A person's word had supreme value, and honour was the most celebrated of virtues.

Christianity was deeply rooted in Yemen, with a major centre in Najran, but here it was torn between a Nestorianism loyal to the Church of Persia and a Miaphysite belief shared with the kingdom of Ethiopia. Judaism, also widespread in Yemen, was more able than Christianity to take root in central Arabia, especially in Medina, where Jewish communities played a leading role in local agriculture. As for Mazdaism, despite the inclinations of the Sassanid authorities, it remained confined to the southern shore of the Persian Gulf. The majority of the inhabitants of Arabia Deserta cared little about religion and mainly sought to win the favours of a supernatural 'master' or 'mistress',[22] whose outbursts of wrath were dreaded. The three 'mistresses' (Al-Lat or Allat, 'the Goddess', Al-Uzza, 'the Mighty One', and Al-Manat, 'Destiny') were the object of a very popular cult in the Hejaz. Allah, in Arabic 'the God', designated both one of the pagan deities thus revered and the unique God of the Christians. The belief in spirits, or jinns, also fed into a long-lasting superstition, with various amulets to ward off the evil eye. Divination

---

[21] The original meaning of sheikh, 'elder' or 'old man', evolved into 'wise', even 'master'. The term *sayyed*, 'sire', is more emphatic.

[22] 'Master' is *rabb*; the feminine form is *rabba*.

interpreted the direction of arrows, the flight of birds, and the progress of camels.

Mecca was the most important pilgrimage (*hajj*) site in Arabia. The Kaaba, literally 'the Cube', is said to house, embedded in its eastern corner, 'the Black Stone', a basalt rock on which multiple legends have been based. The southern corner of the building also contains 'the Yemeni corner', pointing in the direction of Yemen. Where each pagan tribe venerated its own sacred stone, taking it along when necessary in its wanderings, Mecca thus brought together the baetyls (sacred stones) permanently displayed for the devotion of pilgrims. The Kaaba was close to the Zamzam Well, itself associated with immemorial rites. Rebuilt many times over the centuries, the building would have housed a pantheon of idols, including the goddess Manaf and the god Hubal, whose intercession was sought by soothsayers. The faithful would walk around the Kaaba several times, touching the sacred stones, before going to sacrifice animals on the nearby hill of Marwa. As well as this properly Meccan *hajj*, there was, near the city, an autumnal gathering to pray for rain. The religious calendar coincided each year with important fairs, against a backdrop of banquets, libations, and rejoicings. In modern times, militant Islam would strive to erase all traces of this pagan splendour, in an extreme case of archaeology of destruction rather than of preservation.

The Quraysh tribe took control of Mecca towards the end of the fifth century, on the initiative of its chief Qusai, who shared out among his followers the different tasks involved in accompanying the pilgrimage (collection of taxes, planning of rituals, ensuring a supply of water and food). The inviolable character of the sanctuary (*haram*)[23] allowed the Quraysh to pose as mediators between the different tribes of Arabia, which could not fail to promote the attractions of the Mecca *hajj*. Located halfway between Arabia Felix and its Mediterranean outlet of Gaza, the city was also connected by caravans to Al-Hirah, the gateway to Mesopotamia, and to the Persian Gulf. Neither the Byzantines nor the Sassanids ever took it, and the Yemeni expedition launched against it around 570 failed. Meccan prosperity was not, however, equitably distributed among all the Quraysh: Hashim, one of Qussay's

---

[23] *Haram* refers in Arabic to the notion of the forbidden, and thus to the 'sacred'.

grandchildren, was forced to pay homage to his own nephew Umayya, who monopolized the most prestigious and most remunerative functions of the *hajj* for his so-called 'Umayyad' line. Hashim and his 'Hashemite' descendants, including his son Abd al-Muttalib, were obliged to be satisfied with the very modest task of supplying water to the pilgrims. It should be emphasized that this account is based only on late compilations of oral transmissions. This is not enough to invalidate them as such, but it in no way protects them, as for the biography of Muhammad,[24] from the reconstructions of religious apologias.

Muhammad the Messenger

Muhammad, son of Abdullah, grandson of Abd al-Muttalib,[25] was born around 570 into a Hashemite family in Mecca. He lost his father very early on, and then his mother; so his paternal uncle Abu Talib, a fervent pagan devoted to the worship of the goddess Manaf,[26] took charge of his education. Muhammad is said as a teenager to have joined the caravans chartered by his uncle, immersing himself in the picturesque legends and prophecies disseminated by Jews and Christians. Everyone was in no doubt about the punishment that would strike 'Rome' – the Rome of the Romans, punished for having destroyed the Jewish temple in Jerusalem, but also the Constantinople of the Byzantines, punished for having persecuted Nestorians and Miaphysites. What is more certain is that Muhammad, as an adult, was in charge of his own caravans, and married to a wealthy widow from Mecca. The resumption of the war between Persians and Byzantines encouraged apocalyptic ruminations,

[24] The first biography (*sira*) of Muhammad was written more than a century after his death, by Ibn Ishaq. Only in the year 170 had the first of the 'evangelical harmonies' attempted to reconcile the discrepancies between the Gospels in the accounts of the life of Jesus.
[25] In Arabic, Muhammad ibn Abdullah ibn Abd al-Muttalib (ibn/ben means 'son of'). More generally, the designation by paternal ancestry remained in force until the adoption of 'modern' surnames in the nineteenth and twentieth centuries.
[26] Islamic literature prefers to use diplomatic language about the Prophet's uncle by using his *kunya*, a respectful appellation where Abu ('father of') is followed by the name of the eldest son (Abu Talib, 'father of Talib'), rather than his name Abd Manaf, literally 'worshipper of Manaf'.

especially as the Arab pillars of each of the two empires collapsed: after the fragmentation of the Ghassanids, the Lakhmid sovereign was executed in 602 by order of Khosrow II, having been deluded by his expansionist ambitions. In these times of trouble and ruin, several preachers in central Arabia advocated the supremacy of a single deity; they included Musaylima, who proscribed the consumption of alcohol and pork in the name of the 'Merciful' (*Rahman*).

At the age of about forty, Muhammad began to preach a rigorous monotheism in Mecca. According to him, 'there is no God [Allah] but God', an act of faith which involves a commitment of submission (the literal meaning of 'Islam') to the designs of the Most High. This almighty God expressed himself through the mouth of Muhammad, with this revelation taking the form of a recitation (in Arabic *Qur'an*). The Meccan aristocracy, led by the Umayyads, feared that this subversive message would threaten the whole economic system of pilgrimages. It persecuted the first converts, forcing a small group of them to take refuge in Ethiopia. For a long time, Muhammad was protected because he belonged to the dominant tribe of the Quraysh. His uncle, while remaining a staunch pagan, also granted him the protection of the entire Hashemite clan. But the death of Abu Talib in 619 led to the isolation of Muhammad, now forced to depend on the generosity of his neighbours rather than of his relatives. The situation gradually became untenable and Muhammad decided to join the nucleus of his supporters established in the oasis of Medina, 400 kilometres farther north.

This Hijra (or Hegira) occurred in 622 and marks the founding event of the Islamic calendar. Muhammad broke away from tribal solidarity, and promoted in its stead the community of the faithful, the *ummah*, literally the 'motherhood'. The suras, i.e. the chapters of the Qur'an, revealed to him in Medina accuse the Meccans of having perverted the monotheistic nature of the Kaaba: it was Adam himself, according to the Qur'an, who found the Black Stone, and Abraham, the ancestor of the Arabs, who deposited it in Mecca. The veneration of the three mistresses, Al-Lat, Al-Uzza, and Al-Manat, was now caricatured as the sacrilegious adoration of the 'daughters of Allah'.[27] As for Jesus, he was indeed born of

---

[27] The association (*shirk*) of idols with the one God is one of the worst sins denounced in the Qur'an.

Mary/Maryam, who was miraculously a virgin; but he could not be the 'son of God' and it was only his double who was crucified in his place. Muhammad's claim to draw on the prophets of Judaism, and therefore of Christianity, was a challenge for the Jewish population of Medina. The Hijra was transfigured into the Muslim equivalent of the Exodus of Moses. The dispute worsened when Muhammad claimed to be the 'Messenger of God' and the 'Seal of the Prophets'.[28] The crisis broke out in 624 with the expulsion of one of the Jewish tribes (soon followed by others) and the reorientation of the direction of Muslim prayer (*qibla*) to Mecca, when it had hitherto been offered in the direction of Jerusalem.

It was also in 624 that the Muslims won their first victory in Badr against the Meccans, led by Abu Sufyan, the leader of the Umayyads. The latter took their revenge the following year in Uhud. The pagan coalition that gathered in 627 around Medina nevertheless failed to seize the city, protected as it was by a trench that broke the momentum of the enemy cavalry. The idea for this trench was attributed to 'Salman the Persian',[29] probably the son of a Mazdean priest, who converted to Islam in Medina. As soon as the Meccans withdrew, Muhammad turned against the last of the Jewish tribes in the oasis, whose men he ordered to be massacred. Now the undisputed master of Medina, he decided to enter into talks with Abu Sufyan. He brushed aside the objections of the fiery Ali, who was his cousin, his son-in-law,[30] and one of his favourite scribes. Muhammad could count on the unconditional support of Abu Bakr and Omar, two early Muslims who later became his fathers-in-law.[31] Thanks to the truce concluded in 628, he obtained the right to make the pilgrimage to Mecca, sword in sheath, accompanied by hundreds of unarmed partisans.

The manoeuvring of the Muslim leader of Medina was crowned with success: the shock of his return, however temporary, to his native city

---

[28] Jesus, Issa in Arabic, is thus the penultimate prophet of this cycle, initiated by Adam and concluded by Muhammad.

[29] Salman al-Farsi in Arabic, Salman Pak in Persian (*pak* means 'pure' in Persian). His mausoleum was revered at the site of Ctesiphon, the Sassanid capital.

[30] Ali was indeed the son of Abu Talib and the husband of Fatima, daughter of Muhammad; she would be Ali's only wife.

[31] Abu Bakr was the father of Aisha and Omar was the father of Hafsa, both married to Muhammad.

accelerated defections in the Quraysh camp. This time, Muhammad felt powerful enough to break the truce and, in 630, he laid siege to Mecca. In order to avert a very probable defeat, Abu Safyan decided to convert the Umayyads to Islam and to open the doors of Mecca. Muhammad entered the Holy City at the head of his troops, as both victor and peacemaker. He tore down the idols of the Kaaba so that only Allah could be worshipped there. This was the *Fath*, literally the 'Opening' – in fact the Victory, or even the Conquest. Shortly after, the Muslims, whose ranks were swollen by Meccan rallies, defeated the tribes traditionally hostile to the Quraysh at Hunayn. Muhammad's successes coincided with the organization by Heraclius, in Jerusalem, of the solemn return of the True Cross, at a time when Persia had collapsed into civil war. Returning to Medina, the Messenger of God received a delegation of Christians from Najran, to whom he offered his protection in exchange for tribute.

Muhammad's last campaign, when he commanded a contingent of unprecedented magnitude, took him to Tabuk, 600 kilometres north of Medina. This deployment of force was enough to bring over to Islam, without a fight, several Arab leaders from the edges of the Byzantine Empire, in particular the kinglet of the current Israeli port of Eilat. Returning from this expedition, Muhammad reportedly said: 'Here we are, back from the minor jihad so we can now embark on the major jihad.' This quotation has hitherto underpinned the distinction between 'minor jihad', of a military nature, and 'major jihad', of a spiritual nature, as well as the superiority of the latter over the former. In any case, jihad is not one of the five pillars of Islam, namely the profession of faith, prayer, almsgiving, fasting during the month of Ramadan,[32] and the pilgrimage to Mecca. Muhammad, a political, religious, and military leader, also asserted himself as the master of time: he abolished the intercalary month which made it possible to adjust the lunar year by the solar calendar; he thus made the lunar calculation, with the Hijra for founding date, the only valid one. The *hajj* to Mecca and its surroundings, freed

---

[32] Ramadan, the ninth month of the Islamic calendar, is associated with the advent of the Qur'anic revelation. It ends with the 'Feast for the Breaking of the Fast' (*Eid al-Fitr*), also known as the 'Little Feast' (*Eid al-Saghir*).

from the cycle of the seasons,[33] was accomplished in 632 by Muhammad, who fixed the rites over several days; he was followed by a crowd of the faithful. The Muslims who nowadays converge each year on Mecca in their millions strive to observe the prescriptions of what they call the 'Farewell Pilgrimage'. Indeed, shortly after performing this founding *hajj*, the prophet of Islam returned to Medina, where, struck down by illness, he died and was buried.

The first two caliphs

In the absence of any political testament left by Muhammad, but also in the absence of a male heir,[34] the Muslim leaders appointed a 'successor' – the literal meaning of 'caliph' – according to the traditional process of giving tribal allegiance to the best of the notables. Omar, who for a while was the favourite, successfully backed the designation of Abu Bakr. Ali took advantage of his legitimacy as son-in-law and cousin of the Prophet to refuse to take the oath to Abu Bakr. But his muted opposition was quickly overwhelmed by the existential threat that rose against nascent Islam: many freshly converted Arab tribes considered that the death of Muhammad freed them from their commitment, especially when Musaylima relaunched his claims to the prophetic magisterium. Abu Bakr entrusted Khalid ibn al-Walid, the former head of the Meccan cavalry, with the command of the Muslim reconquest in these 'wars of apostasy' (*ridda*). The uprising was crushed, with appalling massacres. The pagan presence, which Muhammad had tolerated outside Mecca and Medina, was fought throughout Muslim territory. The immense peril faced by Islam immediately after the death of its prophet played a significant role in the now absolute prohibition of apostasy. This prohibition remains in force today, punishing with death any denial by a Muslim of his or her faith. Thus, a period unfamiliar with the idea of freedom of conscience bequeathed this disastrous heritage until our

[33] The month of pilgrimage (*dhu al-hijj*a) is the twelfth and last month in the Islamic calendar. The tenth day of this month corresponds to the 'Feast of Sacrifice' (*Eid al-Adha*), also known as the 'Great Festival' (*Eid al-Kabir*), marked by the sacrifice of a sheep, in memory of Abraham's actions. The pilgrimage to Mecca, if performed outside this consecrated period, is called *umrah*, not *hajj*.

[34] Muhammad's sons all died in infancy.

own time, when this freedom has been legitimately erected as one of the fundamental rights of the human person.

Once the Arabian Peninsula had been pacified and converted, expansion by armed jihad seemed the surest way to channel the violence of the tribes under the sole banner of Islam. Khalid ibn al-Walid launched an assault on Mesopotamia, before coming to the aid of two sons of Abu Sufyan, Yazid and Mu'awiya, in their Syrian campaign. Abu Bakr, who died after two years in power, was replaced by Omar, the first caliph to bear the title of 'Commander of the Faithful'. It was under his leadership that the Muslims triumphed in quick succession, in 636–637, first over the Byzantine army on the course of the Yarmuk, then over the Persian troops at Al-Qadisiyyah, on the left bank of the Euphrates. The Sassanid sovereign had to evacuate his capital, Ctesiphon, which was soon looted by the Muslims,[35] who were occupying Mesopotamia. The Battle of Nahavand, fought around 642, opened up the Iranian plateau to the conquerors; a new Sassanid defeat, this time at Isfahan, made their expansion irreversible. The Byzantines, after a short-lived counter-offensive in Homs, preferred to abandon Syria and retreat to the foothills of the Taurus. As for Egypt, it passed into the hands of the Muslims between 640 and 642; they set up a capital at Fustat, on the right bank of the Nile. The different districts of the new city were divided between the Arab tribes who participated in the conquest. This same garrison-city system was applied in Mesopotamia, with the foundation of Kufa, on the banks of the Euphrates, and Basra, at the confluence of the two rivers.

The ravages of the wars that had just been fought between the Persians and the Byzantines largely explain the rapidity of Islamic progress, accelerated by the collapse of the Arab buffer zone which had so long protected the two empires. The relative tolerance of the conquerors towards the 'People of the Book', i.e. Christians and Jews, whose protection was guaranteed on the payment of a tribute (*jizya*),[36] also facilitated accommodation, if not outright support. The Nestorians of the Church of Persia, and even more the Miaphysites of Egypt and Syria,

---

[35] The most beautiful item from the imperial palace of Ctesiphon, a sumptuous carpet measuring 27 square metres, called the 'Garden of Khosrow', was divided between the winners.

[36] The *jizya* is mentioned in the ninth sura of the Qur'an.

were happy to see the Byzantine Empire driven back to the northwest of the Middle East. They sometimes even recovered churches that had been confiscated from them by order of Constantinople. Muslim leaders were less willing to grant the status of People of the Book to the Mazdeans, because the Avesta, their sacred 'book', did not belong to the Judeo-Christian heritage which Islam sought to follow. So they viewed the disciples of Zarathustra as idolatrous 'magi' – in their eyes, the Persian equivalent of sorcerers. Forced conversions of Mazdeans were all the more frequent as their places of worship were often demolished or transformed into mosques. Admittedly, the sanctuary of the sacred fire at Takht-e Soleyman, ransacked by the Byzantines in 623, then restored by the Sassanids, remained active during the first three centuries of Islam.[37] But this was in striking contrast to Syria, where archaeologists even speak of 'invisible conquest', in the absence of any traces of systematic destruction. While Damascus soon flourished under the banner of Islam, Ctesiphon would never recover from the plunder inflicted by the invaders in 637.

The Great Discord

After the death of Omar, assassinated by a resentful slave in 644, Osman succeeded him as caliph. The son of a cousin of Abu Sufyan, he was one of the few Umayyads to have converted to Islam very early on.[38] However, it was a cruel paradox to see the family that had so fiercely fought Muhammad gaining supreme power so quickly. Osman consolidated immense territorial conquests: in 649, he launched an expedition against Cyprus, and forced it to pay tribute; he occupied Azerbaijan and the foothills of the Caucasus; he expelled the last of the Sassanid monarchs, who was killed in 651 in Merv, in what is now Turkmenistan. The caliph endeavoured to impose a single version of the Qur'an in 653;

---

[37] The migration to Gujarat of Mazdeans fleeing persecution with their priests, from the eighth century onwards, would give rise to the current Indian community of the Parsis. Zoroastrianism is now officially recognized by the Islamic Republic of Iran, with a deputy representing this community in Parliament.

[38] Osman was the husband of two of Muhammad's daughters; one, Ruqayya, married during Muhammad's lifetime, and the other, Umm Kulthum, after his death.

tensions had already been aroused by the contradictory transcriptions of the prophetic revelation, themselves the fruit of inevitably complex oral transmissions.[39] But it was the increasingly insolent pomp of the court of Medina and the shameless nepotism of the Umayyads that stirred up trouble in the garrison towns of the jihad, in Egypt and Mesopotamia. Mu'awiya, the son of Abu Sufyan who governed Syria, was unable to protect Osman from the uprisings in Fustat, Kufa, and Basra. In 656, the insurgents converged from the east and the west to besiege Medina. In their vengeful rage, they put the caliph to death and desecrated his remains. The consequences of this sacrilege continue to weigh on internal disputes among Muslims to this day, even though it would take a long time for these differences to structure specific forms of Islam.

It was in this troubled context that Ali, so long a candidate for the 'succession' of Muhammad, finally acceded to the caliphate. But, far from being an undisputed 'Commander of the Faithful', he was immediately subjected to vile accusations from the Umayyads. Uniting around Mu'awiya, Osman's relatives demanded the punishment of his assassins, a punishment which could alone, in their eyes, clear Ali of the suspicion of complicity. The new caliph dithered; a new revolt against him was led by Aisha, Muhammad's favourite wife. Ali managed to stifle the challenge from Aisha's supporters in Iraq, but he seemed increasingly incapable of curbing the scourge of civil war, the dreaded 'Discord' (*Fitna*) between Muslims. The five years of Ali's caliphate are also referred to as the 'Great Discord': the gap widened between loyalist Iraq and Umayyad Syria, each raising an army in the name of their own vision of Islam and the champion who was needed to embody it.

The clash occurred in 657, on the border between Syria and Iraq, on the right bank of the Euphrates, at Siffin, not far from present-day Raqqa. After weeks of fighting, Mu'awiya took advantage of the exhaustion of both sides and convinced Ali to accept arbitration. The caliph agreed that the legitimacy of his power be called into question; this provoked the dissidence of the Kharijites, literally the 'leavers', who were opposed to the very principle of arbitration. Satisfied to have thus

---

[39] The 114 suras of the Qur'an are listed in order of more or less decreasing length, and not according to the sequence of their revelation over some two decades (sura 96 is often considered the first to have been revealed).

divided the opposing party, Mu'awiya dragged out the arbitration over more than a year of endless discussions. Ali exhausted his credit in such talks – he no longer appeared as the supreme leader of all Muslims, but as the leader of a faction, of a party (*shi'a*), hence the term 'Shiites' now attached to those who follow him. The caliph also had to suppress the Kharijite dissidence, resorting to killings for which the Kharijites took revenge in 661 by assassinating Ali himself, at Kufa. The death of Ali removed the hindrance that Muhammad's relations had imposed on the ambitions of the Umayyads. Mu'awiya proclaimed himself caliph, instituted a dynastic succession, and set up his capital in Damascus, far from the intrigues and vendettas of Medina.

An obscure 'golden age'

Over the period since 395 covered in this chapter, the Middle East was, for more than two centuries, divided between two empires ruled from Constantinople and Ctesiphon. The Byzantine Empire controlled Syria and Egypt, while Mesopotamia, seat of the Sassanid capital, extended its domination far beyond present-day Iran towards the Caucasus in the north and Central Asia in the east. This division of the Middle East was relatively stable, with the conflicts that sometimes broke out in Armenia and Upper Mesopotamia being generally confined to these border areas. The Persians, no doubt because of the proximity of their capital, rapidly attached great importance to the reliability of their Arab allies, the Lakhmids, while it took the Byzantines until the sixth century to match the power of the Ghassanids. The schisms tearing Eastern Christianity apart revealingly tended to follow regional borders: the Church of Persia, of Nestorian inspiration, dominated in Sassanid Mesopotamia, while the Miaphysite questioning of Byzantine dogma allowed the Copts of Egypt to constitute a proto-national Church, and a Syriac Church to develop in the Levant.

From 602 onwards, the Sassanid offensive penetrated deeply into Byzantine territory, with the occupation of Syria, then of Egypt, and even the siege of Constantinople. The restoration by the Byzantines of their eastern borders around 630 came at the time when Muhammad had managed to federate in the Hejaz a power freed from its internal quarrels and bearing a universalist message. The rapid expansion of

Muslim territory soon covered the whole of the Middle East, with the exception of most of present-day Turkey. However, from 656 onwards, Medina, the capital of this nascent empire, was shaken by a civil war which ended, five years later, with the transfer of the centre of power to Damascus. This 'exit from Arabia', a generation after an Arab prophet had preached his new religion to Arabs there in Arabic, was impressively rapid. In fact, this was the first and last time that a power from Arabia succeeded in reshaping the Middle East. The Umayyad victory, on the other hand, inaugurated a period of six centuries in which Arab caliphs would dominate the region from bases in Syria, Iraq, or Egypt.

Those people who nowadays wax nostalgic for imperial Christianity or early Islam have a hard time finding evidence for their fantasies in historical reality. The idealized 'golden age' was in fact a cycle of confrontations and splits, of persecutions inflicted by Christians on other Christians, of exactions perpetrated by Muslims against other Muslims. Constantinople's desire to impose a doctrine that was both 'Catholic' and 'Orthodox' threw the Nestorians back into the Sassanid fold and the Miaphysites into internal resistance. The very principle of autocephalous Churches lay in the self-assertion of a specific identity at the expense of the proclaimed unity of believers around the Byzantine throne. As for the first four caliphs, although Islamic tradition describes them collectively as 'rightly guided' (*rashidun*), three died violently, two of them at the hands of Muslim assassins. And the Arab conquerors, barely launched out of the Hejaz, were quick to identify themselves either with Syria or with Iraq, in order to tear each other apart. These contradictions are neither aberrant nor marginal, but constitutive of the very fabric of these crucial events that shaped both Christianity and Islam. The Middle East is steeped in such contradictions, the religious justifications for which cannot hide the deeply political dynamic underlying them.

Chronology

395–408	Arcadius, first Eastern Roman emperor.
399	Peace between Romans and Persians.
405	Completion of the Vulgate by Saint Jerome in Bethlehem.
410	Sack of Rome by the Visigoths.
431	Council of Ephesus and Nestorian schism.
451	Council of Chalcedon and Miaphysite dispute.
457	Blessing of Leo I by the patriarch of Constantinople.
459	Death of Saint Simeon, called the Stylite.
476	End of the Western Roman Empire.
502–506	Limited war between Romans and Persians.
506	Independence of the Church of Armenia from Constantinople.
525	Ethiopian Expedition to Yemen.
527–565	Justinian I, Eastern Roman emperor.
531–579	Khosrow I, Sassanid king-of-kings.
535–565	Abraha, Abyssinian ruler of Yemen.
537	Consecration of Hagia Sophia in Constantinople.
542	Plague epidemic in Constantinople.
573–591	Dara in Persian hands.
Around 575	Persian intervention in Yemen.
591–602	Peace between Byzantines and Persians.
591–628	Khosrow II, Sassanid king-of-kings.
610–641	Heraclius, Eastern Roman emperor.
Around 612	Beginning of the preaching of Muhammad in Mecca.
614	Sassanid conquest of Jerusalem.
622	Hijra of Muhammad from Mecca to Medina.
624	First Muslim victory at Badr.
625	Muslim defeat by the Meccans at Uhud.
627	'Battle of the Trench' in Medina.
628	Peace treaty between Byzantines and Persians.
630	Islamic conquest (*Fath*) of Mecca.
632	Death of Muhammad; Abu Bakr appointed caliph.
634–644	Omar Ibn al-Khattab, the 'caliph of jihad'.
636	Muslim victory against the Byzantines on the Yarmuk.
637	Muslim victory against the Sassanids at Al-Qadisiyyah.

640–642	Islamic conquest of Egypt.
644–656	Osman Ibn Affan, third caliph, assassinated in Medina.
651	Death of the last Sassanid in Merv.
656–661	Ali, fourth and last 'rightly guided' caliph.

Further reading

Anthony, Sean W., *Muhammad and the empires of faith* (Berkeley: University of California Press, 2020).

Bonner, Michael, *Jihad in Islamic history: doctrines and practices* (Princeton, NJ: Princeton University Press, 2008).

Decker, Michael, *The Sassanian Empire at war* (Yardley, PA: Westholme, 2021).

Donner, Fred, *Muhammad and the believers: at the origins of Islam* (Cambridge, MA: Harvard University Press, 2010).

Luttwak, Edward, *The grand strategy of the Byzantine Empire* (Cambridge, MA: Harvard University Press, 2009).

Menze, Volker, *Justinian and the making of the Syrian Orthodox Church* (New York: Oxford University Press, 2008).

Oman, Charles W. C., *The Byzantine Empire* (Yardley, PA: Westholme, 2009).

Rodinson, Maxime, *Muhammad*, translated by Anne Carter (New York: New York Review Books Classics, 2020).

Stephenson, Paul, *New Rome: the empire in the East* (Cambridge, MA: Harvard University Press, 2022).

Wood, Philip, *We have no king but Christ: Christian political thought in Greater Syria on the eve of the Arab conquest* (New York: Oxford University Press, 2010).

TWO

From the Umayyads to the Abbasids
(661–945)

The Umayyads unified the Middle East under their authority and in the name of an Islamic community (*ummah*) reconciled with itself after five years of civil war. The rise of what had been the most fiercely pagan Meccan clan triumphed over the claims of the late Prophet's family. This dispossession of the heirs of Muhammad was reinforced by the transfer of the seat of power from Medina to Damascus, which stripped Arabia of its political pre-eminence. Mu'awiya granted a general amnesty in 661, in return for the acknowledgement of his caliphate by Hassan, Ali's eldest son, and his so-called 'Shiite' supporters. The heart of the Umayyad Empire was Syria, abandoned by the Byzantine aristocracy, whose rites and palaces were now taken over by the new Muslim masters. The construction of mosque-cathedrals and the institution of the Friday sermon (*khutbah*), delivered from the pulpit (*minbar*) in the name of the caliph, were part of this Islamic recycling of Byzantine pomp. But where the sovereign of Constantinople imposed his authority as God's lieutenant on earth, the Commander of the Faithful took care to ensure that his legitimacy was rooted in this world. In 678, Mu'awiya organized a ceremony of allegiance of the great leaders of Islam to his son Yazid, who succeeded him to the caliphate on his death two years later.

A diverse and contested empire

Gathered under a Muslim power, the Umayyad Middle East was, however, only partly Islamized: a majority of the population, especially in Syria, remained Christian, even if the discriminatory taxation against the People of the Book constituted in the long run a powerful spur to conversion; the relic of John the Baptist, a prophet of Islam under the name of Yahya, attracted Muslim and Christian faithful to a sacred space in Damascus that they shared for a long time; and Mu'awiya relied on senior Christian

46

officials, among others, to administer his empire. The permanence, in an Islamized form, of Byzantine practices of power reinforced the persistent significance of Christians in the elite as well as in the population. It was only in the Arabian Peninsula that, ending the protection granted to the Christians of Yemen by Muhammad, a process of systematic Islamization was undertaken – admittedly prior to the Umayyads and nourished by the vengeful dynamic of the wars of apostasy.[1] In general, conversion, despite the Prophet's injunctions, was not enough to ensure full equality: the new Muslims had to join an Arab clan, and their inferior status was expressed by their designation as *mawali*, i.e. 'clients' or even 'servants'.[2] Contrary to the clichés sometimes in vogue today, it is therefore incorrect to assert that the Middle East suddenly became both Arab and Muslim in the seventh century: in this group, which had a very strong Christian component, the Arab conquerors constituted only a small minority, and the Arabization of the populations, especially in urban areas, was not always synonymous with Islamization.

Arab domination took different forms in Syria, Egypt, and Iraq. Bilad al-Sham, designating both Damascus and Syria in the broad sense, was divided into four *ajnad* (the plural of *jund*), military districts whose respective capitals were Damascus, Homs, Lod (for 'Palestine', extending to the deserts of Arabia and Sinai), and Tiberias (for 'Jordan', this province covering Galilee and the coast of Tyre). The Muslim invaders often took the place of the Byzantine owners of latifundia to collect the income from their lands, whose farmers continued to work there. In Egypt, however, the garrison town of Fustat, on the current site of Old Cairo, was the centre of attraction for significant immigration from the Arabian Peninsula and the Nile Valley. This hybrid situation was reflected in the coexistence of tax procedures either inherited from the Byzantine era or brought in by the new regime. In Iraq, the Arab fighters who moved into the cities of Kufa and Basra lived off the farmed income of the surrounding provinces, the social hierarchy corresponding to the different waves of settlement, with the most recent immigrants being the least noble. As for the Iranian countryside and borderlands, they long

---

[1] See above, p. 37. It should be noted that the Umayyad marginalization of Yemen favoured the maintenance of a Jewish community there.

[2] *Mawali* is the plural of *mawla*.

remained in the hands of Sassanid governors who remained in office, subject to the payment of an annual tribute. Again contrary to certain current stereotypes, the Umayyad Empire was a far more empirical than ideological construction, and this empiricism guaranteed its solidity. And the contradictions with which it was riven, as in the caliphate of Medina before it, fundamentally set the factions of Islam against one other.

Thus Yazid, upon his accession to the caliphate in 680 (an accession that had, however, been long prepared by Mu'awiya), was challenged by Hussein, son of Ali and brother of Hassan, who had died ten years earlier. Hussein endorsed Ali's claims to the establishment of a caliphate which would thus be Shiite rather than Umayyad. Following the example of his father, he thought that Kufa, and more generally Iraq, could provide a base for this revolutionary movement. However, only an escort of unconditional supporters accompanied him when he was encircled by the Umayyad army at a place called Karbala, north of Kufa. Hussein and his family were massacred, and the head of Ali's son was carried off as a trophy to Damascus. It was exhibited there in public, to the greater shame of the Shiites, in the same great mosque where the head of John the Baptist/ Yahya was hidden from the sight of the faithful so as to be better revered. It would take centuries for Shia piety to overcome the shock of this sacrilege; Ali and his son Hussein were venerated at the Iraqi site of their martyrdom and their mausoleum (Najaf for Ali, Karbala for Hussein). The painful fervour of martyrdom exalted the figure of Hussein, abandoned by all to his executioners. For the time being, the defeated Shiites fell back on the divine vengeance that a hidden vigilante, the Mahdi (the 'Rightly Guided'), would one day exercise against the Umayyads.

The considerable importance of this founding crime in the subsequent structuring of Islam cannot conceal the fact that, in the eyes of his contemporaries, Hussein's sedition appeared limited and even marginal. Much more formidable was the other challenge to Caliph Yazid in 680, this time emerging from Arabia, and launched by Ibn Zubayr, grandson of Abu Bakr, the first caliph of Islam. The rebels challenged the Umayyads for the right of hereditary transmission of a power which, according to them, should go to the best among the descendants of Muhammad's companions. The contingent dispatched from Damascus stifled the sedition in Medina, but failed to seize Mecca, where Ibn Zubayr, proclaimed caliph by his supporters in 683, would last nearly ten years. Dissidence was fuelled by the vagaries of the Umayyad succession: Mu'awiya II, who became caliph on the death of his father Yazid in 683, himself died after a few months, bringing to the throne one of his distant cousins, Marwan I.[3] The armies of the two competing caliphs clashed on the outskirts of Damascus in 684, a battle that turned largely to the advantage of the Umayyads, despite their numerical inferiority. This conflict led to a profound recomposition of tribal allegiances, each side identifying – often in defiance of real genealogy – with the 'Yemenis', the Kalb (in the case of the Umayyads), and with the 'Arabs of the North', the Qays (in the case of the supporters of Ibn Zubayr). The siege of Mecca by loyalist troops in 692 was accompanied by major destruction, including in the Kaaba, which was hit by catapult fire. It ended with the execution of Ibn Zubayr and the crushing of his dissent, which signalled the submission of Arabia to the power of Damascus; victors and vanquished, aware of the sacrilegious nature of their confrontation in the very heart of Mecca, took care not to keep his memory alive.

Abd al-Malik and his successors

Caliph Abd al-Malik,[4] the son of Marwan I, in power from 685 to 705, was in many respects the most important of the Umayyad rulers. Shortly before finally regaining control of Mecca, he completed the construction in Jerusalem of the sumptuous 'Dome of the Rock', improperly called the 'Mosque of Omar' in reference to the caliph who conquered Palestine. This monument was not, however, dedicated to Friday prayers: it was meant to celebrate the mystical encounter between Muhammad and Abraham, while the myth developed of an Abraham who was the ancestor of the Arabs through his first son Isma'il. Just as Qur'anic revelation purports to close the cycle of prophecy, the Dome of the Rock Islamizes the site where, according to a widely held interpretation of Genesis, Abraham was ready to sacrifice his second son Isaac. This

---

[3] The numbering of sovereigns has no meaning in Islam, where paternal filiation (ibn/ben, 'son of') prevails. They are retained here for clarity of presentation and in conformity with current historiography, as was done above for the Sassanid rulers Khosrow I and Khosrow II.

[4] 'Abdullah' means 'worshipper of God', a title that is varied for each of the ninety-nine names attributed to God, including 'Al-Malik', 'the King/Lord'.

sacred space also corresponds, in Jewish piety, to 'Temple Mount', sacked twice by the Babylonians and then by the Romans. Finally, the grandiose mosaic inscriptions mention Jesus but deny his divine uniqueness and humanity, in sovereign denial of Christian dogma. The Arab Empire definitively proclaimed itself Muslim, even though the majority of its population was still not converted.

This symbolic consecration came with a proactive Arabization of the Umayyad administration, where Greek, Coptic, and Pahlavi continued to be used. Arabization itself went hand in hand with an increase in taxation and a centralizing pressure which provoked regionalist reactions and localized uprisings. The establishment of Syrian settlers in the heart of rebellious areas, particularly in Iraq, was part of this great imperial process. The embryo of a professional army, with ranks and salaries, aimed to replace the mass levies that fuelled expansion through jihad. The homogenization of the manuscripts of the Qur'an on the basis of the vulgate fixed a generation earlier was completed by the methodical destruction of the 'dissident' copies.[5] Where the Byzantines favoured gold coins and the Sassanids silver coins, Abd al-Malik instituted bimetallism, with the gold dinar/denarius and the silver dirham/drachma.[6] The few coins minted in the name of the 'caliph of God' reveal a theocratic temptation of the Byzantine rather than Islamic type.

In any case, such claims no longer applied under the reign of Abd al-Malik's four sons and nephew, who succeeded him on the Umayyad throne. The first of them, Walid, in power from 705 to 715, was distinguished by his activity as a builder, establishing the 'Umayyad mosque' in Damascus, which now devoted the relics of John the Baptist/Yahya solely to Muslim worship; the mosque of Medina, whose courtyard housed the tomb of Muhammad in its eastern corner; and the Al-Aqsa Mosque, which completed the Dome of the Rock in Jerusalem in a 'Noble Sanctuary (Haram al-Sharif)', destined to become the third holiest place in Islam, after the enclosure of the Kaaba in Mecca and the Prophet's Mosque in Medina. Caliph Walid continued the campaigns of expansion of an empire that already extended from Morocco to Central Asia, cracking down on

[5] The Shiites long accused the Umayyads of having 'falsified' a Qur'an whose original text had, they said, been favourable to Ali.
[6] The dinar weighed 4.25 g of gold and the dirham 2.97 g of silver.

commanders deemed too independent. Thus Musa Ibn Nusayr, despite being responsible for the conquest in 711 of most of the Iberian Peninsula, Islamized under the name of Al-Andalus, fell out of favour. The short reign of Caliph Sulayman, from 715 to 717, was marked by the construction of the second Umayyad mosque, this time in Aleppo, alongside the Cathedral of Saint Helena, who was still venerated. Sulayman, a former governor of Palestine, founded the city of Ramla, where he established the capital of this province, which until then had been ruled from Lod. He devoted himself above all to a fierce campaign against the Byzantines, besieging Constantinople in vain by land and sea for a long year. In a final gesture of defiance, Sulayman was buried in Dabiq, north of Aleppo, where he gathered his armies before invading Byzantine territory.

Caliph Omar,[7] nephew and son-in-law of Abd al-Malik, remained in power from 717 to 720. As pious as he was learned, Omar was credited with one of the first compilations of the deeds and sayings of Muhammad, designated under the generic term of 'hadith'. He suspended military expeditions, starting with the siege of Constantinople, in order to better focus on internal challenges to the empire. The most serious was the discrimination against non-Arab converts, the *mawali*, a discrimination which they deeply resented. Omar's reign was too brief to resolve this dispute, but this has not prevented an exceptional aura from surrounding this caliph up until now.[8] The expansionist policy, interrupted by Omar, was taken up with energy by his successors Yazid II (720–724) and Hisham (724–743), both sons of Abd al-Malik. A century after the death of the Prophet of Islam, the Umayyad domain reached its maximum extension, from the Narbonne area in the west to the Indus valley in the east. This immense territory was structured by a postal network on horseback, highly efficient for the time, with supply relays and even caravanserai (*khan*) at each stage. Alongside Kufa for Iraq, Fustat for Egypt, and Medina for Arabia, Mosul asserted itself as the centre of Umayyad power for Upper Mesopotamia and Armenia. Caliph Hisham ordered the construction of palace complexes in the Jordan Valley, in

[7] He is known as Omar Ibn Abd al-Aziz to distinguish him from Omar Ibn al-Khattab, the second caliph of Islam.

[8] Some Muslims, indeed, see him as the fifth and last of the 'rightly guided' caliphs, after the first four caliphs of Islam.

the Palmyra desert, and in his stronghold of Resafa, on the middle course of the Euphrates.⁹ The refinement of these 'desert castles' was the counterpart, in terms of courtly art, of the splendour of the Umayyad mosques of Damascus and Aleppo.

The Abbasid revolution

The Umayyad regime entered a period of crisis during the end of Hisham's reign, a crisis aggravated on his death in 743 by power struggles which saw four caliphs succeed each other in less than two years. Marwan II won the throne in 744 only by trusting unreservedly the so-called 'Northern' Arab tribes, the Qays, at the expense of the so-called 'Yemeni' clans. Although the real ancestries of each group were debatable, the Arab leaders of Syria had organized themselves for half a century around this North/South divide. Abd al-Malik and his successors had been wise enough to co-opt both sets of tribes in order to preserve internal peace. However, Marwan II made the doubtless fatal mistake of leaving Damascus to settle in Harran, in Upper Mesopotamia; here, he was admittedly protected by his followers among the Qays, but in the long term he was isolated from his other subjects. At the same time, the exhaustion of the dynamic of expansion by jihad dried up the resources of the Umayyad Empire, maintained on its borders masses of soldiers embittered by repeated defeats, and fuelled increasingly violent internal revolts in Egypt and the Maghreb.

The most serious threat nevertheless came from the *mawali*, the non-Arab converts who no longer tolerated their second-class status, notably in tax matters, vis-à-vis Muslims of Arab stock. The revolt was particularly virulent in Khorasan, the territory that today would cover the province of the same name in eastern Iran, as well as western Afghanistan and southern Turkmenistan. It was in this area, the far east of Islam, that a Persian agitator of genius, Abu Muslim, produced revolutionary and egalitarian propaganda that soon had tremendous success among the *mawali*. He then gained the support of the Shiite militants for a restoration of the descendants of Ali, militants whom the crushing of a

⁹ From the sixth century onwards, Resafa, where the tomb of Saint Sergius was located, attracted many of the then Christianized Arabs (see above, p. 30).

recent revolt in Khorasan had left relatively powerless. Abu Muslim also recruited from among the ranks of the Arab contingents of the border garrisons, who accused the Umayyads of having abandoned them on the borders of the empire. Finally, he recycled themes linked to the popular imagining of the End of Times, notably the Black Banners, whose advent would mark the triumph of the Mahdi, the 'Rightly Guided', and the restoration of justice in this world by his sabre.

Abu Muslim combined all these components in a language and a movement that challenged the very foundations of the Umayyad Caliphate. He brushed aside the accusations of *Fitna*, discord between Muslims, insisting instead on the religious imperative to overthrow an impious ruler. He let the Shiites believe that he supported their champion, Ja'far, the great-grandson of Hussein. The insurrection broke out in Khorasan in 747, captured Merv the following year, and progressed inexorably towards the west. The triumphal entry of the rebels into Kufa in 749 was accompanied by a dramatic turn of events: Abu Muslim proclaimed as caliph not Ja'far, but Abu al-Abbas, a distant descendant of one of the Prophet's uncles, Abbas (hence the term Abbasid given to this branch of the family). Ja'far accepted the fait accompli, to the dismay of his supporters, who were hoping that Ali's lineage would sweep to a historic revenge. Abu al-Abbas launched his troops against Upper Mesopotamia, tearing the Umayyad army to shreds in 750, at the Battle of the Zab. Marwan II fled to Egypt, where he was captured and executed shortly thereafter. The relatives of the deposed caliph were systematically massacred; only one of them, Abd ar-Rahman, escaped the carnage to find refuge in Andalusia. Abu al-Abbas earned from this series of killings his nickname of al-Saffah, 'the Bloodthirsty'.

The Abbasid triumph, however, merely resulted in replacing one dynastic principle with another. The term '*Dawla*', initially associated with the revolution of the stars, and therefore with revolution of a political type, now took on the meaning of 'state'. This radical institutional change was very different from the Great Discord from which Mu'awiya emerged victorious against Ali in 661. It was in fact part of a dynamic of taking power that Ibn Khaldun, a pioneer of Arab social sciences in the fourteenth century, conceptualized according to the threefold distinction between *assabiyya*, *da'wa*, and *mulk*. *Assabiyya* is a closely united 'group' bound by tribal ties and/or esprit de corps; it spreads a 'preaching' (*da'wa*), establishing its ambition to seize 'power' (*mulk*) and exercise it. The Abbasid 'group' thus imposed its collective interests and prevailed over Shiite pretensions, and it succeeded – thanks to the power of the 'preaching' of Abu Muslim – in substituting its own *mulk* for that of the Umayyads. The *da'wa* was part of the Islamic lexicon, even if it can be translated today as 'discourse' or 'propaganda', because all the actors in these power struggles claimed to be Muslims (and therefore better Muslims than their adversaries). In addition, Ibn Khaldun linked the weakening of central power and the emergence of protest on its periphery – a pattern that was found in the rise to power of the Abbasid alternative, from Khorasan to the heart of the Middle East.

The Umayyad era lasted less than a century, but never would a Muslim empire subsequently control such a vast territory. Leaving Arabia as a base, as did Mu'awiya in 661 – a process completed by the liquidation of Ibn Zubayr in 692 – favoured the long-term establishment of an empire which could not have been managed so effectively from Medina: this was one of the less well-assimilated lessons of the Great Discord. The centrality of Syria under the Umayyads also facilitated the promotion of Jerusalem as the third holy city, alongside Mecca and Medina, with none of these three cities combining a political dimension with its sacred status. The main legacy of the Umayyads to their Abbasid conquerors lay in the dynastic heredity which, by excluding, at the behest of the various factions, the direct descendants of Muhammad, sealed the historic defeat of the Shiite 'party'. However, it would take two more centuries for Shiite dissidence to become a specific dogma of Islam, in opposition to a 'Sunnism' that itself was gradually structured around four canonical schools. As for Arabization, carried out with deliberation since the caliphate of Abd al-Malik, it fostered among the converts of Persia – themselves Arabized – desires for emancipation that the Abbasid insurrection successfully mobilized.

The caliphate of Baghdad

Abu al-Abbas designated as heir his half-brother Al-Mansur,[10] 'the Victorious', who succeeded him on his death in 754. The new caliph

[10] Abu al-Abbas and Al-Mansur had the same father, but the latter's mother was a Berber.

instructed Abu Muslim, governor of Khorasan, to stifle any form of opposition there. Once this mission had been accomplished, he turned against Abu Muslim, who was liquidated with his supporters before they became too powerful. Beyond the quarrels of the inner circle, what was at stake was the stabilization of a dynasty threatened by the messianic fervour of some of those who had brought it to power. This was no longer the time to invoke the Black Banners, nor to exalt a vengeful Mahdi, but to consolidate a truly earthly power. We will see this process repeated during the advent of the Fatimids and the Safavids. As for the Abbasids, once the work of the founder had been accomplished, it fell to the second ruler of the line to eliminate extremists whose enthusiasm, channelled towards the conquest of power, was becoming dangerous in its phase of institutionalization.

Caliph Al-Mansur launched the colossal construction site of a new capital in 758, inaugurated four years later under the name of Baghdad with the nickname of 'City of Salvation' (*Madinat al-Salam*), following a circular plan with a diameter of two and a half kilometres. The caliph then left Kufa, too much in thrall to its Shiite solidarities, after crushing the revolts in Medina and Basra fomented by two distant descendants of Ali. The triumphant dynasty thus imposed its sole legitimacy, with Baghdad marking a clean break from the bases of former rivals and predecessors. The Abbasid Middle East was ruled from Iraq, while Syria, identified with the defeated Umayyads, was often treated as occupied territory. Just as the establishment of the Umayyads in Damascus had seen them take over some aspects of Byzantine pomp, the choice by the Abbasids of a capital close to Ctesiphon was accompanied by the recycling of certain Sassanid rites of power. Henceforth, the caliph, hidden by a veil,[11] received privileged people who had to prostrate themselves and kiss the ground. The sovereign's nickname was associated with the divine person, if only by the invocation of his grace.[12] The title 'caliph of Allah', which only Abd al-Malik had intermittently claimed during the Umayyad era, was increasingly used. The general policy of promoting the *mawali*, the non-Arab converts, mainly benefited Muslims of Persian origin, many of whom gained access to the highest positions in the state. This signalled

[11] The chamberlain in charge of protocol was called *hajib* ('he who veils').
[12] Al-Mansur's full nickname was thus 'Victorious by the grace of God'.

the beginning of the Arab–Persian synthesis which would mark the golden age of this first Abbasid century.

The central administration was organized into different offices (the treasury, the army, the estates, and the postal service),[13] each office (*diwan*) being headed by a secretary (*katib*). It was only gradually that the honorary title of vizier[14] came to designate the coordination of governmental affairs. Tax resources were mainly of three types: land tax (*kharaj*), levied on real estate or land; the tithe (*ushr*), payable on commercial transactions and agricultural production; and the poll tax (*jizya*), paid by non-Muslims. But the Abbasid imagination was fertile in prescribing and collecting new taxes. These various taxes were levied by the governor before being transferred to the Baghdad treasury. Essential to the prosperity of the Abbasid state was the centralization of administration by departments, not territories, with each official reporting to his superior in Baghdad, not to the local governor. So, in the event of a dispute with the representative of such and such a *diwan* in his province, this governor was at the mercy of possible arbitration from the capital that would go against him. Such an arrangement greatly limited centrifugal tendencies in this vast empire[15] (only Andalusia seceded in 756 under the authority of the sole survivor of the Umayyad family).

Harun al-Rashid, the fifth Abbasid caliph, reigned in Baghdad from 786 to 809, even if he often resided in Raqqa, on the Euphrates, from which he would go regularly to war against the Byzantines. The tales in which he appears in the *Thousand and One Nights*, contributing to his legendary reputation, have little connection with reality, since they were written centuries later in Syria and Egypt. These tales often present the viziers of the Barmakid family,[16] whose patriarch, Yahya ibn Khalid,

---

[13] The postal agents were also involved in intelligence via the daily reports sent to the caliph from the provinces (a function carried out in the capital by the Office of Information/*Khabar*).

[14] The term 'vizier' is an anglicized version of the Arabic *wazir*, itself translated as 'minister'.

[15] The Eastern Roman Empire had, for the same reasons, adopted a comparable system of administrative centralization (see above, p. 14).

[16] Prior to their conversion to Islam, the Barmakids were Buddhist dignitaries from the monastery of Balkh in northern Afghanistan.

a veteran of the Abbasid revolution, was one of the confidants of the caliphs Abu al-Abbas and Al-Mansur. Yahya, Khalid's son, was placed in charge of the tutelage of the young Harun and, on his accession to the caliphate, became his highly feared minister. This position favoured the two sons of Yahya, with Ja'far succeeding his father as minister of Harun al-Rashid while his brother al-Fadl held important military commands. The disgrace of the Barmakids in 803 was all the more brutal, with the beheading of Ja'far and the imprisonment of his relatives.

Harun al-Rashid used this torture, which intimidated his contemporaries, to assert the absolute nature of his power. He blocked the overtures of his viziers towards the Shiite movement – after all, he did not hesitate to imprison or even assassinate the descendants of Ali. He also penalized the religious and intellectual tolerance that prevailed at the court of Baghdad: he professed a finicky orthodoxy, alternating, throughout his reign, the years of pilgrimage to Mecca and years of campaigning against the Byzantines. We will see that in 806 he led his troops as far as Ankara, imposing his 'protection' on the Christian emperor. Harun al-Rashid's piety led him to deposit in Mecca the will entrusting the caliphate to his son Al-Amin, born of a legitimate wife of Arab blood. He thus relegated to second position Al-Amin's half-brother, Al-Ma'mun, born a few months before the heir, but of a Persian concubine. Harun al-Rashid thus believed his succession to be guaranteed when, on an expedition to quell a rebellion in Khorasan, he died in 809 and was buried there. His mausoleum in Mashhad is now incorporated into the site, which has gradually become the most sacred of Iranian Shiism. So this caliph had a strange posterity, having constantly repressed the descendants of Ali before resting with one of them.[17]

Despite the precautions taken during his lifetime by Harun al-Rashid, civil war soon broke out between the two half-brothers, Caliph Al-Amin in Baghdad and Al-Ma'mun, governor of Khorasan. Al-Ma'mun finally won in 813, after a particularly bloody siege of Baghdad. A poet of the time describes the use of catapults and incendiary projectiles fuelled by

[17] Mashhad is the site of the mausoleum of Reza, the eighth Imam of Shiism, who died in 818, probably poisoned on the orders of Caliph Al-Ma'mun, son of Harun al-Rashid.

'naphtha', i.e. oil. The desolation was immense, even if Al-Ma'mun's victory over Al-Amin, who was slaughtered and then beheaded, was complete. During the first five years of his reign, Al-Ma'mun set up his court at Merv, in Khorasan, and made bold overtures to Ali's family, whose green he even displayed on his flag, instead of the Abbasid black. But, in 818, Al-Ma'mun brutally returned to his father's anti-Shiite policy. The caliph restored black to his flag and returned to settle in Baghdad. Here he opened a 'House of Wisdom' (*Beit al-Hikma*) dedicated to intellectual exchanges, with translations of Greek and Roman philosophers made from manuscripts acquired in Byzantine territory. Among those participants who stood out were the Nestorian physician Hunayn Ibn Ishaq (the interpreter of Galen) and the mathematician Al-Khwarizmi (whose Latinized name gave us 'algorithm').[18]

Caliph Al-Ma'mun increasingly openly encouraged an interpretation of Islam of a rationalist type, that of a so-called 'Mutazilite' current, literally that 'which keeps itself apart' (to abstract itself from profane considerations and focus on sacred realities). The works of the main authors of this current have disappeared, but we know that they were based on two conceptions that were revolutionary at the time: the created and historical character of the Qur'an, on the one hand, and the free will of human beings, fully responsible for their acts, on the other. It was one thing to deal with these philosophical questions in the inner circles of the court, quite another to establish Mutazilism as an official doctrine of the caliphate and to brutally suppress dissenting opinions. This step was taken in 833, at the very end of the reign of Al-Ma'mun, when he launched the *Mihna*, i.e. the 'Ordeal', the equivalent (albeit without death at the stake) of an Inquisition where clerics reluctant to accept Mutazilism were persecuted. The sudden death of the caliph, on an expedition against the Byzantines, shortly after the outbreak of the *Mihna* was interpreted by opponents of Mutazilism as divine punishment. However, this episode only takes on its full meaning in the context of the formalization of the prophetic tradition, the Sunna, alongside the Qur'anic message.

---

[18] Al-Khwarizmi conceptualized calculation by 'restoration' (*al-jabr*), which became 'algebra'.

The late emergence of Sunnism

The mobilization of a Shiite tendency by the Abbasid revolution and the ambivalence of the caliphs of Baghdad towards the descendants of Ali illustrate the persistent fluidity of dogmatic borders during the first two centuries of Islam. Only by rather illicitly transposing Christian categories can we date an irreconcilable 'schism' between Sunnis and Shiites back to the Great Discord between Ali and Mu'awiya, and then the martyrdom of Hussein in 680. The absence of a Church in Islam prohibits this type of comparison, since the 'Sunni' category only emerged very gradually with the elaboration of the Sunna, i.e. the 'tradition' linked to Muhammad and founded on the hadith, literally the 'quotations' attributed to the Prophet. The discipline of hadith, of which an Umayyad caliph seems to have been one of the pioneers, aimed to constitute a corpus of reference, a process in which validation was as important as exclusion. The task was all the more immense in that apocryphal quotations from Muhammad had proliferated after his death in 632. It was in the middle of the ninth century that a dozen monumental collections of hadith were compiled by Arabized rather than Arab authors. Their selection criterion was the chain of transmission (*isnad*), which must go back continuously to the closest companions of the Prophet. A hadith was said to be more or less 'solid' depending on the reliability of this chain of transmission.

The two most respected collections of hadith, organized by theme, are both entitled 'The Authentic'.[19] They are the work of two Persians Arabized by long stays in Iraq and Arabia, and even in Egypt: Muhammad ibn Isma'il al-Bukhari, who died near Samarkand in 870, and Abu al-Husayn Muslim, who died in 875 in his native city of Nishapur. The normative work of hadith specialists was contemporaneous with the formalization of four legal schools, known in the singular as *mazhab*, which elevated the prophetic tradition, the Sunna, into a source of canonical legitimacy, in the same way as the Qur'an. The divine revelation was thus completed by the deeds attributed to the one who was its Messenger, because of

---

[19] These two 'Authentic' collections were completed in Sunni orthodoxy by the four *Sunan* (the plural of Sunna), written in the same period by Abu Daud, Tirmidhi, al-Nasa'i, and Ibn Majah.

the Abbasid sacralization of the very person of Muhammad. Each Sunni school derives its name from its tutelary figure, mentioned below in chronological order of appearance, so as not to establish a hierarchy between this or that *mazhab*.

The first of these figures who inspired a school of hadith was Abu Hanifa, born in Kufa in a family of Persian *mawali*. It was in this Iraqi city that he delivered a teaching that soon met with great success. But he refused to enter the service of Caliph Al-Mansur, who took revenge by having him imprisoned in Baghdad. Abu Hanifa died in custody in 767, accused of Shiite sympathies. He never suspected that his writings would eventually constitute the body of doctrine of a future Sunni school – one that would be known by his name. This founding work was handed on to his direct disciples, who enjoyed the favour of Harun al-Rashid, one being appointed *qadi* (religious judge) of Baghdad, and therefore head of all the *qadi*s of the empire, the other becoming adviser to the caliph, before being appointed *qadi* of Raqqa. Such strategic positions facilitated the dissemination of the ideas of Abu Hanifa throughout Abbasid territory. Centuries later, it was the adoption of Hanafism by the Seljuks, then by the Ottomans, which allowed this doctrine to become dominant in the Turkish world today. It is distinguished by a relative pragmatism and validates the possible use of personal opinion (*ra'y*) in the service of the lesser evil.

Next came Malik Ibn Anas, nicknamed 'the Imam of Medina', because it was in this holy city that he spent most of his life, until his death in 796. He, too, suffered the whip and the dungeon, before being pardoned by the caliph. Malik wrote the *Muwatta*, 'the well-trodden path', considered to be the first treatise on *fiqh*, as 'Islamic jurisprudence' was called. The different editions of this pioneering treatise allow for a variety of interpretations, justifying both rigour and tolerance towards mysticism. Unlike the brilliant intellectual Abu Hanifa, Malik favoured moral cohesion over logical coherence. He feared that leaving too much scope for personal reasoning would widen the differences between believers, whose general interests were best furthered by consensus (*ijma'*). His most brilliant student, Sahnun, left Medina in 807 and taught in Kairouan until 854. This early establishment contributed to the Maliki school today being the most popular school in the Maghreb and in sub-Saharan Africa.

Muhammad ibn Idris al-Shafi'i was born in Gaza in 767, the same year Abu Hanifa died. An appreciated poet and an outstanding archer, he turned away from these secular considerations to follow the teachings of the imam Malik in Medina. He was closely involved in the controversies in Baghdad, so much so that he was imprisoned there, and then chose to settle in Fustat, where he was buried in 820. Al-Shafi'i published a voluminous 'Fundamental Book' of Islamic jurisprudence, as well as a treatise on the interpretation of the hadith. He put forward reasoning by analogy (*qiyas*), while setting intellectual and legal limits to the consensus of clerics, a consensus that had hitherto been largely undisputed. He believed that the Qur'an should be read in the light of the Sunna, emphasizing the process of foregrounding the prophetic tradition. He thus established the four sources of the Law: the primary sources, i.e. the Qur'an and the Sunna; and the derived sources, i.e. analogy and consensus. Shafi'ism now became the dominant doctrine in Egypt and Yemen, as well as in Indonesia, where Yemeni traders helped to spread Islam.

Ahmad Ibn Hanbal, the latest of the creators of the four Sunni schools, was born in 780 in Baghdad. He spent part of his life studying in the Hejaz, Syria, and Yemen, later composing an ambitious collection of hadith, entitled *Musnad*. He favoured a literalist approach to the Qur'an and the Sunna, and rejected derived sources – a stance that contrasted with the relative flexibility of his predecessors. This dogmatism, closely argued for and asserted, impelled Ibn Hanbal to openly fight the imposition, in 833, of Mutazilism in official doctrine. Arrested in Baghdad, he was taken under guard to the camp of the caliph, who was then campaigning in southern Anatolia. Al-Mamun's brutal death caused Ibn Hanbal, who got no farther than Raqqa, to be sent back to Baghdad. But he was to be imprisoned there by order of the new caliph, Al-Muta'sim, who remained faithful to Mutazilism until the end of his reign, in 842. Ibn Hanbal refused to retract his views, and although he was released after two and a half years, he was expressly banned from preaching.

The symbolism was powerful, even if it might have been forced: Ibn Hanbal's passive resistance drew the respect of the population of Baghdad, which Al-Muta'sim left, establishing in 836 his new capital in Samarra, on the upper course of the Tigris. The Abbasids felt safer there, far from the crowd and its passions, under the protection of a Turkish guard staffed increasingly by converted slaves, called Mamluks. It was not until the reign of Al-Mutawakkil, the son of Al-Muta'sim, that Mutazilism ceased, in 848, to be state dogma. Ibn Hanbal, rehabilitated with great acclaim, nevertheless refused to exercise an official function with the new caliph. Until his death, in 855, he cultivated the image of incorruptibility, insensitive both to the charms and to the threats of the court. The Hanbali school was distinguished by its hostility to Shiism and its exaltation of *hisba*, the obligation imposed on each Muslim 'to order good and forbid evil'. We will see how this doctrine, in its Wahhabi version, would become state dogma in Saudi Arabia.

Major jihad and minor jihad

This multifaceted movement of Sunni self-assertion, far from being limited to the legal context alone, was accompanied by a mystical effervescence, designated by the generic term of Sufism.[20] The pioneers were two ascetics from Basra, the preacher Hasan al-Basri (642–728), famous for his exhortations to renunciation, and the poetess Rabia of Basra (713–801), who sang of annihilation in God. Al-Muhasibi, who died in Baghdad in 857, is often considered the first true Sufi, because he developed the spiritual exercises of 'examination of conscience', the *muhasaba*. He opposed his contemporary Ibn Hanbal, as he thought that the believer must first be accountable to him- or herself, rather than settling accounts with others.[21] The controversy has since remained open, setting the proponents of the priority of inner ecstasy against those of the outer moral order. Junayd, a disciple of Muhasabi, tried to reconcile the two approaches by prescribing secular respect for Islamic morality, regardless of the believer's degree of spiritual advancement.

Al-Hallaj, one of Junayd's students, nevertheless sought to disseminate to the mass of believers the teachings reserved for an esoteric elite. The agitation he thus fuelled led him to be imprisoned for many years in Baghdad. He was executed in 922 for having questioned the obligation of the pilgrimage to Mecca, on the grounds that the believer is free to

[20] None of the etymologies put forward for the term 'Sufi' are fully convincing.
[21] The two terms *hisba* and *muhasaba* are derived from this notion of 'accounts'.

meet God in his or her heart. The mausoleums of these various mystics in Iraq attracted popular fervour, with a veneration that endured and even grew over the centuries. This popularity fuelled hostility from fundamentalists, who accused Sufism of being a perverse manifestation of Islamized paganism. These same extremists today deny any validity to the major jihad – namely the spiritual struggle of the mystic against the forces of evil. Their modern obscurantism recognizes only the military form of jihad, even though this is considered to be a minor jihad.

The formalization of the four Sunni schools led, in the Abbasid era, to the progressive codification of the rules of engagement and conduct of this kind of armed jihad, in a form of an Islamic 'law of war'. The fundamental distinction lies between so-called 'offensive' jihad and so-called 'defensive' jihad. Defensive jihad is imposed on everyone: this obligation can become 'individual' (*fard 'ayn*) in the event of the need to defend a threatened population in the 'land of Islam'. Offensive jihad, on the other hand, is an obligation that can be delegated and thus 'collective' (*fard kifaya*), under the authority of the caliph or his representative. In either case, the doctrine and practice of Islam establish a fundamental link between military jihad and a specific territory, to be defended or conquered, as well as with the population of this territory, to be protected or conquered.

This link between minor jihad and territory contributed to the relative stabilization of the Abbasid borders, with the de facto abandonment of the ambition of a universal Islam. The Umayyad polarization between the 'domain of Islam' and the 'domain of war' (or 'of impiety') was now nuanced by an intermediate category of the 'domain of conciliation' (or 'of the pact'), where local agreements justified the lasting suspension of hostilities. The truce concluded by Muhammad himself in 628 with the Meccans was invoked to legitimize the multifaceted exchanges between former belligerents in these border areas. As for the major jihad of the mystical current, it remains highly respected – as much as, if not more than, armed struggle, sometimes carried out by proxy, with the hiring of mercenaries for this purpose. Islam is therefore neither a 'religion of war', as its detractors insist, nor a 'religion of peace', as its apologists fantasize. It is a religion which, like the others, gradually formalized its relationship to war and peace, from initial expansion through military conquest to Abbasid consolidation.

Politics and religion in Islam

Faced with the divine right of Shiism, from which some Abbasids sought in vain to derive their legitimacy, Sunnism built up its problematic relationship to power in successive touches and layers. The weariness of the mass of the faithful in the face of cycles of civil wars conferred genuine popularity on a doctrine that rejected both blind obedience to the authorities and systematic dissent. To understand this reality, we must beware of misleadingly projecting Christian concepts onto Muslim reality. Seeing the caliph as comparable to the pope is merely the most frequent of these confusions, together with the recurring aspiration to spread from above a 'good Islam', as opposed to the so-called 'bad Islam'. Apart from its muscular paternalism, this vision is based on the all too widespread myth of an Islam organized into Churches, with a clearly formulated dogma and a clerical hierarchy responsible for ensuring its application. The Umayyad and then Abbasid periods, however, had no equivalent to the councils that were then being regularly convened by the Byzantine emperor (and even by Charlemagne in Frankfurt in 794). The only attempt from Baghdad to impose a state dogma, Mutazilism, came to an end after about fifteen years. It was thus less the rationalist character of this official doctrine that caused its loss than the state repression which, by attempting to disseminate it by force, undermined its popular legitimacy.

The cliché according to which, since Muhammad was at the same time a prophet, a warlord, and a head of state, there can be no distinction between politics and religion in Islam leads straight to an intellectual impasse. The historical reality, on the contrary, was a result of permanent tension: the caliphs have always sought to subjugate the clerics of Islam, designated by the generic term of 'ulama',[22] literally 'scholars'; these ulama in return constantly strive to preserve their autonomy, with the exception of the minority of ambitious and greedy men who, as at all times and in all places, associate themselves with the throne to accumulate power and wealth. These are the 'court ulama', as the other clerics call them, without much respect. Each camp of the executive power and the religious power insists that 'Islam is religion and state' (*al-Islam din wa dawla*), but each

[22] 'Ulama' is the anglicized form of the Arabic plural of *alim* ('scholar').

camp uses this maxim against the other: the caliphs to invalidate all religious preaching outside the state, the ulama to call on the caliphs to respect the prescriptions defined by the professionals of the religious sphere. And we have seen that the four founders of the Sunni schools all experienced Abbasid prisons, where, indeed, Abu Hanifa met his death.

The mastery of sacred sources in Islam is a matter of science (*ilm*), the very science that gives the ulama their name. And it is in a jurisprudential mode, by deduction, commentary, and interpretation (*ijtihad*), that these ulama elaborate the foundations (*usul*), then the branches (*furu*), of Islamic law, the *fiqh*. These Arabic terms are all the more difficult to translate as they belong to a specific register, which itself has variant forms in each of the four schools of Sunnism. For example, the Hanafi, Maliki, and Shafi'i schools recommend that women stay at home for Friday prayers, while the Hanbali school, despite being deemed more rigorous, encourages women to go to pray collectively at the mosque. In addition, the Hanafi, Shafi'i, and Hanbali schools allow a woman to lead the prayers of other women, while the Maliki school, often considered more tolerant, restricts this privilege to male believers. Add to this the fact that practice in Shafi'ite Egypt entrusts men with the direction of women's prayers, and one can measure the complexity of the relationship of these various groups to the Islamic norm.

A question as fundamental as that of the verses of the Qur'an abrogated by a later revelation continues to be debated even now, even though it involves the invalidation of one part of the sacred book in favour of another. There is therefore no sharia,[23] no definitively fixed 'Islamic law' on each subject, but a range of interpretations and uses resulting from a balance of power both political and social. This was how all Abbasid attempts to establish a Muslim equivalent of the Code of Justinian were defeated by the ulama. In general, political powers can, at a given time, take advantage of this or that aspect of sharia, or even of sharia as such, with the active or passive support of the ulama concerned. In return – a dimension that is all too often forgotten – some ulama go so far as to set the standards of sharia against the arbitrariness of a particular power at a given moment. As for Christians and Jews, they retain their own

---

[23] The term 'sharia' appears only once in the Qur'an.

jurisdiction: sharia is imposed on them only in the event of a dispute with Muslims.

For Caliph Al-Mansur, the founder of Baghdad in 762, the four pillars of his power were the *qadi*, the prefect of police, the director of the treasury, and the head of the postal service (because of his intelligence function). However, it was not until Harun al-Rashid that his *qadi* exercised hierarchical authority over the other religious judges of the empire. Abu Yusuf, the first incumbent, from 791 to 798, employed his talents as a casuist on very profane matters; in particular, he published a treatise on land tax. This grand *qadi* was literally called '*qadi-of-qadis*', a title that resonated with that of the '*mowbed-of-mowbeds*' under the Sassanids. But while state Mazdaism was organized in a pyramid fashion, Islam does not lend itself well to this type of configuration, even in the case of a fatwa, or a legal opinion, issued under the pressure of the political authorities. The persecution carried out from 833 to 848 by a grand *qadi* who looked like a grand inquisitor permanently discredited him in the eyes of the mass of the faithful. While the grand *qadi* could still appoint his subordinates in the provinces, henceforth he had to spare local sensitivities and avoid doctrinal controversies. As for his fiscal interventionism, it often came up against a Muslim institution, the *waqf*, i.e. inalienable property that escaped taxation and requisitions. Thus, the Abbasid caliph, even supported by a grand *qadi* under his authority, sometimes found the arguments and achievements of Islam were being held against him.

The birth of Shiite messianism

While Sunnism established the canons of its legal schools during the third century of Islam, Shiite sensibility was divided on the attribution of the supreme title of 'imam',[24] chosen by God, to one or the other descendants of Ali. The death in 740 of Zayd, Ali's great-grandson, at the head of an anti-Umayyad revolt in Iraq led his 'Zaydi' supporters to advocate armed struggle alone. Nine years later, the acceptance of the

[24] The notion of imam ('the one who stands in front') was swathed in mystical respect in Shiism, whereas in Sunnism it refers rather to the direction of prayer and to the moral magisterium.

Abbasid Caliphate by Ja'far, even though he was the declared champion of the Shiites, was rejected by a diehard dissidence, which supported one of his sons, Isma'il. This 'Isma'ili' protest engaged in long-term underground activism before establishing itself as the 'Fatimid' dynasty in Tunisia and then Egypt.[25] Legitimist Shiism, meanwhile, continued with the line of imams inaugurated by Ali, then by his sons Hasan and Hussein. Hussein's youngest son, Ali, is revered as the fourth imam under the name of Zain al-Abidin, the 'ornament of worshippers' of Allah, and his own son, the very studious Muhammad, assumed as the fifth imam the title of Baqir al-ilm, 'he who deepens knowledge'. The imamate continued to be transmitted from father to son, this time to Ja'far, who is thus therefore revered as the sixth imam. His submission to the new Abbasid order, condemned by the Isma'ilis, was lauded by the Shiites as a model of integrity, hence his nickname of Al-Sadiq, 'the Faithful'.

These three successive imams lived and died in Medina, but the Abbasid rulers, concerned for the popularity of Ali's descendants, now decided to confine them among their entourage. The seventh imam, Musa, earned his nickname Al-Kadhim ('the Reserved') for his stoicism in this ordeal. He was assassinated in Baghdad on the orders of Harun al-Rashid. His son Ali, known as Reza ('the Approved'), was buried in eastern Iran, where pilgrimages to his tomb led to the foundation of a veritable city, Mashhad. Ali Reza's son, Muhammad, became the ninth imam with the sobriquet of Al-Jawad ('the Generous'). He rests with his grandfather Musa in Baghdad, in the district named, in their memory, Al-Kadhimiyah. The following two imams lived on the fringes of the Abbasid court, installed in its new capital of Samarra: Ali and his son Hasan were both nicknamed Al-Askari, as their lives were entrusted to the military camp (*askar*) of the Commander of the Faithful.

When Hasan al-Askari died in 873, this eleventh imam seems not to have had any descendants. Some insiders claimed, however, that he had left a four-year-old son, Muhammad, securely hidden. This was the time of the 'minor occultation', in which Muhammad, having become an adult, communicated through four successive 'ambassadors'. They identified the figure of this twelfth imam with the Mahdi, the instrument of the fulfilment of the prophecies, already invoked with his Black

---

[25] The Fatimid phenomenon will be studied in the following chapter.

Banners during the Abbasid revolution. In 941, the last of the 'ambassadors' stated that the Hidden Imam, theoretically seventy-two years old, had decided to withdraw completely from the world. This was the 'major occultation', in which Shiism has existed up until today. The Hidden Imam was transfigured into the 'awaited Mahdi', whose physical absence has not stopped people describing his radiant beauty, his long black hair, and his dark beard. The Mahdi can manifest himself at a given period as the 'master of time', and his definitive return will mark the end of the cycle of creation.

This Shia vision of the Mahdi amalgamated different elements that had emerged over three centuries of millennial angst. The theme of occultation, born during the darkest times of Umayyad oppression, dramatized this complex dynamic. It was during the tenth century that this notion imposed itself on other interpretations of the imamate; Shiism was described as 'Twelver', in reference to the infallible line of the twelve imams. Shiite scholars drew on a prophetic hadith already validated by Sunni tradition: 'If there was only one day left in the world to exist, Allah would lengthen this day, until a man of my posterity appears whose name will be my name.' In Shia dogmatics, the major occultation corresponds to the day that will never end until the return of the Mahdi. This major occultation was the basis on which Shiite clerics endeavoured to identify, in voluminous collections, the sayings attributed not only to the Prophet Muhammad, but also to each of the twelve imams. Like those who had shaped the Sunni tradition in the previous century, they accomplished a colossal task of selection, commentary, and compilation.[26] A Shiite *mazhab* was thus born; this was in fact the fifth in Islam alongside the four Sunni schools.[27] The Shiite ulama strove in their treatises to refute the extremist deviations (*ghulat*) that had flourished in

---

[26] Just as six Sunni collections have canonical value (see above, p. 59), four compilations have this status in Shiism; two were established by the sheikhs Kulayni (who died in Baghdad in 939) and Ibn Babawayh (who died in Ray in 991) respectively, and the two remaining collections were drawn up by sheikh Abu Ja'far Tusi (who died in Najaf in 1067).

[27] One difference between the Shiite and Sunni systems is that, according to Shiite law, a couple having only daughters bequeath their entire inheritance to them, whereas, in Sunnism, grandparents, uncles, and paternal cousins can in this case benefit from it.

previous centuries. They now refused to accredit the idea that there had been a 'falsification' of the Qur'an by the Umayyads to the detriment of Ali. On the other hand, they underlined the esoteric dimension of the revealed text, of which the successive imams of Shiism, they said, held the key, contrary to the literalist interpretation of the Qur'an dominant in Sunnism.

Minorities and rebels

The diversity of the Abbasids cannot, however, be reduced to the dialectic between Sunnism and Shiism, both engaged in a laborious process of doctrinal consolidation. Lower Mesopotamia, where the new caliphs set up their capital after the Sassanids, was, during the first century of their reign, the scene of intense activity among the Christian Churches, in the forefront of which was the Nestorian Church, but also among various Gnostic sects. It was against this backdrop that the court of Kufa, soon transferred to Baghdad, was swept by a wave of intellectual libertinism in which many dogmas were questioned. Caliph Al-Mansur decided to crack down; in c. 756/759 he executed Ibn al-Muqaffa,[28] who had had the audacity to send him a public epistle on the application of sharia. The inquisitors branded free thought under the generic term of *zandaqah*.[29] They considered it a pernicious form of apostasy from Islam, an offence punishable by death. Anyone condemned for *zandaqah* was obliged, if he wanted to avoid beheading, to abjure his errors; this saved the life of the poet Abu Nuwas, famous for his bacchic odes and his blasphemous deviations from orthodoxy. The *zandaqah*, far from representing an established doctrine, referred to a critical posture which Abbasid orthodoxy gradually shook off with more or less success. This intellectual effervescence, hidden from view in the history of the second century of Islam, remained all the livelier in that, legitimizing rebellion against the caliphate, it echoed certain Sufi provocations.

[28] Ibn al-Muqaffa, of Persian and Mazdean origin, was also famous for his Arabic adaptation of the Indian tales *Kalila* and *Dimna*.
[29] In this repressive idiom, a follower of *zandaqah* was a *zindiq*. The offence of *zandaqah*, which had long fallen into disuse, was exhumed at the end of the twentieth century by Colonel Gaddafi to crush opposition to his dictatorship (see below, p. 288).

At the beginning of the Abbasid era, Egypt was probably still predominantly Christian, even if Islamization was much more noticeable here than in Syria. The Coptic Church remained the institutional interlocutor of the provincial authorities of Fustat, while conversions were often part of an individual process among uprooted rural people; urbanization was increasingly associated with Islamization. The gradual development by Abbasid jurists of a status of *dhimmi*,[30] where the Christian (or Jew) was 'protected' though subject to numerous prohibitions (on the bearing of arms or proselytism), established a discrimination more visible than heretofore. The construction of churches, which had hitherto been perfectly possible, including in Fustat, became very problematic. But it was mostly the pressure of taxes, aggravated by the rapacity of governors who served an average term of two years, which pushed the Coptic peasants of the Nile delta to revolt in 830. The insurrection was crushed after two years, with Caliph Al-Ma'mun leading an implacable crackdown in the area. Baghdad now played the other Churches against the Copts. This latent conflict ended only with the autonomy assumed, from 868 to 905, by a line of governors of Turkish origin, the Tulunids, who made many overtures to the Copts. The heavy trend towards Islamization nevertheless seemed irreversible, with the majority of the Egyptian population converting, by the beginning of the tenth century at the latest.

The Abbasid Caliphate, established in Samarra from 836 to 892, had to deal not only with the remoteness of Egypt, but also with an unprecedented uprising in southern Iraq. Tens of thousands of slaves, deported from the eastern coast of Africa and designated by the collective term of Zanj, laboured to cultivate land reclaimed from the marshes and the sea. A preacher of Shiite inspiration, whose egalitarian message had the greatest impact on the Zanj, managed to foster their emancipation in a mass uprising which, from 869 to 883, controlled Lower Iraq and the now Iranian province of Khuzestan. At the height of their power, the Zanj coined money, set up their 'capital' south of Basra, and proposed that the other rebels join in an anti-Abbasid alliance. It took the

---

[30] This status of *dhimmi*/'protected' is apocryphally described as the 'pact of Omar', in reference to the Umayyad caliph Omar Ibn Abdelaziz (717–720), or even to the second caliph Omar Ibn al-Khattab (634–644).

intervention of the army and the caliph's fleet to curb this movement, in which the poor peasantry joined the freed slaves in a common fight against the landowners. This crisis underlined the dependence of the Abbasid sovereign on his generals, designated under the generic term of 'emirs'.[31] The caliphate was now much more absorbed by the internal troubles within its immense territory than by the challenge represented on its northern border by the Byzantine power. A form of status quo prevailed between the two empires, far from the clichés of the supposedly 'perpetual' war between Islam and Christianity. To understand this new regional balance, it is necessary to follow the thread of the evolution of the Eastern Roman Empire, going back to the end of the seventh century.

The Byzantines in Asia Minor

Constantinople, besieged by Umayyad troops from 674 to 678, then from 717 to 718, resisted successfully, in particular because of the mastery of Greek fire by the Byzantine defence. In Asia Minor, the contingents which fell back in the face of the Arab conquest gave birth to the politico-military organization of 'themes', soon extended across the rest of the empire: the theme of the Armeniacs and that of the Anatolics[32] corresponded respectively to the armies withdrawn from Armenia and the Orient; their soldiers received a plot of land, sometimes taken from the domains of the Crown, to encourage them to settle on the Umayyad border. The expeditionary force of the Roman *limes* was replaced by a theme rooted in its soil, with the recruitment from father to son of a permanent cavalry; this was supported, as needed, by peasants enlisted as infantry. A naval theme was also established in the port of Antalya to counter the development of the Muslim fleet. The 'strategist' at the head of each theme gradually assumed the administrative management of the province concerned; this function was strictly supervised so as to avoid the creation of personal fiefdoms. This system proved effective in containing Umayyad pressure, which suffered a major setback in 740 with the Byzantine victory of Akroinon, the current Afyon.

---

[31] *Amir*/'emir' can also sometimes be translated as 'prince', or even as 'commander' (in the expression 'Commander of the Faithful').
[32] *Anatolè* means 'Orient' in Greek.

Just as Muslim expansion had been seen as God's punishment, the triumph of Akroinon reflected to the glory of Emperor Leo III and his son, the future Constantine V, both present on the battlefield.[33] They quickly saw it as a providential encouragement for their 'iconoclastic' policy of suppressing the worship of images, a policy which set the sovereign up as the sole intercessor with the deity. The supporters of icons accused their opponents of espousing the Jewish and Muslim ban on divine representation. John Damascene (676–749), the son and grandson of senior Christian officials of the Umayyad Caliphate, was paradoxically freer to refute iconoclastic theses from his Palestinian monastery than were the bishops residing in Byzantine territory. Iconoclasm became the official doctrine of the Church in 754 and remained so until the Second Council of Nicaea, in 787,[34] when the pendulum swung to the other extreme by instituting the worship of icons. This allowed Charlemagne, seven years later, to convene a council in Frankfurt, invalidating Nicaea II and thus casting the Byzantine Empire into the darkness of heresy. At Christmas 800, Charlemagne proclaimed himself Emperor of the West in Rome.

Nikephoros I, who seized power in Constantinople in 802, suffered the shock of the exchange of embassies between Harun al-Rashid and Charlemagne. The arrival in Aix-la-Chapelle of a white elephant, a present from the caliph, caused a stir at the court of Charlemagne. The Byzantine ruler, or *basileus*, feared he would have to bear the brunt of this rapprochement, especially in 806 when Harun al-Rashid led a huge army to attack Anatolia. The fortress of Heraclea, in Cilicia, fell into the hands of invaders who devastated Cappadocia and threatened Ankara. Nikephoros I therefore had to swallow the humiliation of placing himself under the symbolic 'protection' of Harun al-Rashid and paying him considerable tribute.[35] The Byzantine emperor did not have to respect these commitments for long, as the troubles in Khorasan absorbed the Abbasid caliph and his army, followed by the civil war which, on his

---

[33] Constantine V succeeded his father on his death in 741.

[34] The First Council of Nicaea, in 325, laid the foundations of Trinitarian dogma (see above, p. 11).

[35] Islamic sources claimed that Nikephorus I agreed to pay six gold coins as *jizya* for himself and his son.

death in 809, set his two sons against each other. Nikephoros I himself had to face the threat of the Bulgarians in the Balkans. The expedition he led against them ended in disaster, with the death of the *basileus* and the annihilation of his troops.

The Bulgarian siege of Constantinople led to a palace revolution in 813, bringing to the throne Leo V, the strategist of the Anatolian theme. The new emperor succeeded in clearing the capital and, attributing his success to divine favour, in 815 he reinstated the prohibition of icons. The Asia Minor front seemed calm, especially since confrontation with Baghdad now shifted to the Mediterranean, where, in 827, Abbasid vassals seized Crete and others landed in Sicily. It was not until 837 that the *basileus* Theophilus, a fervent iconoclast, launched a devastating expedition to Malatya and Edessa. The Abbasid counter-offensive ended the following year with the sack of Amorium, the chief town of the Anatolic theme and thus the cradle of the reigning dynasty. This crushing defeat of the Byzantines was, however the last of its kind, as the caliphs now installed in Samarra were absorbed by their own internal troubles. As for iconoclasm, it was discredited by its excesses and definitively abandoned by the council of 843.

A so-called 'Macedonian' dynasty settled in Constantinople in 867 and retained power for two centuries. This long-term presence allowed the new masters of Byzantium to wait until the Abbasid Caliphate had fallen into a deep crisis before launching the beginning of a 'reconquest'. In 909, Eastern Cappadocia was organized as a theme around a contingent transferred from Armenia. This was the beginning of the Armenian adventure in southeastern Anatolia, which would lead, two centuries later, to the establishment of the principality of 'Little Armenia', as a counterpoint to the historical 'Greater Armenia'. Several border skirmishes followed, until the Byzantines managed, in 934, to break through the Abbasid lines in the centre of the Taurus massif. The 'reconquest' of Malatya was then accompanied by the expulsion of all Muslims who refused to convert. As for the siege imposed on Edessa in 944, it was lifted only in return for the recovery by the Byzantines of the Mandylion, a fabric supposed to preserve the imprint of the face of Jesus. The relic of the Holy Face was transported with great pomp to Constantinople. This celebration of the Byzantine restoration marked the end of a cycle of three centuries in Asia Minor.

A caliphate under tutelage

The contestation of the caliphate by Ali's supporters was itself deeply divided between his various descendants: the legitimist Shiites abandoned all political agitation to cultivate the messianic expectation of a saviour, ultimately identified with the Hidden Imam; in 897, the Zaydites, who instead supported armed struggle, managed to settle in the mountains of North Yemen, from where the Abbasid troops refrained from trying to dislodge them; the Isma'ilis, more discreetly, maintained their networks of propaganda and proselytism, for example in a Syria that had been despoiled by the reigning dynasty. In 899, the leader of the Isma'ilis claimed to be the Mahdi, the righter of wrongs of the End Times, from his base in the oasis of Salamieh on the edge of the Palmyra desert. This messianic uprising was quickly suppressed by the Abbasid army, while the self-proclaimed Mahdi fled to North Africa. The failure of the insurrection in Syria was made more inevitable by the refusal of the other Isma'ili hub, established in the territory of present-day Bahrain, to recognize the Mahdi of Salamieh. These rebels were called 'Qarmatians', a name derived from that of their first leader, and they would prove to be much more dangerous for the Abbasid order than the Zaydites, entrenched in their sanctuary in North Yemen, and the Isma'ilis, orphans of their 'Mahdi' exiled in the Maghreb.

The Qarmatians carried out repeated and destructive incursions into Iraq, looting Basra and Kufa and then fomenting discord in Baghdad. The intrigues which subsequently shook the Abbasid capital culminated, in 908, with the accession to the throne of the 'caliph for a day', assassinated just after taking power. In this menacing climate, the Qarmatian threat was used by some to cast aspersions on their adversaries, and brandished by others to reject any arrangement with those heretics. In 929, the raid of the Qarmatians on Mecca was all the more traumatic as they captured, for more than twenty years, the Black Stone, associated by the Muslims with the prophet Abraham. In 939, Caliph al-Radi bi'llah was forced to negotiate with these formidable rebels over the smooth running of the *hajj*, guaranteeing them comfortable rights of protection. Such an admission of weakness led, in reaction, to the appointment in Baghdad of a grand emir, literally a 'commander of commanders', whose military power now eclipsed that of the Commander of the Faithful.

In 945, the internal struggles in Baghdad were decided in favour of General Ahmad Ibn Buya,[36] who took the title of 'Grand Emir', overthrew the reigning caliph, and replaced him with a more accommodating monarch. This marked the beginning of the so-called 'Buyid' dynasty of military leaders, who exercised power in the name of the caliph, but actually in his stead. The new Buyid masters needed this support from the caliph all the more because they were themselves Shiites, a religious affiliation that did not entail any proselytism on their part. Thus, where today's fables paint a Dantesque picture of an inexpiable war between Sunnis and Shiites, supposed to have lasted fourteen centuries, history presents us with the lasting and, on the whole, benevolent tutelage of a Shiite authority over a Sunni caliphate. It also took long generations for Sunnis and Shiites to agree on their respective dogmas, often persecuting the extremists of their own camps with more aggressiveness than the opposing orthodoxy. Nonetheless, 945 was a pivotal date, which justifies our closing this chapter with it, because it marked the replacement in Baghdad of the power of the titular caliphs by that of non-Arab emirs.

A Middle East under one caliph

With all due respect to current revisionists, the Arab caliphate as the supreme institution of Islam lasted only three centuries, from 632 to 945, first in Medina, then in Damascus, and finally in Baghdad, with the interlude of the Abbasids of Samarra. It was during this period, and this period alone, that this Middle Eastern power was able to assert its unchallenged domination over most of the region. The fact that this imperial order was repeatedly challenged takes nothing away from this unparalleled continuity. The fact that this Muslim domination only belatedly translated into the Islamization of populations also provides us with food for thought. And finally, the fact that official Arabization,

---

[36] Buya was a mountain dweller from Daylam, a range to the southwest of the Caspian Sea, where Islam was implanted only very late by Shia missionaries. He was the father of three 'Buyid' emirs who carved up Persia between 932 and 936. It was one of them, Ahmad Ibn Buya ('son of Buya'), who seized Iraq, in 945, from his base in southern Persia.

from the end of the seventh century, remained more cultural than ethnic is essential to invalidate prejudices and stereotypes. This formidable synthesis, made possible by the Arabic language, continued during the second Abbasid century, distinguished by, among others, the works of the philosopher al-Farabi, the historian al-Tabari, the geographer al-Masudi, the writer Jahez, and the philologist Qudama. Their original contribution was considerable, and went far beyond the transmission, adaptation, and interpretation of the Greco-Latin heritage, assiduously carried out at the Abbasid court.

In addition to numerous localized uprisings, the period covered by this chapter was marked by three major civil wars between Muslims: the longest, from 683 to 692, set the Umayyads against the supporters of the 'anti-caliph' Ibn Zubayr, who was defeated after great devastation in Arabia, and especially in Mecca; the second, from 747 to 750, saw the Abbasid revolution carry off the Umayyad dynasty, after similar devastation in Syria, and especially in Damascus; and the third, from 809 to 813, was literally fratricidal, with one of the sons of Harun al-Rashid finally triumphing over the other, with yet more devastation in Iraq, and especially in Baghdad. In the last two cases, an army from Khorasan seized Iraq to impose its champion at the head of the empire, contrary to the cliché of a Persia passively subjected to 'Arab invasions' ever since the fall of the Sassanids. Even more important was the shift of the pole of the caliphs' power from Umayyad Syria to Abbasid Iraq, even if the Byzantine influence was more marked under the first dynasty than the Sassanid heritage under the second. Egypt played little part in all these conflicts over central power, divided as it was, from 813 to 826, by its own factional dynamics. The autonomy of the governors of Fustat was recognized from 868 to 905, and was simply a confirmation of this distance.

The Umayyad order, then that of the Abbasids, was based on free, male Muslims. There followed a variety of discriminations against free female Muslims, then 'protected' people of the Jewish and Christian faiths, and finally slaves, who were better treated if they were Muslims and not 'infidels'. But the caliphs' courts brought together figures whose legally inferior status did not hamper their political importance, whether they were the Christian collaborators of Mu'awiya, the wives of Harun al-Rashid, or the Mamluks of the Samarra guard. The deepest dividing line was in fact between the 'elite' (*khassa*) and the 'masses' (*amma*):[37] whether this elite was political, economic, military, or religious, it was able to overcome its internal differences in order to maintain its influence on the 'masses' of free or servile condition. Attempts to seize power were settled on the battlefield or else by coups d'état, the defeated 'elites' being eliminated or granted amnesty. Only twice did the Abbasid Caliphate waver before the irruption of the 'masses': in 836, it had to leave Baghdad for Samarra, when faced with popular rejection of the imposition of a state dogma; and in 869, the alliance of self-emancipated slaves and destitute peasants enabled the Zanj to govern southern Iraq for fifteen years. The urban uprising in the first case, and the rural insurrection in the second, were the two sides of the same nightmare that plagued the 'elite', an elite that Abbasid decline would force to evolve very significantly.

[37] *Khassa* literally means 'special' (plural) and *amma* 'ordinary' (also plural).

Chronology

661–680	Mu'awiya, first of the Umayyad caliphs.
678	Yazid, the son of Mu'awiya, designated as future caliph.
680	Martyrdom of Hussein, son of Ali, in Karbala.
683–692	Ibn Zubayr, grandson of Abu Bakr, master of Mecca.
685–705	Abd al-Malik, Umayyad caliph, with Arabic as the state language.
699–767	Abu Hanifa, founder of the Hanafi *mazhab*.
708–714	Construction of the Umayyad mosque in Damascus.
711–796	Malik Ibn Anas, founder of the Maliki *mazhab*.
712	Umayyad capture of Samarkand.
713–801	Rabia, the mystic from Basra.
715	Completion of Al-Aqsa Mosque in Jerusalem.
718	Failure of the Muslim siege of Constantinople.
724–743	Hisham, Umayyad caliph.
740	Byzantine victory of Akroinon.
744–750	Marwan II, last of the Umayyad caliphs.
749–754	Abu al-Abbas al-Saffah, first Abbasid caliph.
c. 756/759	Execution at Kufa of Ibn al-Muqaffa.
762	Foundation of Baghdad by Caliph Al-Mansur.
767–820	Ibn Idris Shafi'i, founder of the Shafi'i *mazhab*.
780–855	Ahmad Ibn Hanbal, founder of the Hanbali *mazhab*.
786–809	Harun al-Rashid, fifth Abbasid caliph.
808–877	Hunayn Ibn Ishaq, Nestorian medical pioneer.
809–870	Bukhari, major author of hadith.
813	Victory of Caliph Al-Ma'mun over his half-brother Al-Amin.
814	Death in Baghdad of the poet Abu Nuwas.
820–875	Muslim, major author of hadith.
833–848	Mutazilism, official doctrine of the caliphate.
836–892	Interlude of Samarra as Abbasid capital.
838	Byzantine defeat at Amorium.
850	Death in Baghdad of the mathematician Al-Khwarizmi.
867	Beginning of the Macedonian dynasty in Constantinople.
868–905	Autonomy of the Tulunid governors of Egypt.
869–883	Zanj rebellion in southern Iraq.

897	Beginning of the Zaydite imamate in North Yemen.
899	Proclamation of the Isma'ili Mahdi in Salamieh.
922	Execution in Baghdad of the mystic al-Hallaj.
929	Qarmatian raid on Mecca.
934	Byzantine 'reconquest' of Malatya.
941	'Major occultation' of the Mahdi, twelfth imam of the Shiites.
945	Seizure of power in Baghdad by a Buyid grand emir.

Further reading

Bernheimer, Teresa, *The 'Alids, the first family of Islam (750–1200)* (Edinburgh: Edinburgh University Press, 2013).

Bressand, Fanny, *Caliphs and merchants: cities and economy of power in the Near East (700–950)* (New York: Oxford University Press, 2020).

Cook, David, *Understanding jihad* (Berkeley: University of California Press, 2005).

Filiu, Jean-Pierre, *Apocalypse in Islam*, translated by M. B. DeBevoise (Berkeley: University of California Press, 2011).

Haldon, John, *The Empire that would not die: the paradox of Eastern Roman survival (640–740)* (Cambridge, MA: Harvard University Press, 2016).

Hallaq, Wael, *Shari'a: theory, practice, transformations* (New York: Cambridge University Press, 2009).

Hibri (el-), Tayeb, *The Abbasid Caliphate, a history* (New York: Cambridge University Press, 2021).

Hurvitz, Nimrod, *The Formation of Hanbalism: piety into power* (London: Routledge, 2002).

Marsham, Andrew (ed.), *The Umayyad world* (London: Routledge, 2022).

Popovic, Alexandre, *The revolt of African slaves in Iraq in the 3rd/9th century* (Princeton, NJ: Princeton University Press, 1999).

THREE

The era of the two caliphates (945–1193)

After 945, the Abbasid Caliphate no longer exercised anything more than a show of the supreme power which the Arab caliphs had displayed during the three previous centuries. The Buyid emirs held real authority (*sulta*) in Baghdad, and had Friday prayers said throughout the empire in the name of the reigning monarch. The loss of effective power by the Abbasid sovereigns, at the cost of formal respect for its norms and forms, was irreversible. This shift came as Isma'ili dissidents, persecuted throughout the Middle East, were gaining a foothold in the Maghreb, where, indeed, in 909, they established a caliphate with legitimacy derived from Imam Ali, via his wife Fatima. This caliphate, which is thus known as 'Fatimid', controlled the territory of present-day Tunisia, and seized Sicily and then all of North Africa. In 969, it launched an assault on Egypt and expelled the Abbasid troops. The Fatimids decided to establish the seat of the caliphate in their new province. The city they founded, north of Fustat, was called 'the Victorious' (*al-Qahira*), anglicized as Cairo. The Middle East was now divided between two caliphates based in Iraq and Egypt, while the Byzantine Empire pushed forward its 'reconquest' in northern Syria. A third caliphate was proclaimed in 929 in Córdoba by an Umayyad emir, a descendant of a survivor of the massacre of this family by the Abbasids. But this far-western caliphate was centred on Al-Andalus, i.e. Islamic Spain, and it stayed outside Middle Eastern affairs.

Fatimid ambitions

Isma'ili propagandists, as well as Abbasid agitators a century and a half before them, drew to their advantage on a combination of messianic fervour and popular resistance. As early as 899, in Syria, their leader claimed to be the Mahdi and he presented his victory ten years later in Tunisia as the sign of the fulfilment of the prophecies. But the politico-military triumph of the Abbasids in the Middle East in the eighth century, then of the Fatimids in the Maghreb in the tenth, invalidated this countdown to the millennium. The End of Times, indefinitely postponed, gave way to the institutionalization of a new caliphate based on a dynastic principle. The revolutionary messianists, who had become not only outmoded but also dangerous, were liquidated in the first years of Abbasid power in Iraq, and then of Fatimid power in Tunisia. Ibn Khaldun's triptych of group/preaching/power, as well as his dialectic between centre and periphery already mentioned in the case of the Abbasids, are just as relevant for understanding the process that happened among the Fatimids: the 'group' of Isma'ili missionaries was rooted in the Maghreb, where it won over several powerful Berber tribes; Isma'ili 'preaching', broadcast in the name of the Mahdi of that time, was even more powerful and structured than the propaganda of Abu Muslim; Fatimid 'power', established on the Tunisian 'periphery', spread to consolidate its hold over the rest of North Africa before seizing the Egyptian 'centre'. Fatimid expansionism also aimed to divert outward millennial energies that could jeopardize dynastic stabilization.

In 966, the Nubian eunuch Kafur assumed supreme power in Egypt and went so far as to have Friday prayers said in his name, a scandal that, three years later, facilitated the conquest of the country by the Fatimids. The new masters were astute enough to shed their North African antecedents so as to add lustre to their glory by borrowing from the aura of timeless Egypt. This was the first time since the end of the Ptolemies, a millennium earlier, that Egypt had gone from being the province of an empire to a centre of imperial power. The caliph Muïzz, born in Tunisia, finally established his sumptuous palace in Cairo, in 973, not far from the great mosque of Al-Azhar ('the Radiant'),[1] inaugurated the previous year. He relied militarily on a Berber guard from North Africa, and on Turkish defectors recruited on the spot or poached from the Abbasid troops. The court, whose pomp soon eclipsed that of Baghdad, gave pride of place to senior Coptic and Jewish officials. The caliph appointed a grand *qadi* of the Isma'ili rite

---

[1] The term 'radiant' took up that attributed to Fatima, wife of Ali and mother of Hussein; she was the eponymous ancestor of the 'Fatimid' dynasty.

to assist him, but he also appointed a person in charge of preaching (*da'wa*),[2] who was responsible for the widest dissemination of Isma'ili doctrine.

Unlike the Abbasids, who were unwilling to impose a state dogma (apart from the fifteen years of the Mutazilite interlude), the Fatimids were meant to promote the Isma'ili message, especially since the founder of their dynasty proclaimed himself Mahdi and his successors claimed the title of 'imam'. The routinization of the caliphate, however, unexpectedly meant that the Isma'ilis, hitherto an exception, became more widely accepted; their teaching actually cohabited with that of the four schools of Sunnism. The caliphs of Cairo never ceased to swing, sometimes during the same reign, between organized pressure in favour of state Isma'ilism and tolerance towards a Sunnism that was still in the majority in the population. They were determined to overthrow the caliphs of Baghdad, who in their view were 'heretics', but in 970 they were obliged to limit their conquests to Damascus and to the south of Bilad al-Sham. They accepted the autonomy of the governor of Mecca and Medina on the express condition that prayers be said in their name alone in the two Holy Cities. The ruse of history would make Cairo and its great mosque of Al-Azhar, set up to ensure the influence and even the domination of Isma'ilism, appear today as a bastion of Sunni orthodoxy. As for the mosques of Hussein and Zaynab bint Ali,[3] still very popular in Cairo, they are in fact late duplicates of Shiite sanctuaries in Damascus, where the Fatimid dynasty constructed the myth of an existence in Egypt in order to exalt the primacy of Isma'ilism in that country. These two mediaeval mosques, now poles of Sunni piety in Cairo, reflected an Egypt that had buried its two centuries of heterodox heritage under a supposedly uncontested Sunnism. However, it took this lengthy detour

---

[2] Just as the grand *qadi* was literally the '*qadi*-of-*qadis*' (see above, p. X), the head of Isma'ili preaching was called 'preacher-of-preachers'.
[3] Zaynab, buried in Damascus in 682, was the sister of Hussein, killed two years earlier in Karbala, where his mausoleum is one of the holiest sites of Shiism; his severed head had been transported to Syria as a trophy for the Umayyads (see above, p. 48). In 1153, the Fatimids accredited the fable that Hussein's severed head had been transferred to Cairo, after being – they claimed – stolen from Damascus and long hidden in Palestine. As for Zaynab, despite never having set foot in Egypt, she is today considered the patron saint of Cairo.

through Isma'ilism for Egypt to emancipate itself from its subjection to Damascus and then Baghdad, finally acquiring, in Cairo, an authentic imperial capital.

The battle for Syria

The Byzantines firmly held on to eastern Anatolia from Malatya, which had come under their control in 934. But they faced a formidable adversary in northern Syria in the person of Sayf al-Dawla, 'Sword of the Dynasty'. This Shiite emir took command of Aleppo in the year 945 when other Shiites, the Buyid emirs, placed the caliphate of Baghdad under their supervision. Sayf al-Dawla was no less loyal than them to this Abbasid 'state' which conferred on him his title of 'Sword' (i.e. *Sayf*). The brilliant court of the emir of Aleppo welcomed Muslims of all persuasions, but also free-thinkers such as the poet al-Mutanabbi, survivor of a millenarian insurrection.[4] Sayf al-Dawla's regular campaigns into Byzantine territory resulted in no more lasting gains than the raids carried out in northern Syria by imperial troops. In 962, they managed to seize the city of Aleppo, which they ransacked. Sayf al-Dawla owed his salvation to his retreat to the citadel which dominated his capital; from here, he gazed helplessly at the looting. The massacre perpetrated by the Byzantines, including among the Sunni ulama, had the unforeseen result of favouring the spread of Shiism, hitherto the minority branch in Aleppo. However, the Christian victory was short-lived and Sayf al-Dawla was still master of a northern Syria that was very impoverished by hostilities but remained anchored in the Abbasid domain.

Sa'ad al-Dawla, who succeeded his father Sayf (who died in 967), maintained an itinerant court and entrusted Aleppo to one of his Turkish officers. He was a self-effacing personality, little versed in the art of war, and he let the garrison of Antioch fall in 969 to a Byzantine siege. The reconquest of the City of God, more than three centuries after its capture by the Arabs, was celebrated with pomp in Constantinople. It coincided with the Fatimid invasion of Egypt and with the founding of Cairo, exposing the unparalleled fragility of the

[4] Al-Mutanabbi means 'the one who proclaims himself a prophet'.

Abbasid Caliphate on its two western fronts. The Byzantines pushed forward their advantage with the methodical occupation of Cilicia, then the imposition in 970 of a treaty of protection of Aleppo, whose customs duties were paid to them. In 975, Emperor John Tzimiskes launched a lightning campaign in Syria from Antioch, where Damascus and Sidon were spared in return for a one-off tribute. The *basileus*, having arrived in the north of Palestine, did not dare to advance as far as Jerusalem for fear of a Fatimid counter-offensive. He ordered his troops to return to Antioch, contenting himself with consolidating Byzantine authority in the port of Latakia. Constantinople was happy with the new status quo in Syria, where the buffer zone of Aleppo, placed under its protectorate, guaranteed the security of its southern border.

It was during this last quarter of the tenth century that the Abbasids lost their footing in Syria. The Fatimids may have had difficulty controlling a rebellious Damascus, but their authority extended over most of Bilad al-Sham, up as far as the latitude of Homs. The Friday prayer was said in the name of the caliph-imam of Cairo in all the mosques of Syria, including in the territory of the emir of Aleppo, the vassal of Constantinople. The Fatimids mobilized to their advantage the sources of Islamic legitimacy: these were, on the one hand, the organization of the pilgrimage to Mecca and, on the other, the jihad against the Byzantines. This explains the prudence of the *basileus* during his retreat of 975. The main Fatimid port on the Syrian coast was fortified at Tripoli, on the edge of the Byzantine domain, and supported farther south by Sidon and Acre. Middle Eastern trade, so long structured around Mesopotamia and the Persian Gulf, was shifting its focus to the eastern Mediterranean and the Nile Valley, with Cairo supplanting Baghdad as the region's most populous metropolis. This geopolitical shift from Iraq to Egypt was inconceivable without Fatimid control over a large part of Syria. It was once again the Euphrates which marked the most stable boundary between the declining caliphate of the East and the ascending caliphate of the West. The Middle East, still ruled from Baghdad by the Abbasids in the middle of the tenth century, was profoundly reconfigured, with the Fatimid occupation of Egypt and the Levant, the Byzantines having imposed their de facto protectorate over northern Syria.

The imam of all excesses

The Fatimid Caliph Aziz, in power in Cairo from 975 to 996, organized the imperial ceremonial around the main dates of the Muslim calendar, as well as the Christian festivals of New Year and Epiphany, and even a Canal Festival, marking the cycle of irrigation by the waters of the Nile. This ecumenism drew on the Isma'ili claim to ensure equitable 'protection' not only for the People of the Book, but also for Muslims who had not yet been convinced of the divine mission of the caliph-imam. One can thus draw a parallel between the Umayyads governing a predominantly Christian and Mazdean Middle East in the middle of the seventh century and the Fatimids coming to terms with a predominantly Sunni Egypt three centuries later. The administration of Caliph Aziz was centralized under the authority of his vizier Ibn Killis, a converted Jew, a native of Baghdad, whose religious tolerance and bureaucratic efficiency curbed Isma'ili proselytism: the Fatimid missionaries were gradually removed from Egypt to go to preach their doctrine to the northeast of distant Persia. In Cairo, the theologians of the Al-Azhar mosque conceptualized the virtuous circle of a just government where the caliph guaranteed equity, which itself guaranteed wealth, which in return ensured the tax revenues which allowed the army and the administration to carry out the will of the caliph. Far from these irenic patterns, Aziz tried in vain to neutralize the polarization in his army between the 'Maghrebis' and the 'Orientals', involving the rivalry between the Berbers, architects of the Fatimid conquest of Egypt, and the Turks, who had come over after the foundation of Cairo. The court of Aziz was also marked by the importance of his sisters, his mother, and his daughter, Sitt al-Mulk,[5] whose considerable wealth and generous endowments favoured the development of the suburb of Qarafa.[6]

The sudden death of Aziz in 996 left the Fatimid throne to his eleven-year-old son, crowned caliph under the title of Al-Hakim bi-Amr Allah, 'the ruler by the order of God'. Real power, however, was exercised by the tutor of the young monarch, the eunuch Barjawan, who relied first on the Berber factions, then on the Turkish generals, in order simultaneously

---

[5] Sitt al-Mulk literally means 'the lady of power'.
[6] Qarafa today corresponds to the City of the Dead in the Egyptian capital.

to consolidate his own authority and to resist the new Byzantine push into Syria. In 1000, Caliph Al-Hakim had his over-powerful regent assassinated and commissioned the patriarch of Jerusalem to negotiate a peace agreement with Constantinople, concluded the following year. This was the beginning of a reign of two decades, one of the most controversial in Islam, since Al-Hakim sowed confusion among his contemporaries as much as among historians. Quick to liquidate his closest associates, pursuing his successive goals with obsessive rage, he had all the attributes not of an enlightened but of a fanatical despot. The incursions of the adolescent caliph into the souks of Fustat initially conferred on him the aura of an accessible sovereign, attentive to the complaints of his subjects. But they were quickly followed by a series of decrees on clothing, food, and trade which went beyond the strictest interpretation of Islamic law and were confusing in their arbitrariness; certain prohibitions on music and travel by night were cancelled shortly after their proclamation.

In 1003–1004, Al-Hakim broke with the tolerance of his Fatimid predecessors by enacting a whole series of discriminations against Christians and Jews, then by imposing anti-Sunni sermons in the mosques (the first three caliphs of Islam, accused of having done harm to the 'Imam' Ali, were thus ritually insulted). Tensions with the Sunni population, the vast majority in Fatimid territory, were so serious that the caliph swung from one extreme to the other, ruling in 1009 that Sunni doctrine had the same value as Isma'ili dogma. This decision, incompatible with the very principle of the Fatimid imamate, was disavowed after a year, with a return to the formal supremacy of Isma'ilism, but without official proselytism against the Sunnis. On the other hand, state intolerance was increasing against Christians and Jews, with the destruction of many churches and synagogues. In 1009, Al-Hakim even ordered the demolition of the Holy Sepulchre of Jerusalem, which was partially implemented after the sacking of the sanctuary. The Byzantine Empire chose not to make this sacrilege a *casus belli* and in 1012, wagering on the inconstancy of Al-Hakim, obtained permission for the Christians of Jerusalem to begin initial reconstruction of their holy place.[7]

The beginning of the fifth century of Islam in 1009 has been used to explain the enthusiasm of Al-Hakim, who could thus revivify the

---

[7] The Holy Sepulchre was fully rebuilt only in 1048.

messianism of the founders of the Fatimid line.[8] In 1013, however, the unpredictable caliph went to strike at the very heart of dynastic legitimacy by appointing one of his cousins as heir, instead of the succession from father to son which had prevailed until then. He intensified his provocation with the appointment as grand *qadi* of a Sunni ulama, of the Hanbali rite, thus excluding Isma'ili theologians from the supreme function of the empire. Al-Hakim, not content to alienate one and then another group, now affected ascetic inclinations, dressing with ostentatious modesty and refusing to ride on anything but a donkey. In 1021, the caliph did not return from one of his frequent nocturnal escapades outside his palace in Cairo. Long before the official announcement of his death (and the execution of the Bedouins who allegedly murdered him), his elder sister, Sitt al-Mulk, took charge of the succession: the designated heir was put to death and one of the sons of Al-Hakim became caliph with the title of al-Zahir, 'he who appears openly', a deliberate assertion of the restoration of Fatimid principles. Sitt al-Mulk was supported in this palace revolution by her steward Al-Jarjara'i,[9] who, after years of patient intrigues, rose to the post of vizier in 1028. He remained in office until his death in 1045, guaranteeing that the Fatimid Caliphate would enjoy invaluable stability after the turbulence of the Al-Hakim era.

Dissidents and endogamous practices

Al-Hakim's passions may have caused an unprecedented scandal, but they were interpreted by circles of visionaries as the manifestation of divine inspiration. In 1019, they went so far as to hail the caliph as a living God, right in the Fustat mosque, leading to riots of popular protest against such presumption. The leader of these messianics, Darazi, fled into hiding with the other moving spirits of the sect, whose members, admitted after an initiation process, called themselves 'unitarians'. The term 'Druze', derived from Darazi, was first used by supporters of those

[8] Variations traditions prophesied the advent of a 'Renovator' of Islam, even of the Mahdi, at the beginning of each century of the Hijri calendar. The Fatimids marked the opening of the fourth century, in 912, by founding, in Tunisia, their capital of Mahdia, the 'city of the Mahdi'.
[9] Al-Jarjara'i was nicknamed 'The Amputee' because he had at least one hand severed in 1013 by order of Caliph Al-Hakim.

who repressed this dissident movement, though it was then assumed by the dissidents themselves.[10] The disappearance of the caliph in 1021 convinced the faithful of this sect that Al-Hakim was now the Hidden Imam. Persecuted throughout Egypt, they found refuge in Syria; here, Fatimid authority was more or less solid in the south but largely symbolic in the north. The Druze developed their doctrine during the next generation, after which any conversion was supposed to be prohibited. Within the group itself, only a minority of 'wise men'[11] were initiated into the mysteries of the dogma, the majority of Druze being encouraged to observe the trappings of Muslim piety.

Syria, where the diversity of environments had already favoured the plurality of Christian Churches, thus became a veritable breeding ground for the different branches of Islam. Sunnism, associated with Umayyad glory, often suffered from the disgrace of Bilad al-Sham under the Abbasid reign; Shiism took advantage of this to establish itself, including in the city of Aleppo; Isma'ilism at the end of the ninth century found in the oases of the Syrian desert the breeding ground for the earliest Fatimid preaching; the Druze, themselves descended from Isma'ilism, flourished in the Syrian heights during the first half of the eleventh century; they were merely the latest arrivals in an acclimatization of dissidence which also affected the disciples of Ibn Nusayr. This Shiite preacher, active in Iraq at the end of the ninth century, presented himself as the intercessor of the eleventh imam, Hasanal-Askari, according to him the last of the mystical line opened by Ali, cousin and son-in-law of the Prophet of Islam. These 'Nusayri' believers would later be called 'Alawites' because of their particular devotion to Ali, but also their refusal to believe in the Mahdi, the Hidden Imam of the Twelver Shiites. Their concentration in the mountain ranges dominating the Syrian coast would then give its name to these 'Alawite mountains', even if there was a significant Christian and Isma'ili population in this rugged massif.

The Alawites shared with the Druze the same initiatory elitism, which left the mass of the faithful of the group in ignorance of the reality of its creed. This esoteric exclusion nourished endogamous practices found, in

---

[10] The Wahhabis (see below, p. 168) would also call themselves 'unitarians', before adopting a name popularized by their opponents.
[11] In Arabic *uqal*, singular *aqil*.

an attenuated form, among the Isma'ilis. According to a process already observed during the schisms of the Church of the East, the dissident minorities give absolute priority to their collective cohesion. Dogmatic subtleties were therefore less important than the conviction of belonging to a community of the elect, united as much by a specific liturgy as by the relentless persecution it faced from the 'Orthodox' authorities. The transmission from generation to generation of a heritage so rooted in celebrations and trials was in itself an act of faith and a way of establishing themselves in the narrative of history. Where Christianity flourished in a plurality of divergent patriarchates, Islam cultivated its own diversity, one which could not be limited to a bipolarity between Sunnis and Shiites, itself the result of a sedimentation lasting nearly three centuries. This is why the Isma'ili, Alawite, and Druze communities must each be considered as branches of Islam in their own right, despite modern anathemas against the Druze or the misleading identification of Alawites with Twelver Shiites.

As for current militants who defend 'minorities' in the Middle East, they generally focus their activism on Christians alone, neglecting the plurality of minorities in Islam. They also forget that the profound heterogeneity of the Levant often relativizes the notions of 'majority' and 'minority': a group can be both a 'minority' in a larger space and a 'majority' in a smaller territory. Finally, the conviction of the followers of a given group, Christian or Muslim, that they belong to a community of elected officials contributes powerfully to the perpetuation of this group through the centuries, but it does not necessarily encourage within it the virtues of tolerance towards other groups. We must therefore be careful not to idealize, in the Middle East as elsewhere, a minority simply because it is a minority. And we must not be surprised, in the Middle East perhaps more than elsewhere, that a 'minority', suddenly intoxicated by a shift in its favour of the balance of power, behaves with the same brutality as the 'majority' that has hitherto been denounced for its excesses.

Abbasids under tutelage

Faced with the Fatimid glory of Cairo, even though it was given a rough ride in the reign of Al-Hakim, the Abbasid caliphs paled in comparison to Baghdad. In 945, the first of the Buyid grand emirs took the title of Mu'izz al-Dawla, 'He who strengthens the dynasty', and was soon entreating the reigning caliph to replace him with an even more docile sovereign. Breaking with the centralizing tradition of the Abbasid Empire, the Buyids divided up the Iranian strongholds of Ray/Tehran, Isfahan, and Hamadan, while setting up vassals, such as Sayf al-Dawla in Aleppo. The son of Mu'izz al-Dawla, Adud al-Dawla, 'Pillar of the dynasty', maintained a brilliant court in Shiraz from 949 before gaining control of the rest of Persia and then seizing Iraq. In 977, in Baghdad, he managed to unify under his sole authority all the Buyid possessions. He even had his name mentioned after that of the caliph in Friday prayers, as well as marrying one of his daughters to the Commander of the Faithful. Despite his Shia beliefs, Adud al-Dawla limited celebrations of the imams Ali and Hussein in Baghdad, thus appeasing the mostly Sunni population of the capital. In 1007, one of his successors crushed the attempt by the Shiite governor of Mosul to go over to the Fatimids. Political allegiance to the Sunni caliphs thus consistently took precedence over sectarian affiliation.[12] The loyalty of the Buyids did not, however, hinder the progressive fragmentation of the Abbasid territory between the different emirs. This division was aggravated by the leasing of entire estates to senior officers whose greed impoverished the peasantry and drained the state coffers. More generally, the historic Mesopotamia/ Persian Gulf axis was, as we have seen, supplanted in regional trade by the Fatimid Mediterranean/Red Sea axis.

However, it would be wrong to associate the Buyid period with an inexorable decline. Admittedly, the court of the caliph in Baghdad faced competition from the various princely courts, but artists and scholars often benefited from this rivalry between patrons, while the provincial capitals were enriched with new monuments. Ibn Sina/Avicenna cultivated the favour of the powerful with his talents as a doctor, even occupying the functions of vizier in Hamadan. Wandering from one court to another, he extended the philosophical work of al-Farabi to structure an authentically 'Oriental' *falsafa* (philosophy) whose ultimate

---

[12] It was also during the Buyid period that the Shiite ulama ceased to support the idea that the Qur'an had been 'falsified' by the Umayyads (see above, p. 50, n. 5 and p. 69).

aspiration was 'illumination'.[13] The geographers Ibn Hawqal and Maqdisi, despite their Fatimid sympathies, criss-crossed the Abbasid domain to draw up the most complete 'description of the earth'.[14] Ibn al-Nadim, on the other hand, stayed in Baghdad to compile, in 988, an encyclopaedic 'Repertory' of all the books supposed to have been published in Arabic until then (only six of the ten volumes of this summa concern works on Islamic themes). Arabic remained the common language of a political and cultural elite with profoundly diverse ethnic and linguistic origins. This intellectual effervescence fed on the rivalry between the Buyid courts, while Cairo centralized the theological legitimation of the Fatimids around the Al-Azhar mosque.

Two Abbasid caliphs, Al-Qadir and Al-Qa'im, each in power for four decades, took advantage of this exceptional longevity to endeavour to reaffirm their supreme magisterium, without, however, emancipating themselves from Buyid tutelage. Al-Hakim's ravings in Cairo gave Al-Qadir the opportunity to vigorously denounce the usurpation of the Fatimids in 1011. Seven years later, he published an 'Epistle', rather like a profession of faith, in which he subscribed to the rigorous interpretation of Sunnism by the Hanbalite school, the very one against which his distant predecessor of 833 had unleashed the state's persecution. In 1029, he renewed his condemnation of the doctrine of a created Qur'an and affirmed the supremacy of the first three caliphs of Islam over Ali. By opposing both rationalism and Shiism, Al-Qadir asserted his rights to choose his own successor, in the person of his son Al-Qaïm. The new caliph, in office from 1031 to 1075, continued his symbolic showdown with the Buyids. He appointed Mawardi, a brilliant Shafi'i theologian, grand *qadi* of Baghdad, before entrusting him with missions to the Persian and Turkish princes who ruled entire sections of this sham empire. Mawardi drew from this a treatise on Islamic governance, one that was rather lenient towards the great feudal lords at a time when Sunni emirs had supplanted the Buyids in Baghdad.

---

[13] In Arabic, the term *ishraq* ('enlightenment') is indeed derived from *sharq* ('east').
[14] This was the title of Ibn Hawqal's treatise, the successive versions of which date from between 977 and 988.

The Seljuk restoration

The rise in power of the Turkish guards dates from the temporary establishment of the Abbasid Caliphate in Samarra, in the middle of the ninth century. The Fatimid rulers relied on Turkish defectors to push forward their advantage in Syria and neutralize their own Berber generals. Whatever the effective power of these Turkish commanders, they then mobilized it for the benefit of this or that caliph. This formal subordination was no longer appropriate given the rise, to the east of the Abbasid domain, of full-fledged Turkish principalities which shared the same Sunni orthodoxy. From the conflicts between these different emirs emerged the Seljuk family, one of whose members, the ambitious Toghrul, seized Khorasan in 1038. This marked the start of a methodical advance towards Iraq, slower than that of Abu Muslim in 747 or Al-Ma'mun in 809, but just as determined. Toghrul expelled the Buyids from Baghdad in 1055 and forced the caliph to give him the unique title of 'sultan', or official holder of executive power (*sulta*), which the Shiite emirs exercised de facto and not de jure. Toghrul, pompously nicknamed the 'Pillar of Religion', in fact based his claims on a proactive policy of restoring Sunnism. Ibn Khaldun's triptych group/preaching/power, already relevant in the dynamics of the Abbasid and Fatimid conquests, again sheds light on the rise of the Seljuk 'group', united around a Sunni 'preaching' until it won 'power' with the 'sultanate' of Baghdad, against a backdrop of the takeover of central Iraq by the periphery of Iran.

The Seljuk sultans, by the very fact of their reaffirmation of Sunni dogma, defended the symbolic supremacy of the Abbasid caliph, in whose exclusive honour the Friday prayer was solemnly said.[15] Their dynastic logic, where the ruling clan was collectively the holder of power, nevertheless combined the factors of both expansion and segmentation. Toghrul's nephew and successor, Alp Arslan, inflicted a crushing defeat on the Byzantines in 1071 at Manzikert, north of Lake Van, thus opening up Anatolia to Islamization. Malik Shah, the son and successor of Alp Arslan, triumphed at Damascus in 1076, reintegrating Syria into the

---

[15] From 1081, it was also in the name of the Abbasid caliph, and no longer of his Fatimid rival, that the Friday prayer was said in Mecca and Medina.

Abbasid domain, after a century when Bilad al-Sham had been divided between Fatimids and Byzantines. Malik Shah, however, was forced to concede Anatolia to distant cousins, who, deeply involved in the power struggles in Byzantium, managed to consolidate a 'Sultanate of Rum' (*Rum* was the designation in Arabic and Turkish of the second 'Rome' of Constantinople, and by extension of Anatolia). But Malik Shah opposed the ambitions of his own brother, Tutush, who, on the former's death, consolidated Syria into an increasingly autonomous stronghold of Baghdad. With the quarrels between the two sons of Tutush, one reigning in Aleppo and the other in Damascus, Bilad al-Sham, theoretically reunited under Abbasid authority, drastically fragmented and finally collapsed.

The Seljuk restoration was therefore in many respects paradoxical. The establishment in Baghdad of the madrasa (literally 'school') system aimed at spreading a Sunni dogma that was all the more combative as it was associated with the refutation, by the Shafi'i theologian Al-Ghazali, of the eastern philosophy (*falsafa*) of al-Farabi and Avicenna.[16] This dominant orthodoxy contrasted with the pluralism and diversity that prevailed in the Buyid courts, even if it was attenuated by the popular wave of mystical Sufism to which even the severe Al-Ghazali succumbed. State Sunnism was therefore both restored and impoverished under the Seljuk sultans, in line with the seemingly inexorable decline of the figure of the Abbasid caliph. A parallel decline then struck the Fatimid caliphs in Cairo, who were forced to abandon the reality of power to viziers who held military power. An exhausted dynastic legitimacy in Egypt was contested by the Isma'ili missionaries of Persia. Led by the charismatic Hassan-i Sabbah, they seized the citadel of Alamut in 1090 and, four years later, definitively broke with Cairo. Neither of the two competing caliphates was now capable of keeping Jerusalem, which passed from the Fatimids to the Seljuks, only to return to the former in 1098. This zero-sum game around the third holiest city of Islam prepared the ground for the irruption in the Middle East of a new type of invasion, the Crusade.

---

[16] This refutation of *falsafa* by Al-Ghazali would itself be 'refuted' by Averroes/Ibn Rushd in the Muslim 'West' of the Maghreb and Al-Andalus.

Byzantines and Crusaders

The ecumenical and therefore universalist ambitions of the Byzantine Empire were challenged, symbolically, by the establishment of the Holy Roman Empire and, in Mediterranean affairs, by the gradual reconquest of Fatimid Sicily by the Normans, who were increasingly active in the Italian peninsula. Constantinople nevertheless remained the most brilliant metropolis of Christianity, where Byzantine administration and its military power were preeminent. This feeling of superiority largely explains the indifference of contemporaries to a dogmatic quarrel over the Holy Spirit: the original version of the founding council of Nicaea, in 325, stated that the Spirit proceeds from the Father, while the Roman papacy endeavoured to promote a version in which the Spirit proceeds from the Father 'and the Son' (*filioque* in Latin). The controversy escalated with the reciprocal excommunication of Roman and Byzantine bishops in Constantinople in 1054. But it was only very much later that this controversy over the *filioque* would take on the dramatic form of a schism between the Churches of the West and the East in which the authority of the pope of Rome, previously associated with that of the patriarch of Constantinople, was now opposed to the latter. It was political considerations, and not religious ones, that left the Byzantines isolated in the face of the Seljuk invasion in 1071, and it was palace intrigues in Constantinople that favoured the establishment in 1077 of the Sultanate of Rum in Nicaea. The loss of Asia Minor and its immense resources fuelled a multifaceted crisis from which there emerged in 1081 a new dynasty, the Komnenoi, after two centuries of 'Macedonian' emperors.

In Clermont-Ferrand, in 1095, Pope Urban II launched an appeal for a Crusade to 'combat the infidels' and to wrest the Holy Sepulchre from them. He thus intended to consolidate the 'peace of Christ' in Europe and to mobilize chivalry in the East under the sole banner of the Cross. There was, however, no particular urgent need in the Middle East for such an expedition: Christian pilgrimages to Palestine were admittedly complicated by the Seljuk conquest of Anatolia, but there was no obstacle to journeys by sea; as for the Christians of the Holy Land, they were often rather less affected than their Muslim neighbours by the political troubles then shaking the Levant.[17] If the Komnenians welcomed the Crusade, it was in the hope that it would lead to the repression of the Turkish invaders from Asia Minor. The campaign initially unfolded according to this logic, with the reconquest of Nicaea in 1097 and its restoration to the authority of Constantinople.[18] But the Crusaders accused the Byzantines of having abandoned them during the victorious siege of Antioch and they used this as a pretext, in 1098, to keep the City of God in their hands alone. The same manoeuvre took place in Edessa, where the Crusaders, called to the aid of the Byzantine garrison, eliminated it shortly after driving back the Seljuks. Alexios, the first Komnenian emperor, realized too late that the Crusaders were less allies than conquerors of a new kind.

The Muslims drew an increasingly sharp distinction between 'Byzantines' and 'Franks';[19] the savagery of the latter made a deep impression (cases of cannibalism by starving foot soldiers in northern Syria are reported even in Christian chronicles). In fact the Crusaders, unlike the Byzantines familiar with Islam, were convinced that Muslims were merely the pagan worshippers of Muhammad; the knights and their infantry were supported by an extremely fanatical populace. Caricaturing the Crusades as a clash of civilizations between Christianity and Islam is therefore as reductive as it is misleading. In fact, this was the first expedition of the Christian West to the very heart of the territory attributed in 395 to the Eastern Roman Empire, while Justinian had from the sixth century occupied a good part of the Roman Empire of the West. As for the 'liberation' of the Holy City, neither Heraclius, even after the capture of the True Cross in 614, nor John Tzimiskes, during his incursion in 975, had demonstrated the obsessive ferocity that drove the Crusaders. Their entry into Jerusalem on 15 July 1099, after a month's siege, was accompanied by the massacre of thousands of Muslim and Jewish inhabitants.[20]

The Fatimid garrison, which negotiated its withdrawal, had, in anticipation of the battle, expelled the local Christians, whose return

[17] For instance, in 1078, the Abbasids spared the Christian population of Jerusalem during the repression of an uprising led by Muslim agitators.
[18] The Seljuks of Rum moved their capital to Konya in central Anatolia.
[19] In Arabic, *Rum* and *Franj* respectively.
[20] Shortly afterwards, the Jews of Haifa were also massacred by the Crusaders for having actively contributed to the city's resistance.

was prevented by the Crusaders, in order to leave room for the new occupants. In the same spirit, the Holy Sepulchre came under the exclusive control of the Catholic clergy, with the expulsion of 'Oriental' priests. The Holy City was thus transformed, by fire and blood, into a so-called 'Latin' city, the capital of a 'Latin' kingdom independent of the 'Greek' empire of Constantinople. This was in striking contrast to the relative but undeniable tolerance shown by the Muslim authorities since the seventh century, except during the dark interlude of Caliph Al-Hakim. The parallel between Islam and Christianity is especially baseless in that the fall of Jerusalem, celebrated throughout Catholic Europe, caused only a moderate stir in the Muslim Middle East. It would take decades of maturation and propaganda for the Muslim counter-Crusade to invest Jerusalem with an intensity comparable to that of the 'Latins', and to channel collective energies commensurate with this challenge into its 'liberation'.

Half a century of coexistence

The Crusaders organized their occupation of part of the Levant around three entities: the Latin kingdom of Jerusalem, established by Godfrey of Bouillon, which chose feudal autonomy rather than theocratic integration into the domain of the papacy; the county of Edessa, whose first chief, Baldwin of Boulogne, brother of Godfrey, became, on the latter's death in 1100, King of Jerusalem (he set up his palace there four years later in the Al-Aqsa mosque, which had been disused ever since the banishment of all Muslims from the Holy City); and the principality of Antioch, which alternated between conflict and alliance with the feudal Armenians of neighbouring Cilicia.[21] These Latin States methodically extended their territory: the kingdom of Jerusalem stretched out to the coast, the county of Edessa temporarily extended as far as Malatya, and the principality of Edessa permanently

---

[21] From the beginning of the tenth century, an Armeniac 'theme' had existed in eastern Cappadocia (see above, p. 73). In the eleventh century, Byzantine offensives against the kingdom of Armenia followed by the Turkish invasions in Asia Minor led to a significant displacement of the Armenian population towards Cilicia, in the southeast of Anatolia.

extended to Latakia. The continuous stretch of Crusader territory on the Mediterranean coast was acquired with the conquest of Acre in 1104, then of Tripoli, five years later. The now fully established county of Tripoli provided the link between the principality of Antioch and the kingdom of Jerusalem, itself suzerain of the county of Edessa.[22] The four Crusader States thus guaranteed their place in the Middle Eastern region because they could be supplied by sea without having to depend on Byzantine support.

The Fatimids, though directly challenged by the fall of Jerusalem, compensated for their conspicuous passivity with aggressive rhetoric. Their very late intervention in Tripoli did not manage to save this port from conquest by the Crusaders. Indeed, the caliphs of Cairo viewed the Latin invasion as far less worrying than the pressure from the Seljuks and, above all, the Isma'ili dissidents led by Hassan-i Sabbah from his base in the Persian fortress of Alamut. These dissidents are sometimes called Nizaris, because, during the Fatimid succession of 1094, they supported Nizar, son of the deceased sovereign, whom the manoeuvres of the viziers had excluded in favour of his half-brother Al-Mustali. (Nizar, who led an insurrection in Alexandria, was captured by the new caliph and walled up alive in Cairo.) But these diehard Isma'ilis have gone down in history under the name of the 'Assassins', derived from hashish,[23] which their opponents accused them of being intoxicated by. Even if there is no evidence for this mythical addiction, the 'assassination' came to designate the spectacular but targeted attacks perpetrated on Sabbah's orders. The terrorism inspired by Alamut struck high Abbasid and Fatimid dignitaries, viziers and generals, governors and preachers. In addition to northeast Persia, Sabbah's supporters established themselves in Syria in the eyries of the coastal range, wedged between the principality of Antioch and the county of Tripoli. They respected a form of non-aggression pact with their Crusader neighbours in order to concentrate their blows against the two caliphates. Sabbah fomented a

---

[22] The two French houses of Boulogne (in the *langue d'oïl* area) and Toulouse (in the *langue d'oc* area) respectively controlled the states of Jerusalem and Tripoli, with the Normans of Sicily dominating the principality of Antioch.

[23] 'Assassin' is the anglicized version of *hashshashin*, the term that designates regular consumers, and even addicts, of hashish.

millenarian propaganda in which his own sect would end up imposing its vision of Islam as the only one permitted.

As for the court of Baghdad, it was no more affected than Cairo by the fall of Jerusalem. The *qadi* of Damascus, sent to the Abbasid capital in 1099 to warn of the Crusader danger, was quickly appointed grand *qadi* to quell the local unrest. The caliph of Baghdad was in any case quite powerless in the face of his Seljuk overseers, themselves bogged down in bloody power struggles and overwhelmed by the surge of Turkmen hordes as far as Anatolia. The petty kings of Damascus and Aleppo often feared the intervention of the sultan's troops, which would be fatal to their autonomy, much more than the rise in power of the Crusaders, with whom mutually beneficial arrangements were concluded, including revenue sharing from the lands bordering their respective domains. The quarrels between Latin feudal lords overlapped with those between Syrian emirs; indeed, Muslim–Christian coalitions occasionally confronted Christian–Muslim alliances. Faced with this compromise, the populations of Damascus, and even more of Aleppo, sometimes rose up to affirm the imperative need to fight against the Franks. In Aleppo, the Sunni and Shiite dignitaries formed a common front, twice obtaining the deposition of the local emir in favour of a general ready to do battle with the Crusaders (in 1118 the governor of Diyarbakir, and in 1125 that of Mosul). The Isma'ili dissidents, accused of colluding with the Crusaders, were massacred in the course of collective lynchings in Aleppo in 1114 and in Damascus in 1129.

Arab city dwellers in Syria felt at the mercy of alliances between Franks and Turks, and sometimes had no recourse but to rely on another Turk to save them from the Crusaders' threat. The Arab peasants of Bilad al-Sham continued to pay their tithes to an officer who gave them to the Franks or the Turks; the product of their harvest was sold in the Crusader ports or on Muslim markets. The knights from Europe, whose somewhat crude brutality had already shocked the Byzantines, became civilized in the East, where they took root and glady adopted the local ceremonies. They ensured the protection of the caravan from Damascus to Mecca, admittedly in return for tribute – but this at least guaranteed that the most important pilgrimage of Islam could be safeguarded. Crusader intolerance, with systematic Christianization of the mosques during the first decade of the Latin States, softened somewhat after the fall of Sidon in 1110. The Fatimids, gradually pushed out of Palestine, clung to the port of Ashkelon, saved by the resistance of its population in 1111. This city was the last line of defence for Egypt, once the oasis of Gaza, at the gates of the Sinai, had fallen into the hands of the Franks.

The caliphs of Cairo, however, persisted in considering the threat from the Crusaders as much less serious than that from the Isma'ili dissidents, even after the death, in 1124, of Hassan-i Sabbah: the 'new preaching' (*da'wa*), spread from the citadels of Alamut and Syria, fuelled its calls for murder with a fervent eschatological anxiety; the Crusader invasion was only one of the signs heralding the End of Times, and therefore the imminent advent of the New Law. In 1130, the Fatimid imam was slain in Cairo, in the middle of an official ceremony, by a commando of Assassins. But Abbasid power was no less vulnerable to this threat rooted in its territory. In 1135, the caliph himself was 'assassinated' south of Tabriz. His son, who had succeeded him on the throne before being deposed by the Seljuk sultan, was also 'assassinated' in 1138 in Isfahan. Each time, these murders were celebrated for seven days and seven nights in Alamut. Never had both caliphates, clearly unable to protect themselves from determined extremists, seemed so fragile.

This weakness contrasted with the rise to power of a Turkish general, the *atabeg* Zengi.[24] Having become master of Aleppo and Mosul, this tireless warrior took the nickname of Imad al-Din, 'the Pillar of Religion', to highlight his fight against the Franks. The discipline he imposed on his troops contrasted with the previous excesses of the Muslim soldiers. In 1144, Zengi reconquered Edessa, the seat of one of the four Latin States, thereby winning the first victory of the counter-Crusade. He expelled the Franks from the city and, among the Christian residents, favoured the Syriacs over the Armenians.[25] He then preferred to consolidate his achievements rather than to embark on a new offensive. While it was thus several decades before the Muslim reaction to the Crusades took shape, the fall of Edessa caused a shock wave in Western Europe: the Second Crusade was preached in 1146 in Vézelay, on Easter

---

[24] *Ata* ('father') and *beg* ('lord') was the title given by the Seljuk sultans to the guardians of their sons.
[25] Zengi then settled in Edessa 300 Jewish families, whose loyalty he had secured.

Sunday, in the presence of the king of France, Louis VII, then in Speyer, on Christmas Day, before the German sovereign Conrad III.

The Light of Religion

The assassination of Zengi in 1146 left Aleppo to one of his four sons, Nur ad-Din, 'the Light of Religion', with Mosul returning to the eldest of this 'Zengid' sibling, Sayf ad-Din, 'the Sword of Religion'. Nur ad-Din's son needed to quell a Frankish attempt to capture Edessa, an attempt whose terrible repression led to the ruin of the city. He then took advantage of the erratic conduct of the Second Crusade which Conrad III and Louis VII had led into the Seljuk trap in Anatolia, before Conrad reached Jerusalem and Louis reached Antioch, both by sea. The Crusaders, gathered in assizes in Acre in 1148, decided to attack Damascus rather than Aleppo. Nur ad-Din, freed from any direct threat, was thus able to come to the aid of the emir of Damascus. Faced with this solid Muslim front, the Crusaders were divided over the ambitions of the count of Flanders to establish a stronghold in Damascus comparable to that of the Toulousans in Tripoli. The siege of Damascus was finally lifted and the status quo between Franks and Turks was restored, but the prestige won by Nur ad-Din, who protected the city without trying to seize it, was immense. The Second Crusade ended in 1149 with this acknowledgement of failure, and the return to their thrones of the French and German monarchs. The myth of Frankish infallibility had been destroyed, while the Crusaders compensated for their numerical inferiority by consolidating several imposing fortresses, often entrusted to the fighting orders of the Hospitallers and the Templars.

During the next five years, Nur ad-Din the Zengid gradually seized the eastern part of the principality of Antioch, while eliminating the last pockets of resistance in the county of Edessa. He cultivated his image as a pious sovereign leading a minor military jihad against the Crusaders and a major mystical jihad of Sunni fervour. Where the first Seljuks were distinguished by their intolerance and rigour, Nur ad-Din, also of Turkish ethnicity, preferred to favour Sufi personalities, encourage institutions of study, and manage negotiated solutions. It was as a champion of Islam that he succeeded, first, in stifling in Aleppo the centres of a Shiism which had already become a minority sect, then, after two unsuccessful sieges, in conquering Damascus without a fight in 1154. In the ancient capital of the Umayyads, he staged the demonstrations of force which preceded and followed his operations against the Crusaders. Nur ad-Din could count on a solid intelligence service and on the loyalty of his Kurdish general Shirkuh, appointed governor of Damascus. The pressure exerted by Nur ad-Din on the Crusaders, but also on the Seljuks, allowed the Byzantine Empire to restore its suzerainty over the principality of Antioch in 1159 and to receive, two years later, the symbolic submission of the sultan of Anatolia. Constantinople thus directly benefited from the Muslim counter-Crusade – a new illustration of the deep antagonism between the Byzantines and the Crusaders.

In 1163, a Syria reunited under Nur ad-Din, and backed by Abbasid Iraq, faced, in Jerusalem, the Latin kingdom of Amalric, to whom the Crusader conquest of Ashkelon, ten years earlier, and the fortification of Gaza by the Templars, had opened the way to Egypt. After the battle for Syria which set the Byzantines against the Fatimids during the second half of the tenth century, it was a battle for Egypt which was now being played out between Damascus and Jerusalem. Caliph al-Adid, who ascended the throne of Cairo in 1160, at the age of eight, was marginalized by the bloody quarrels between his various viziers, who did not hesitate to seek the intervention of Amalric and Nur ad-Din. In 1164, the master of Damascus dispatched to Egypt an army commanded by his faithful Shirkuh, himself assisted by his nephew Saladin.[26] This campaign ended with the negotiated withdrawal of Syrian and Crusader troops, both cheated of victory. Here again, the myth of a frontal clash between Islam and Christianity does not hold up in the face of the vagaries of this battle for Egypt, during which the masters of Cairo never obeyed a religiously based logic.

In 1167, the caliph of Baghdad, convinced that he could finally get rid of the Fatimid 'usurpation', encouraged Nur ad-Din to send Shirkuh and Saladin back to Egypt. This second expedition was countered by the parallel intervention of the kingdom of Jerusalem, which ended up imposing its tutelage on Egypt. But the Franks proved to be as brutal as they were rapacious, and thus sparked an uprising among the people of Cairo. While his capital was set on fire so as not to have to surrender to

[26] Saladin is the anglicized version of the Arabic nickname 'Righteous of the Faith'.

the Crusaders, al-Adid, the Fatimid ruler, sent Nur ad-Din a heartfelt appeal for help. Amalric, fearing attack from the rear, retreated at the head of his troops to Palestine. Shirkuh, welcomed in Cairo as a liberator in 1169, was soon named vizier, a function which, after his natural death, fell to his relative Saladin. The young general abandoned his dissolute life to adopt the asceticism dear to Nur ad-Din. In 1171, he officially forbade the Isma'ili rite and appointed a Sunni grand *qadi*, of the Shafi'i school, whose founder is buried in Cairo. Soon after, even as al-Adid lay dying, a poignant embodiment of Fatimid death-throes, Saladin ordered Friday prayers to be said in the name of the caliph of Baghdad in all the mosques of Egypt. Cairo was adorned with black Abbasid flags, while Nur ad-Din in Damascus received the sumptuous rewards of the now one and only Commander of the Faithful.

The rise of the Ayyubids

It was undoubtedly thanks to the Crusader invasion that the Fatimid Caliphate prolonged by three-quarters of a century an existence that the Seljuk restoration might have threatened much earlier. Having tolerated a buffer state in northern Syria which protected it from the assaults of Byzantium, Cairo had accommodated itself to a Latin belt which, on the Levantine coast, neutralized the ambitions of the Turkish Zengids. Saladin, resolved to consolidate his own power in Egypt, both Kurdish and Ayyubid,[27] now took his turn to exploit the Crusaders' buffer zone to avoid being deposed by Nur ad-Din. In 1173, he obeyed the order from Damascus to deploy his army at the foot of the Frankish citadel of Kerak, which overlooked and threatened the pilgrimage route to Mecca. But he retreated when Nur ad-Din moved in with his own troops, thus saving the kingdom of Jerusalem from a coordinated offensive with potentially devastating effects. Saladin also preferred to divert part of his military resources to Yemen, where his nephew conquered an Ayyubid stronghold

---

[27] From the name of Ayyub (Job), the father of Saladin. A province of 'Kurdistan', also known as the 'country of the Kurds', existed in the Seljuk sultanate in the middle of the twelfth century. It lay north of Mosul, in the Zagros range, and the Ayyubid family was, rather significantly, not from there, as Kurdish tribalism was marked by conflict and division.

in 1174, on the pretext of re-establishing there, as in Egypt, the Friday prayers in the name of the Abbasids. Nur ad-Din, to whom Saladin formally remained subordinate, obtained recognition by the caliph of his authority over all the Abbasid territories from Upper Mesopotamia and Syria to Egypt. (Zengid, by biding his time, was in fact able to seize Mosul just as peacefully in 1171 as he had Damascus in 1154.)

The natural death of Nur ad-Din in Damascus, in 1174, led Saladin to drop his mask, while repeating pledges of posthumous loyalty to his former sovereign. He took control of southern Syria, leaving Aleppo and Mosul in the hands of Zengid heirs. He was content with the title of 'king' (*malik*), inferior to that of 'sultan', reserved for the Seljuk protector of the caliph of Baghdad. Saladin was in no more of a hurry to attack Jerusalem than Nur ad-Din had been before him, and he devoted the next twelve years to gradually subjugating Homs, Aleppo, and Mosul. As he intrigued and waged war against his Muslim rivals, he fostered a multifaceted propaganda campaign on the reconquest of Jerusalem and the imperative of jihad to 'liberate' it. Once he had consolidated an empire that, from Upper Mesopotamia to Egypt, Nur ad-Din had never fully controlled, Saladin finally decided to strike the Crusaders at the heart of their domains. In 1187, the breaking of the truce for the pilgrimage to Mecca was a worthy *casus belli*. Saladin's victory at Hattin, on the heights of the Sea of Galilee, enabled him to seize Acre, then Jerusalem, whose Frankish garrison negotiated its evacuation. The magnanimity of this surrender contrasted with the bloodbath of the Frankish conquest of 1099. Furthermore, Saladin portrayed himself as an imitator of the Prophet Muhammad, before whom the gates of Mecca had opened without a fight in 630. From one holy city to another, this piece of dramaturgy, which crowned decades of increasingly fervent invocation of Jerusalem, undoubtedly contributed more to the sanctification of Al-Quds[28] than acts of faith alone.

It was during the ascending phase of this counter-Crusade that one Church of the East chose, in 1182, to go over collectively to the authority of Rome. These were the Maronites of Mount Lebanon, who take their name both from Saint Maron, a hermit of the Orontes valley in the fifth century, and from his disciple John Maron, who organized this

---

[28] Al-Quds is the Arabic name for Jerusalem, and means literally 'the Holy'.

community in the seventh century. The two Marons were as opposed to Byzantine dogma as to Miaphysite dissidence, even if local solidarities weighed much more than any theological positions. This was true of the Maronites as much as of the other minorities in Bilad al-Sham, whether Christian or Muslim, as we have seen. Uncertainty about the real beliefs of the first Maronites is all the greater as their hierarchy has long fostered the fable of historically 'Catholic' Maronites. This autocephalous Church, organized like its peers around a patriarch, in fact waited more than a century after the schism of 1054 between Constantinople and Rome to swear allegiance to the pope's representative in Antioch. It was only in 1213 that a synod meeting in Tripoli, under the authority of a cardinal sent by Rome, formalized the Catholicism of the Maronites, whose patriarch since then has claimed the rank of cardinal.

Towards the Third Crusade

While the Crusaders encouraged the 'Latinization' of the clergy under their control as early as 1099, the adhesion of the Maronites to Catholicism, however belated, gave them access to religious leadership and combatant orders. This choice, facilitated by the establishment of the overwhelming majority of Maronites in the Latin States, contrasted with the attitudes adopted by the other Eastern Christians: the Armenians, punished by Zengi after the fall of Edessa, consistently adopted an autonomous stance within the Christian camp, wagering on the Franks rather than the Byzantines, until, in 1197, they obtained recognition for their 'kingdom' of Cilicia (called 'Little Armenia' as opposed to the original 'Great Armenia'); the Orthodox 'Greeks', very largely Arabized, remained loyal to Constantinople,[29] which earned them various slights from the Crusaders, but gained them a certain leniency from Muslim leaders; the Syriacs/Assyrians, however, appeared to be the most loyal in the eyes of Nur ad-Din and Saladin, taking advantage of the retreat of the Crusaders. As for the Copts, their clergy and notables remained sufficiently neutral to cushion the shock of the Frankish expeditions

[29] The Arabic term *Rum* continued to designate both Constantinople (the 'new Rome') and Anatolia, as well as the Byzantines and the (often Arab) Christians of the Byzantine rite.

to Egypt, then of the fall of the Fatimids. This contrasting picture demonstrates once again the profound inanity of any presentation of the Crusades as a confrontation between two homogeneous blocs, one Christian and the other Muslim.

It was in Saladin's Egypt that Moses Maimonides (1138–1204), known as 'the Rambam', one of the greatest Jewish thinkers of the Middle Ages, produced his work. Born in Córdoba, he moved to Cairo in 1166, where he became the head of the Jewish community, its *naggid*. The status of *dhimmi* ('protected'), granted to Jews as well as to Christians, was obviously discriminatory, imposed by the dominant religion of Islam, but it was based on the internal autonomy of the administrative and religious organization of these minorities. Maimonides was thus both the chief rabbi of Egypt, an intermediary with the Ayyubid authorities, and the judge recognized by his co-religionists for contracts, arbitration, and litigation. A renowned doctor, he successfully intervened at the court of Saladin and drew on this privileged access to Muslim dignitaries for his functions as a community representative. He developed the work of Avicenna, itself inspired by Galen, with a *Treatise on Medical Aphorisms*. But it was his theological summaries, written in Hebrew (*Repetition of the Torah*) or in Arabic (*A Guide for the Perplexed*), which had the greatest impact. Maimonides maintained a rich correspondence with the Jewish communities of Yemen, Syria, and Palestine, where he was buried, in accordance with his last wishes.

If the shock of the fall of Edessa in 1144 had been intense enough to trigger the Second Crusade in Western Europe, the emotions aroused by the Muslim reconquest of Jerusalem in 1187 could not fail to lead to a Third Crusade. The German Emperor, Frederick I Barbarossa, led an immense army which, on the edges of Europe, seized the Byzantine places of Plovdiv and Edirne. Faced with this terrible threat, Constantinople was obliged to consent to the passage of the German contingent to Asia Minor, where the accidental drowning of Barbarossa and the ravages of an epidemic in Antioch led to the rout of the expedition. Philippe Auguste and Richard the Lionheart, the French and English sovereigns, chose the sea route, wintered in Sicily, and contributed to the recapture of Acre in 1191. The King of France returned to his lands, leaving the Crusade under the sole direction of Richard, whose face-to-face encounter with Saladin was tinged with chivalric respect. The shared values of the two fighting elites contrasted with the enthusiasm and indeed the fanaticism of the Frankish and Muslim masses. It led to the conclusion of a lasting truce in 1192, in which the Crusaders agreed to hand over the dismantled fortress of Ashkelon in return for a guarantee of unhindered Christian pilgrimage to Jerusalem. The 'Latin Kingdom' retained the name of the Holy City, even if it had surrendered it to the Muslims. Its capital was now Acre, from where it controlled the coast from Jaffa to Tyre; the rear base of Cyprus was acquired by the Crusaders. Shortly after Richard's departure for England, Saladin died in Damascus in 1193. The Third Crusade had not affected his essential achievements in the Holy Land.

The Egyptian question

The sudden ending of the caliphate of Egypt, after two centuries, revealed the relative fragility of the Fatimid structure. The Isma'ili imams certainly restored to Egypt not only its autonomy, already acquired during the second Abbasid century, but also the ability to influence the rest of the Middle East, which it had enjoyed until the eve of the Christian era. The caliphs of Egypt, however, failed to transform their control of the commercial axis between the Mediterranean and the Red Sea into a lasting power, just as their fleet, already outclassed by the Byzantine navy, failed to stem the rise of the Normans of Sicily. But the main weakness of the Fatimids was probably ideological: they never tried to implant Isma'ilism in the Egyptian population, which remained both Sunni and loyalist; the caliphate of Baghdad, whatever the straitjacket imposed by its successive sultans, continued to be in tune with the piety of its subjects. The gap between the Islam professed by the 'elite' and the Islam lived by the 'masses' continued to widen in Egypt during the Fatimid era, to the point where the abolition of this caliphate by Saladin, its last vizier, did not arouse any noticeable reaction.

The decline of the Fatimids worsened with the Nizari dissent of 1094, which attracted the most fervent of the Isma'ili missionaries, but trapped them in the terrorist impasse of the Assassins. From being an imperial religion under the caliphs of Tunisia and Egypt, Isma'ilism was reduced to no more than the creed of a marginalized minority, which found in Bilad al-Sham a refuge comparable to that of the Druze and the Alawites. As for Saladin's Egyptian campaign, it followed the ternary dynamic of

Ibn Khaldun, although on a smaller scale than for the Abbasids, the Fatimids, and the Seljuks: the Ayyubid 'group' relied on Sunni 'preaching', hostile to the Crusaders and the Fatimids, to establish its 'power', first in Egypt, then in Syria, Yemen, and Upper Mesopotamia. As soon as Nur ad-Din had died, Saladin transferred his capital to Damascus, returning Egypt to the status of a subordinate province-resource, enriched by the agricultural production of the Nile Valley and its delta, as well as by the flourishing commerce in Alexandria. The Euphrates remained the dividing line between Bilad al-Sham and the Iraq of the Buyid emirs, then of the Seljuk sultans, until Nur ad-Din and Saladin succeeded, in Upper Mesopotamia, in extending their domain to the Tigris.

Once the Sunni Sultanate was established in Baghdad, Turkish identity, common to the Seljuks and the Zengids, could not hide the differences between the increasing fragmentation of the former and the counter-Crusade mobilization of the latter. The Turkish Zengids were as linguistically and politically Arabized as the Ayyubid Kurds – an Arabization that allowed them to recruit contingents of very diverse origins under the black banner of the Abbasids. From 1161 to 1175, the Seljuks of Rum, based in Nicaea, then in Konya, went so far as to accept the suzerainty of Byzantium, while a dissident movement, also Turkish, challenged them for the domination of part of Anatolia.[30] Turkish ethnicity therefore has no interpretative value per se, at least at this stage in the history of the Middle East. It is just as erroneous to project onto the leaders of the counter-Crusade the categories of modern nationalism: the pretensions of Nasser in Egypt, Assad in Syria, and Saddam Hussein in Iraq[31] to pose as twentieth-century Saladins in the face of 'Zionism' and 'imperialism' tell us more about their autocratic regimes than about mediaeval Islam. Finally, if Nur ad-Din the Turk is more revered by popular piety these days than Saladin the Kurd, this is because the former, having failed to 'liberate' Jerusalem, did not have to negotiate the conditions of this 'liberation' with the Crusaders, thus preserving his aura of integrity intact. Such considerations, needless to say, simply did not arise during the lifetimes of these characters.

---

[30] These were the Danishmends, based in Sivas from 1071 to 1174.
[31] The Iraqi despot liked to recall that he was born, like Saladin, in Tikrit.

Thinking the unique in the plural

The aberration of the coexistence of two caliphates in the Middle East persisted for two long centuries (the Umayyad Caliphate, established in Córdoba from 929 to 1031, had no impact on the evolution of the eastern Mediterranean). Such an aberration was, from an Islamic point of view, a kind of blasphemy, since it divided the supposedly united community of the faithful between different commanders of the faithful. It should have shattered once and for all the myth of a monolithic Islam, especially since the polarization between Sunni Abbasids and Isma'ili Fatimids was complicated by the Shiite tutelage exercised by the Buyids in Baghdad and the fact that the Egyptian population was very largely Sunnite. These multiple hybridizations blurred the dogmatic borders between different Muslim trends: the symbol of this interbreeding was Al-Azhar, later described as the 'Sorbonne of Islam', even as the 'Lighthouse of Sunnism', even though this mosque-university was actually founded by a schismatic caliph.

The other paradox of the standoff between Abbasids and Fatimids was that the initially most vulnerable caliphate, that of Baghdad, outlived the originally most dynamic caliphate, that of Cairo. This should not be seen as a strategic victory for Iraq over Egypt, but rather as marking the rise to power, focused on Nur ad-Din and then Saladin, of a Syrian bloc backed by Upper Mesopotamia. Nur ad-Din seized Mosul in the same year, 1171, as his general Saladin abolished the Fatimid Caliphate. And it was the capture of Mosul, in 1186, by a Saladin who had become king, which enabled him to launch the 'liberation' of Jerusalem the following year. The displacement of the northern border between the powers of Syria and Iraq from the Euphrates towards the Tigris by these two champions of Islam was the key to their hold on Egypt from the Levant.

As for the Assassins, their dark legend would attract a resurgence of interest after the attacks on New York and Washington on 11 September 2001. They were then presented as the precursors of modern terrorism, the elusive leader of Al-Qaeda being likened to the 'Old Man of the Mountain' who inspired 'assassinations' from his eyries in Syria and Persia. This would be to forget that these dissidents of Isma'ilism, targeting a clearly defined political object, practised a mediaeval form of 'surgical strike', and not the mass terror of the beginning of the present millennium. The most relevant comparison between the Assassins and the jihadists – a comparison too rarely expressed today – would involve the structuring of these two movements into millenarian sects. Hassan-i Sabbah, like Osama bin Laden and then Abu Bakr al-Baghdadi, preached the beginning of a new era of which his terrorist sect would represent the vanguard. A militant of this sect would undergo an authentic conversion, convinced as he was of the imminence of the End of Times. He was reborn under a new identity by joining a group that demanded from him a blind obedience, even the worst violence against his community of origin. The contemporaries of the Assassins, unlike many modern commentators, clearly perceived the sectarian nature of such terrorist groups and would never have made the mistake, now too widespread, of seeing in them the fruit of a 'radicalization' of majority Islam.

The Crusades, of which only the first century has been covered in this chapter, were deeply European in their concept and development. It was not until the nineteenth century that Arab historians substituted the term 'Crusaders' for that of 'Franks', in an explicit parallel between these mediaeval expeditions and the heyday of expanding colonialism of their own time. The bias of this re-reading was then accentuated by a highlighting of the religious dimension of the counter-Crusade and a caricature of the rapacity of the Crusaders, deemed to have been 'imperialists' *avant la lettre*. This 'grand narrative' tends to magnify the spiritual power of an eventually triumphant Islam in the face of a West that was more materialistic than Christian. It fits perfectly into the mirror-narrative of a Europe which tries to deny, now as before, the loss of its Christian values by confronting a decadent Islam in the Holy Land. Such fables shed more light on those who feed on them and disseminate them than on historical reality.

On the other hand, it is true that the shock of the Crusades sometimes led the populations of Bilad al-Sham to disrupt the power games of Muslim 'elites'. This was especially the case in the two major urban centres of Damascus and Aleppo, where the interaction between religious dignitaries, high-ranking merchants, a youthful militia, and refugee dissidents could occasionally encourage a more combative posture. These were already no longer the rebellious 'masses' of ninth-century Iraq, the nightmare of the Abbasid property owners; but to speak in this case of 'public opinion', or even of a 'people in arms', is still an exaggeration. If there is indeed an affinity to be explored between the mediaeval and the current Middle East, it lies in the instrumentalization of 'holy wars' by powers which, Muslim as well as Christian, use them as an argument to impose their will on their peers, long before they turn against their designated enemies. This dialectic of hegemony and conflict, of which the careers of Nur ad-Din and Saladin are impressive examples, would tragically recur in the following and terminal phase of the Abbasid Caliphate: the end of the Fatimid era and the restoration of a single caliphate would not be enough to save this regime from a truly existential threat.

Chronology

945–967	Sayf al-Dawla, Shia emir of Aleppo.
969	Foundation of Cairo by the Fatimids.
969	Byzantine reconquest of Antioch.
972	Opening of the Al-Azhar mosque in Cairo.
975–996	Aziz, Fatimid caliph in Cairo.
977–983	Adud al-Dawla, Buyid Grand Emir in Baghdad.
980–1037	Avicenna/Ibn Sina, master of medicine and *falsafa*.
988	Final version of Ibn Hawqal's *Description of the Earth*.
991–1031	Al-Qadir, Abbasid caliph in Baghdad.
995	Death in Baghdad of the encyclopaedist Ibn al-Nadim.
996–1021	Al-Hakim, Fatimid caliph in Cairo.
1001	Peace between Fatimids and Byzantines.
1009	Partial destruction of the Holy Sepulchre in Jerusalem.
1028–1045	Al-Jarjara'i, Fatimid vizier in Cairo.
1031–1075	Al-Qaïm, Abbasid caliph in Baghdad.
1054	'Great Schism' between the Churches of the West and the East.
1055	First Seljuk 'sultan' in Baghdad.
1058	Death in Baghdad of the theologian Mawardi.
1071	Seljuk victory of Manzikert over the Byzantines.
1072–1092	Malik Shah, Seljuk sultan.
1076	Capture of Damascus by the Seljuks.
1077–1097	'Sultanate of Rum' in Nicaea/İznik.
1084	Capture of Antioch by the Seljuks.
1090	Hassan-i Sabbah established in Alamut.
1094	Split between Fatimids and Sabbah's supporters.
1098	Capture of Antioch by the Crusaders.
1099	Capture of Jerusalem by the Crusaders.
1109	Capture of Tripoli by the Crusaders.
1127–1146	Zengi, governor of Mosul, then of Aleppo.
1130	'Assassination' of the Fatimid Caliph.
1135	'Assassination' of the Abbasid Caliph.
1144	Recapture of Edessa by Zengi.
1146–1149	Second Crusade.
1153	Capture of Ashkelon by the Crusaders.

1154	Capture of Damascus by Nur ad-Din.
1171	Abolition of the Fatimid Caliphate by Saladin and capture of Mosul by Nur ad-Din.
1174	Death of Nur ad-Din in Damascus, where Saladin succeeds him.
1182	The Maronites of Lebanon go over to Catholicism.
1187	Muslim victory at Hattin and reconquest of Jerusalem.
1189–1192	Third Crusade.
1193	Death of Saladin in Damascus.

Further reading

Brett, Michael, *The Fatimid Empire* (Edinburgh: Edinburgh University Press, 2017).

Eddé, Anne-Marie, *Saladin*, translated by Jane Marie Todd (Cambridge, MA: Harvard University Press, 2014).

Halm, Heinz, *Shi'ism*, translated by Janet Watson and Marian Hill, second edition (Edinburgh: Edinburgh University Press, 2004).

Lemire, Vincent, *Jerusalem: history of a global city*, translated by Juliana Froggatt (Oakland, CA: University of California Press, 2022).

Lewis, Bernard, *The Assassins: a radical sect in Islam*, new edition (London: Phoenix, 2003).

Maalouf, Amin, *The Crusades through Arab eyes*, translated by Jon Rothschild (London: Saqi Essentials, 2006).

Morton, Nicholas, *The Crusader states and their neighbours, a military history (1099–1187)* (New York: Oxford University Press, 2020).

Peacock, A. C. S., *The Great Seljuk Empire* (Edinburgh: Edinburgh University Press, 2015).

Prawer, Joshua, *The Latin kingdom of Jerusalem: European colonialism in the Middle Ages* (London: Weidenfeld and Nicolson, 1973).

Walker, Paul E., *Caliph of Cairo* (Cairo: American University Press, 2010).

FOUR

Sultans and invaders (1193–1501)

The aberration of the coexistence of two rival caliphates, which had dominated the previous period, was followed, for most of the next three centuries, by the aberration of the accession of former slaves, the Mamluks, to the now supreme power of the sultanate. The succession of theatrical twists that allowed this shift cannot, unless we write history in the future perfect tense, be captured by any pre-established conceptual scheme. So this chapter, which often endeavours to untangle a complex sequence of situations, will be filled with events, leaving to others the charms of alternative histories. (What would have happened, for example, if the Mongols were not stopped in Palestine in 1260 or if Constantinople had fallen to the Ottomans long before 1453?) Ideological and religious positions no longer held much value in this vast whirlwind of alliances and betrayals, where Christians and Muslims exchanged Jerusalem, where the Crusaders sacked Constantinople, where the Ottomans joined forces with the Byzantines, and where the conquerors converted to the Islam of the conquered. The confusion was such that even the brilliant Ibn Khaldun, when translating his concepts into action, would fail dismally. But we need to return to the state of the Middle East in 1193, when Saladin died.

Despite his victories over the Fatimids in Cairo and the Crusaders in Jerusalem, Saladin was content with the relatively modest title of 'king', which he bequeathed to his descendants. The Ayyubid sovereigns were, however, much more entitled to proclaim themselves sultans than their Seljuk contemporaries: the Anatolian sultanate of Rum, whose capital, Konya, was sacked by the Crusaders in 1190, was shaken, two years later, by terrible quarrels over succession; in 1194, the Seljuk master of Baghdad was dethroned by a new dynasty of Turkish sultans, the Khwarazmians, originating from a Central Asian region that is now shared between Uzbekistan and

Turkmenistan.¹ These Khwarazmians were as fervent as their Seljuk predecessors in defending the Sunni orthodoxy of the reunited caliphate. But they were just as exhausted as the latter by their family disputes over the distribution of the fiefdoms of the Abbasid Empire. As for the Latin States, reduced to a coastal strip in the Levant, they could not threaten the metropolises of Syria and Egypt, despite the repeated campaigns in their support launched from Europe. In fact, the Fourth Crusade was marked by an unleashing of Western violence not against the Muslim states, but paradoxically against the Christian East.

The Crusade against Byzantium

In 1198, Pope Innocent III preached a new Crusade for the liberation of Jerusalem. The mobilization was difficult to arrange: it was not until 1202 that a contingent, largely from Champagne and Flanders, arrived in Venice to embark. In return for their transport to the Holy Land, the Crusaders agreed to pay the city of the Doges a considerable sum, but they managed to pay only half. This was the beginning of a sordid cycle in which a pretender to the Byzantine throne dangled before the Crusaders the carrot of paying off their debt to Venice, as well as ensuring the union of the Churches of East and West, if they supported his coronation. The Crusaders seized Constantinople in 1203, but they had seriously overestimated its wealth. The new emperor they installed proved unable to meet their financial demands. He was soon overthrown, against the backdrop of a popular uprising against the Latins. The Crusaders and Venice, determined to take back the Byzantine capital, signed a treaty enacting the 'partition of Romania': a Latin sovereign would reign over Constantinople and a quarter of the empire, while Venice and the Crusaders would each take half of the rest of the territory. The crudeness of such partitioning underlines how much this Fourth Crusade was hijacked into being an expedition for the colonial appropriation of Christian territory by other Christian powers. Thus the pope's calls for tolerance did little to counterbalance the anti-Greek fanaticism of the priests who had embarked with the Crusaders.

---

¹ These sultans were also called Khwarazmshahs, literally 'Kings of Khwarazm', the region in question.

The second capture of Constantinople, in 1204, was accompanied by a veritable orgy of bloodshed and systematic looting, especially of relics. The churches were desecrated and the tombs of the emperors gutted. The Crusaders imposed one of their own number on the throne of Constantine and set up a Venetian patriarch alongside him, before dividing up the other territorial spoils with the city of the Doges. In Asia Minor, Byzantine resistance was organized around two poles, first in Trebizond, on the Black Sea, and then especially in Nicaea, where a new emperor contrived to be crowned in 1208. There was a heavy symbolism in seeing the city of the first ecumenical council presided over in 325 by Constantine becoming the bastion of 'Greek' resistance to the 'Latin' invasion. But it was the violence perpetrated in the name of 'Western' Catholicism that created a much deeper rift with 'Eastern' Orthodoxy than the dogmatic schism of 1054. The trauma of the sack of Constantinople struck at the very heart of a Church of the East already sorely tested by the Latinization imposed by the Crusaders during the previous century. Once again in the Middle East, doctrinal disputes mattered less than political disputes and expansionist ambitions.

The Ayyubids regroup

Before his death in 1193, Saladin organized the distribution of his vast domain between each of his three sons, who were given respectively Cairo, Damascus, and Aleppo, while one of his brothers controlled Yemen and another, Adil, ruled Upper Mesopotamia. This division of the heritage between these different 'kings' of Kurdish origin could have quickly encouraged a process of fragmentation comparable to that which undermined the Turkish 'sultanates' – first the Seljuks, then the Khwarazmians. This process was initially contained by the intervention of Adil, who methodically succeeded in imposing his authority on his three nephews in 1200. The restoration of Syrian–Egyptian unity, at a time when Christians were tearing each other apart in Constantinople, was formally recognized by the Abbasid caliph in 1207. Adil was nicknamed Sayf ad-Din, 'the Sword of Religion', hence the name Saphadin by which he was known in the Frankish chronicles. Until his death in 1218, he conducted a policy of appeasement with the Latin kingdom of Acre and with the Italian cities which controlled Mediterranean trade: Venice, of course, but also Pisa and Genoa.

Kamil, Adil's son and successor, ascended the Ayyubid throne when a new Crusade, the fifth, targeted Egypt and seized the strategic city of Damietta in the Nile delta in 1219. Francis of Assisi joined the expedition and preached the evangelization of the 'Saracens', even if this would mean suffering martyrdom if he did not obtain their conversion. He was probably taken for an emissary of the invaders, brought to the Kamil camp, and treated with respect, despite the fiery language he used about Islam. This meeting, which no Arabic source reports, was embellished after his death by the story of an ordeal in which Francis – by now a saint – was said to have proposed a trial by fire to Muslim 'priests', who refused. In the seventeenth century, Bossuet was even more strident, presenting a Saint Francis who had preached in vain to 'barbarians', the followers of a 'monstrous religion'. The French *philosophes* took a completely opposite view: in 1756, Voltaire transfigured Kamil into a model of the enlightened monarch, while he cast Francis as the incarnation of religious fanaticism. A new shift occurred: on the one hand, there were the supporters of colonial expansion, who, in the nineteenth century, exalted Francis as an exemplar of the superiority of White people and, on the other hand, there was Pope John Paul II, who, in 1986, portrayed the founder of the Franciscans as a pioneer of interreligious dialogue. This is a very fine case study of the relativity of the interpretation of an event, especially when its historical reality is full of grey areas.

Let us return to the indisputable facts of this Fifth Crusade. The Crusader troops, who had recklessly ventured outside the walls of Damietta in 1221, were trapped by the breaking of the dykes of the Nile. The invaders, surrounded by Kamil's forces, were forced to capitulate, evacuate Egypt, and conclude an eight-year truce. The Ayyubid victory owed much to the procrastination of the German Emperor Frederick II Hohenstaufen, whose expedition to reinforce Damietta arrived too late to save the Crusaders from crushing defeat. As the heir to Germany through his father, and to Sicily through his mother, Frederick II was then the most powerful sovereign of the West. Raised in a Sicily deeply marked by a century of Fatimid reign, he mastered Arabic among other languages, and he maintained a close correspondence with Kamil. The Holy Land was for him just a prize to be seized and monetized, above all in defiance of the Holy See, in the service of his vast imperial purpose. He manoeuvred so adroitly that, in 1225, he contrived to win for himself the title of 'King of Jerusalem', a kingdom whose capital was now Acre. But he broke his promise to organize a new Crusade; in 1227, this earned him excommunication by the pope.

The exclusion from Christianity of the leader of the Holy Empire coincided with rising tensions between Kamil and his own relatives in Syria. Talks were engaged in which Kamil offered Jerusalem to Frederick II, in return for his support against the other Ayyubids. Where Saladin had unified his Syrian–Egyptian domain on the basis of the need to reconquer Jerusalem, his nephew Kamil reversed the argument by sacrificing Jerusalem in advance to the need to preserve Ayyubid unity. To understand this reversal, it is necessary to accept that the Holy City was obviously less holy in the eyes of certain Muslims than it was in the eyes of the Crusaders. On the Christian side, the excommunicated Emperor Frederick II led the Sixth Crusade in 1228 much more as a theatrical operation than as a military expedition. He landed in Acre with only 3,000 men and, after a few very limited engagements, in 1229 he signed a treaty with Kamil granting, in addition to Jerusalem, a corridor linking the Holy City to Jaffa, as well as Bethlehem and Nazareth. Although Kamil had ensured his control of the mosques in the Old City of Jerusalem, the third holiest site in Islam, the Muslim population largely fled the city when the Crusaders arrived. Frederick II stayed only three days in the Holy City, where his respect and tolerance impressed Arab chroniclers. The emperor, embittered by the confirmation of the papal anathema against him, soon left Palestine, leaving behind him the Latin States divided between the supporters of the Hohenstaufens and those of the Holy See. Jerusalem, isolated in the face of the openly hostile regions of Hebron and Nablus, remained in Crusader hands until the death of Kamil in 1238. The Holy City, which the rulers of Acre were unable to populate and fortify, then changed masters several times, in a confusing and destructive sequence.

From one Egyptian sultanate to the next

Even if the great manoeuvres over Palestine mobilized some of the highest leaders of Christianity and Islam, they concerned only reduced contingents on small territories. On a completely different scale were the upheavals generated by the emergence, in the steppes of northern China, of the Mongol Empire of Genghis Khan. The dramatic expansion of his hordes, initially turned towards the east, ravaged Khorasan and Azerbaijan in 1219–1221, before the invaders retreated to Central Asia. But Khwarazm, the province from which the sultans of Baghdad had emerged, was devastated and remained under Mongol occupation. Jalal al-Din Mangburni, the last of the kings of Khwarazm, escaped the débâcle by taking refuge in Afghanistan, and then in India. He returned at the head of his troops in Persia in 1224, and waged war against some groups and made pacts with others before setting up his capital in Tabriz. In 1230, his all-devouring ambitions aroused against him the victorious alliance of the Ayyubids and the Seljuks of Rum.

It was the resumption of the Mongol expansion in 1231 which dealt the final blow to Khwarazmian power, with the assassination of Jalal al-Din. This time, the armies from the steppes established themselves perma- nently in northern Persia, Azerbaijan, and Georgia. They were merely the advanced wing of an immense empire ruled, from 1235 onwards, from the court of Karakorum, in the centre of present-day Mongolia. Mongolian shamanism tolerated Muslims, Buddhists, and Christians in its capital. The Christians were Nestorians – a distant heritage of the missionaries of the Church of Persia sent along the Silk Road. As for the Khwarazmian contingents, deprived of a leader, they put their fighting spirit at the service of the Muslim sovereigns still in power. Some joined the ranks of the Seljuks of Rum, but could not avoid a crushing defeat in 1243 against the Mongols, who imposed their de facto protectorate on Anatolia. The others enlisted under the banner of the Ayyubids, seizing Jerusalem in their name, in 1244, with terrible bloodshed.

The credit for this grim victory belonged to Salih, the son of Kamil, and sovereign of Egypt since 1240; it was, he hoped, a way of erasing fifteen years of compromise with the Crusaders on the part of his family and himself. Salih was also the first of Saladin's descendants to officially bear the title of 'sultan', which he mainly flaunted so as to impose himself on the other Ayyubids of Damascus, Aleppo, and Upper Mesopotamia. (In 1229, the lineage lost control of Yemen.) In these multifaceted conflicts, Salih increasingly relied on veritable praetorian guards; as they were recruited from many different nations, their enduring loyalty was assumed. The servile origins of these shock troops were echoed in their name 'Mamluks', literally those who are 'owned', i.e. slaves. Captured on the shores of the Black and Caspian Seas, and even in Central Asia, these Mamluks, sought and bought on the markets of Anatolia and Syria, were then subjected to intense religious and military training. This re-education by Islam, under the authority of an exclusive master, meant that once they were freed they were immune to local intrigues, especially since they often spoke Arabic very badly. In addition to the Mamluk units already formed by his predecessors, Salih established his own, in a dedicated citadel on the banks of the Nile.[2]

The Ayyubid sultan's wager was crowned with success when, in 1244, a few months after the recapture of Jerusalem, the Mamluks led by Baybars cut the Crusader army to pieces not far from Gaza. This triumph meant that he could rapidly seize Damascus, before letting the Syrian generals eliminate the Khwarazmians, who really were proving far too intractable. Salih now had an army at his disposal in Cairo, based on his loyal Mamluks, and in 1247 he managed to neutralize the Crusader bastions of Tiberias and Ashkelon. However, the vulnerability of the Latin States in itself would not have been enough to rekindle the spirit of the Crusade in Europe, which the pope himself had hijacked in 1245 when he proclaimed it against Frederick II. It took all the ardour of the king of France, Louis IX, obsessed by the idea of a holy war, to mobilize a seventh Crusade with the designated objective of Egypt.

The future Saint Louis landed in Damietta in 1249, at the head of a contingent ten times greater than that led by the German emperor during the previous Crusade. The Sultan Salih, drastically weakened by tuberculosis, proposed to the invaders that he would deliver Jerusalem to them to save Egypt; the king of France rejected the proposal. The death of Salih, in this dramatic context, sowed panic in the Ayyubid court. Shajar al-Durr, literally 'the Tree of Pearls', the favourite wife of the deceased sultan, may well have been merely a freed slave, but she then succeeded in ensuring that the death of the sovereign was kept secret until her son Turanshah, Saladin's great-grandnephew, returned from

---

[2] These Mamluks were thus called 'Bahri' Mamluks (in Egypt the Nile was referred to as 'the sea'/'al-bahr').

distant Diyarbakir, in present-day Turkey. The decisive battle was fought in 1250 at Al Mansurah, about 60 kilometres southwest of Damietta, on the road to Cairo. Baybars, once again at the head of the Mamluks, won a resounding victory. Shortly after, the Egyptian galleys dealt a serious blow to the Crusader fleet, blocking any prospect of withdrawal. Louis IX was taken prisoner, and obliged to order the unconditional departure of his troops. He himself was released only on the payment of a considerable ransom. He then went to the Holy Land, where he would remain for nearly four more years, largely devoted to the consolidation of the fortifications of Acre, Jaffa, and Sidon. Still as unskilled in diplomacy as ever, he never sought to take advantage of the recurring tensions between Cairo and Damascus. In Europe, in the meantime, the rout of the Seventh Crusade had provoked the popular uprisings of the 'Shepherds' Crusade', with preachers accusing the knightly forces of having displeased God by their pride.

Turanshah was back in Egypt by 1250, but, after the turning point of Al Mansurah, he failed to gauge the new situation created by the rise of the Mamluks. He believed himself to be a full-fledged sultan, while his generals considered him to be dependent on the throne. The crisis soon erupted and ended with his assassination. No sooner had the regicide been perpetrated than the Mamluks recoiled from the prospect of a direct seizure of power. They decide to entrust the sultanate to Shajar al-Durr, the widow of the highly respected Salih. In Baghdad, the Abbasid court fumed at such sacrilege and, throughout the Muslim world, the lack of virility of the Egyptians was mocked. After three months, the Mamluks proclaimed one of their emirs, Aybak, as sultan; he was recognized as such by the caliph. But real power remained in the hands of the ephemeral Sultana, Aybak's mistress and then officially his wife. The de facto reign of Shajar al-Durr ended tragically in 1257. Anxious about Aybak's desires for emancipation, she had her husband assassinated, before being put to death herself. Ali, Aybak's still young son, was named sultan at the age of eleven. It was the Emir Qutuz who held real authority this time, because he controlled the most important Mamluk troops and had reconciled with his rival Baybars, after years of estrangement. This position of strength was sealed by the formal accession of Qutuz to the sultanate, in 1259.

The end of the Baghdad Caliphate

In Baghdad, the Abbasid caliphs, now rid of the obstacle of the Fatimids, embodied the symbolic restoration of a potentially universal Sunnism. The tutelage of their Turkish sultans was all the more bearable as the latter were often absorbed in endless quarrels with their own relatives, then diverted from Iraq by Mongol pressure. The long reign of Caliph Nasir, from 1180 to 1225, also enabled him to carry out an ambitious policy of teaching the four schools of Sunnism,[3] accompanied by demonstrations of respect for Shiite piety (with the development, in Samarra, of a shrine on the supposed site of the occultation of the Twelfth Imam). Nasir also encouraged the Sufi brotherhood of the Suhrawardiyya in Baghdad, which came to present the caliph as the mystical intercessor between believers and God. The caliphate of his grandson Al-Mustansir, from 1226 to 1242, was both shorter and duller, despite the construction in Baghdad of a sumptuous madrasa dedicated to the Commander of the Faithful.[4] But the Ayyubids did not bother to consult the caliph when they made a pact with the Crusaders over the fate of Jerusalem. And the brilliance of the Baghdad court was no longer enough to attract the great minds of the time: it was in Aleppo that the geographer Yaqut wrote his encyclopaedic work, and it was in Cairo and Damascus that the historian Ibn Khallikan composed his biographical dictionary.

Al-Musta'sim became, on the death of his father Al-Mustansir, the thirty-seventh Abbasid caliph. The Commander of the Faithful could not imagine that his fate depended on decisions being made thousands of miles away, in the Mongolian court of Karakorum. Möngke Khan, grandson of Genghis, sent his two brothers Hulagu and Khublai to conquer the Middle East and China respectively. Hulagu's huge army entered Persia in 1256 and soon eliminated Alamut, the Persian stronghold of the Isma'ili dissenters, the Assassins. An ambitious Shiite scholar, Nasir al-Din al-Tusi, then pledged allegiance to Hulagu, convinced that the Mongols were the instrument of divine vengeance against Baghdad

---

[3] The favouring of Hanbalism, which Nasir inherited from his predecessor, ended with the exile of the preacher Ibn al-Jawzi in 1194.

[4] This was the Mustansiriya, established in 1233, and fortunately preserved to this day.

and its unholy power. A certain Shiite messianism, associating Khorasan with the End of Times, as in the preaching of Abu Muslim five centuries earlier, saw the fulfilment of prophecies in the emergence, in the Far East of Islam, of an existential threat to the Sunni Caliphate. But the Mongol generals did not attach any more importance to these disputes between Muslims than to the proposals for a reverse alliance against Islam brought by various emissaries of the Christian powers. Tusi, an eager collaborator of the invading hordes, would later be rewarded by the foundation of an observatory where he continued to pursue his astronomical studies for more than a decade. It is a fine parable: history proves that, often, ambitious advisers to the current ruler are less skilful in guiding him here below than in scrutinizing the constellations above.

In 1258, Hulagu ordered his armies, reinforced by the contingents provided by his Middle Eastern vassals, to converge on Baghdad. The Abbasid caliph, visibly unaware of the balance of power, responded with bluster to the khan's ultimatums. The Muslim troops who attempted a bypass manoeuvre were crushed between the Tigris and the Euphrates. The siege of the capital, supported by a massive catapult bombardment, continued for a whole week. The capture of the Abbasid chief of staff and his execution, as well as that of all his relatives, impelled Al-Musta'sim to capitulate. Hulagu entered Baghdad in triumph and compelled the humiliated caliph to surrender the greater part of his treasure and his harem. Outside the palace, the carnage and looting lasted even longer than the battle itself. The toll of tens if not hundreds of thousands of victims was meant to sow terror throughout the Middle East and hasten its submission. Hulagu also strove, in the ruins of Baghdad, to erase all traces of Abbasid grandeur. As for Al-Musta'sim, in accordance with the Mongolian custom which forbade the shedding of a king's blood, he was rolled up in carpets and trampled to death by horses.

Never had the Muslim world experienced such a catastrophe, the impact of which facilitated the Mongol advance on all fronts. The message put out by Hulagu was cruelly simple: only unconditional capitulation could save you from massacre. Thus the garrison of Aleppo was spared in 1260, while the rebellious city was methodically sacked. Informed of Möngke's disappearance, Hulagu decided to return immediately to Karakorum to play his part in his brother's succession. He entrusted the command of his troops to General Kitbuqa, who, despite being a Nestorian, was not in the least inclined to leniency towards the Crusaders, as he proved by devastating Sidon as punishment for resisting him. Hama, Homs, and Damascus fell one after the other. The road to Egypt seemed open to the Mongols, who sent an ultimatum to the sultan of Cairo. Baybars advised Qutuz to go for an all-out fight and execute the emissaries. The confrontation, which had become inevitable, took place in Ain Jalut,[5] in Galilee, and the Mamluks were victorious. Baybars covered himself with glory in the front line and allowed Qutuz to capture Kitbuqa and then put him to death.

The Muslim victory at Ain Jalut marked not only the end of the Mongol advance, but also the tipping of the military balance, with a dazzling reconquest of Syria and the retreat of the invaders east of the Euphrates. The hasty withdrawal of Khan Hulagu and his army certainly played a role in the Mamluk success, even if it had not previously halted the Mongol drive south of Aleppo. It was nonetheless a historic turning point, little known in Europe but celebrated in the Middle East. From there to claiming that Qutuz and Baybars saved in Palestine the whole of the 'civilized world' from the onslaught of the hordes would be a bridge too far, however, as the objective assigned to Hulagu was indeed Egypt, not Europe. Moreover, the Mongols were far from having relinquished the Middle East: they were in firm control of Iraq and Persia. The Turkish Sultanate of Rum did not merely pay them tribute but was under constant pressure from them. This long-lasting weakness on the part of Muslim Anatolia enabled the Byzantines of Nicaea to concentrate their forces around Constantinople, from which they expelled the Latins in 1261. Three years after the disappearance of the Abbasid Caliphate, it was indeed the whole of the Middle East which had been radically reconstructed.

The Mamluk laboratory

Qutuz was perhaps hoping that the Mongols would eliminate the overweening Baybars at Ain Jalut. He refused to give him the governorship of Aleppo, even though the other Mamluks were dividing up the

---

[5] Literally, 'the spring of Goliath'.

fiefdoms of Syria. Baybars concluded that he must kill or be killed. He organized the assassination of the sovereign during a hunting party, and seized the throne. The new sultan realized, however, that he could not base his power on force of arms alone. In 1261, he decided to take under his wing a survivor of the massacre of the Abbasids[6] by Hulagu and to have him proclaimed 'caliph'. Where the previous 'sultans' had settled in Baghdad for three centuries to impose their tutelage on the caliph, Baybars reversed the process by transplanting to Cairo a line of caliphs who would owe him everything. It was in their name that the Friday prayer continued to be said, but attached to the name of the 'Sultan of Islam and Muslims', a title whose universal vocation eclipsed that of the caliphate. The Abbasid dynasty no longer existed except through the artifice and arbitrariness of a Mamluk sultan who diverted its prestige and authority for his own exclusive benefit.

Baybars made a pilgrimage to Mecca in 1269, where the splendour of his retinue was matched only by his generosity towards the faithful and the sanctuary. On this occasion, he affirmed his authority over the dynasty of the *'ashraf* (plural of *sharif*), the descendants of the Prophet who governed the Hejaz and had often ruled it in the past as an autonomous principality. In Egypt itself, Baybars appointed four grand *qadis* to assist him, one for each of the four schools of Sunnism, in order to curb the Shafi'i, who were then in the majority in that country.[7] This division at the top of the religious hierarchy was designed to avoid the constitution of a clerical counter-power. The sultan also appeared in public with Sufi personalities, whose disciples organized teaching and celebrations within their lodges.[8] Baybars thus reinforced his legitimation by official Islam, derived from a caliph who was under his thumb, by fostering his political charisma as a sultan among the population by linking it with the spiritual charisma of the mystics. In the same spirit,

---

[6] The first of these caliphs died in 1261 during an improvised expedition to reconquer Baghdad. The second, proclaimed in 1262, was a distant descendant of Caliph Al-Mustarshid, in power in Baghdad from 1118 to 1135. He never left Cairo, where his successors would also generally remain confined.

[7] In 1171, at the end of the Fatimid Caliphate, Saladin had appointed a single grand *qadi*, of the Shafi'i rite (see above, p. 103).

[8] The Arabic word *zawya* (plural *zawaya*) literally means 'corner'.

he created, in Palestine and Syria, many pious foundations,[9] all stamped with the symbol of a leopard, his personal coat of arms (Baybars means 'lord panther'). He built up his own myth during his lifetime, and it has been perpetuated to the present day by the oral transmission of the fabulous *Sirat al-Zahir Baybars* (*Biography of al-Zahir Baybars*), an epic both picaresque and edifying.

Baybars was in many ways the real founder of the Mamluk regime, after a decade of post-Ayyubid chaos and the Mongol demolition of the Baghdad Caliphate. He replaced the family dynamics of previous sultanates with the logic of a military elite, culturally and ethnically foreign to the local population, which renewed itself through a constant flow of acquisition and integration of new Mamluks.[10] This regime of former slaves, who had now become generals, militarized the supreme power as well as the political and administrative hierarchy. Its central-izing purpose was underpinned by a tight network of post offices,[11] sometimes backed by the commercial nodes of the caravanserais/khans. Baybars also paid particular attention to propaganda and intelligence, and had no hesitation in rewriting the history of the sultanate to erase the troublesome Qutuz. He thus appears as a highly gifted precursor of modern dictators in the Arab world – those putschist officers who reach the higher echelons of the state after years of intrigue. The major difference was that Baybars was a formidable warrior, whereas the Mamluks of our time pile up defeats abroad so as to turn their firepower against their own populations.

The last chapter of the Crusades

During his seventeen years of reign, Baybars eliminated one after the other the eyries of the Assassins in the Syrian mountains, thus putting a definitive end to these Isma'ili dissidents, whose Persian branch had

---

[9] These foundations were endowed in the inalienable mode of the *waqf* (see above, p. 66).
[10] Baybars acquired 4,000 new Mamluks during his reign, from 1260 to 1277, and Sultan Qalawun 6,000, from 1279 to 1290.
[11] Damascus, for example, was four days by horse from Cairo, and Aleppo five. The transmission of instructions and information was further accelerated by the Mamluk use of messenger pigeons for state purposes.

already been annihilated by the Mongols. He also methodically seized a string of Crusader fortresses; then, in 1268, he conquered the city of Antioch and cracked down on Little Armenia (i.e. Cilicia), both of which were punished for having collaborated in the Mongol invasion. The successors of Baybars on the Mamluk throne completed the liquidation of the Latin States, until the capture of Acre, the capital of the kingdom of Jerusalem, in 1291. Thus ended the long sequence of two centuries of Crusades, often reduced to its first part, with the Crusader conquest of Jerusalem in 1099 and its recapture in 1187, after the Muslim victory at Hattin. Even with regard to the Holy City, we need to broaden the focus by at least half a century to restore the effective periodization of 1099–1244, opened and closed by two bloodbaths, the first perpetrated by the Crusaders, the second by the Khwarazmians, and punctuated by two negotiated surrenders, one by Saladin, the other by Frederick II in 1229. When the cycle of the Crusades began, Islam was divided into two competing caliphates: the one in Cairo was more powerful than the one in Baghdad. By the time of the fall of Acre, the caliphate as a seat of power was well and truly gone, replaced by a sham institution legitimizing the Mamluks. This considerable turning point in Muslim history, however, owed nothing to the Crusades, and everything to the hordes commanded by Hulagu.

Of the seven Crusades that were launched in the Middle East (the eighth and final one being aimed at Tunisia), one of the most comprehensive resulted in the sacking of Constantinople in 1204, contributing more to setting the Churches of the West and of the East against each other than had all the theological splits. Far from being a head-on clash between Christianity and Islam, the Crusades saw the Latin States become involved in a regional equation where the Crusader leaders, themselves often divided, played one Muslim camp (in Egypt) against another (in Syria) and vice versa, not counting all the arrangements made with the local kinglets. If there was one constant in the Crusades of the twelfth and thirteenth centuries, it was the immense disappointment of the Crusaders who had come from Europe to discover the Frankish reality in the Levant.[12] As for Frederick II, the excommunicated emperor,

---

[12] In 1251, the papal legate had to prohibit the imitation by the Crusaders of Muslim coins – an imitation which, for commercial reasons, resumed seven years later.

he made substantial gains in a few months, whereas Louis IX, the canonized king, proved powerless to alter the status quo, despite several years in the Holy Land. Added to this was the fundamental weakness of the Crusader enterprise, which most of the fighters abandoned once their military and spiritual pilgrimage had been accomplished. The Latin States held out only because their maritime outlets compensated for the absence of colonial settlements. It is therefore understandable that the Crusader enterprise tells us more about the Europe from which it spread than about the Middle East, where it was, in many respects, peripheral.

'True' and 'false' Islam

The Mongol power that persisted east of the Euphrates from 1260 gradually weakened its ties with the court of the Grand Khan, itself transferred to Beijing. It marked the emergence in Tabriz of a so-called 'Ilkhanid' kingdom, to distinguish it from the original khans, which assumed full autonomy with the conversion in 1295 to Sunni Islam of its Nestorian sovereign, Ghazan, soon followed by the senior dignitaries. As one more illustration of the relative relevance of religious amalgams, the Islamization of the Ilkhanid kingdom resulted not in an easing of its relations with the Mamluk regime, but, on the contrary, in a revival of Mongol expansion in Syria. In 1299 and 1303, Ghazan led campaigns that were ultimately defeated before Damascus, on the very site where the conquerors from Arabia had defeated the Byzantines in the seventh century. Among the volunteers then enlisted in the Mamluk army was Sheikh Ibn Taymiyyah, a flamboyant preacher of the Hanbali school. He committed an unprecedented transgression of the doctrine of jihad, hitherto proscribed among Muslims, by ruling that Ghazan and his soldiers were authentic 'infidels', despite their conversion to Sunnism. To this end, he forged the concept of *takfir*, literally 'branding as infidel', which could be transcribed into Christian categories as anathema or excommunication, though these are, as ever, imperfect translations. The bottom line was that Ibn Taymiyyahh justified war against other Muslims for the first time in the name of jihad. His doctrine, marginal at the time due to its extremism, would flourish again later on, first with the Wahhabism of Arabia in the eighteenth century, then with contemporary jihadism.

For the time being, Ibn Taymiyyah, already severe with the supposedly 'infidel' converts, showed himself even more implacable when it came to the minorities of Islam: he took part in the Mamluk escapades against the Shiites of Lebanon in 1300 and 1305, and he encouraged the appalling repression of the Alawite jacquerie of 1317. This brought him into line with a Mamluk power which was brutally reorganizing the sectarian mosaic of Syria, less for religious reasons than out of hostility towards any form of dissidence. Ibn Taymiyyah, on the other hand, undermined the strategies of the sultanate by violently attacking the very principle of Sufism. He denied any value to major jihad of the spiritual type in order to exalt jihad by arms alone. He could not fail to clash with the Mamluks, who, like Nur ad-Din and following Baybars, sponsored the mystical brotherhoods to reinforce a militarized order. Ibn Taymiyyah was ordered to tolerate Sufism, but he adamantly refused to be silent and, five centuries after Ibn Hanbal in Baghdad, rigorously upheld his master's irreducible posture. He paid for it with his freedom, ending his days in the prison of Damascus in 1328. Fundamentalists these days exalt the figures of Ibn Hanbal and Ibn Taymiyyah as examples of the politico-religious resistance to leaders and to ulama guilty, in their eyes, of perverting Islam.

As for the Mongol khans of Tabriz, driven out of Syria on two occasions, they compensated for this setback in 1307 by delivering the coup de grâce to the Turkish sultanate of Konya, already their vassal for decades. The disappearance of Seljuk power left the Mongols masters of part of Anatolia, while the rest of Asia Minor broke up into a series of principalities, called beyliks, because they were each governed by a bey, the Turkish equivalent of the Arab emir.[13] We will briefly mention the Karamanids, the Germiyanids, the Hamidids, and the Saruhanids, without claiming to exhaust the subject of this generalized breakdown, even if each of these beys strove to provide the capital of his fiefdom with prestigious monuments. We need simply to remember that in 1302 one of these beys, by the name of Osman, received from the last Seljuks a fief in western Anatolia and successfully defended it against the Byzantines.

---

[13] Just as the emir, initially the commandant/commander, became the prince, the bey/beg was first a lord, and ended up being identified with the prince. The Turkish beylik therefore largely corresponds to the Arabic emirate.

Orhan, his son and successor, seized Bursa in 1326; this was the first capital of a power called 'Ottoman' in memory of Osman. He would gradually encroach on Byzantine territory, first in Nicaea, then in İzmit. In 1346, as a result of the civil war that was tearing Byzantium apart, Orhan married the daughter of the usurper John Cantacuzene, whose claims to the throne of Constantinople he successfully supported. From this very political marriage stemmed an alliance between Byzantines and Ottomans, who waged war together for a decade. Orhan, at the request of his father-in-law, embarked on repeated expeditions against the emperor's Christian rivals. It was these conflicts between Christians, and not an irrepressible impulse for 'holy war', which led the Ottomans to gain a foothold in Europe.

The grim reaper

In the middle of the fourteenth century, the Middle East was organized around the Euphrates as a dividing line, with Mamluk power in the west and Mongol power in the east. This polarization was only marginally affected by the quarrels of the beyliks in Asia Minor, with the emergence in the northwest of Anatolia of a hub bringing together Byzantines and Ottomans. But it was a phenomenon that ignored borders, religions, and ethnic groups that was to upset the region in 1348, before ravaging Europe and North Africa. The plague pandemic of 1347–1350, which reached its highest death rate that year, killed at least an eighth of the population, with some (inevitably hazardous) estimates producing even more terrible figures. It was particularly visible and destructive in the major centres of Cairo, Alexandria, and Constantinople. It did not spare the countryside either, despite the great uncertainty of sources as to the extent of the carnage, which was apparently heavier in urban areas and coastal regions. The Maghrebi chronicler Ibn Battuta, who travelled the Muslim world from 1325 to 1353, was a privileged witness to the horror caused by the plague in Damascus and Gaza. Baghdad, which was slowly recovering from the devastation of the Mongols, was again plunged into mourning.

Murad, son of Orhan, and the latter's successor in 1362, was the first of the Ottomans to proclaim himself sultan, thus displaying ambitions far beyond the horizon of the beys of Asia Minor. He significantly transferred his capital from Bursa to Edirne/Adrianople – and thus from Asia to Europe. He did not neglect Anatolia, however, where a policy combining matrimonial alliances and military campaigns enabled him to progress towards the east and to ensure, among other things, control of Ankara. His reign also saw the systematic organization of the janissaries (from the Turkish *yeŋiçeri*, literally 'new soldier'). This troop was new insofar as it recruited from among young Christian subjects, converted to Islam before being placed at the service of the sultan. This practice, known as *devshirme*,[14] differed from Mamluk dynamics both because it concerned free children, not slaves, and because it could lead to careers other than the military. Thus the administrative hierarchy of the Ottoman sultanate would often be occupied by converts from Anatolia and Rumelia[15] rather than by native Muslims or ethnic Turks. As for the janissaries of the army, the real shock troops of the sultanate, they largely contributed to the historic victory of 1389 against Serbian troops in Kosovo.[16] Murad, who died in combat, was succeeded on the battle-field by his son Bayezid, sometimes anglicized as Bajazet and nicknamed Yildirim, 'the Thunderbolt'. The vassalized Serbs now provided contingents to the Ottoman army, which resumed the offensive against the various beys and their principalities in Asia Minor.

As for the improbable regime of the Mamluks, it continued to keep a firm grip of Egypt and Syria, while the rulers of Yemen sometimes challenged it for control of Mecca, with local governors playing on these rivalries to restore a form of autonomy. Baybars' successors ensured a steady supply of slaves destined to join the militarized elite, a flow that depended on the free passage of ships laden with captives through the ports of the Black Sea. This organized slave trade was based on pacts concluded between Cairo and Constantinople; the latter city thus collaborated not only in the transfer of such prisoners, but also in their future Islamization. Such a lasting collusion between a Christian empire and a Muslim sultanate once again invalidates essentialist clichés about

[14] Literally 'picking' or 'gathering'.
[15] Rumelia designates the European territories under Ottoman domination.
[16] This was the battle of Kosovo Polje, in Serbian 'the blackbird's field'. While Serbia would remain faithful to Orthodox Christianity, the province of Kosovo itself was very gradually Islamized.

the two monotheisms. Moreover, the Mamluk regime was still plagued by a tension between the dynamics of promoting former slaves, on the one hand, and the dynastic temptation of the sultan in office, on the other. This contradiction led to a whole series of power plays between freed or free-born Mamluks, against a backdrop of sometimes bloody successions, until the advent, in 1382, of sultans of Circassian/Cherkess origin.[17]

The ravages of Timur the Lame

The Mongol kingdom of Persia, which for a time went over to Shiism with the khan Oljeytu between 1310 and 1316, returned to Sunni orthodoxy under the reign of his son and successor, Abu Sa'id, who remained on the throne until his death in 1335. The absence of a male heir then opened up a confused period from which the Ilkhanid regime would never recover, disappearing completely in 1353. Its territory was dismantled between various dynasties whose origins were Mongol (the Jalayirids, masters of Baghdad), Arab (the Muzaffarids, based in Shiraz), and Turkmen (the Aq Qoyunlu, a tribal confederation known as the 'White Sheep', in Diyarbakir and their rivals the Qara Qoyunlu, the 'Black Sheep', in Tabriz).[18] This fragmentation, even if it fell short of the degree of atomization of the beyliks in Anatolia, occurred at a time when, in Samarkand, from 1369, a central Asian power was consolidating that would soon have all-devouring ambitions: Timur the Lame, also known as Tamerlane, presented himself as the heir of Genghis Khan, even if this genealogy was more political than biological; he professed, moreover, not the shamanism of Genghis Khan, but a Sunni Islam of the Hanafi type, the dominant school in the Turkish world, while relying on the Sufi networks of the Naqshbandi, a very influential brotherhood in the region. For a long time, Timur claimed only the title of 'Grand Emir', but this ostentatious modesty failed to conceal an expansionist project

---

[17] These Circassian Mamluks were called 'Burjites', in reference to the 'tower' (*burj*) of their barracks, just as the sultans of the previous period were called 'Bahrites', i.e. 'of the Nile', again because of their home garrison (see above, p. 121, n. 2).
[18] These 'sheep', white or black, might refer to the rallying totem of these tribal alliances.

whose abominable massacres, symbolized by the famous pyramids of skulls, aroused the same terror as the hordes of Hulagu.

Timur led many campaigns in Persia, marked by the bloodbath perpetrated in Isfahan in 1387. Five years later, he launched his armies against the Middle East. By 1393, his dazzling progress had brought him to the gates of Baghdad, which surrendered without a fight, to spare itself a horror comparable to that of 1258. The former Abbasid capital was nonetheless methodically plundered, while the conqueror, displaying a very hypocritical piety, had the provisions of wine discovered by his troops poured into the Tigris. Timur continued his campaign of destruction in Upper Mesopotamia and Azerbaijan, before turning to the north and the Russian steppes. In 1398, he set off again in the direction of the east and India, where he sowed terror in Delhi, before switching back to the west the following year, this time devastating Georgia, followed by the Anatolian cities of Sivas and Malatya. The Grand Emir then called on the Mamluks, weakened by one of their recurring succession crises, to recognize his authority. The foreseeable rejection of this ultimatum led to a battle in Aleppo in 1400 in which Timur, armed with his combat elephants brought back from India, defeated the Mamluks. There would be no repeat of the way the hordes had been brought to a halt at Ain Jalut in 1260 because this time the Mamluks, crushed on the outskirts of Damascus, abandoned Syria to the invaders and retreated to their Egyptian domain.

Ibn Khaldun, whose cyclical vision of Muslim history has already been mentioned several times, was at that time one of the four great *qadi*s of the court of Cairo, where he represented the Maliki rite, the majority rite in his native Maghreb. Remaining in Syria after the rout of the Mamluk sultan, in 1401 he was commissioned by the notables of Damascus to negotiate the clemency of Timur. Convinced that the decadence of the Mamluks was as irreversible as the rise of the Turco-Mongols, he actually offered his services to the invader. Blinded by his dreams of grandeur, he forgot the logic of his own theory: the 'group' led by Timur was admittedly bubbling with an energy surging up from the Asian 'periphery' towards the Middle Eastern 'centre', but this did not make it the bearer of a 'preaching' that could establish a lasting 'power' over the immense territories thus occupied. The Islamic casuistry with which the sovereign dressed up his crimes, for example his torturing of Syrian sheikhs over questions of doctrine, seemed very fragile in the face of the past power of the messages of Abbasid, Fatimid, Seljuk, or Ayyubid propaganda. Ibn Khaldun, who had been so lucid in the past, was doubly mistaken this time: assuming that Timur's Middle Eastern project had a future, the invader had no interest in associating himself with such an adviser.

Ibn Khaldun was already on his way back to Egypt when Timur, violating all the commitments made during the surrender of Damascus, sacked the city with fire and bloodshed. Then he turned to Baghdad, which had been surrendered to him in 1393, but which a Mongol sultan had since dared to take back. This presumptuous leader fled in the face of the return of the hordes, which overwhelmed Baghdad after six weeks of siege. Timur ordered each of his soldiers to bring him two decapitated heads, on pain of being killed themselves. The chroniclers of the time speak of 120 pyramids of skulls and 90,000 deaths. According to these horrified testimonies, the Tigris, saturated with corpses, ran red. Once the carnage and the looting were over, Timur paid his respects at the tomb of Abu Hanifa, the founder of the school of Sunnism to which he was attached. This show of bigotry cannot compensate for the fact that he left nothing but ruins in Syria and Iraq, from which he deported thousands of craftsmen to beautify his capital of Samarkand. It was not some new order that Timur aimed to impose on the Middle East, but rather its liquidation and the transfer of its wealth to Central Asia. In this sense, his enterprise was even more devastating than that of Hulagu, whose commanders had eventually settled in Persia and Mesopotamia, building cities and regimes.

The Turkish principalities had collapsed one after the other, and a clash was now inevitable between Timur and Bayezid the Thunderbolt, who, after his 1389 victory over the Serbs, had won many successes in Asia Minor. This time the Ottomans were defeated, in 1402, not far from Ankara, and their sultan was taken prisoner; he died in captivity a year later. This tragic outcome seemed to seal a final defeat for the Ottomans, especially since what had been their first capital, Bursa, as well as the port of Izmir/Smyrna, were sacked by Timur's troops. But this was far from being the case. Certainly, the dynamism of the Ottomans seemed much more affected by the capture of Sultan Bayezid in Ankara than it had been by the death of his father Murad in Kosovo. The impact was traumatic and Bayezid's sons aggravated it by tearing each other apart, before Sultan Mehmed imposed his authority on his brothers. For now, Ankara's victory had exhausted Timur's forces, who did not push their advance any farther westward. This battle therefore saved Constantinople, first from what would have been an appalling attack by the hordes of Timur, and second, of course, from an offensive by the Ottomans, who would take half a century to reconstitute their war machine.

The Ottoman defeat of 1402 paradoxically led to a result comparable to the Mamluk victory of Ain Jalut. The invasion launched from the heart of Asia was stopped before reaching Africa and Europe respectively. Either way, the outcome of the battle mattered less than the internal dynamics of the empire of the steppes and the shift of its centre of gravity towards the east: the return of Hulagu, in 1260, to take part in the succession of Möngke Khan; the invasion of China launched in 1404 by Timur, who was swept away shortly after by fever, in the south of present-day Kazakhstan. The power of his successors, known as 'Timurids', soon ebbed out of the Middle East, with the exception of Khorasan. The procession of destruction that had accompanied the two waves of Mongol invasion, in 1256–1261 and in 1393–1404, left lasting consequences in Syria and Iraq, even more so than in Iran and Anatolia. Egypt was spared in each of these cycles of devastation. On the other hand, the entire region was affected by the Black Death of 1347–1350, followed by returns of the epidemic at regular intervals over the following decades. The century and a half that ended with the withdrawal of Timur, therefore, was marked in the Middle East by stagnation and even demographic depression. This affected both the large urban centres and the cultivated areas, which were eroded by the return of a nomadism that was pastoral as well as predatory.

The fall of Byzantium

Sultan Murad, in power from 1421, was called 'the second' to distinguish him from his great-grandfather, who was killed in 1389 in Kosovo, though these numbers did not hold much meaning for contemporaries. In 1422, Murad II tried in vain to seize Constantinople, whose emperor had supported another pretender to the sultanate. In order to avoid any succession quarrel himself, he abdicated in 1444 in favour of his fourth son, Mehmed, aged only twelve, who now became the second sovereign with this first name. This daring formula proved to be impracticable after two years, and Murad II returned to the throne until his death in 1451. Mehmed II, again sultan, intended to erase the failure of his premature accession to power. He was determined to eliminate the power of Byzantium, lying right in the heart of the Ottoman possessions, on both banks of the Bosphorus. He established Rumelia, on the European side of the Bosphorus, as a fortress to complement the fortress of Anatolia already built by Bayezid on the Asian side. In 1453, he relied massively on heavy artillery to break through the defences of the Byzantine capital. During this fifty-four-day-long siege, Mehmed II ordered the transfer across the mountains of part of the fleet – a titanic manoeuvre. The Ottoman ships, having thus circumvented the Byzantine defences, sowed destruction by shelling the defences from the Golden Horn, the estuary located in the heart of the city.

Mehmed II issued an ultimatum to the Byzantine emperor, Constantine XI, who rejected it and died in battle; the sultan took this as a pretext to authorize the looting of the city for a whole day. On the evening of the final attack, Mehmed II went to Hagia Sophia to give thanks to Allah and thus mark the transformation of the basilica into a mosque.[19] Some Christian quarters, including Fener, however, were spared by the sultan, who granted them his official protection, the *aman*. But the counterpart of this protection was the appointment of an Orthodox patriarch responsible for the Greek community under the power of the new authorities. This 'Ecumenical Patriarchate of Constantinople' had only a symbolic primacy, inherited from Byzantium, as the so-called 'autocephalous' Orthodox Churches were each managed by their own patriarch. This patriarchy foreshadowed the institution of the *millet*, i.e. the community designated as a 'nation', whose autonomy of internal organization was guaranteed by its submission and its integration into the Ottoman order. This system would be extended to Armenians in 1461, then to other Christian denominations and Jewish communities. The Genoese of the Galata district had to content themselves with the *aman* for the time

[19] In 1934, Atatürk's Republic decided to secularize the monument into a museum; in 2020, President Erdoğan restored the religious status of the Ayasofya mosque (Turkish for Hagia Sophia/Divine Wisdom).

being; it was then granted to the Venetians, once they were reconciled with the Sublime Porte.

In 1458, Constantinople became the new capital of a sultanate which now saw itself as an empire and recovered all of Byzantium's pomp for its own glory. Mehmed II launched, near Hagia Sophia, the construction of a 'New Palace' (Yeni Saray), which at the beginning of the eighteenth century would take the name of Topkapi. Thousands of people were settled inside this 'city within the city' that became the Seraglio/Saray. The sultan also had the city walls rebuilt and consolidated, placing all the power of his state at the service of repopulating his capital. Constantinople continued to be called by this name (Kostantiniye in Turkish), a phenomenon comparable to that experienced, on a smaller symbolic scale, for the Algerian city of Constantine, even after its Islamization. The name of Istanbul, despite its Oriental appearance, comes from the Greek *eis-tên-polis*, 'to the city', and for long designated just one part of the historic city, south of the Golden Horn. It was only very late that Istanbul came to be the Turkish equivalent of Constantinople. This toponymic change was not formalized until the end of the Ottoman era, hence the decision in this book not to use the name of Istanbul before this date.

Mehmed II deserves his nickname of Fatih, 'the Conqueror', all the more since, after Constantinople, he seized Trebizond, the last Byzantine redoubt. At the same time, he eliminated the last principalities of Anatolia, expelling the Karamanids as far as Aleppo. In Europe, he annexed Serbia, already vassalized, and broke the resistance of Bosnia and then of Albania. As well as being a warrior and builder, Mehmed II was a brilliant organizer who set standards and consolidated a bureaucracy. He ordered the first recension of a *Kanoun-nâmé*, the 'book of regulations' of the Ottoman state in the political, military, fiscal, penal, and formal domains. These provisions had their own legitimacy, independently of sharia, starting with the famous 'law of fratricide', which authorized the sultan to eliminate his own brothers. This terrible 'law', dedicated to putting an end to succession disputes, remained in force for almost a century. As for the Byzantine Empire, it had existed for more than a millennium, a unique longevity in the history of the Middle East. It was true, however, that, after having controlled a good part of the region for two and a half centuries, Byzantium had, since the advent of Islam, been no more than an Anatolian power, a power already reduced to the margins of Asia Minor by the Seljuks and the Crusaders.

The Ottomans versus the Mamluks

Mehmed II was celebrated as the 'sultan of the two continents', Europe and Asia, and as the '*khaqan*', or the grand khan of the 'two seas', the Black Sea and the Aegean Sea, in order to underline the centrality of Constantinople, which he conquered when he was only twenty-one. The Mamluk sovereign, Inal, although he was an illiterate septuagenarian at the time, pretended to write two poems to the glory of the young conqueror of Islam and sent them to him through one of his emirs. He decked out Cairo with flags to better associate himself with the Ottoman victory. But the Mamluks hoped above all to direct the ambitions of Mehmed II towards Christian Europe and thus away from them. They drew no lesson from the fall of Byzantium in terms of military doctrine and continued to cultivate cavalry as the noblest weapon, without paying due attention to artillery. Shortly before his death in 1461, Inal appointed as his successor his son Ahmed, a genuine servant of the state, determined to restructure the sultanate in depth. These desires for reform were coupled with Ahmed's refusal to follow the practice of his predecessor sultans on acceding to the throne of paying a gratuity to the various factions in order to buy peace from the militia. The Mamluks, for once united, deposed Ahmed and, though sparing his life, placed him under house arrest in Alexandria. A historic opportunity to revitalize the Mamluk Sultanate in the face of the Ottoman challenge was well and truly wasted.

The new sovereign, Khoushqadam, was too closely identified with a single Mamluk clan to really impose himself on the other factions. He also committed repeated blunders with regard to Mehmed II, who was fortunately too busy on other European fronts. Carried away by dysentery in 1467, Khoushqadam was finally replaced by the chief of his guard, Qaitbay, who remained in power for thirty-eight years, a remarkable achievement in the pitiless universe of the Mamluks. The most powerful emirs were in fact considered at the time as 'miniature sultans', because they had a fief (*iqta*') transferred by concession, itself measured by their rank in the military hierarchy (emirs 'of a Hundred', 'of Forty', and 'of Ten'). The sultan endeavoured to limit his subordinates' capacity to stir up trouble by reducing command posts and transferring the resources thus freed up to the central treasury. The emirs endeavoured in return to ensure the hereditary transmission of offices, with very limited success. The persevering and tenacious Qaitbay emerged victorious from this showdown, but did not take advantage of it to reform the army and the administration. In addition, he interfered in the conflict for the succession of Mehmed II, who died in 1481. The new Ottoman sultan, Bayezid II, did not have time to apply the law of fratricide to his younger brother, Cem, who was already raising the banner of revolt and taking refuge in Egypt, having been warmly greeted on his way via Aleppo, Damascus, Hebron, and Gaza.

Qaitbay went so far as to welcome the rebel suitor to his court. Hostilities between the Ottomans and Mamluks opened with border clashes in southern Anatolia in 1485. The victories won by Qaitbay forced Bayezid II to conclude a favourable peace in Cairo in 1491, in particular for access to Black Sea slave markets. This shows what a formidable adversary the Mamluks could have constituted if they had seized the opportunity to regenerate themselves in time. Instead, it was a new plague epidemic that struck Egypt and decimated the Mamluk ranks, a plague aggravated by an epizootic that ravaged livestock. Qaitbay, who died in 1496, designated as heir his son Muhammad, who turned out to be as sadistic as he was debauched, hence provoking an all too predictable Mamluk uprising. The sultans then followed one another in Cairo at an accelerated pace: one was tortured and thrown out onto the roadside, another was beheaded, a third managed to save his life, if not his throne, by disguising himself as a woman. From all these storms emerged, in 1501, Qansuh al-Ghuri, who of course could not have seen himself as the penultimate Mamluk sultan. It was during this period that the Portuguese opening of the sea route to India dealt a severe blow to Mamluk finances, significantly reducing European trade with Alexandria.

In their face-to-face encounters in the Middle East, the Ottomans and Mamluks never forgot the Turkmen tribes who had established their power east of the Euphrates. But these tribes were divided into the two rival confederations mentioned above: the 'White Sheep', bordering the Ottoman Empire in Upper Mesopotamia; and the 'Black Sheep', the masters of Azerbaijan and central Iraq. This division ruled out the constitution of a Turkmen alternative to the powers of Constantinople and Cairo. Even when Uzun Hasan,[20] at the head of the White Sheep, inflicted a definitive defeat on his 'black' rivals in 1467, setting up his capital in Tabriz and seizing Baghdad, it was towards the east that he pursued his offensive. He came to control most of Persia, leaving Khorasan in the hands of the descendants of Timur. On the other hand, his attempts to break into Anatolia were crushed by the Ottomans and he was careful not to cross the border of the Euphrates with the Mamluks. In his shock troops, Uzun Hasan mobilized Sufi fighters from the Safavid brotherhood,[21] followers of a military rather than spiritual jihad. This mystical and fighting order was originally Sunni, of the Shafi'i rite, but the leaders who succeeded one another from father to son belatedly proclaimed themselves descendants of Muhammad. This claim accompanied the conversion of the order to Shiism, with Safavid supporters now wearing a red cap with twelve tassels, meant to correspond to the twelve imams, hence their nickname of Qizilbash ('Red Head'). The spectacular successes of Uzun Hasan fostered in the Turkmen world a messianic anguish, exacerbated by the chaos which, in 1478, followed the death of the conqueror. It would nevertheless take another generation for the Safavid 'group' to refine its Shiite 'preaching' for the benefit of a new imperial 'power'.

A militarized Middle East

During the three centuries covered by this chapter, Egypt imposed itself as a centre of stability, and even of structural cohesion, in the Middle East. It was the Ayyubid rulers of Cairo who took control of their rivals in Syria, themselves divided between, at least, Damascus and Aleppo. They were also the ones who absorbed the shock of the two Crusades that landed in the Nile delta, each time managing to repel them spectacularly. It was again from Egypt that the Mamluks launched their

---

[20] In Turkish, Uzun Hasan means 'Hasan the big/the tall'.
[21] The Safavid order takes its name from its founder Safi ad-Din Ishaq (1252–1344). Safi ad-Din means 'sincere friend of religion'.

campaign to stop and then push back the Mongol hordes. The transfer of the seat of the caliphate from Baghdad to Cairo in 1261 – even if the supreme function of Islam was emptied of its substance on this occasion – confirmed the pre-eminence of Egypt in the region as a whole. Bilad al-Sham, devastated by the two waves of Central Asian invasion, was no more than one component, admittedly brilliant but still submissive, of the sultanate ruled from Cairo. The Euphrates border was never really called into question, with a striking contrast between, in the west, the long-term Mamluk presence and, in the east, the entanglement of regimes and conflicts (the Mongol khanates of Tabriz, then of Baghdad, the Muzaffarid emirate of Shiraz, and the Turkmen confederations that were implacably hostile to one another).

The period 1193–1501 also completed the process, launched by the first 'sultans' of Baghdad, whereby the civil Arab and Arabized elites were dispossessed in favour of upstart mercenaries or freed slaves, who collectively were the holders of armed force. The fact that none of the three emblematic figures of mediaeval jihad, Nur ad-Din, Saladin, or Baybars, was an Arab is just one indication among others of this shift at the top. The Mamluk consecration of the primacy of the sultanate over the caliphate meant the marginalization of the former dominant class in the administrative and religious field, hence the muted resistance of the ulama and their attempts, generally in vain, to impose their standards on the current regime. Arabic remained the language of legitimization, the language of worship, and the language of the people, but for the Mamluks, who were poor Arabists, it often retained a dimension of otherness which cut them off from the society under their domination. The gap in classical Islam between 'elites' and 'masses' was widened by this additional alienation. The militarization of power reached such a degree that populations no longer played a part except in the Syrian cases of abandonment by their sultan when faced with invaders. The Ottomans followed a radically different dynamic, as they were rooted in the historical depth of two and a half centuries of Turkish power in Asia Minor, ever since the Seljuks of Rum. Once they had conquered Constantinople, the Ottomans occupied vis-à-vis the Mamluks the Middle Eastern position of the Byzantines against the Umayyads, namely that of an Anatolian power established in the northwest of Bilad al-Sham, but primarily turned towards Europe.

The preceding three centuries, finally, were marked by the disappearance of political Shiism in the Middle East, apart from the interlude of a few years of conversion to Shiism of one of the Mongol khans. The messianic expectation of the Hidden Imam, whose reappearance alone could restore justice on earth, weighed heavily in this Shiite inability to reconcile itself to political action and thus to emerge from a tetchy quietism. As for the Isma'ilis, they were satisfied with their status as a minority in Islam, their political project having been ruined by the fall of the Fatimids and then by the extremism of the Assassins. All the Muslim regimes in the Middle East thus followed a Sunnism necessarily posed as orthodox, a unanimity that the fall of the Abbasid Caliphate did not call into question. The formidable development of Sufism can then be understood as a wave of popular reappropriation of a religion that was too closely identified with power, which in turn strove to win over the brotherhoods. These three centuries of undisputed Sunnism invalidate, once again, the simplistic vision of a bitter and never-ending confrontation between Sunnis and Shiites since the dawn of Islam. On the other hand, the conflicts between Sunni powers, already very violent, culminated with the carnage perpetrated by the devoutly Sunni Timur against Sunni populations. If this Sunni era came to an end at this point, it was not because of a more or less spontaneous Shiite reaction, it was because a Middle Eastern power was about to constitute itself as a conquering empire in the name of a new state religion, forcing the Ottoman sultanate to establish itself in the very heart of the region so as to block its way.

Chronology

1193	Ayyubid principalities of Damascus, Aleppo, and Cairo.
1194	First Khwarazmian sultan of Baghdad.
1200	Restoration of Ayyubid unity around Adil/Saphadin.
1202–1204	Fourth Crusade against Constantinople.
1218–1221	Failure of the Fifth Crusade in Egypt.
1229	Treaty between King Kamil and Emperor Frederick II.
1244	Return of Jerusalem to Ayyubid sovereignty.
1249–1250	Failure of the Seventh Crusade in Egypt.
1250	Shajar al-Durr, ruler of Egypt for three months.
1250–1257	Aybak, first Mamluk sultan in Cairo.
1256	Mongol conquest of Persia by Khan Hulagu.
1258	Mongol destruction of Baghdad and end of the Abbasids.
1260	Mamluk victory over the Mongols at Ain Jalut.
1260–1277	Baybars, Mamluk Sultan of Egypt and Syria.
1261	Byzantine reconquest of Constantinople.
1295–1304	Ghazan, first Mongol khan converted to Islam.
1302–1326	Osman, first Ottoman bey.
1307	End of the Seljuk Sultanate of Rum.
1326–1362	Orhan, Ottoman Bey, with Bursa as his capital.
1328	Death in prison in Damascus of Sheikh Ibn Taymiyyah.
1348	Peak of the plague pandemic.
1362–1389	Murad, first Ottoman sultan.
1366	Edirne/Adrianople, Ottoman capital.
1369	Samarkand, capital of Timur.
1389–1402	Bayezid I Yildirim (the Thunderbolt), Ottoman sultan.
1393	First capture of Baghdad by Timur.
1401	Destruction by Timur of Damascus and Baghdad.
1402	Victory of Timur over the Ottomans in Ankara.
1405	Death of Timur, on campaign towards China.
1406	Death of Ibn Khaldun in Cairo.
1444–1446 and 1451–1481	Mehmed II Fatih, Ottoman sultan.

1453	Ottoman capture of Constantinople.
1453–1478	Uzun Hasan, Turkmen leader of the 'White Sheep'.
1461	Ottoman capture of Trebizond.
1468–1496	Qaitbay, Mamluk sultan.
1481–1512	Bayezid II, Ottoman sultan.
1491	Peace between Ottomans and Mamluks.
1501–1516	Qansuh al-Ghuri, penultimate Mamluk sultan.

Further reading

Foss, Clive, *The beginning of the Ottoman Empire* (New York: Oxford University Press, 2020).

Grousset, René, *The Empire of the Steppes: a history of Central Asia*, translated by Naomi Walford (New Brunswick, NJ: Rutgers University Press, 1970).

Humphreys, Stephen, *From Saladin to the Mongols* (Albany, NY: SUNY Press, 1977).

Manz, Beatrice Forbes, *The rise and rule of Tamerlane* (New York: Cambridge University Press, 1999).

Petry, Carl F., *The Mamluk sultanate, a history* (New York: Cambridge University Press, 2022).

Philippides, Mario and Walter Hanak, *The siege and the fall of Constantinople in 1453* (Farnham: Ashgate Publishing, 2011).

Queller, Donald, Thomas Madden, and Alfred Andrea, *The Fourth Crusade: the conquest of Constantinople* (Philadelphia: University of Pennsylvania Press, 1997).

Rapoport, Yossef and Ahmed Shahab, *Ibn Taymiyya and his times* (Oxford: Oxford University Press, 2015).

Raymond, André, *Cairo*, translated by William Wood (Cambridge, MA and London: Harvard University Press, 2000).

Tolan, John, *Saint Francis and the sultan: the curious history of a Christian–Muslim encounter* (Oxford: Oxford University Press, 2009).

FIVE

Ottomans and Safavids (1501–1798)

Today, Shiism is spontaneously associated with Iran, though this identification goes back to an imperial policy, with the advent of the Safavid shahs at the beginning of the sixteenth century. This imposition of Shiism as a state religion followed a complex course, arising from a messianic insurrection which ended, after a period of serious unrest, in the establishment of a new dynasty. In 749, the Abbasids were the first to hijack a millenarian uprising and place it in the service of their family's aims. Abu al-Abbas's kinship with the Prophet of Islam may have been distant, but it was undeniable.[1] The Isma'ili Mahdi had more difficulty validating a 'Fatimid' line, going back to the daughter of Muhammad, when, in 909 in the Maghreb, his dynastic project brought decades of subversion to a climax. The same process of genealogical transfiguration took place with the Safavids; as we have seen, for a long time, they fought in the ranks of the Turkmen White Sheep. Their late conversion to Shiism was accompanied by the claim of prophetic ancestry, through the seventh imam Musa al-Kazim. The death in combat of their leader in 1499 brought to their head a twelve-year-old boy, Isma'il, who proclaimed himself to be the long-awaited Mahdi who had finally reappeared after five and a half centuries of occultation. This apocalyptic context made it possible to channel, then fully mobilize, Turkmen aggression within the Safavid shock troops. With the support of these formidable Kizilbachs, Isma'il managed to seize Tabriz as early as 1501.

As master of the capital of the Mongol khans, which then became the capital of the 'black' Turkmens and their 'white' rivals, Isma'il granted himself the Persian title of 'shah'.[2] He decreed Shiism to be the official religion and publicly cursed the first three caliphs, whom he accused of

---

[1] The first Abbasid Caliph was the great-great-grandson of Muhammad's uncle.
[2] Even if the Persian term shah means 'king', the notion of emperor and empire would be more relevant for the Safavids, in an echo of the Ottoman dynamic.

having robbed Ali of the supreme magisterium of Islam. Isfahan and Shiraz fell into his hands in 1503, followed by Baghdad, five years later.[3] Everywhere, the Safavid militias broke down Sunni resistance to the new state religion and they killed, right in the heart of the mosque, the faithful who refused to insult Ali's predecessors in the caliphate. The Muslim profession of faith now had to be followed by the Shia invocation that 'Ali is the ally [*wali*] of God'. Still a minority sect in the population, this Shiism – imposed from above and by constraint – was sorely lacking in theological reference points. These gaps were filled by military zeal and by the invocation of the shah as Mahdi. The new power also used Shiite clerics from the holy cities of Iraq to preach and implant the state dogma in Persia. It was the emergence of this unprecedented challenge on their Asian border that drove the Ottomans, hitherto turned towards Europe, where more than half of their subjects were to be found, to become more and more deeply involved in the Middle East.[4] The two empires, one Sunni and the other Shiite, soon divided up the region in terms comparable to those of the Byzantines and Sassanids a millennium earlier.

The Custodian of the Two Holy Cities

Sultan Selim ascended to the Ottoman throne in 1512, overthrowing his father Bayezid II, before eliminating his brothers and nephews. Faced with Shiite agitation in eastern Anatolia, he led his troops in 1514 against those of Shah Isma'il, whose army was overcome by Ottoman artillery at the Battle of Chaldiran. Selim's army pushed on to Tabriz, which was temporarily occupied, before turning to Upper Mesopotamia and settling, this time permanently, in a buffer zone between the Safavid and Mamluk territories. The Ottoman sultan embarked on an assault on Syria in 1516 to avoid a Safavid breakthrough from Iraq, or even an alliance between Mamluks and Persians. The Ottoman and Mamluk armies clashed at Dabiq, about 40 kilometres north of Aleppo, where

---

[3] The Safavid conquest of Baghdad in 1508 was accompanied by the destruction of the tomb of Abu Hanifa, the founder of the Sunni school to which the Ottomans belonged (see above, p. 60).

[4] The Ottoman population was then evenly divided between Christians and Muslims.

the Umayyads habitually gathered their forces during the campaigns against the Byzantines. The betrayal of the governor of Aleppo hastened the Ottoman victory, which was all the more glorious as the Mamluk sultan, Qansuh al-Ghuri, who had come from Cairo at the head of his army, perished on the battlefield. The city of Aleppo and then its citadel were handed over without a fight to Selim, in whose honour festivals were organized for several days. The Ottoman sovereign staged the support of the 'caliph' al-Mutawakkil, whom the Mamluks had brought with them. Selim gave him a large sum of money and a robe of honour, while ironically swearing to resettle him in the former Abbasid capital of Baghdad, then under Safavid domination. In Cairo, Mamluk power was reorganized around a new sultan, Tuman, who pledged allegiance to al-Mutawakkil's father, designated 'caliph' in his stead.

Selim seized Bilad al-Sham in a few months, before directing his offensive against Egypt. The Ottoman troops, in a hurry to see an end to the matter, did not linger in Palestine. In Gaza, the notables, even more than the population, believed that Mamluk power might suddenly erupt. Rumours of a defeat for Selim led to an uprising in the city. But the sultan, who in fact had proved victorious over the Mamluk army, turned in fury against the insurgent city. The massacres he perpetrated there lived up to his nickname of the 'Terrible'. The punishment of Gaza contributed to the surrender of Cairo, which Selim triumphantly entered alongside 'his' caliph al-Mutawakkil. Tuman, the last of the Mamluk sultans, was publicly humiliated before being handed over to the executioner. His supporters were beheaded and their heads stuck on wooden poles throughout the city. The former Mamluk governor of Aleppo, whose defection had been decisive at Dabiq, became the first Ottoman governor of Cairo.

As for al-Mutawakkil, he fulfilled his office as caliph by legitimizing the overthrow of the Mamluks who had kept him in power for so long. Selim no longer had any interest in this figure but, rather than get rid of him, he transferred him with his retinue by boat to Constantinople. The gilded cage of the so-called 'caliphs' was merely moved from the banks of the Nile to those of the Bosphorus, where while in captivity they continued to bequeath a caliphal title without substance to their successive heirs. It was not until the eighteenth century that the Ottomans invented the fable of an Abbasid voluntarily transmitting his 'caliphate' to them. After

Baybars transformed the caliph into a simple instrument of legitimation of Mamluk power, Selim finished the process of ruining the credit of this institution by moving al-Mutawakkil around, from Aleppo to Cairo and then to Constantinople. The Friday prayer, pronounced for generations in the name of the Ottoman sultan, and of him alone, was now also said in Syria, Egypt, and Arabia – in spite of those who claim, in defiance of historical reality, that Muslims cannot live without a caliph. It was in Cairo that Selim symbolically received the keys to Mecca and Medina, before his troops physically occupied the Hejaz. The sultan was now celebrated as 'Custodian of the Two Holy Cities',[5] guarantor of the organization of the *hajj*, the annual pilgrimage carried out either by caravan from Damascus, or over the Red Sea from Egypt. The dynasty of the *ashraf*, the descendants of the Prophet Muhammad who succeeded one another in power in Mecca, was kept in place, but it was integrated into the hierarchy of the Sublime Porte.

Two state religions

Shah Isma'il's claims to be the incarnation of the Hidden Imam were swept away in 1514 by his failure at Chaldiran. This was his first defeat, but it was a resounding one – and against a Sunni sultan to boot – and so ruined his reputation for invincibility. Since it was now impossible for him to appear as the Mahdi, he claimed to be at least his representative, responsible for establishing divine justice in his name. This new legitimization of the Safavids, moreover, corresponded more closely to their Turkmen origin, while the Mahdi could only be an Arab. It accompanied the consolidation of an empire stretching to Khorasan, based on the support of a large part of the Persian nobility and on the pugnacity of the Turkmen leaders, who were rewarded for their loyalty in line with the conquests they accomplished. When Isma'il died in 1524, his son Tahmasp, then ten years old, succeeded him for a reign of half a century, a longevity essential for the Safavids if their dynasty was to flourish. Sheikh Al-Karaki brought his immense prestige from Najaf to ensure the shah's power, before settling in Persia with many Shiite ulama. In return,

[5] The term *khadim* literally means 'servant', the 'two holy cities (or places)' of Mecca and Medina being in Arabic *al-haramayn*.

Tahmasp granted Karaki, in the matter of religious affairs, a 'delegation' of the Hidden Imam, of whom the sovereign was thus set up as a temporal arm. The minority within the Kizilbachs who still associated the shah with the very person of the Mahdi were liquidated in 1532, just as the first Abbasids and Fatimids had, in their time, crushed the millennial agitation of their own diehards. Safavid power was henceforth stabilized around the sovereign, the intercessor of the Hidden Imam, protector and guarantor of state Shiism. Shah Tahmasp transferred his capital from Tabriz to Qazvin in 1548, 150 kilometres west of Tehran, and so closer to the centre of Persia, in order primarily to protect himself from the Ottoman Empire, but also to break with the Turkmen heritage.

The triptych of Ibn Khaldun, although rarely referred to in the case of the Safavids, was nevertheless of great relevance: without Shiite 'preaching', the Safavid 'group' would never have been able to establish, from the 'periphery' of Azerbaijan, an imperial 'power' over the whole of Persia. The Ottoman dynamic was very different since it emerged during the period of intense competition between the different beyliks; there was no specific 'preaching' to distinguish Osman and his descendants. On the other hand, the role of the state religion in consolidating the Safavids was fundamental, as it contrasted with the neutrality shown by the Fatimids, who were not concerned with promoting Isma'ilism in the face of the dominant Sunnism in the Middle East. The aggressiveness of the imposition of Shiism on a majority of the Persian population was unprecedented in the history of Islam, where sovereigns of different faiths had led populations of various persuasions, admittedly with waves of repression, but never with such a systematic campaign of conversion. This marked the irruption in the Middle East of the principle of correspondence between the religion of the monarch and that of his subjects, a principle that Europe then adopted to settle the wars between Catholics and Protestants.[6] In return, the Ottoman power launched a campaign of methodical repression of the Shiites of Anatolia, perceived as a dangerous tool of Safavid ambitions. These dissident populations, thus cut off from the Persian clergy and forced into clandestine worship, developed

---

[6] This was the principle *cujus regio, ejus religio* ('to each kingdom, the religion of its king'), which was the basis in 1555 of the Peace of Augsburg between the Catholic and Lutheran states of the Holy Roman Empire.

an esoteric dogma, known as 'Alevi', which differed just as much from Twelver Shiism as the beliefs of the Alawites, Isma'ilis, and Druze. The Kurdish emirs, who negotiated their submission to Constantinople one after the other, formed an anti-Safavid buffer zone in the southeast of Anatolia; the heterogeneity of their statutes and their bitter and never-ending quarrels mean they were unable to represent a pole of autonomy.

Selim made the Ottoman Empire the major power in the Middle East, but it was his only surviving son, Suleiman, who completed his work in his forty-six-year-long reign, from 1520 to 1566. Suleiman is known as 'the Magnificent', though his Ottoman title was *Kanouni*, or 'the Legislator'.[7] Suleiman resumed the offensive in Europe, bringing it to the gates of Vienna in 1529. He then turned against the Safavids, from 1532 to 1536, seizing Baghdad and Iraq, as well as part of Azerbaijan. The sultan led the Ottoman armies against the Persians in 1548–1549 in Van, then in 1553–1555 in Erzurum. Only then did he finally seal peace with Tahmasp. The Ottomans withdrew from Azerbaijan, but this was to better ensure their control over Iraq. Suleiman undertook to facilitate the transit of Persian pilgrims to Mecca and Medina, which could not fail to reinforce his status as Custodian of the Two Holy Cities. The same aid was granted to Shiite pilgrims bound for Najaf and Karbala. Out of respect for Ottoman Sunnism, the Safavids undertook in return to stop stigmatizing the caliphs Abu Bakr, Omar, and Osman. This imperial peace, however, was compromised by the intrigues of the seraglio. Suleiman was so intensely in love with his favourite Hürrem Sultan[8] that he freed her so as to make her his only legitimate wife. The way to the throne was then open to their two sons, the older, Selim, and the younger, Bayezid. Suleiman favoured Selim over Bayezid, who rose up against his father in 1559 and fled to Persia after his supporters were crushed. The shah spared Bayezid the rebel for a long while, before having him assassinated by emissaries of the sultan. The peace between Constantinople and Qazvin would not be disturbed for six decades.

[7] This term, derived from the Greek *kanoun*, actually means 'regulator', as in the *Kanoun-nâmé* of Mehmed II (see above, p. 138), but it is the meaning associated with the 'law', and therefore the 'legislator', that imposed itself.

[8] She was the daughter of a Polish priest, and was nicknamed Roxelana by the Europeans.

The Franco-Ottoman alliance

In 1536, the Ottoman Empire experienced its maximum east–west extension, from Austria to Azerbaijan. Constantinople then had nearly half a million inhabitants, of whom approximately 40% were Christians and 5% Jews. This was the moment that Suleiman chose to forge a veritable anti-Habsburg alliance between Paris (François I was then King of France) and Constantinople. It was not a treaty in the proper sense,[9] but the recognition of shared interests, both against Charles V and in the structuring of trade in the Levant. This basically strategic rapprochement between the 'eldest daughter of the Church' (France) and the main power in Islam ignored religious considerations. The French fleet cooperated in the western Mediterranean with the ships of Hayreddin Barbarossa, master of Algiers, in the name of Sultan Suleiman.[10] The collaboration between Paris and Constantinople was not even affected by the conclusion of a five-year truce between the Ottomans and Habsburgs in 1547. The other European states, unable to compete with France, strove to obtain commercial privileges, referred to by the misleading term 'capitulations'.[11] Granting *aman*, protection, was for the Ottoman Empire a demonstration of power, and not a sign of weakness. These immunities and facilities, from which local intermediaries benefited,[12] remained limited to the cities open to trade known as the '*échelles du Levant*', i.e. Constantinople and Izmir, Aleppo and its outlet of İskenderun/Alexandretta, the Lebanese ports of Tripoli and Sidon, and Alexandria and Cairo.

After the primarily military phase of his reign, Suleiman the Magnificent launched a monumental policy of unprecedented ambition.

[9] Indeed, the French project was never signed by the Ottoman side.

[10] In 1543, a Franco-Ottoman fleet, setting out from Marseille, seized Nice, before withdrawing against the Savoyard counter-offensive. Ten years later, another Franco-Ottoman fleet managed to occupy Corsica, which was returned to Genoa in 1559. As for the French ambassador to Constantinople, he accompanied Suleiman during his anti-Safavid campaign of 1548–1549.

[11] France did not conclude formal capitulations with the Ottoman Empire until 1569, long after the opening of its diplomatic representations in Constantinople, Aleppo, and 'Eastern Tripoli'.

[12] These intermediaries were called 'drogmans', an anglicized version of the Arabic and Turkish term for 'translator'.

Sinan, a former janissary who had accompanied the sultan on many campaigns, became the court architect. He supervised the construction of nearly 500 buildings, including 100 large mosques. *Külliye*-type complexes joined a whole series of buildings to the mosque itself. One of them in Constantinople, called Suleymanye in honour of the sovereign, included seven madrasas, an institute for the study of hadith, a medical school, a hammam (public steam bath), and a hotel. Suleiman also ordered the construction, from 1537 to 1540, of the wall that has enclosed the 'Old City' of Jerusalem until the present day. No military imperative justified such a formidable project, carried out under the aegis of three architects, from Aleppo, Constantinople, and Jerusalem. More than 3 kilometres of ramparts bristled with thirty-four towers and were pierced by seven monumental gates. There is no doubt that Suleiman aspired to perpetuate his glory, in an echo of his namesake Solomon/Suleyman, the emblematic king of Israel, considered one of the prophets of Islam.[13]

Viziers, janissaries, and sheikhs

The grand vizier, the most powerful man in the empire after the sultan, was also the most vulnerable, as he could be sacrificed at any time. For example, Yunus Pasha, the grand vizier of Selim, was executed in 1517 for having dared to criticize the appointment of the former Mamluk leader of Aleppo as leader of Egypt. Sometimes the sultan also gave in to pressure from the janissaries who 'overturned the cauldron', using this symbolic gesture as a threat of revolt.[14] The monarch could also eliminate the grand vizier if the latter became an alternative pole of power; the former could then lay his hands on the wealth accumulated by his former right-hand man. From 1453 to 1614, out of fifty-seven successive grand viziers, only five were ethnic Turks and many were converts, which made them even more vulnerable to the sultan's whims. The grand vizier presided, in

---

[13] During the consecration of the Hagia Sophia in 537, a millennium earlier, the Byzantine Emperor Justinian had already claimed to have 'surpassed' Solomon (see above, p. 24).

[14] The 'cauldron' in which the soldiers accepted food from the sovereign was the daily guarantee of their obedience, and 'overturning' it was tantamount to insubordination.

the name of the sovereign, over the divan,[15] the Ottoman equivalent of the council of state. The *defterdar*, responsible for the cadastre, occupied a strategic position, in part because of land taxation, but also because of the allocation of plots in usufruct (*timar*) to retain the loyalty of the local lords and a portion of the army. The practice of buying high office was tolerated, if not formalized, in order to feed the coffers of the empire.

The result was a vicious circle where administrators like the grand vizier strove to amass the biggest fortunes they could as quickly as possible before their dismissal, even if it meant 'financing' a possible return to favour. Apart from its intrusive bureaucracy, this system could thrive only as long as predatory practices were wagered successfully on the realm's expansion, hence its recurring crises in phases when borders were stabilized or even contracting. To counter the spiral of corruption, Ottoman ethics actively set up a virtuous circle of justice, summarized thus: 'no state without an army, no army without a sword, no sword without wealth, no wealth without *reaya*, no *reaya* without justice'. The *reaya*, a term derived from Arabic, referred to the people, literally the 'herd'.[16] It was from this people that the state drew its substance through taxation and production, hence the imperative need to show justice towards the population and limit oppression. This dialectic between state and people contrasted with the flamboyant militarism of the Seljuk, Mamluk, and Turkmen Sultanates. It is also striking that it came in the name of an ethic of the higher interests of the state, without calling on religious legitimacy.

The Ottoman army was made up of two distinct bodies: the spahis, horsemen authorized to operate a *timar* (or recruited by a local notable on the basis of his own *timar*), and the janissaries, rounded up from the Christian minorities of the empire and then converted. Selim was the first sultan to grant janissaries the right to marry. Their number reached 25,000 in 1528, under Suleiman, and continued to swell under the reign of his successors, representing approximately two-thirds of the

[15] The term 'divan' is derived from the Arabic *diwan*, which at the beginning of the Abbasid era designated one of the components of the administration (see above, p. 56), before being applied to the government as such.
[16] This Muslim notion corresponds to the priest's 'flock' in Christian terminology. This 'circle of justice' differed from the comparable model set up in Al-Azhar five centuries earlier, centred on the Fatimid Caliph (see above, p. 86).

professional army over this period. The janissaries were very often linked to a Sufi brotherhood, which allowed them to assert their autonomy, even their distrust of the state apparatus. As for the ulama, the Ottoman regime tried to make them civil servants within the framework of a hierarchy of *qadi*s and muftis,[17] whose supreme head was the *sheikholeslam*, the 'sheikh of Islam'. Ebussuud, the first holder of this post from 1545 to 1574, brought his clerical support to Sultan Suleiman's elimination of his rebellious son Bayezid. Ottoman formalism thus made a fatwa from the *sheikholeslam* essential to legitimize the execution of a high dignitary, even if this fatwa was often obtained a posteriori. More generally, Ebussuud and his successors used their legal expertise to subordinate the application of sharia to the designs of the ruler.[18] Sunnism in its Hanafi variety permeated this religious hierarchy, thereby depriving the Shiites of legal rights, especially around the holy cities of Najaf and Karbala in Iraq, but also the Alevis.[19] These minorities within Islam actually organized their own internal affairs in matters of worship and personal status. Their relations with the Sublime Porte were not codified like those of the various Christian Churches or Jewish communities.

An empire of seas and lands

In 1566, when Suleiman died, his son Selim ascended to the Ottoman throne and became Selim II in European historiography. (As all the brothers of the new sultan had already died, there was no longer any need to apply the appalling law of fratricide.) Five years later, in 1571, Selim II suffered a crushing defeat on the seas at Lepanto, in the Gulf of Corinth, against the Spaniards allied with the Venetians and the Genoese. As a result, the Ottoman Empire lost its uncontested domination in the Mediterranean, even if it compensated for this serious

---

[17] Fatwas were issued by a mufti, the latter term being derived from the former. The mufti in the Ottoman system was more in charge of religious affairs, as compared with the judge of the temporal realm, who was generally the *qadi*. The *sheikholeslam* was both the greatest of the *qadi*s and the most important of the muftis.

[18] This is how tobacco, which was long prohibited, was 'legalized' in 1652 by a fatwa from the *sheikholeslam*, thereby legitimizing the significant tax revenues.

[19] The Alevis were long called Kizilbach by the Ottoman bureaucracy, in reference to the Safavid shock troops.

setback by negotiating with Venice over the ceding of Cyprus in 1573. In addition, Ottoman vassals in Algiers seized Tunis shortly afterwards, followed by Tripolitania. Rather than witnessing large naval battles, the Mediterranean was now the scene of piracy and counter-piracy, carried out in the name of the Christian sovereigns by the 'corsairs' and of the sultan by his 'Barbary' subjects from the Maghreb.[20] As well as the booty itself, Europeans and Ottomans seized prisoners, and freed them only after fierce negotiations. The relationship of reciprocal predation was not, however, symmetrical, thanks to the advantages of conversion to Islam, which facilitated release on the spot and even promotion in the administration and the army. The result in Europe was a lasting phobia of 'renegades', the terms used to stigmatize Christians who became Muslims.

It would be tedious to list the successive sultans. Murad III, who succeeded his father Selim II in 1574, exhausted a dozen grand viziers in twenty years of his reign, and executed several of them. His prestige was tarnished by court intrigues, with his mother and one of his wives supporting two opposing parties. Subsequent sultans faced rampant instability in Anatolia, where bands of deserters joined local rebels. Ottoman order was not fully restored until 1608, with the shipment to Constantinople of thousands of decapitated insurgents' heads. Osman II, who ascended to the throne in 1618 at the age of fourteen, was, despite his young age, an ambitious reformist as well as an authentic polyglot. But in 1622 his plan to radically overhaul the army provoked the uprising of the janissaries, who assassinated him in his own palace. His brother Murad IV, faced with a new revolt of the janissaries in 1631, restored order with methodical brutality. He relied on the most rigorous ulama to curb the multifaceted influence of the Sufi brotherhoods. The empire was then organized into about thirty provinces (*eyalets*), themselves subdivided into some 300 districts (*sanjaks*), half of these structures being in the Middle East. A complex system, like all imperial constructions, the Ottoman Empire thrived on the contradictions it generated. It sought to be centralized, but continued to grant derogatory statuses so as to establish its authority in sensitive areas. It fixed and settled its

---

[20] The term 'corsair' is derived from the 'letter of marque' (*lettre de course*), which was an official warrant to attack an enemy ship, while 'Barbary' is derived from 'Berber'.

subject populations to tax them more efficiently, but reserved the right to move them collectively in the event of war or absolute need. It publicly proscribed conflict, but benefited from the management and arbitration of these same conflicts.

A frontier of empires

The most powerful of the Safavid rulers, the Persian equivalent of Suleiman the Magnificent among the Ottomans, was Shah Abbas, in power from 1587 to 1629. He methodically undermined the power of the great feudal lords, relying on an English adventurer, Robert Sherley to reorganize his military institutions. The modernized Persian army was based on the amalgamation of three forces: first, a professionalized contingent, whose Persian officers sometimes belonged to the same families as the high administration; then, the shock troops of the Kizilbachs, perpetuating the warlike tradition of the Turkmens (though the shah regularly forced them to fall into line); and, finally, a guard dedicated to the very person of the sovereign and composed of Armenians, Georgians, and Circassians. This military power enabled Shah Abbas to repel Uzbek attacks in the east of the country, and then to regain control of the two main cities of Khorasan, namely Herat and Mashhad, where he solemnly went on pilgrimage in 1601 to the tomb of the eighth Shia Imam. But the shah also extended his influence to the south of the Persian Gulf, playing the English against the Portuguese,[21] until the latter were expelled from the Strait of Hormuz. He finally turned against the Ottomans, violating the peace of 1555 to seize Baghdad in 1624, whose Sunni population he persecuted.

This war, devastating for Iraq, also weighed very heavily on the resources of Persia, which repelled two campaigns of reconquest conducted by Murad IV in 1626 and 1630, before yielding to the third, in 1638. Baghdad, besieged for more than a month, was this time forced to suffer the massacre of much of its Shiite population. The peace concluded in 1639 drew a border between Ottoman Iraq and Safavid Persia that is

---

[21] The English were rewarded for their assistance against the Portuguese by being given facilities in the Persian port of Bandar Abbas; these facilities were soon also granted to the Dutch.

largely the same as the one that now exists between Iraq and Iran. It was a frontier of empires, defined by a balance between powers and stabilized after a century. This division was neither ethnic, nor linguistic, nor religious: Turkish, Kurdish, and Arab populations lived on either side, while a Sunni minority persisted in Persia, and Iraq was the home of the two holiest cities of Shiism. The persistence of this border over the past four centuries, despite the terrible conflict between Iraq and Iran from 1980 to 1988, should be pondered by all sorcerer's apprentices who believe they are 'solving' the problems of the Middle East by separating the supposed territories of each community.

The Safavid court

In 1598, Shah Abbas chose Isfahan – already the economic and cultural centre of the kingdom – as his capital. He endowed it with imposing monuments, hence the Persian proverb that 'Isfahan represents half of Creation'.[22] The magnificent Shah Mosque overlooks the no less superb Shah Square, now an 'Imam' Mosque and Square, in reference to Ayatollah Khomeini. The Safavid court impressed ambassadors and travellers with its splendour. The suburb of Joulfa was populated by Armenians transferred collectively from the locality of the same name in the Caucasus.[23] They were authorized to cultivate vines, officially for their 'communion wine', but they supplied the entire capital with alcohol. These Armenians were industrious craftsmen, prosperous traders, and, in some cases, loyal militiamen. Shah Abbas's marked tolerance towards his Christian and Jewish subjects contrasted with the discrimination he continued to inflict on Sunnis. The sovereign cultivated his status as the embodiment of Safavid Shiism; his 1601 pilgrimage to Mashhad celebrated the centenary of the dynasty. As for the arts, they lost in quality what they gained in quantity; this was tangible in the case of the famous 'Persian miniatures', which were increasingly imitated and commonplace.

---

[22] In Persian: *Isfahân nesf e-Jahân.*
[23] Shah Abbas even planned to move the Etchmladzin church, still today the seat of the Armenian patriarchate, and situated north of Yerevan, stone by stone, but he finally gave up on his project.

Abbas II, in power from 1642 to 1666, is considered the last of the three great Safavid sovereigns, after the founder Isma'il and the first Abbas, who built on his predecessor's achievements. The peace that prevailed during his reign, on the Ottoman border as well as at home, is largely credited to him. Abbas II continued to shower the Christians of the kingdom with his favours, while frequently subjecting the Jews of Isfahan to insults as he tried in vain to drive them to conversion. The shah also firmly defended his religious pre-eminence against the ulama, who were trying to divert for their exclusive benefit the delegated authority derived from the Hidden Imam. On the other hand, the two successors of Abbas II, either out of weakness or out of bigotry, gradually succumbed to the pressure of the Shiite ulama. Sheikh Baqer Majlesi, promoted to the head of the clerical hierarchy in 1687, fiercely persecuted Sufism, which had hitherto been as highly developed in Shiism as in Sunnism. He thereby attacked the way Safavid authority was based on this kind of brotherhood, and also criticized a form of mystical ecumenism, all in the name of a combative Shiism.

Jean Chardin, a French jeweller in search of precious stones, stayed three times at the court of Shah Suleyman, the son of Abbas II, between 1666 and 1677. His travel accounts were widely distributed in Europe, and Montesquieu drew on them for the local colour of his own *Persian Letters*, published in 1721. The court of Isfahan, shrouded in exoticism, gave birth to ever more fantasies as the 'Grand Turk' was, at the same time, set up as the archetype of the 'Oriental despot'. Shah Hussein, who succeeded his father Suleyman in 1694, proved to be a very poor ruler. He preferred to legitimize the intolerance of the ulama so as to better indulge his own vices. The harem alone absorbed a tenth of the imperial budget, with thousands of women, including dozens of wives and concubines, each accompanied by their daughters and slaves. The fiscal pressure on the provinces was such that, in 1722, no regional contingent came to the aid of Isfahan when it was surrounded by Afghan tribes. After six months of siege, Shah Hussein was forced to capitulate, then to abdicate in favour of the invader. We will see later that a fiction of Safavid power survived this rout for a few decades. But the dynasty founded by Shah Isma'il had reigned for a little more than two centuries over a Persian Empire where state Shiism, the base of the Safavid edifice, had also favoured the consolidation of the clerical structure.

1.1 The Middle East between Byzantines and Sassanids (395-630)

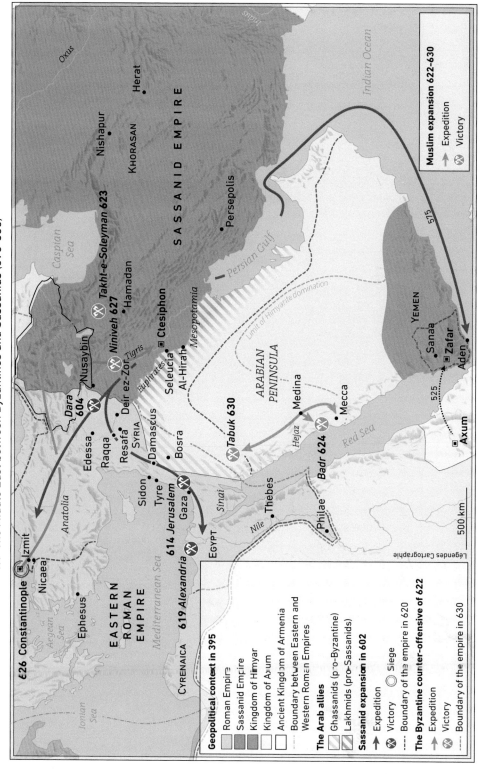

Geopolitical context in 395

- Roman Empire
- Sassanid Empire
- Kingdom of Himyar
- Kingdom of Axum
- Ancient Kingdom of Armenia
- - - Boundary between Eastern and Western Roman Empires

The Arab allies

- Ghassanids (pro-Byzantine)
- Lakhmids (pro-Sassanids)

Sassanid expansion in 602

- ↑ Expedition
- ⊗ Victory
- ◎ Siege
- - - - Boundary of the empire in 620

The Byzantine counter-offensive of 622

- ↑ Expedition
- ⊗ Victory
- - - - Boundary of the empire in 630

Muslim expansion 622-630

- ↑ Expedition
- ⊗ Victory

500 km

Légendes Cartographie

1.2 The spread of Islam in the Arabian Pensinsula (612–632)

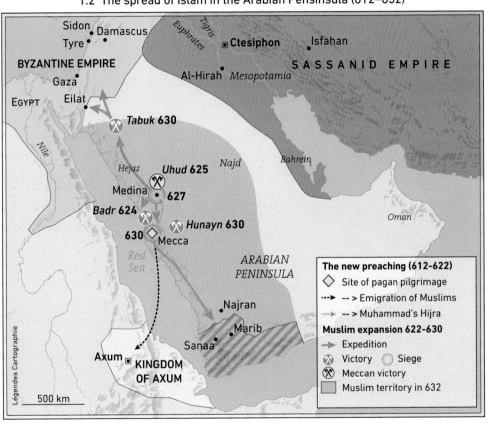

Sidon
Tyre
Damascus
Euphrates
Tigris
□ Ctesiphon
Isfahan

BYZANTINE EMPIRE

SASSANID EMPIRE

Gaza
Al-Hirah   *Mesopotamia*

EGYPT   Eilat

Nile

⊗ *Tabuk* **630**

Hejaz   *Najd*   *Bahrein*

⊗ *Uhud* **625**
Medina **627**

Badr **624**   ⊗   ⊗ *Hunayn* **630**

630 ◇   Mecca

Red Sea   *ARABIAN PENINSULA*   *Oman*

Najran

Marib

Sanaa

Axum ◻ **KINGDOM OF AXUM**

500 km

Légendes Cartographie

The new preaching (612–622)
◇ Site of pagan pilgrimage
⋯▶ Emigration of Muslims
⋯▶ Muhammad's Hijra

Muslim expansion 622–630
➤ Expedition
⊗ Victory   ○ Siege
⊗ Meccan victory
▨ Muslim territory in 632

2.1 The Umayyad Middle East (661–750)

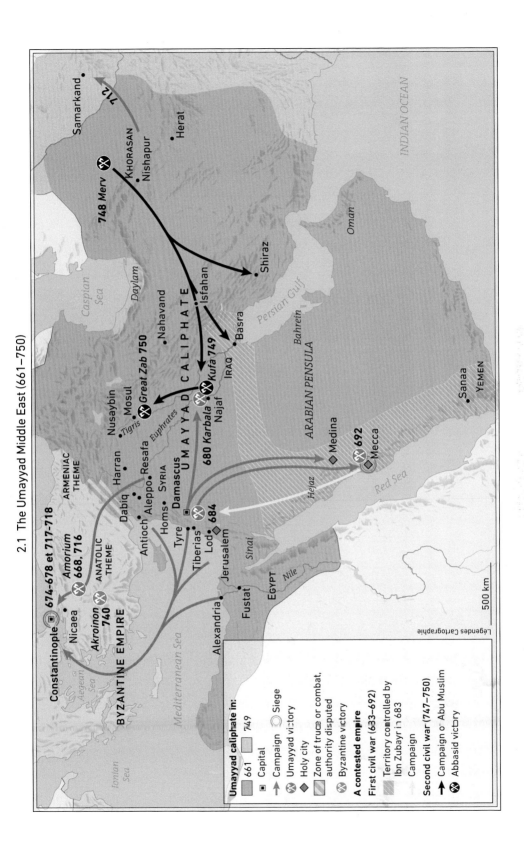

Umayyad caliphate in:
- 661
- 749
- ■ Capital
- ↑ Campaign   ◎ Siege
- ⊗ Umayyad victory
- ◆ Holy city
- Zone of truce or combat, authority disputed
- ⊗ Byzantine victory

A contested empire

First civil war (633–692)
- Territory controlled by Ibn Zubayr in 683
- Campaign

Second civil war (747–750)
- Campaign of Abu Muslim
- ◆ Abbasid victory

Legendes Cartographie

500 km

Constantinople ◎ 674–678 et 717–718
Amorium 668, 716
Akroinon 740 ⊗
BYZANTINE EMPIRE
Nicaea
ANATOLIC THEME
ARMENIAC THEME

712
Samarkand
Herat
KHORASAN
Nishapur
748 Merv ⊗
Shiraz
Isfahan
Nahavand
Basra
Kufa 749 ⊗
Great Zab 750 ⊗
Mosul
Nusaybin
Tigris
Euphrates
680 Karbala ⊗
Najaf
IRAQ

Caspian Sea
Daylam

INDIAN OCEAN
Oman

Harran
Resafa
Aleppo
Antioch
Homs SYRIA
Dabiq
Damascus ■
684 ⊗
Tyre
Tiberias
Lod ◆
Jerusalem
Sinai
Jerusalem

Mediterranean Sea
Aegean Sea
Ionian Sea

EGYPT
Nile
Fustat
Alexandria

UMAYYAD CALIPHATE

Medina ◆
692 ⊗
Mecca ◎
Hejaz
Red Sea
ARABIAN PENSULA
Bahrein
Persian Gulf

Sanaa
YEMEN

2.2 Abbasid Iraq (749-945)

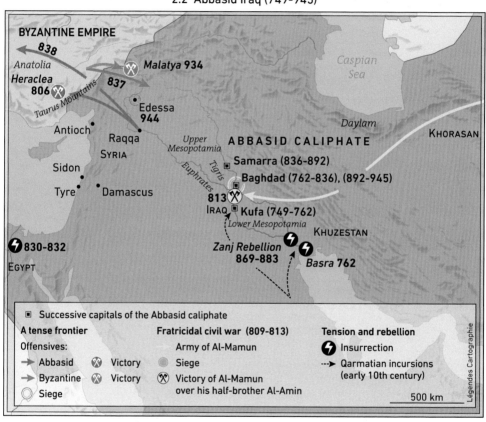

Legend:

◼ Successive capitals of the Abbasid caliphate

A tense frontier
Offensives:
→ Abbasid   ⊗ Victory
→ Byzantine ⊗ Victory
◯ Siege

Fratricidal civil war (809-813)
Army of Al-Mamun
◯ Siege
⊗ Victory of Al-Mamun over his half-brother Al-Amin

Tension and rebellion
⚡ Insurrection
⇢ Qarmatian incursions (early 10th century)

500 km

Légendes Cartographie

Map labels: BYZANTINE EMPIRE; 838; Anatolia; Heraclea 806; 837; Malatya 934; Taurus Mountains; Edessa 944; Antioch; Raqqa; SYRIA; Upper Mesopotamia; Caspian Sea; Daylam; ABBASID CALIPHATE; KHORASAN; Sidon; Tyre; Damascus; Euphrates; Tigris; Samarra (836-892); Baghdad (762-836), (892-945); 813; IRAQ; Kufa (749-762); Lower Mesopotamia; KHUZESTAN; 830-832; EGYPT; Zanj Rebellion 869-883; Basra 762

3.1 The Middle East of the two caliphates (969–1095)

Samarkand

Balkh

KHORASAN
1038

Herat

Nishapur

Caspian
Sea

Caucasus

INDIAN OCEAN

Oman

Shiraz

Rayy

Ispahan

BUYID EMERATE
(945–1055)

1055

Basra

Persian Gulf

Bahrein

Hamadan

Manzikert **1071**

Mosul

Baghdad

IRAQ

Najaf

ABBASID
CALIPHATE

ARABIAN
PENINSULA

ZAYDITE EMIRATE

Saada

Sanaa

Yemen

Tigris

Euphrates

SULTANATE OF RUM
(SELJUK)

Anatolia

Malatya

Aleppo

EMIRATE OF ALEPPO

Homs

1076

Damascus

SYRIA

Medina

Mecca

Hejaz

Red Sea

Antioch

Latakia

Tripoli

Sidon

Acre

975

Jerusalem

Constantinople

Nicea

BYZANTINE EMPIRE

Aegean
Sea

Ionian
Sea

Mediterranean Sea

Sinai

EGYPT

FATIMID
CALIPHATE

Cairo

Alexandria

Nile

Ionian
Sea

500 km

Légendes Cartographie

The geopolitical context at the end of the 10th century

- Abbasid Caliphate
- Fatimid Caliphate
- Byzantine Empire
- Byzantine Protectorate
- Capital
- Byzantine campaign

Seljuks' rise to power in the 11th century

- Seljuk Khorasan (1038)
- Seljuk campaign
- Seljuk victory
- Western boundary of the Abbasid Caliphate in 1095

The Byzantine reconquest

- Expansion during the first half of the 11th century

3.2 The first two crusades (1095-1149)

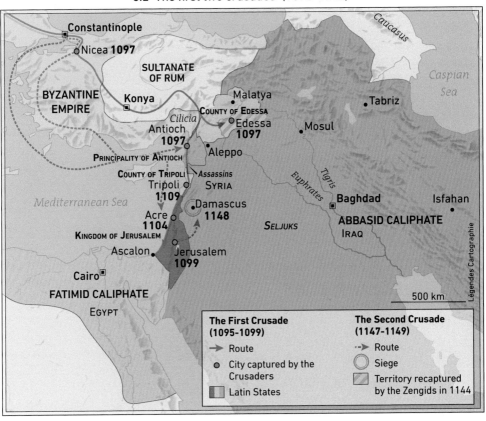

Constantinople

Nicea **1097**

SULTANATE
OF RUM

Caucasus

BYZANTINE
EMPIRE

Konya

Malatya

Tabriz

Caspian
Sea

Cilicia

COUNTY OF EDESSA

Antioch
1097

Edessa
1097

Mosul

PRINCIPALITY OF ANTIOCH

Aleppo

COUNTY OF TRIPOLI

Assassins

Euphrates

Tigris

Tripoli
1109

SYRIA

Baghdad

Isfahan

Mediterranean Sea

Damascus
1148

Acre
1104

SELJUKS

ABBASID CALIPHATE
IRAQ

KINGDOM OF JERUSALEM

Ascalon

Jerusalem
1099

Cairo

FATIMID CALIPHATE

EGYPT

500 km

Légendes Cartographie

**The First Crusade
(1095-1099)**

→ Route

◉ City captured by the
Crusaders

▨ Latin States

**The Second Crusade
(1147-1149)**

⇢ Route

◯ Siege

▨ Territory recaptured
by the Zengids in 1144

4.1 The Middle East from the Ayyubids to the Mamluks (1193–1260)

The Fourth and Fifth Crusades

→ The Fourth Crusade (1202–1204)

⇢ The Fifth Crusade (1217–1221)

✖ Crusader victory

✖ Ayyubid victory

The geopolitical context in 1230

Abbasid Caliphate

including Ayyubid Sultanate

Byzantine Empire

Mongol territory

'Frankish' territory

→ The Seventh Crusade (1249–1254)

Mongol expansion until 1260

→ Campaign ✖ Victory

▬ Mongol Expansion in 1260

▬ Mamluk counter-offensive

✖ Mamluk victory

---- Border to which Mongols withdrew after the defeat of Ain Jalut

Légendes Cartographie

500 km

4.2 The invasion of Timur the Lame (1387–1404)

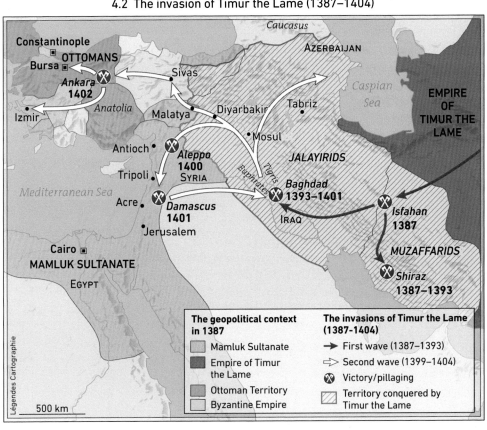

Constantinople
OTTOMANS
Bursa
Ankara **1402**
Anatolia
Izmir
Sivas
Malatya
Diyarbakir
Tabriz
Caucasus
AZERBAIJAN
Caspian Sea
EMPIRE OF TIMUR THE LAME
Antioch
Aleppo **1400**
SYRIA
Mosul
JALAYIRIDS
Tripoli
Acre
Damascus **1401**
Jerusalem
IRAQ
Baghdad **1393–1401**
Euphrates
Tigris
Mediterranean Sea
Cairo
MAMLUK SULTANATE
EGYPT
Isfahan **1387**
MUZAFFARIDS
Shiraz **1387–1393**

The geopolitical context in 1387
- Mamluk Sultanate
- Empire of Timur the Lame
- Ottoman Territory
- Byzantine Empire

The invasions of Timur the Lame (1387–1404)
- → First wave (1387–1393)
- ⇨ Second wave (1399–1404)
- ⊗ Victory/pillaging
- ▨ Territory conquered by Timur the Lame

500 km

Légendes Cartographie

5.1 The Middle East from 1501 to 1555

5.2 The 1629 border between the Ottomans and the Safavids

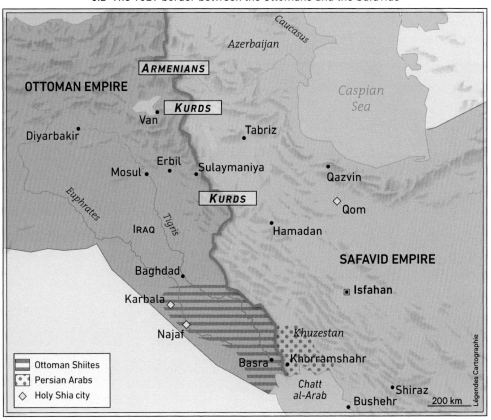

6.1 The Middle East from 1798 to 1810

The geopolitical context at the beginning of the 19th century
- Ottoman Empire
- Quadjar State
- Russian Thrust (1801)

The Egyptian expedition
- French campaign
- French victory
- French defeat
- Retreat

The Wahhabi challenge
- Cradle of the Saud
- Expansion
- Wahhabi Emirate in 1808
- Limit of the Ottoman Empire in 1810

OTTOMAN EMPIRE

QUADJAR STATE

WAHHABI EMIRATE

ARABIAN PENINSULA

OMAN

YEMEN

EGYPT

Constantinople

Izmir

Anatolia

Diyarbakir

Mosul

Aleppo

Tripoli

Damascus

Acre 1799

Alexandria 1798

Cairo 1801

The Pyramids 1798

Van

Tabriz

Hamadan

Baghdad

Karbala

Najaf

Isfahan

Shiraz

Kerman

Tehran

Nishapur

Dariya

Medina

Mecca

Caucasus

Caspian Sea

Aegean Sea

Mediterranean Sea

Red Sea

Persian Gulf

INDIAN OCEAN

Tigris

Euphrates

Nile

Hejaz

1798

1801

1802

1803

1805

1810

500 km

Légendes Cartographie

6.2 The United States at war in Libya (1801–1805)

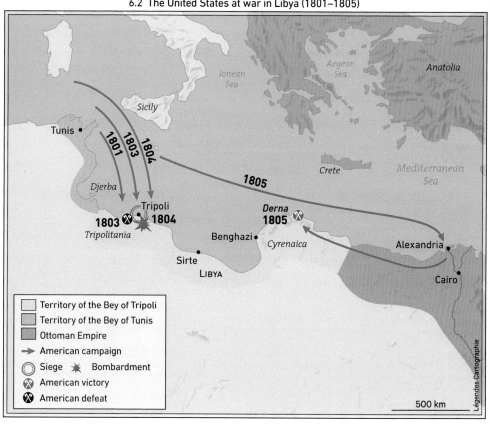

Anatolia

Ionean
Sea

Aegean
Sea

Sicily

Tunis •

1801
1803
1804

Crete

Mediterranean
Sea

1805

Djerba

Tripoli

Derna

Tripolitania

1803 ⊗   ☀ 1804

1805 ⊗

Benghazi •

Cyrenaica

Alexandria •

Sirte •

Cairo •

Libya

▢	Territory of the Bey of Tripoli
▨	Territory of the Bey of Tunis
▩	Ottoman Empire
→	American campaign
◎ Siege	☀ Bombardment
⊗	American victory
⊗	American defeat

500 km

Légendes Cartographie

7.1 The Middle East in 1882

RUSSIAN EMPIRE

- Samarkand
- Balkh
- Herat
- Nishapur

AFGHANISTAN

Indus

Towards Bombay

INDIAN EMPIRE

- BALUCHISTAN
- Karachi

INDIAN OCEAN

QAJAR EMPIRE

- Bandar Abbas
- Kirman
- Shiraz
- Teheran
- Hamadan
- Isfahan
- Tabriz

Caspian Sea

Caucasus

- Tbilissi
- Van

Tigris

Euphrates

- Mosul
- Baghdad
- Diyarbakir
- Aleppo

Persian Gulf

OMAN 1861

TRUCIAL COAST (FORMERLY PIRATE COAST) 1853

BAHRAIN 1880

Saud

ARABIAN PENINSULA

HADHRAMAUT 1874

Aden 1839

1869

Red Sea

- Medina
- Mecca

Hejaz

OTTOMAN EMPIRE

- Constantinople
- Izmir
- Damascus
- Limassol

Anatolia

1878 Cyprus

Mediterranean Sea

Aegean Sea

Crete

GREECE

Suez Canal

Nile

- Cairo

EGYPT 1882

500 km

Légendes Cartographie

The geopolitical context in 1882

- Ottoman Empire
- Qajar Empire
- British Empire
- Russian Empire
- Afghanistan
- Territory of the Saud

Zone of control

- British
- Russian
- 1882 Date of British settlement
- --- Major maritime route

1907 Covention on Persia

Zone of influence
- British
- Russian

7.2 From the 'Armenian Crisis' to the genocide (1894–1916)

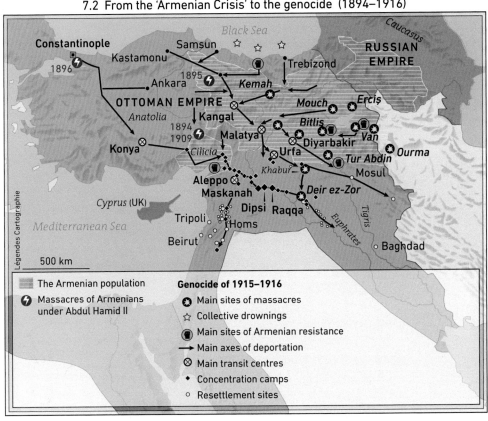

Black Sea

Caucasus

RUSSIAN
EMPIRE

Constantinople

1896

Kastamonu

Samsun

Ankara

1895

Trebizond

Kemah

OTTOMAN EMPIRE

Anatolia

1894
1909

Kangal

Malatya

Mouch

Erciş

Bitlis

Van

Cilicia

Konya

Diyarbakir

Urfa

Tur Abdin

Ourma

Khabur

Mosul

Aleppo

Maskanah

Deir ez-Zor

Cyprus (UK)

Mediterranean Sea

Tripoli

Dipsi

Raqqa

Euphrates

Tigris

Homs

Beirut

Baghdad

500 km

Légendes Cartographie

The Armenian population

Massacres of Armenians
under Abdul Hamid II

Genocide of 1915–1916

Main sites of massacres

☆ Collective drownings

Main sites of Armenian resistance

→ Main axes of deportation

⊗ Main transit centres

◆ Concentration camps

○ Resettlement sites

8.1 The Middle East in 1923

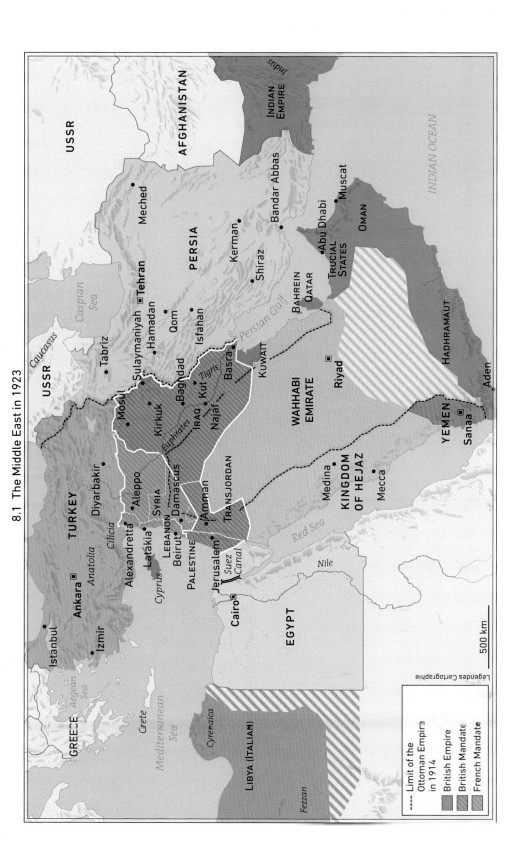

Legendes Cartographie

- - - Limit of the Ottoman Empire in 1914

British Empire

British Mandate

French Mandate

500 km

8.2 The formation of Saudi Arabia (1902–1932)

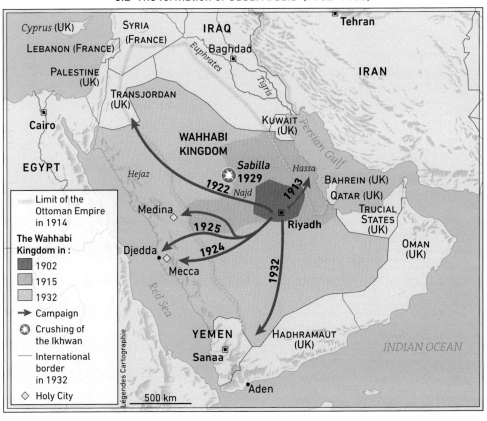

Cyprus (UK)

SYRIA (FRANCE)

IRAQ

Tehran

LEBANON (FRANCE)

Baghdad

IRAN

PALESTINE (UK)

Euphrates

Tigris

TRANSJORDAN (UK)

Cairo

KUWAIT (UK)

Persian Gulf

WAHHABI KINGDOM

EGYPT

Hejaz

Sabilla 1929

Hassa

BAHREIN (UK)

1922

Najd

1913

QATAR (UK)

Medina

TRUCIAL STATES (UK)

1925

Riyadh

OMAN (UK)

Djedda

1924

Mecca

1932

Red Sea

YEMEN

HADHRAMAUT (UK)

INDIAN OCEAN

Sanaa

Aden

Légendes Cartographie

Legend:

Limit of the Ottoman Empire in 1914

The Wahhabi Kingdom in:
- 1902
- 1915
- 1932

→ Campaign

✸ Crushing of the Ikhwan

— International border in 1932

◇ Holy City

500 km

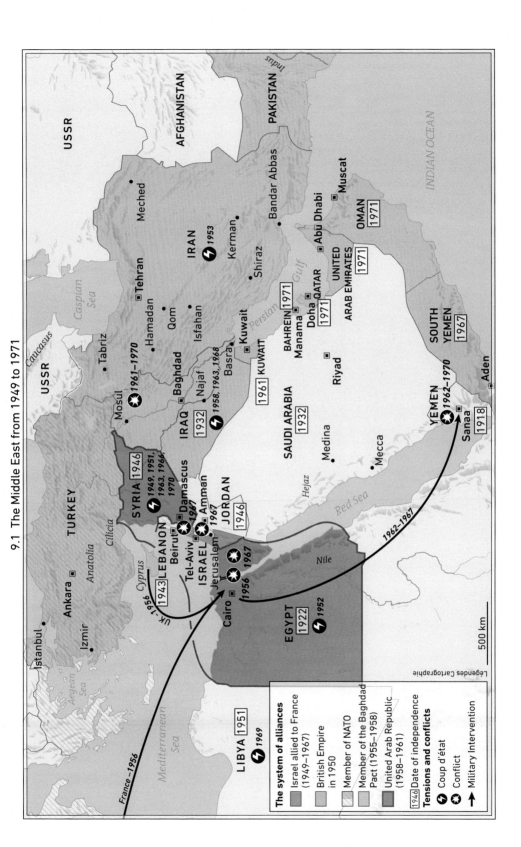

9.1 The Middle East from 1949 to 1971

The system of alliances

- Israel allied to France (1949–1967)
- British Empire in 1950
- Member of NATO
- Member of the Baghdad Pact (1955–1958)
- United Arab Republic (1958–1961)

1946 Date of independence

Tensions and conflicts

- Coup d'état
- Conflict
- Military Intervention

Légendes Cartographie

500 km

USSR
AFGHANISTAN
PAKISTAN
Indus
INDIAN OCEAN
Meched
Tehran
Hamadan
Qom
Isfahan
Kerman
Shiraz
Bandar Abbas
IRAN 1953
Muscat
OMAN 1971
Abū Dhabi
UNITED ARAB EMIRATES 1971
QATAR 1971
Doha
Persian Gulf
BAHREIN 1971
Manama
Riyad
Kuwait
KUWAIT 1961
Basra
Najaf
Baghdad
IRAQ 1932
1958, 1963, 1968
1961–1970
Mosul
Tabriz
USSR
Caspian Sea
Caucasus
SAUDI ARABIA 1932
Medina
Mecca
Hejaz
Red Sea
SOUTH YEMEN 1967
YEMEN 1962–1970
Sanaa 1918
Aden
1962–1967
SYRIA 1946
1949, 1951, 1963, 1966, 1970
Damascus
LEBANON
Beirut
TURKEY
Ankara
Anatolia
Cilicia
Istanbul
Izmir
Aegean Sea
Cyprus
UK–1956
1943
France–1956
Mediterranean Sea
LIBYA 1951
1969
Tel-Aviv 1967
ISRAEL 1956, 1967
Jerusalem
Amman 1967
JORDAN 1946
Cairo
EGYPT 1922
1952
Nile

9.2 The 'Six-Day War' in 1967

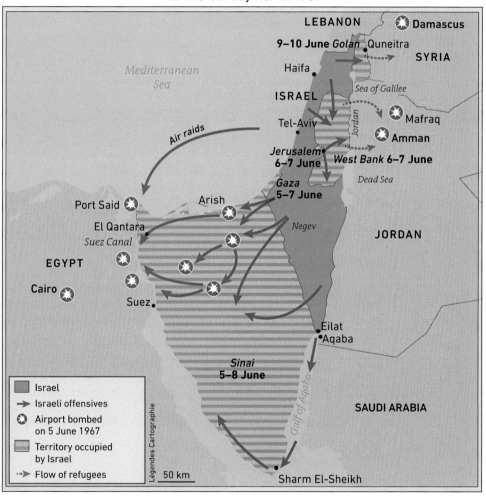

LEBANON

Damascus

9–10 June *Golan* Quneitra

SYRIA

Mediterranean Sea

Haifa

ISRAEL

Sea of Galilee

Mafraq

Tel-Aviv

Jordan

Amman

Jerusalem
6–7 June

West Bank **6–7 June**

Dead Sea

Air raids

Gaza
5–7 June

Port Said

Arish

Negev

JORDAN

El Qantara

Suez Canal

EGYPT

Cairo

Suez

Eilat
Aqaba

Sinai
5–8 June

SAUDI ARABIA

Gulf of Aqaba

Sharm El-Sheikh

	Israel
	Israeli offensives
	Airport bombed on 5 June 1967
	Territory occupied by Israel
	Flow of refugees

Légendes Cartographie

50 km

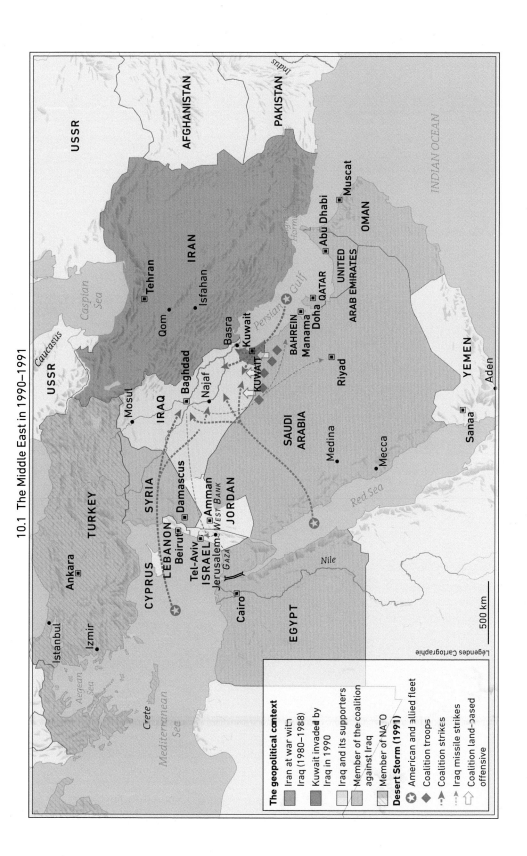

10.1 The Middle East in 1990–1991

The geopolitical context

Iran at war with Iraq (1980–1988)

Kuwait invaded by Iraq in 1990

Iraq and its supporters

Member of the coalition against Iraq

Member of NATO

Desert Storm (1991)

✪ American and allied fleet

◆ Coalition troops

Coalition strikes

Iraqi missile strikes

⇧ Coalition land-based offensive

Légendes Cartographie

500 km

USSR

AFGHANISTAN

PAKISTAN

Indus

USSR

Caucasus

Caspian Sea

TURKEY

Ankara

Istanbul

Izmir

Aegean Sea

Crete

Mediterranean Sea

CYPRUS

LEBANON

Beirut

SYRIA

Damascus

Amman

ISRAEL

Tel-Aviv

Jerusalem

WEST BANK

GAZA

JORDAN

EGYPT

Cairo

Nile

Red Sea

IRAN

Tehran

Qom

Isfahan

Mosul

IRAQ

Baghdad

Najaf

Basra

Kuwait

KUWAIT

Persian Gulf

Strait of Hormuz

BAHREIN

Manama

QATAR

Doha

Abū Dhabi

UNITED ARAB EMIRATES

OMAN

Muscat

INDIAN OCEAN

SAUDI ARABIA

Riyad

Medina

Mecca

YEMEN

Sanaa

Aden

10.2 The Syrian crisis (2011–2021)

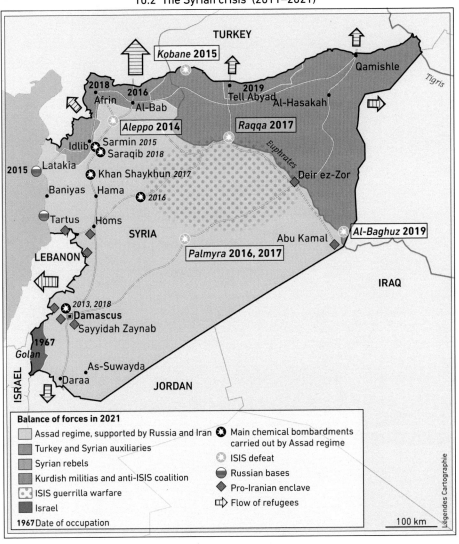

TURKEY

Kobane 2015

Qamishle

Tigris

2018
Afrin
2016
Al-Bab

2019
Tell Abyad
Al-Hasakah

Aleppo 2014

Raqqa 2017

Idlib
Sarmin *2015*
Saraqib *2018*

Euphrates

2015 Latakia

Khan Shaykhun *2017*

Deir ez-Zor

Baniyas
Hama
2016

Tartus
Homs

SYRIA

Abu Kamal

Al-Baghuz 2019

Palmyra **2016, 2017**

LEBANON

2013, 2018
Damascus
Sayyidah Zaynab

IRAQ

1967
Golan

As-Suwayda

ISRAEL

Daraa

JORDAN

Balance of forces in 2021

- Assad regime, supported by Russia and Iran
- Main chemical bombardments carried out by Assad regime
- Turkey and Syrian auxiliaries
- ISIS defeat
- Syrian rebels
- Russian bases
- Kurdish militias and anti-ISIS coalition
- Pro-Iranian enclave
- ISIS guerrilla warfare
- Flow of refugees
- Israel
- **1967** Date of occupation

100 km

Légendes Cartographie

Syria seen from Aleppo

After the Ottoman conquest of 1516, Bilad al-Sham was divided between the two governorates of Damascus and Aleppo, the latter having pre-eminence over the former because of its strategic importance: Aleppo was the crossroads of the road leading from Constantinople to India, either via Armenia and Azerbaijan, or via Baghdad and the Persian Gulf. The province of Aleppo covered Antioch, as well as a large part of the former Little Armenia of Cilicia, and extended to the Euphrates, the boundary with the governorate of Diyarbakir. Aleppo, the most disputed *échelle*, saw the successive opening of the consulates of France, England, and Holland,[24] which implanted the 'nation' of their traders in the caravanserai of the fortified city, at the foot of the citadel. This term of English or French 'nation' refers to the Ottoman concept of *millet*/community: the Europeans enjoyed, with their consulates, an autonomy of jurisdiction comparable to that of the minorities of the empire. The predominance of Aleppo was preserved during the administrative reorganization of 1579–1586, which created the two governorates of Tripoli (in central Syria) and Raqqa (east of the Euphrates), at the expense of Damascus and Diyarbakir respectively. The demographic dynamism of Aleppo particularly affected minorities, and the number of dwellings of the inner Jewish quarter doubled between 1570 and 1683, while a Christian suburb was created in Al-Jdayde.

The economic calendar of Aleppo was soon organized around the gathering of silk cocoons in the summer; the weaving of textiles in the autumn; and the sale, at the very beginning of winter, of bales of silk, shipped to Europe from the port of İskenderun/Alexandretta. The rest of Bilad al-Sham, in particular Mount Lebanon, also benefited from the craze for silk, but to a lesser extent than Aleppo. This trade flourished until the last third of the eighteenth century, before declining under the effect of Indian competition and Western production. The population of Aleppo, structured in sometimes multi-sectarian corporations, rose up against a continuing heavy tax burden. The revolt was led by the *ashraf*, the so-called 'descendants of the Prophet', who put their

---

[24] In 1562, 1583, and 1613 respectively. These three countries had opened their embassies in Constantinople in 1535, 1580, and 1612.

religious prestige at the service of the anti-Ottoman protest: in 1770, they prohibited the Ottoman governor from entering Aleppo for more than a month; in 1775, they legitimized the riots which forced the representative of Constantinople to leave the city in humiliation; in 1784, along with the local contingent of janissaries, they organized the autonomous administration of the city for a year; and in 1791, the Ottoman governor had to evacuate after being besieged in the citadel by the populace. Such disturbances, while doubtless being part of a general context of Ottoman crises (we shall return to this), nevertheless reflected the assertion of a very strong local identity in Aleppo even before it spread to Syria as a whole.

The great game of the minorities

At the beginning of the Ottoman era, some sources make it possible to estimate the Christian population at around one-tenth of that of Bilad al-Sham. Its demographic growth was tangible over the next three centuries, both in urban centres and in Mount Lebanon, where the Maronite peasantry took full advantage of the 'sultan's peace'. The representatives of the Sublime Porte were happy to treat their Christian subjects with some favour, even though the latter, as people of the Book, were much more heavily taxed than their Muslim neighbours. It was in this spirit that in 1591 the governor of Damascus entrusted the Druze emir Fakhr al-Din II[25] with the management of Mount Lebanon. This astute feudal official quickly became the privileged interlocutor of the European powers in the *échelle* of Sidon, while setting up his winter residence in Beirut.[26] He even joined the revolt of the Kurdish governor of Aleppo, Ali Janbulad, in 1606, abandoning him shortly before he was crushed:[27] this earned him the indulgence of the Ottomans. Fakhr al-Din consolidated his Lebanese autonomy and his relations with the court of the Medici in Florence, to which, having become rather too

[25] His name means 'honour of religion'.
[26] His summer residence was located in the Maronite locality of Deir al-Qamar ('the Monastery of the Moon'), in the heart of the Lebanese mountain district of Chouf.
[27] Relatives of Janbulad, welcomed by Fakhr al-Din in Chouf, were authorized, exceptionally, to convert to the Druze religion, their surname being Arabized as Jumblatt.

ambitious, he was exiled in 1613. Returning to Lebanon in 1618, Fakhr al-Din dominated an increasingly extensive stronghold for a decade, especially after his 1623 victory over the governor of Damascus and the Shiite tribes of the Beqaa. He nevertheless continued to raise taxes rather than troops in the name of Constantinople; his refusal to contribute to the Iraq campaign led, in 1635, to his execution.

In 1623, King Louis XIII sent a consul to Jerusalem, responsible for protecting pilgrims and French interests, but also for representing Catholics during the recurring quarrels with the Church of the East over the holy places of Christianity. However, he did not manage to establish a permanent mission, contenting himself with encouraging the development of the Franciscan order within the 'custody of the Holy Land'. Generally, the French consulates in the Middle East supported the proselytism of Catholic missionaries aimed at local Christians as the Ottomans prohibited any form of apostasy on the part of Muslims. In 1639, Louis XIII proclaimed himself 'protector' of the Catholics of the Levant, especially the Maronites, a claim reaffirmed by Louis XIV in 1649 and 1701 without ever being recognized by the Sublime Porte. France's direct and indirect activism led, from 1656, to the emergence of 'Catholic' dissidence within three 'Orthodox' Churches of the East: first the Syriac, then the Greek, and finally the Armenian. Each of these new Churches was attached to Rome under the authority of a patriarch and on the model already adopted by the Maronites. Though in the renegotiation of the capitulations in 1740 Louis XV posed, like his predecessors, as a protector of his co-religionists in the Middle East, he unilaterally exploited the ambiguity between the French 'nation' and the Catholic *millet*.

England, which proved commercially more powerful than France in the *échelle* of Aleppo, could not claim to be protecting a local minority. The London delegates therefore cultivated the favour of the Ottoman authorities and the Levantine notables, the *ayan*, sometimes with a marked interest in Jewish communities. The expulsion of the Sephardim[28] from Spain and Portugal after the fall of Granada in 1492 was followed by similar persecutions in the Italian cities in the

---

[28] In mediaeval Hebrew, the term *Sefarad* designated the Iberian Peninsula, then the Jews who originated there.

sixteenth century, swelling the ranks of Middle Eastern Judaism. The Jewish world of the Levant was profoundly shaken, in the middle of the seventeenth century, by the messianic preaching of Sabbatai Zevi, a native of Izmir, but active in Constantinople and Cairo. The support he gained from Rabbi Nathan of Gaza in 1665 was decisive in the face of the virulent hostility of the Talmudic seminaries in Jerusalem. Eastern communities were divided between supporters and opponents of the so-called 'messiah', whose conversion to Islam in 1666, probably to avoid abuse at the hands of the Ottomans, meant the loss of his credibility. Millenarian fervour waned as quickly as it had arisen and collective disillusion spread to all except small groups of diehards who were rejected in the Middle East and spread to Poland in the following century.[29]

Ottoman crises

Sultan Mehmed IV, who ascended to the throne at the age of six in 1648, would reign for nearly forty years. During the sovereign's childhood, power was exercised in his name by the queen mother and the janissaries. It took all the skill of the octogenarian Mehmed Köprülü, appointed grand vizier in 1656, for the sultan to finally free himself from court intrigues. In order to consolidate the effective authority of the sovereign, Köprülü suppressed all forms of dissent and in 1658 bloodily crushed an uprising at the gates of the capital. Thousands of heads of decapitated insurgents were presented to the grand vizier, who eliminated the last rebel leaders by inviting them to a so-called 'reconciliation dinner'. He also obliged the clerical hierarchy to disavow the strict ulama, who had ended up imposing their own moral order. When the grand vizier died in 1661, Mehmed IV appointed one of his sons, the governor of Damascus, to succeed him. However, Ahmed Köprülü, despite his solid background as a scholar, had to postpone any reforms and became absorbed in pressing military affairs. He led a campaign against Austria in person, before devoting himself in 1669 to the conquest of Crete, a possession of Venice since the Fourth Crusade.

---

[29] This was the 'Frankist' movement, named after Jacob Frank, who claimed to be the heir of Sabbatai Zevi.

Louis XIV's support for Venice in this crisis led to the dismissal of the French ambassador to Constantinople. This breaking of the Franco-Ottoman pact did not, however, prevent Venetian defeat. French diplomats hoped this difficulty had been overcome when it became known that an Ottoman dignitary had been sent to Paris. But this man was simply in charge of an exploratory mission, whereas the French had thought they would be welcoming a plenipotentiary ambassador from the sultan.[30] The splendour deployed at Versailles to honour the Ottoman guest was therefore wasted. Hence the great annoyance of the Sun King, who, it seems, took his revenge by commissioning Molière to write the scathing satire on the farcical 'Mamamouchi' figure in *Le Bourgeois gentilhomme* (*The Bourgeois Gentleman*). The French craze for Turkish fashions was then so intense that Racine wrote his tragedy *Bajazet* shortly after, inspired by the dark destiny of Bayezid, assassinated in 1635 on the order of his brother Murad IV. As for the Franco-Ottoman alliance, it was fully restored with the Venetian evacuation of Crete.

The death of the second Grand Vizier Köprülü, in 1676, opened a more sombre chapter in the reign of Mehmed IV, no doubt because this sultan never fully took charge of state affairs. This crisis of authority, palpable in Constantinople, was also felt on the battlefields. In 1683 came the resounding failure of the Ottoman siege of Vienna and, four years later, the defeat at Mohács in Hungary. Mehmed IV, held responsible for these repeated humiliations, was deposed by the insurgent soldiers and replaced by his half-brother Suleiman, until then a recluse in a luxurious prison in the imperial palace.[31] Sultan Suleiman II and his two successors, however, failed to stem the spiral of military setbacks. The peace concluded with Austria, Poland, and Venice in Karlowitz in 1699 sealed the loss by Constantinople of Hungary, Croatia, and Transylvania. The Europeans would henceforth continue to push back the Ottoman Empire. During the following century, the Ottomans confronted the Russians in a series of four exhausting and destructive conflicts in 1710, 1735, 1768, and 1787. Of these four conflicts, only the first, triggered by

[30] The first Ottoman ambassador to Paris was not appointed until 1720.
[31] The law of fratricide had been abandoned in favour of house arrest, lasting, in this case, thirty-six years.

the asylum granted by the Ottomans to Charles XII of Sweden, turned to the advantage of Constantinople.

The most severe defeat resulted in the Russian occupation of Crimea, ratified by the Treaty of Küçük Kaynarca, signed in northern Bulgaria in 1774. It was the first time that the Ottoman Empire had ceded a territory overwhelmingly populated by Muslims, in this case the Crimean Tatars. Catherine II, advised by well-informed Orientalists, introduced into the treaty the distinction between the executive authority of the Ottoman Sultanate, eventually supplanted by the Tsarist Empire in the Crimea, and the religious authority of the Ottoman Caliphate, still in force with the Crimean Tatars. This move, both diplomatically and theologically astute, echoed the more general desire of the Ottoman sultans to revive the lustre of the Sublime Porte by flaunting the title of 'caliph', which had until then fallen into disuse. This involved creating the fable of an alleged 'transmission' of the caliphal title by Abbasids who felt gratitude towards their Ottoman hosts. Although the ulama were unanimous in considering that an Arab origin was essential in any claim to the supreme dignity of Islam, they bowed before the theological dictate of the sultan. The caliphate, which had simply disappeared for two and a half centuries, thus reappeared thanks to an international treaty with an 'infidel' power, on the basis of a distinction between the temporal power of the sultan and the spiritual power of the caliph.

The Tulip Era

Beyond these military setbacks, in the long term the 'world economy' that the Ottoman Empire represented for many years, straddling three continents, inserted itself with great difficulty into the globalized world economy, itself governed by Anglo-Dutch financial mechanisms. The Sublime Porte hunkered down in Constantinople, relying on its *Nizam*, literally its 'regime', where a thousand leaders and officials were paralysed by the evolution of the outside world, stuck in an outdated protocol and prone to never-ending quarrels. The loyalty maintained by the dominant Sunnism was aggravated by a real fear of change, which would inevitably be a source of conflict, branded as a 'discord' (*fitna*) fatal to Islam. People frequently quoted the saying that 'better a thousand years of tyranny than *fitna*'. In fact, only eleven families controlled the religious hierarchy, in the three successive capitals of Bursa, Edirne, and Constantinople, as well as in Cairo, Aleppo, Baghdad, and Damascus. However, there was great diversity within the Sufi brotherhoods: the Mevlevis and the Naqchabandis were favoured at court, the former for their elitist refinement, the latter for their quietist rigour; the Bektashis were linked to the janissaries; and the Halvetis were associated with popular unrest.

However, we must beware of ascribing too early a date to Ottoman decline. The 'Tulip Era' (*Lale Devri*), from 1718 to 1730, was marked by great cultural effervescence, with the introduction of the printing press. This era was associated with tulips imported from Holland, which the Ottoman notables loved at the time, so much so that they crammed the urban landscape with these flowers. This Tulip Era ended when an Ottoman defeat in Azerbaijan led to a new revolt of the janissaries, supported by the common people of Istanbul, and the deposition of the sultan. The new sovereign, Mahmud Ghazi, or 'the Conqueror', made promises to the rebels, but only in order to liquidate them more efficiently. He drew on the services of a French artilleryman, the Comte de Bonneval,[32] who developed the 'bombards', large-calibre guns. The sultan arrested the erosion of the Ottoman domain on his borders, while carrying out major infrastructure works in his capital. This brilliant reign, lasting a quarter of a century, proved the empire's undeniable ability to adapt, even if the decline in caravan traffic and the growing independence of the Barbary 'regencies' gradually reduced its financial base.

The rebels of Arabia

The Ottomans, concentrated on controlling the pilgrimage to Mecca and Medina, had to relinquish three areas of the Arabian Peninsula: northern Yemen, governed by a fiercely independent Zaydite imam; Oman, whose sultans had emerged from among the first dissidents of Islam; and eastern central Arabia, where a so-called 'Wahhabi' pact was belatedly drawn between an extremely intolerant Sunni preacher and the head of the Saud family. The Yemeni theocracy, by far the oldest,

---

[32] Claude-Alexandre de Bonneval, who converted and took the name Ahmed, was officially Khumbaradji Pasha (chief bombardier).

based its pugnacious originality on an impressive longevity. Indeed, a continuous line of imams could be traced back to 897 in Yemen. They claimed to be descendants of Zayd (son of Zain al-Abidin, himself the fourth imam of Twelver Shiism), hence their name Zaydites. However, theological considerations were less important than the appointment, at the head of this isolated community, of the chief best able to defend it thanks to his warlike merits and effectiveness as a preacher. This was how the Zaydite imamate established itself over the long term, with Saada or Sanaa as capitals, the sovereign being revered as the imam of that period.

This theocracy, protected by nigh inaccessible mountains, remained independent, except from 1174 to 1454, when it fell under the control of Sunni dynasties, then from 1517 to 1636, when it was subject to the Ottoman Empire. The population of the Yemeni Imamate was divided roughly evenly between Sunnis from Taiz, the highlands, and the Red Sea coast, on the one hand, and Zaydis from the northern and eastern mountains, on the other. But Sunnis were excluded from real power, which was exercised by the Zaydites, and more precisely by the small minority of the supposed descendants of the Prophet and Ali.[33] Most of the imam's income came from Sunni areas, controlled with an iron fist by the Zaydi tribes. The jihad proclaimed by the imam against the Portuguese invaders allowed the Zaydites to consolidate their religious legitimacy and justify their warlike activities. As for the devoutly Sunni Ottomans, they readily forgot their dogmatic opposition to the Zaydites and contributed their assistance in the fight against the European 'infidels'.

In the northeast corner of the Arabian Peninsula, the Omani mountains offered sanctuary to followers of the Kharijite schism, which split the camp of Caliph Ali's followers between 657 and 661. Persecuted under the Umayyads and the Abbasids, the dissidents who had taken refuge in Oman formed an 'Ibadi' population whose quietism contrasted with the revolutionary tension of the original Kharijites.[34] The Omanis were skilled sailors and competed with the Portuguese at the entrance to the Persian Gulf and on sea routes of the Indian Ocean, setting up their

---

[33] In Arabic *sayyid*, plural *sada*.

[34] Outside Oman, two Ibadi communities exist today on the Tunisian island of Djerba and in the Algerian oasis of M'zab (hence the name 'Mozabite' often given to Algerian Ibadis).

trading posts as far away as Java. In 1749, the House of Busaid or Al Said dynasty led the resistance to the Persian invasion. They became the masters of Muscat as well as the hinterland, and established a dynasty of sultans, in power in Oman to this day. The Al Said dynasty also settled along the eastern coast of the African continent. This was the origin of Swahili, literally the language 'of the coast', largely derived from Arabic. In addition to the various ports controlled in present-day Somalia and Kenya, the sultans of Muscat seized the island of Zanzibar and its very lucrative clove trade. Oman was remarkably well integrated into the circuits of globalization at the time, while the third of these spaces outside Ottoman authority, on the contrary, fell back into its reclusive, tetchy rectitude.

Muhammad ibn Abd al-Wahhab, born in 1703 in central Arabia, was a preacher of the Hanbali rite, the most intransigent of the four schools of Sunnism. He founded a so-called 'unitary' sect that was very aggressive towards any form of theological 'innovation' (*bid'a*), as well as against the 'heresies' he felt were represented by Shiism and Sufism. He became the guest and the dependant of Muhammad Ibn Saud, the emir of the modest oasis of Diriyah, in Najd. These two marginalized leaders decided around 1744 to unite their forces and their ambitions in the name of 'Wahhabism', as the new sect was quickly designated by its opponents. Their pact legitimized jihad against 'bad Muslims' – in fact all Arabs who rejected Wahhabi dogma. Thus it depicted tribal raids as endowed with the virtue of the noblest of combats, justifying not only the elimination of their adversaries but also the destruction of mausoleums and 'idolatrous' writings. It was in the texts of Ibn Taymiyyah, who, four centuries earlier in Damascus, had prescribed jihad against 'false' Muslims, that Ibn Abdelwahhab found arguments in favour of the so-called 'jihad' of the Saud family against the other Muslim tribes of central Arabia. For the time being, Wahhabi preaching remained confined to Najd and thus escaped the attention of Ottoman decision-makers, and a fortiori of the outside world.

The vassalized Mamluks

We left Egypt in the hands of the former Mamluk governor of Aleppo, installed in 1517 by order of the conqueror Selim. Eight years later,

Suleiman the Magnificent sent his own grand vizier, Ibrahim Pasha, to Cairo to thoroughly reorganize the administration of the country. The Mamluk units were maintained, but they functioned alongside the janissaries and other forces dispatched by the Sublime Porte. The Mamluk emirs were demoted to the rank of bey, while they lost ownership of their fiefs, recovered on a case-by-case basis as concessions. It was a *beylerbey*, a bey-of-beys, who was responsible for the government of Egypt, in the name of the sultan and with the rank of pasha. His main mission was to contribute to the imperial treasury and provide fresh troops for the Ottoman campaigns. He also had to ensure the regular supplies for Mecca and Medina. The cadastre, drawn up in 1528 for tax purposes, was never updated; it was a way of managing Egypt that seemed forever frozen. Struggles between 'houses', the local name for military factions, whether Mamluk or janissary, nevertheless broke out at regular intervals. These struggles, as in the time of the Mamluk sultans, remained confined to the military elite, and their impact, though destructive for certain districts of Cairo, did not affect the rest of the city and the country.

The Arab notables, who were not allowed to pursue army careers, managed to follow instead a religious course that offered serious possibilities of promotion, either in the Ottoman bureaucracy (only the posts of *qadi* and deputy were reserved for the Turkish sheikhs) or in the vast world of Sufi brotherhoods and pious foundations. As for the population, it was often overwhelmed by epidemics and food shortages. It was then grateful to the Ottoman power for ensuring a sphere of relative prosperity throughout the empire. Egypt's trade with Europe was now in relative decline, contrary to the trend in Aleppo and the Levant, but trade with the other Ottoman provinces was progressing steadily. The city of Cairo saw the number of its inhabitants double during this period, going from 150,000 to 300,000 inhabitants, with an unequalled extension of its area. This development contrasted with the perception of Western observers, who often saw in Egypt only decadence and decay. Volney, one of the most respected Orientalists in France under Louis XVI, travelled to the Middle East between 1782 and 1785. His description of an Egypt torn between 'the rapacity of tyranny and the defiance of slavery' was scathing. Such devastating clichés would provide ample fuel for the imagination of those in Paris who one day would invade. Moreover, while the two Ottoman expeditions launched against Egypt, in 1773 and 1786, shattered the insolent autonomy that the Mamluk governors had established, they proved to be evanescent, the cycle of power struggles resuming in Cairo as soon as the contingents dispatched by the Sublime Porte withdrew.

From the Safavids to the Qajars

Just as this chapter opened with the imposition of Shiism as the state religion of Persia, it will end with the institutionalization of the hierarchy of the ayatollahs, even after 1798, as religious processes do not always follow the chronology of political changes. The poles of influence of Shiite Islam corresponded to cities sanctified by the mausoleum of one of the twelve imams or of a close relative. This was how Najaf and Karbala in Iraq came to be considered as the two holiest cities of Shiism as they hold, respectively, the tombs of Ali and his son Hussein. Samarra, still in Iraq, and the district of Al-Kazimiyyah in Baghdad are also revered for their mausoleums of imams, as is Mashhad in eastern Persia. It was only later that Qom, not far from Tehran, became an important Shiite centre due to the tomb of the sister of Imam Reza, himself buried in Mashhad. These cities of pilgrimage sometimes assumed a teaching mission, something of crucial importance in a Shiism that valued *mojtaheds*, literally 'interpreters'. A whole university-type curriculum governed the *hawzas*, or Shiite seminaries, with a hierarchy ranging from the mullah, the basic cleric, to the *hojatoleslam*, the 'proof of Islam', and culminating with the ayatollah, the 'sign of God', a distinction involving decades of study. Unlike Sunnism and its four canonical schools, Shiism went beyond the Qur'an and the tradition (*Sunna*) of the Prophet Muhammad to incorporate into its corpus the traditions associated with the twelve imams. It was the considerable nature of this corpus that justified years of apprenticeship, followed by equally long years spent refining theological dissertations and supporting contradictory theses before finally earning the title of '*mojtahed*'.

The Safavids had been but a shadow of their former selves since their capitulation at Isfahan in 1722, a decadence which also eroded the founding conception of state Shiism. Nadir Shah, the Turkmen leader of eastern Persia, was tasked with containing the Afghan threat, but his victorious campaigns led him to turn against his Safavid masters and replace them on the throne in 1736. Nadir Shah even began a reform of Shiism, whose messianic aspect was to be eliminated in favour of support for the sixth imam[35] and thus integration into Sunnism as the fifth canonical school. But the project was cut short: although this formidable warrior extended his territory from the Caucasus to India, he himself fell, in 1747, the victim of a conspiracy. There followed a confused period when a dynasty based in Shiraz, the Zands, maintained the fiction of a restoration of the Safavids. The disintegration of the state encouraged border conflicts and generalized insecurity. Many Shiite clerics left Persia to take refuge in the holy cities of Najaf and Karbala, even though these were under Ottoman domination. It was here that, traumatized by Nadir Shah's attempt at an authoritarian recasting of Shiism, they prepared the weapons for a reconstitution of the Twelver dogma.

The power struggles that tore Persia apart during the second half of the eighteenth century turned to the advantage of the Qajars, a Turkmen tribe south of the Caspian Sea. Their leader, Agha Mohammad, chose Tehran as his capital and, in 1794, he had himself crowned shah there. Unlike the Safavids, the Qajars did not claim any mandate from the Hidden Imam and they relied on the Shia clergy to interpret the Mahdi's plans during his occultation. This transfer of religious legitimacy significantly increased the authority of the ayatollahs, especially if they resided in Ottoman Iraq, which was beyond the reach of Qajar power. Fath Ali Shah, who reigned over Persia from 1797 to 1834, was also a devout Shiite. He made frequent visits to Mashhad and Qom,[36] generously endowing the various religious institutions of Persia and Iraq. During the two disastrous conflicts with Russia, in 1804–1813, and then again in 1826–1828, the Qajar throne requested fatwas from the ayatollahs to legitimize jihad against the tsarist forces. In Shia theology, jihad was indeed a prerogative of the Hidden Imam, which the Safavids used for their own declarations of war. This move was impossible for the Qajars, who were obliged to turn to the religious authorities.

This rise in power of the Shiite hierarchy led to the formalization of the prerogatives of the *marja al-taqlid*, the 'authority to be followed':

[35] This was the imam Ja'far (see above, p. 53), hence the term 'Ja'fari' sometimes given to Shiite ulama to distinguish them from their Sunni counterparts.
[36] Indeed, Fath Ali Shah was buried in Qom.

each faithful Shiite was led to choose a 'model' ayatollah, whose opinions as a *mojtahed* would reflect the intentions of the Hidden Imam. This choice committed him to a chain of hierarchical authorities, from the mullah to the *hojatoleslam*, then to the ayatollah, and finally to the 'grand ayatollah', who had become a *marja*. This chain was also responsible for the collection and distribution of the tithe paid by believers on behalf of the Mahdi. The first *marja* recognized throughout the Shia world was based in Najaf and nicknamed Sahib al-Jawahir, or the 'author of the pearls'. Beyond the dogmatic prescriptions, a profound divergence was thus introduced with the Sunnis into daily practice. In the Shiite case, what was now a tight network of clerics ensured the allegiance of the faithful, as well as the resulting financial transfers, with the Qajar Empire giving the ayatollahs the last word in religious matters. In the Sunni case, the Ottoman sultan was only a very part-time caliph and the state religious apparatus involved only one of the four schools of Sunnism, the Hanafi school, and also failed to rein in the Sufi brotherhoods, who themselves were in charge of inalienable foundations in the *waqf* mode. In both cases, and in spite of what essentialists these days may claim, Shiite and Sunni piety was organized in accordance with relatively recent logics which appeared nearly a millennium after the consolidation of their respective dogmas.

The Iraqi question

The parallel between the division of the Middle East by the Byzantines and Sassanids, on the one hand, and by the Ottomans and the Safavids, on the other, is illuminating. Each of these empires based its authority on a state religion, which ensured control of its vast territories. Byzantines and Ottomans in Constantinople engineered their power in the Middle East and their ambitions in Europe and the Mediterranean. Sassanids and Safavids affirmed the Persian character of their empire, one that was even more marked with the installation of the Safavid capital in Qazvin, then in Isfahan. On the other hand, the conflicts between the Ottomans and Safavids were much more circumscribed than those between Byzantines and Sassanids, concentrating, after the victory of Sultan Selim against Shah Isma'il in 1514, on the battle for Iraq, which was conquered by the Ottomans two decades later. Where the Sassanid influence spread out from their Mesopotamian capital of Ctesiphon, the Safavids held Baghdad, despite it being very close, only from 1508 to 1534 and then again from 1624 to 1638. The peace between the Ottomans and Safavids, concluded in 1555, and finally confirmed in 1639, traced a frontier between the empires of Iraq and Persia, as noted above, thus shifting to the east the dividing line which for so long had corresponded to the Euphrates. This move permanently brought the three Middle Eastern poles of Egypt, Syria, and Iraq under a single effective authority, that of the Ottoman Sultanate, for the first time since Abbasid domination over these same three poles had been broken in 969 by the installation of the Fatimids in Cairo.

The collapse of the Safavids and the rise of Nadir Shah reopened hostilities on the Ottoman front in Iraq. In 1736, after several terrible battles, a peace was concluded on the same basis as a century earlier. Nadir Shah, however, left in 1743 to attack Mosul, whose population and garrison, united against the invader, resisted with courage and success. A new treaty was signed between the Ottomans and Persians, again on the basis of the 1639 pact. Hussein Djalili, governor of Mosul since 1730, his prestige enhanced by the epic of the siege of his city, managed to keep the title in his family, and it stayed there practically until 1834. The Ottomans, unable to get rid of the Djalili, put up with this provincial dynasty to maintain their authority, however theoretical, on their eastern border. It was a comparable reasoning that led them to abandon the governorate of Baghdad to the Mamluks; these were becoming ever more independent but proved to be fierce defenders of Basra in the face of the Persian offensive of 1775. The border drawn between the Ottoman and Safavid Empires was thus preserved, despite the blows inflicted by the chaotic transition towards the Qajars in Persia. The counterpart of this resilience was, for Constantinople, the de facto recognition of Iraq as a buffer state, led in Mosul by a family with very strong local legitimacy, and in Baghdad by Mamluks following the same militaristic logic as their predecessors in the Middle Ages.

Both the Ottoman and the Safavid Empires were characterized by their ethnic and sectarian diversity, despite the Islamic state dogmas imposed in both cases, with the same claim of exclusive 'orthodoxy' for Sunnism as for Shiism. They both proved to be more tolerant towards Christians and, to a lesser extent, Jews than towards Muslims of another persuasion, who were at best ignored, at worst discriminated against and even persecuted. The universalist claim of the Ottoman sultans, noticeable in their ceremonial arrogance towards European sovereigns,[37] was not an attribute claimed by the Safavid throne, despite the narcissism inherent in all empire-building. The successors of Shah Isma'il gradually emancipated themselves from their onerous Turkmen companions, linking their regime to the glory of Persia, a process completed by the transfer of the capital to Isfahan. As for the sultans of Constantinople, they cared little about the ethnic origins of their wives or concubines, thus diluting the 'Turkish' component of the reigning family. Moreover, although the Ottoman sovereign boasted of being the Custodian of the Two Holy Cities, he refrained from physically making the hazardous pilgrimage to Mecca. The Safavid shahs, deprived by the Ottomans of access to Najaf[38] and Karbala, transferred their favours to Mashhad and the mausoleum of Reza, the eighth imam, as well as to Qom and the mausoleum of his sister. The Ottoman rulers abstained from *hajj*, while their Safavid counterparts encouraged substitute pilgrimages; piety in the higher echelons of the two Middle Eastern empires seems to have fallen short of its proclaimed objectives.

The populace, obviously absent from these imperial chronicles, made their mark through urban riots, which sometimes proved of decisive importance in Constantinople, where they supported a janissary uprising. The people had much greater impact in Aleppo and Mosul, as their episodic uprisings, even if they were channelled into the framework of factional struggles, led to the consolidation of forms of local autonomy more attentive to their urban base. Notables and 'masses' then mobilized against a Muslim enemy perceived as an invader, or against a Muslim power rejected as a usurper. These mobilizations, despite their often religious tenor, were rooted in local solidarities, invoking the collective honour of a city rather than belonging to any larger community. The inhabitants of Cairo and Alexandria were no less proud of their cities,

[37] Suleiman the Magnificent treated his ally, the French king François I, as his younger brother, and not his equal, while refusing the title of emperor to Charles V, who was merely described as 'King of Spain'.
[38] Only Shah Tahmasp, in 1527, visited Najaf during the four decades of Safavid occupation of Iraq in the sixteenth and seventeenth centuries.

but even during phases of violent unrest they never managed to overcome the gap which separated them from their Mamluk rulers. Worse still, they were condemned to impotence when these same Mamluks were tearing each other apart at regular intervals in the struggle for power. This structural blockage aggravated the marginalization of Egypt, which, having been the structuring pole of the Middle East during the previous period, was now reduced to the status of an in many respects peripheral Ottoman province. The strategic decline of this country would make it all the more vulnerable to the imperialist thrust, which, for the first time in the Middle East, would leave a direct imprint on its soil.

Chronology

July 1501	Isma'il proclaimed Safavid shah in Tabriz.
October 1508	Shah Isma'il enters Baghdad.
August 1514	Ottoman victory over the Safavids at Chaldiran.
August 1516	Ottoman victory over the Mamluks at Dabiq.
January 1517	Entry of the Ottoman sultan Selim into Cairo.
September 1520–September 1566	Suleiman, Ottoman sultan.
May 1524	Death of Shah Isma'il, succeeded by his son Tahmasp.
August 1543	Siege of Nice by a Franco-Ottoman fleet.
May 1555	Peace between the Ottoman Empire and Safavid Persia.
September 1566–December 1574	Selim II, Ottoman sultan.
October 1571	Ottoman defeat at Lepanto.
October 1587–January 1629	Shah Abbas in Persia.
September 1623–February 1640	Murad IV, Ottoman sultan.
April 1635	Execution of the Lebanese emir Fakhr al-Din.
May 1639	Peace between the Ottoman Empire and Safavid Persia.
May 1642–October 1666	Shah Abbas II in Persia.
August 1648–November 1687	Mehmed IV, Ottoman sultan.
September 1666	Conversion of Sabbatai Zevi to Islam.
October 1670	Molière, *Le Bourgeois Gentilhomme*.
January 1672	Racine, *Bajazet*.
August 1687	Ottoman defeat at Mohács in Hungary.
January 1699	Peace of Karlowitz, very unfavourable to the Ottomans in Europe.
July 1718–September 1730	Ottoman 'Tulip Era'.
May 1721	Montesquieu, *The Persian Letters*.

October 1722	Afghan conquest of Isfahan.
October 1730 –December 1754	Mahmud I, Ottoman sultan.
Around 1744	'Wahhabi' pact of the Saud family.
September 1746	Peace between Ottomans and Persians, confirming that of 1639.
June 1747	Assassination of Nadir Shah in northeastern Persia.
June 1749	Advent of Al Said dynasty in Oman.
July 1774	Russian–Ottoman Treaty of Küçük Kaynarca.
December 1775	Popular uprising in Aleppo.
June 1797 –October 1834	Fath Ali Shah, second Qajar shah.

Further reading

Abdullah, Thabit, *Merchants, Mamluks, and murder: the political economy of trade in eighteenth-century century Basra* (Albany, NY: SUNY Press, 2001).

Barkey, Karen, *Empire of difference: the Ottomans in comparative perspective* (New York: Cambridge University Press, 2008).

Chardin, Jean, *Travels in Persia: 1673–1677. Selections* (New York: Dover Publications, Inc., 1988).

Courbage, Youssef and Philippe Fargues, *Christians and Jews under Islam*, translated by Judy Mabro (London and New York: I.B. Tauris, 1998).

Degeorge, Gérard, *Damascus*, translated by David Radzinowicz (Paris: Flammarion, 2005).

Hanna, Nelly, *Ottoman Egypt and the emergence of the modern world* (Cairo: American University Press, 2014).

Husain, Faisal H., *Rivers of the sultan: the Tigris and Euphrates in the Ottoman Empire* (New York: Oxford University Press, 2021).

Kunt, Metin, *The Sultan's servants: the transformation of the Ottoman provincial government, 1550–1650* (New York: Columbia University Press, 1983).

Melville, Charles (ed.), *Safavid Persia: the history and politics of an Islamic society* (London: I.B. Tauris, 1989).

Winter, Stefan, *The Shiites of Lebanon under Ottoman rule, 1516–1788* (New York: Cambridge University Press, 2010).

SIX

Colonial expansion (1798–1912)

The 'long nineteenth century' in the Middle East was one of both colonial expansion and a process of modernization. A certain historiography, nourished by Western sources, including diplomatic ones, considers the latter only in the mirror of the former. This methodological bias often leads to the diagnosis of an inevitable decadence of the Ottoman and Persian Empires, a decadence that is said to have nourished imperialist aims on the basis that nature abhors a vacuum. This circular argument ignores the powerful currents that transformed regimes and societies, as a Middle Eastern equivalent of the Enlightenment. It is clear that the intervention of European powers, themselves in competition with one another, developed in opposition to these emancipatory aspirations, willingly caricatured as a resistance to 'progress'. This chapter will therefore be devoted solely to the complex sequence of Western interferences in the Middle East, before turning in the following chapter to the study of reformist movements and societal evolutions during the same period. This differentiated approach makes it possible to focus on processes external to the region, and only then on its internal processes, without denying the dialectical relationship between the two. The 'Eastern question', which agitated the European chancelleries so much in the nineteenth century, then appears in many respects as a 'Western question', one that was to weigh increasingly heavily on the future of the region.

General Napoleon Bonaparte's expedition to Egypt in 1798 was launched to strike at Great Britain's route to India and weaken that sworn enemy of the French Republic. Added to these European considerations was the unprecedented desire, nourished by French messianism, to establish a new regime in the Nile Valley, in the name of 'civilization', and even the 'liberation' of the Arabs from Turkish domination. This premature nationalist discourse was given a chilly reception in an Egypt where Islamic identity took precedence in the face of the irruption of such 'infidels', despite the proclaimed respect of the future Napoleon I for the 'Prophet Muhammad and the glorious Qur'an'. Having landed in Alexandria, the invaders won a decisive victory over the Ottoman troops at the Battle of the Pyramids. They tried to win the notables over to their control of Cairo, if only to finance their own occupation from local sources. Bonaparte nevertheless had to crush an anti-French riot in the capital, before being able to embark, in 1799, on the conquest of Palestine.[1] He dreamt of raising the Eastern 'third estate' against the despotism of Constantinople and already pictured himself seizing Syria in order to attack the Ottomans from the rear. This grandiose plan was shattered before the citadel of Acre, which successfully resisted a two-month siege. Bonaparte withdrew with his troops to Egypt, from where he returned to Paris to take power on 18 Brumaire, Year VIII of the revolutionary era.

General Kléber, now in command of Egypt, put down a second uprising in Cairo, before being himself assassinated in 1800 by a Syrian student from Al-Azhar. His successor, General Menou, converted to Islam with the first name of Abdullah and married an Egyptian woman of noble origin. This union was supposed to symbolize the shared destiny of the two peoples. But an English landing at Aboukir, combined with an Ottoman offensive in the Sinai, led to the capitulation of the French in Cairo in 1801, followed by that of Menou in Alexandria. The fiery 'Army of the Orient' was no more than a shadow of its former self and left the country on British ships. The showdown between Paris and London ended with the official restoration of Ottoman authority. The three-year French interlude did, however, leave a lasting legacy with the *Description de l'Égypte*, an encyclopaedic work involving the collaboration of dozens of scientists from all disciplines whom Napoleon brought to Egypt.

The first war of the United States

After the start of the 'Egyptian expedition' in 1798–1801, it was a very young Western power, the United States, which carried out its own

---

[1] A messianic group from the 'Frankist' movement (see above, p. 164, n. 29) accredited in Eastern Europe the fable of a Bonaparte who was offering Palestine to the Jewish people.

intervention in the Middle East. This episode is often forgotten in studies devoted to the wave of imperialism, on the pretext that the United States, a colony of Great Britain until 1783, could not be identified with the colonizing camp. The same moralizing prejudice still prevails today in the American collective memory, where this first war in the distant Middle East is overlooked in favour of the second war of 1812–1815 against Great Britain, echoing the ' War of Independence' of 1776–1783. The conflict with the 'regency' of Libya, constituted by the pashas of the Karamanli family as an autonomous fiefdom of the Ottoman Empire, nevertheless marked the founding years of the United States, with the endeavour swallowing up about a third of the federal budget. It further revealed the antagonism between the worldviews of George Washington's two successors to the presidency: the 'dove' John Adams (1797–1801) and the 'hawk' Thomas Jefferson (1801–1809). This opposition appeared as early as 1786 when Adams and Jefferson, then ambassadors in London and Paris respectively, negotiated together with a Libyan plenipoten-tiary to obtain the suspension of attacks on American ships. These talks failed because of the contradiction between Adams the conciliator and Jefferson the hard-liner.

We have seen that, for centuries, Christian and Muslim corsairs had traded blow for blow in the Mediterranean, with orders from sovereigns conveyed by letters of marque, the forced labour of captives who were sometimes ransomed, and the incorporation of seized vessels into the victorious fleet. The independence of the United States stripped their ships of the protection of British power. The American Congress then passed a substantial budget in order to buy the non-aggression of the Barbary navies. After Morocco, the signatory of the first agreement in 1786, it took nine years for the dey of Algiers to agree to conclude a comparable treaty with President Washington, whom Adams succeeded in 1797, with Jefferson occupying the vice-presidency. From the first year of his presidency, Adams signed treaties with the bey of Tunis and the pasha of Tripoli, whose financial clauses weighed heavily on the finances of the young state. New demands from the master of Libya led Jefferson, no sooner had he been elected president in 1801, to send an American squadron to blockade the port of Tripoli. Congress was furious at not having been consulted over this expedition, the cost of which was twice the tribute demanded by the Libyan sovereign.

Jefferson, faced with the ineffectiveness of the blockade of Tripoli, was forced to lift it. The new squadron he dispatched in 1803 lost its flagship, whose crew was imprisoned by the Libyans; this resulted in solidarity campaigns in the press and in Congress. The offensives of the American fleet in 1804 led nowhere, despite the bombardment of Tripoli. The United States then fell back on a land operation from Egypt, officially so that the brother of the pasha of Tripoli, presented by American propaganda as the only legitimate sovereign, could be installed on the throne. In 1805, the US Marines seized the stronghold of Derna, in Cyrenaica, where they hoisted the American flag. This time, the pasha of Tripoli agreed to negotiate and released his prisoners on payment of a ransom, with the proviso that the United States withdraw their expeditionary force and abandon the pretender to the throne. This marked the end of the 'Barbary War', in which the main ingredients of contemporary American policy could be found: the tension between the Jeffersonian hawks and the doves who followed the Adams line, the former emphasizing power, the second trade, while the two camps agreed on the strategic importance of the Middle East; the decisive role of public opinion, which intensified if American citizens were held hostage; the desire of Congress not to be marginalized by the presidency; and, last but not least, a deep cultural misunderstanding, compounded by the US betrayal of its local allies.

France's Egyptian gamble

The re-establishment of Ottoman power in Egypt in 1801, after the shock of the French expedition, remained a sham. One of the officers sent by the Sublime Porte, Muhammad Ali,[2] ended up imposing his personal authority in Cairo in 1805. Two years later, he successfully repelled a British landing in Alexandria sent to overthrow him. In 1811, the new ruler of Egypt ordered the massacre of the Mamluks in Cairo, eliminating this last counter-power represented by the distant heirs of Baybars, heirs who had been vassalized for three centuries by the Ottomans. Muhammad Ali methodically built up his Egyptian power, for whose decisive aid Constantinople was obliged to negotiate, first in the face of the Wahhabi challenge in Arabia, then in the face of the nationalist insurrection in

---

[2] Mehmed Ali Paşa in the Turkish spelling.

Greece. In 1827, France, Great Britain, and Russia committed themselves by treaty to supporting the Greek claims, 'as much out of a feeling of humanity as in the interest of the peace of Europe'. Shortly after, their united navies destroyed the Egyptian–Ottoman fleet. In compensation for his losses, Muhammad Ali claimed the government of the Ottoman provinces of Syria. The foreseeable refusal on the part of Constantinople further widened the gap with Cairo.

Muhammad Ali, who presented himself as the continuator of the work of 'civilization' launched by Bonaparte, was seen by the France of the Restoration as increasingly important for its own designs. This pro-Egyptian policy was accentuated in 1830 under the July Monarchy of Louis-Philippe, which sought the support of Cairo for its conquest of Algeria. But it was towards the east that, in 1831, Muhammad Ali turned, sending his son, Ibrahim Pasha, to attack Syria. The barrier city of Acre fell in 1832, opening the road to Anatolia to the Egyptian troops. Panic spread to Constantinople, where in 1833 Sultan Mahmud II reconciled with the Russian enemy to protect his capital. The landing of tsarist troops in the Bosphorus halted the Egyptian advance. Ibrahim Pasha nevertheless demanded recognition of the rights of an 'Arab nationality', as legitimate as the Greek or the Belgian, to establish his domination over Syria, in line with his father's rule over Egypt. It was then that the term the 'Eastern question' became commonplace in diplomatic correspondence, illustrating the centrality of this crisis for the European chancelleries.

In 1835, the Ottoman Sultanate, strengthened by the Russian intervention, regained the initiative in the Mediterranean by restoring – this time effectively – its authority over Libya. At the same time, Ibrahim Pasha continued his overhaul of the Syrian administration, with the promotion of Christians within local councils.[3] The extension of conscription and an increase in taxation certainly provoked several localized revolts. But this rapid modernization contrasted with the cautious reforms in Constantinople, which became truly ambitious only after the death of Mahmud II in 1839 – and only under European pressure. The following

---

[3] On the other hand, a European-type anti-Semitism developed in the Syria of Ibrahim Pasha: in 1840, an accusation of ritual crime was brought against the Jews of Damascus.

year, Britain obtained the support of Russia, Austria, and Prussia for its pro-Ottoman policy, isolating France in its support of Ibrahim Pasha. King Louis-Philippe, despite the warmongering wave that was sweeping across his country, resigned himself to abandoning his Egyptian ally, who was soon expelled from his bastion in Acre. Under the threat of an English landing in Alexandria, Muhammad Ali agreed to withdraw all his forces from Syria in 1841. He obtained in return the recognition of the hereditary government of his family in the Nile Valley.

Grand imperial manoeuvres

The Qajar dynasty, which reigned over Persia from 1794, tried in vain to stem the Russian thrust on its northern border with the tsarist annexation of Georgia in 1801. The two wars waged for this purpose by Fath Ali Shah ended in two crushing defeats, with the loss of all Persian access to the Black Sea in 1813 and the Russian conquest of new Caucasian territories in 1828. The unconscionable treaty concluded that year granted Russian nationals extraterritorial privileges comparable to the Ottoman capitulations, and provided for the resettlement in Russia of Armenians transferred by the Qajars to their territory. The plenipotentiary dispatched to Tehran in 1829 to supervise this operation granted consular protection to three Christian fugitives.[4] The local populace, whipped into a rage by the harangues of the ayatollahs, stormed the Russian embassy and massacred the staff. The tsarist regime, then absorbed in an offensive against the Ottomans on the Danube, was reluctant to open a second front in Persia and accepted the shah's apologies for the Tehran massacre.

The British Empire, always concerned about access to India, was anxious about the way Persia was falling into the Russian orbit. This is why, on the death of Fath Ali Shah in 1834, it supported both financially and militarily the enthronement of his designated heir, Muhammad, rather than either of the brothers of the deceased sovereign. The new shah, crowned in Tehran in 1835, was torn between Russian encouragement to commit himself to the east and English pressure in the opposite direction. There followed a complex sequence in which the

---

[4] These were two women, the slaves of a wealthy merchant, and one of the shah's eunuchs.

Persian siege of the Afghan city of Herat in 1837 led, the following year, to a British expedition to the Persian Gulf, with the occupation of the island of Kharg, which was restored to the shah only in return for Persian withdrawal from Afghanistan. These politico-military ricochets were part of what would soon be called the Anglo-Russian 'Great Game', in which each of the two empires endeavoured to counter the expansionist aims of the other. The Qajars, caught in the middle of this standoff, did, however, learn to play one interfering power against the other in order to preserve the territorial integrity of Persia, and even obtain some small new wiggle room. But British nationals, soon followed by other Europeans, obtained the same exceptional status as the Russians.

As for France, its occupation of Algeria, a relatively easy process on the coastal fringe in 1830, came up against fierce resistance from the interior provinces two years later, under the leadership of the emir Abdelkader. Russia faced a comparable challenge in the Caucasus where, in 1834, once Persian defeat was assured, Imam Shamil, himself of Avar ethnicity, united the struggle of Chechens and Circassians against the invader. In both cases, a young and charismatic leader at the head of a Sufi brotherhood[5] organized a popular campaign of anti-colonial jihad, in which the Ottoman caliph abandoned Muslims[6] to 'infidel' armies. Abdelkader resisted France for fifteen years, Shamil held out for another decade, and both laid down their arms only in the context of an honourable surrender. Their capitulation led, in Algeria as in the Caucasus, to an escalation in the number of colonial settlements, against the backdrop of a repression and dispossession of the masses of defeated natives. In 1848, the Second Republic decreed the annexation of 'French Algeria' organized around the three departments of Algiers, Oran, and Constantine, the rest of the country being a militarized zone. As for the Russification of the North Caucasus, with the installation of Cossack garrisons to protect the Christian settlers, it intensified with the systematic expulsion of local Muslims, a policy favoured by the resumption of war with the Ottomans.

---

[5] The Qadiriya in the case of Abdelkader and the Naqshabandi in that of Shamil.
[6] The French occupation of Constantine in 1837 marked the end of the Ottoman presence in Algeria.

The Crimean War

Ever since Louis XIII, France had claimed that it held a mission to 'protect' Catholics in the Middle East, a role that the Republic, the Restoration, and the July Monarchy continued to assume with tenacity, in particular by encouraging missionary orders in the region. Ibrahim Pasha's decade of domination over the Levant, from 1831, was all the more favourable to French aims as the Egyptian administration lifted the Ottoman veto on the appointing of European consuls to Jerusalem. But it was Great Britain that first seized this opportunity by installing a legation in the Holy City in 1839. The Protestant and a fortiori Anglican presence was very limited in Palestine, and the instructions of the British consul prescribed 'the protection of the Jewish nation'.[7] Prussia opened its representation in Jerusalem in 1842, followed by France the following year. Russia sought to counteract French 'rights' of protection over Catholics and, henceforth, the British equivalent when it came to Jews, and vigorously demanded a comparable 'right' for the Orthodox, drawing on an identification between the patriarchate of Jerusalem and the Church of Russia, although the latter was founded a millennium later.

The claims of Saint Petersburg on the Ottoman Orthodox were all the more unacceptable since these *Rum* represented more than a third of the population of the empire. But the Greek Orthodox of Jerusalem had an effective precedence in the Holy Places, as they were there earlier and Ottoman jurisprudence weighed in their favour. The quarrel with the Catholics that broke out in 1847 in the Church of the Nativity in Bethlehem would gradually become international, with President Louis-Napoleon Bonaparte taking sides against Tsar Nicholas I. The Ottoman sultan took many years before settling the dispute in favour of the Orthodox in a firman of 1852. This decree, soon supplemented by other decisions, constituted the basis of the status quo which has since governed the Holy Places of Jerusalem, both Christian and non-Christian. It was, moreover, in 1853 that the first map appeared demarcating, in the old city of Jerusalem, Muslim, Christian, Armenian,

---

[7] The term 'nation' referred to the Ottoman concept of *millet*, which designated each of the different communities of the empire (see above, p. 137).

and Jewish 'neighbourhoods', even though the population of these different neighbourhoods remained mixed.

Tsar Nicholas I, receiving the British ambassador at the very beginning of 1853, described the Ottoman Empire as a 'sick man' and tacitly envisaged a partition of its territories, from which France would be excluded. Shortly afterwards, he demanded from the Sublime Porte an intrusive 'protection' of the Orthodox populations which would amount to a form of co-management of the empire by himself. The refusal of the Ottoman sultan was expected and led to the destruction of his Black Sea fleet by the tsarist navy. In 1854, Napoleon III, who had just founded the Second Empire, decided to establish the first Franco-British alliance in more than a century, with the aim of countering this Russian expansion. London and Paris focused most of their efforts on the Crimean peninsula, while Ottoman forces tried in vain to regain the initiative in the Caucasus. Russia, handicapped by deficient logistics, was forced to acknowledge defeat in 1856. The conflict left nearly a million dead, mostly civilians, and led to the flight to Anatolia of a comparable number of Crimean Tatars and Caucasian Muslims. The peace treaty signed in Paris guaranteed the territorial integrity of the Ottoman Empire, demilitarized the Black Sea, and ensured the validity of the status quo in Jerusalem.

Poorly 'protected' Christians

Just as the challenge of Egypt forced the Ottoman Sultanate into a first set of reforms in 1839, the threat of Russia forced it to extend them in 1856, with the abolition of discrimination against Christians and Jews. The Treaty of Paris, which associated Constantinople with the combined European effort to settle the Crimean War, officially recognized the emancipation of the Ottoman Christians. However, it avoided referring to the Jews, who did not at the time enjoy equal rights in many European countries. In the next chapter, we will study this Ottoman dynamic of emancipation, but here I would like to emphasize the logic of internationalization that underlay it. This logic was accentuated with the demands for 'protection' of certain minorities made by France and Great Britain, now that defeated Russia had been obliged to give up its great pan-Orthodox design. London, which had tried to extend its influence beyond an ultra-minority Protestantism by playing the Jewish card, now came up against the activism of the Alliance Israélite Universelle, established in Paris in 1860, whose Francophile and anticlerical networks were developing in the Middle East. English diplomacy therefore turned to the feudal Druze, whose unrest it had already fomented during the Egyptian occupation of Syria.

Thus, the alliance between Paris and London prevailed only during the Crimean War, before a proxy war set them against one another in Mount Lebanon. Maronites and Druze had lived there for centuries, the former being the majority in the north, the latter in the south, in the Chouf region. The demographic growth of Eastern Christianity, then widespread in the Ottoman Levant, was particularly noticeable in the Chouf, where the low Druze birth rate contrasted with Maronite fertility. Added to this physical pressure on the land was a class conflict between the Druze landowners and the Maronite peasantry. What might have been merely a localized peasants' revolt, as in 1841 and 1845, would, however, become a major conflict between communities, due to European rivalries, on the one hand, and the opposition of local administrators to the reforms dictated by Constantinople, on the other. The hostilities, which opened in May 1860 in the Chouf, quickly turned to the advantage of the Druze, more or less openly supported by the Ottoman forces. Thousands of Christians were massacred in a few weeks, while Catholic institutions, even under the French flag, were ransacked, although the rioters spared the Protestant missions. Parisian newspapers reported this tragedy in detail, attacking the cruel 'Muhammadans' and 'perfidious Albion' with equal indignation.

Fuad Pasha, the Ottoman Minister of Foreign Affairs, received full powers to restore order in Mount Lebanon, at the head of a large contingent. In July 1860, this decision provoked a new bloodbath against the Christians, this time in Damascus, whose governor had joined forces with the rebels. The toll, again running into thousands of victims, would have been much heavier without the intervention of Emir Abdelkader. The former leader of the Algerian insurrection, exiled in Damascus since 1855, took under his wing thousands of civilians, as well as the consuls of France, Greece, and Russia. As in Lebanon, the rioters openly spared British interests. Fuad Pasha launched a fierce crackdown, with a hundred people being shot (including the governor of Damascus) and about fifty hanged. But only once order had been restored did Napoleon III obtain from his European peers and from the Sublime Porte the authorization to dispatch 6,000 soldiers to Beirut. The French general was quickly rendered powerless by the determination of Fuad Pasha. There was no longer any question of going to 'punish' the Druze or of laying the foundations of an 'Arab kingdom' in Syria,[8] whose Francophilia Abdelkader would guarantee: while the exile from Damascus was happy to accept the Grand Cross of the Legion of Honour, he categorically refused any political office.

The French expedition to Lebanon, the prototype in 1860 of more recent 'humanitarian interventions', was a resounding failure: not only did it achieve none of the objectives assigned to it by the public campaign in favour of 'our Christian brothers', but it also revealed how, when executioners were in control, the protection of a Muslim notable turned out to be much more effective than that of distant France. As for British diplomacy, it accredited a distinction between the 'massacres' in Damascus and the 'civil war' in Lebanon, for which it blamed the Maronites, in order to clear the Druze of responsibility. In the same month of June 1861, when the French contingent left Beirut, an 'organic regulation' of Mount Lebanon was adopted by the European powers and ratified by Constantinople. A Christian governor, chosen outside Lebanon by the central power, was to govern the province with the assistance of a council composed equally of Christians and Muslims.[9] In practice, the obsession with inter-community balance resulted in an arithmetically sectarian distribution of representative and adminis-trative positions. This legacy would weigh very heavily, and still does, on a Lebanon unable to promote an authentic citizenship going beyond religious affiliations. It is also important to emphasize that this institu-tionalization of Lebanese sectarian identities, under European pressure,

[8] This plan for an 'Arab kingdom' in Syria in 1860 echoed a comparable project of Napoleon III in Algeria, destined to remain equally unrealized.
[9] This council had twelve members, including two Maronites, two Greek Orthodox, two Greek Catholics, two Druze, two Sunnis, and two Shiites. The revision of the statute in 1864 gave a slight majority to Christians, with four Maronite members, two Greek Orthodox, and one Greek Catholic, against three Druze, one Sunni, and one Shiite.

flew in the face of a modernization that would erase any distinction between Ottoman subjects.

The Suez Canal

Abbas Pasha, who ascended to the throne of Egypt in 1848 on the death of his grandfather Muhammad Ali, maintained the fiction of Ottoman tutelage over his country. He mandated the British to build the railway between Cairo and Alexandria, even if this project meant straining Egypt's budget. The spiral of debt worsened, from 1854 to 1863, under the reign of his successor, Said Pasha, who had lived for a long time in Paris. Ferdinand de Lesseps, the former consul of France in Egypt, won the concession for the digging of a canal between the Mediterranean and the Red Sea, work on which began in 1859. Great Britain took a very dim view of this great French design, which, in terms of technical progress, it viewed as an echo of Bonaparte's desire to carve out his own road to India. The British campaign was waged in the name of a 'humanitarian' denunciation of the corvée imposed on Egyptian peasants for this huge construction site. A ruling by Napoleon III in 1864 abolished the corvée, so making London's objections superfluous. Isma'il Pasha, the new master of Egypt, obtained the restitution of vast irrigable territories, but at the cost of a compensation which increased the country's debt. The inauguration of the Suez Canal took place in 1869, with great fanfare, in the presence of the Austrian emperor and the French empress. This sumptuous ceremony marked the apogee of Isma'il, recognized as 'khedive' of Egypt by the Ottoman sultan in 1867, a title that he was able to pass on to the eldest of his sons. The master of Cairo was nevertheless obliged in return to double the tribute paid to Constantinople, which further accentuated the dependence of his country on Western creditors.

European imperialism increasingly drew on its financial clout in the Middle East. The Ottoman Empire, partially bankrupt from 1875 onwards, was declared completely bankrupt in 1881. A Public Debt Administration was established under the alternating presidency of France and Great Britain, with the participation of Germany, Austria-Hungary, Italy, and the Netherlands. This guardianship used the income from the state monopoly on salt, as well as taxes on tobacco, silk, and fishing, to pay off creditors. In Egypt, the debt burden forced the

Khedive Isma'il, in 1875, to cede Egyptian shares in the Suez Canal to Great Britain. Three years later, he had to entrust the finance portfolio to a Briton and the public works portfolio to a Frenchman. When the sovereign dared to dismiss this 'European ministry' in 1879, he was forced by London and Paris to abdicate in favour of his son Tewfik.

Western control over Egypt was accompanied by the recognition, in the name of a very extensive interpretation of the capitulations, of privileges granted to the Greeks, Levantines, and Maltese who came to settle in their tens of thousands. They were particularly numerous in the cosmopolitan city of Alexandria, where riots between 'natives' and 'Europeans' claimed hundreds of victims in June 1882. The British fleet responded by bombarding the port, which was being pillaged; they then occupied the city with the support of the khedive, who relied on foreign intervention to quell the nationalist insurrection. The bey of Tunis had made the same calculation the previous year, preferring to keep his throne against his people's wishes, and under the protectorate of France. In September 1882, Egyptian resistance was brutally put down and Great Britain took control of the Suez Canal, whose company remained under French management, but the majority of whose shareholders were British, while three-quarters of the traffic was carried by British ships. His Royal Highness's representative in Cairo admittedly had only the modest title of 'agent' and 'consul', but he was now the true master of the country.[10]

The Great Game between Britain and Russia

Let us go back a generation to gain a better grasp of the intensity of the rivalry, described as 'the Great Game', between Britain and Russia in the eastern Middle East. The crushing of the sepoys' revolt in 1857 led London to dissolve the East India Company and to establish the imperial structure of the Raj, which, under the direction of a 'viceroy', combined direct domination and indirect control of the subcontinent. This meant that Great Britain was all the more determined to prohibit any Persian advance towards Afghanistan, considered as a buffer state

---

[10] Evelyn Baring, the future Lord Cromer, governed Egypt from 1883 to 1907, with only 3,000 soldiers and a few hundred British administrators.

to be neutralized at all costs. The Qajar occupation of Herat in 1856 provoked, as in 1837, a British expedition to the Persian Gulf, this time with the occupation of the ports of Bushehr and Khorramshahr. The showdown ended with the simultaneous withdrawal of the two armies, together with a formal recognition by Persia of the independence of Afghanistan.

Russia, which, after its defeat in the Crimea, no longer had military access to the Black Sea, concentrated on absorbing the methodically colonized territories of the Caucasus. It then extended its positions to the east of the Caspian Sea, and on to Central Asia; in 1865, it seized Tashkent, promoted to the capital of the Russian governorate of Turkestan. As for British ambitions, they were made clear in Parliament in 1876 by the vote proclaiming Queen Victoria Empress of India, whose border with Persia was consolidated by the vassalization of Balochistan. The Indian army became as indispensable to the colonial ventures of London as the 'Armée d'Afrique'[11] was to those of Paris. These Indian contingents played a decisive role in the British occupation of Egypt in 1882.

The Middle East once more became the focus of Anglo-Russian rivalry thanks to the war that the tsarist regime, allied with the Serbs and the Bulgarians, declared in 1877 against the Ottoman Empire, which was quickly overwhelmed. The bloodbath was again appalling, with nightmarish population displacements. Russia, whose troops had bivouacked 10 kilometres from Constantinople, came to the Congress of Berlin in 1878 in a position of strength.[12] But the concert of Europe settled the conflict in favour of Great Britain: it occupied Cyprus as the price of its 'mediation' in favour of the Sublime Porte; the Russian plan for Greater Bulgaria was abandoned and Prime Minister Benjamin Disraeli could boast of having stopped Russia in its tracks.[13] Chancellor Otto Bismarck, the great architect of the Congress of Berlin, preferred to encourage the Mediterranean aims of Britain (and of France, which would thus be diverted from Alsace-Lorraine) rather than the continental expansionism

---

[11] This was actually the French Army of Algeria, where European units of *chasseurs*, *zouaves*, and legionnaires rubbed shoulders with 'indigenous' units of skirmishers, spahis (light cavalry units), and *méharistes* (camel companies).
[12] The Ottoman negotiator in Berlin was a Greek diplomat, born in Constantinople.
[13] His oft-quoted expression was 'thus far and not farther'.

of the tsarist regime. Russia took revenge by expelling en masse the Muslim populations of the Ottoman provinces in the southwest of the Caucasus: Kars, Ardahan, and Batumi, all annexed in 1878.

The Great Game continued the following year in Afghanistan, with Russia encouraging riots in Kabul, where the British consul and his guard were massacred. But Britain successfully pursued a campaign of reprisals and in 1880 deposed the Afghan emir in favour of his cousin, who recognized British control over his foreign policy in return for the withdrawal of the expeditionary force. In order to consolidate this major victory in the Great Game, London established a buffer zone of 'tribal areas' on the northwestern border of its Indian empire. These were populated by tribes of the same Pashtun ethnic group as the dominant group in Kabul, which thus became weakened. The buffer state of Afghanistan was now bordered by these frontier territories, managed autonomously by tribal chiefs, under the distant tutelage of a British administrator. The establishment of these zones of lawlessness was sealed by the drawing, in 1893, of the Indo-Afghan border. This Pashtun Far West would persist in postcolonial Pakistan, until it became, at the end of the twentieth century, the cradle of Al-Qaeda and, thus the crucible of modern jihadism.

The invention of the Middle East

The fiction of Egyptian sovereignty, preserved despite the British occupation of 1882, also applied to Sudan, controlled by Egypt since 1821.[14] London was soon obliged to face the challenge of a millenarian rebellion which, starting in the west of the country, now threatened its capital, Khartoum. The leader of this insurrection claimed to be the Mahdi, who was expected at the beginning of Islam's fourteenth century.[15] In 1884, he besieged the Egyptian contingent, commanded by Britain's General Gordon, for ten months in Khartoum. The reinforcements

[14] It was on the orders of Muhammad Ali that the city of Khartoum was founded in 1822, at the strategic confluence of the White Nile and the Blue Nile.
[15] The fourteenth century of the Hijri calendar began in 1883. Islamic messianism believed that the beginnings of a century was favourable to the advent of a Mahdi, both a saviour and a vigilante.

dispatched by London arrived too late to prevent the capture of the city by the Mahdi, who crushed all opposition. This imperial setback of 1885 was all the more resounding in that it contrasted with the capitulation of Abdelkader to France in 1847 and of Shamil to Russia in 1859. The Mahdi led the prayers in the largest mosque in Khartoum before setting up his capital in Omdurman, on the other bank of the Nile. His death a few months later did not hinder the structuring of a 'Mahdist' state which resisted London's desire for revenge for a dozen years. The carnage inflicted on the Sudanese by British machine guns in Omdurman, in 1898, would make a lasting impression on a young lieutenant by the name of Winston Churchill. The expeditionary force then obliged a French detachment from the Congo to evacuate the fort of Fashoda, 600 kilometres south of Khartoum, on the course of the White Nile. The north–south axis of British domination of the African continent thus neutralized the French desire for an unbroken territory from west to east, from Brazzaville to Djibouti. Sudan was transformed in 1899 into an 'Anglo-Egyptian condominium', actually subject to the sole authority of London.

The consolidation of the Indian Empire and of these great African designs was accompanied by a methodical advance on the shores of the Arabian Peninsula. First, the strategic port of Aden was occupied by British forces in 1839, before being incorporated into the Raj and finding itself at the centre of a series of 'protection' deals with the surrounding tribes. Then, the dreaded 'Pirate Coast' was pacified in 1853 as the 'Trucial Coast', on the current territory of the United Arab Emirates. The power of the Sultanate of Oman was weakened in 1861 by the British takeover of Zanzibar, the source of the precious supply of cloves. London also arbitrated in the rivalries between the Al-Thani family in Qatar and the Al-Khalifa family in Bahrain, with the latter having to recognize the former's independence in 1868, before Bahrain became a British protectorate in 1880. A series of treaties gradually increased London's control over the southern shore of the Persian Gulf. This system was consummated in 1899 when the Emirate of Kuwait came under the tutelage of London. This was a scathing snub for the Ottoman Empire, whose province of Iraq no longer had access to the Persian Gulf except through the narrow mouth of the Shatt al-Arab, the 'Shore of the Arabs', i.e. the shared estuary of the Tigris and the Euphrates. The Sublime Porte nursed a virulent irredentism against this 'protected' Kuwait. These annexationist demands would be taken up in Iraq by Arab nationalists in the second half of the twentieth century.[16]

This imperial apogee inspired an unprecedented conceptualization of the Middle East by the future American admiral Alfred Mahan. In 1898, Mahan, a highly influential professor of military academies, threw his weight behind the US annexation of the archipelago of Hawaii, strategically located in the middle of the Pacific Ocean. Four years later, he asserted, in the *National Review*, a major British conservative publication, that the key to world hegemony lay in control of the 'Middle East'. This crossroads of three continents was indeed located at the junction of the Suez Canal and the route to India, in other words the land and sea axes of communication between Europe and Asia. This geographical space was then given the generic term of 'the East', in reference to the 'Eastern question', after long having been called the 'Levant', as in the *échelles du Levant*. The East and the Levant both correspond to the Arab notion of Mashriq, the region where the sun rises, as opposed to the Maghreb, the Arab West, located in North Africa. Mahan, from his perspective in the Western hemisphere, highlighted the geopolitical centrality of an Eastern region that had thereby become the 'Middle' East. His vision of the Middle East as a source of power, long before the tapping of the region's oil, remains disturbingly topical.

The birth of Zionism

Ottoman Palestine did not have a territorial or administrative existence of its own. It was divided into three *sanjaks*/districts, to distinguish them from the upper echelon of *eyalets*/provinces. The *sanjak* of Jerusalem was attached directly to Constantinople in 1872 because of the sensitivity of the Eastern question. To be its ruler was not an envied post owing to the endless quarrels between the local churches and the regular interventions of the European consuls. The Sublime Porte settled the question of the keys of the Holy Sepulchre by entrusting them to one of the Muslim

---

[16] In 1961, Iraq opposed the admission of Kuwait to the United Nations and Saddam Hussein invaded and then annexed Kuwait in 1990 (see below, pp. 310 and 313).

notables of Jerusalem, which relieved him of having to decide between the different Christian sects. The constituency of Jerusalem was extended to Nazareth so as to facilitate European pilgrimages, which were now booming, with a new railway linking the port of Jaffa to the Holy City from 1892. The two other *sanjaks* of Palestine, Acre and Nablus, came under the governorate of Damascus, then, from 1888, that of Beirut. It was not until 1906 that an empire border was drawn between the Negev and Sinai deserts, i.e. between Ottoman Palestine and an Egypt subject to Great Britain. The British ensured that this line crossed the town of Rafah itself, in order to control the outlet of the Egyptian Sinai on the Mediterranean coast. It was recognized that the Bedouin tribes could continue to lead a nomadic existence on either side of a border widely perceived as artificial.

In this Palestinian area, made up of the three entities of Jerusalem, Acre, and Nablus, the population was estimated in 1880 at 400,000 Muslims, 40,000 Christians, and 25,000 Jews. The majority of these Jews devoted their lives to Talmudic studies, with the assistance of wealthy patrons in the Diaspora. The main centres of rabbinical learning were Jerusalem, Safed, and Hebron, where a Jewish presence was attested over a very long period. As an alternative to these religious centres, the Alliance Israélite Universelle (AIU) opened 'French-style' educational schools. Founded in 1860 and chaired for twenty years by Adolphe Crémieux, who attached his name to the Frenchification of the Jews of Algeria, the AIU contrasted the rabbinic curriculum with the virtues of republican assimilation. The pogroms of 1881 in Eastern Europe and Russia led to the first stream of significant Jewish emigration to Palestine, called in Hebrew *aliyah*, meaning 'ascent' to the Promised Land. The first *aliyah* lasted until 1890 and preceded the foundation of Zionism proper. In 1882, the group of the *Hovevei Zion* (Lovers of Zion) established the Palestinian colony of Rishon LeZion, based on a kernel of Ukrainian immigrants. They advocated redemption through work, in this case agriculture, even if their endeavours depended on the support of the French banker Edmond de Rothschild. It was in this first *aliyah* that *Ha-Tikva* ('The Hope'), which has since become the Israeli national anthem, was composed. These pioneers opened Hebrew schools in order to impose modern Hebrew as the national language, and thus emancipate it from rabbinical influence.

The Viennese activist Nathan Birnbaum was the first to use the term 'Zionism', but it fell to Budapest-born Theodor Herzl to formalize this doctrine for the 'Jewish people'. He drew on the same people/language/land triptych that structured the different nationalisms of the Austro-Hungarian Empire and the post-Ottoman Balkans. In 1896, Herzl wrote, in German, *The State of the Jews*. On this basis, the following year in Basel, he chaired the founding congress of the Zionist movement, which set itself the objective of 'the creation in Palestine, for the Jewish people, of a national home guaranteed by public law'. In 1901, the Zionist writer Israel Zangwill invoked, in defiance of demographic realities, a 'land without people for a people without land'. Palestine was lauded as the 'land of Israel', in Hebrew *Eretz Yisrael*. The movement's centre of gravity, initially located with Herzl in Vienna, moved to Berlin in the hope of gaining the sponsorship of Wilhelm II, then to London; here, the Zionists could count on the indulgence of the Protestant millennials, in whose eyes the 'return' of the Jewish people to 'its' land was part of the fulfilment of the prophecies.

The Zionist movement, tempted for a while to settle in Uganda, a British protectorate since 1894, rejected this option after Herzl's death in 1904. The second *aliyah*, launched that year, was marked in 1909 by the founding of Tel Aviv, the 'Hill of Spring', as a Jewish quarter separated from the Arab port of Jaffa. The Yishuv[17] – Zionist, militant, and hard-working – sought to be the modernist antithesis, open to the Mediterranean, of the rabbinical seminaries of inland Palestine. This proactive policy brought the number of Jewish inhabitants of this territory to 75,000 in 1914, for approximately 600,000 Muslims and 40,000 Christians, i.e. Jews formed one tenth of the population. The real 'promised land' remained the United States, however, which absorbed forty times more Jewish immigrants than Palestine in forty years.[18] As for Zionist colonization, it came up against increasingly strong local resistance; in the transfer of land, the complicity of the Ottoman authorities and the laxity of the absent landowners were denounced. This rise in

[17] This Hebrew term, which means 'settlement', designates the Jewish community in Palestine before the founding of Israel.
[18] About 2 million Jews emigrated to the United States between 1881 and 1920, mainly from Eastern Europe and Russia, compared to some 50,000 to Palestine.

tensions was paradoxically less tangible in Jerusalem, whose population had quintupled in half a century, reaching 70,000 inhabitants in 1914, half of them outside the historic walls. Diversity prevailed in many neighbourhoods, even within the Old Town, and municipal autonomy was a daily reality, partly transcending sectarian affiliations.

The kill

Germany, unified in 1871, set out to impress the Ottoman Empire with its difference from France and Great Britain. It posed as an 'honest broker' at the Congress of Berlin of 1878, and displayed its support for the sultan in his policy of modernization and infrastructural development, investing in the railway line which would soon link Constantinople to Ankara. German officers held important leadership and command positions in the Ottoman army. Berlin frequently insisted on its absence of colonial aims and counted on the elites who had been disappointed by the model of the French Revolution, or simply by liberalism in the broad sense. In 1898, Emperor Wilhelm II completed a month-long tour of the Middle East: in Constantinople, he celebrated his friendship with the sultan-caliph, who was nevertheless denounced as a bloodthirsty despot in the European press; in Damascus, he financed the embellishment of Saladin's mausoleum; and in Jerusalem, where the wall of the Old City was pierced for his solemn entry, he inaugurated the Lutheran Church of the Redeemer in close proximity to the Holy Sepulchre.

Two years later, German engineers took part in the launch in Damascus of the 'Hejaz railway', which reached Medina in 1908. They worked in parallel with the *Bagdadbahn* (Berlin–Bahgdad railway), which linked Anatolia to Iraq. Thus strengthened in the Middle East, Germany tried in 1905 to stand up against France in Morocco, while draping its ambitions in the anti-colonial speech Wilhelm II gave in Tangier. But in this crisis the Great Britain supported France, in line with the very recent 'Entente cordiale' and in return for the abandonment of Paris's last claims in Egypt. The stage was set for a conference convened in 1906, under the aegis of the United States, in the Spanish city of Algeciras. This sealed France's dominant position there, opening the way to the proclamation, in 1912, of its protectorate over the majority of Moroccan territory, with the recognition of a Spanish zone and the international character of Tangier.

The cycle of colonial expansion ended with Italy, which, forty years after its unification, launched an assault on Libya in October 1911. As had been the case for France in Algiers in 1830, the landing, and the conquest of the capital, were relatively easy, which delighted the interventionist movement.[19] But the failure of the Ottoman command was counterbalanced by the determination of the young officers who organized the fierce resistance soon put up by the local tribes. One of these officers, Mustafa Kemal, distinguished himself in the fighting in Tobruk. In general, Cyrenaica resisted better than Tripolitania, to the point that the Italians, forced to mobilize tens of thousands of soldiers, lost control of Benghazi. Rome thereupon extended hostilities to the coast of Yemen; this favoured the imam of Sanaa against the Ottoman troops. The Italian victory was recognized by the Sublime Porte in a treaty signed in Lausanne, at the Château d'Ouchy. As with the loss of Crimea in 1774 to Russia, the prerogatives of the Ottoman caliph in Libya were formally preserved by the new Italian power. But the transfer to Constantinople of Rhodes and the neighbouring islands would never be realized. It would take more than a century for President Erdoğan's 'neo-Ottoman' plans to present Turkish intervention in Libya, alongside the internationally recognized government of Tripoli, as revenge for the humiliation inflicted in 1911–1912 by Italy.

Let us recap the situation on the eve of the First World War: France has occupied North Africa, 'French Algeria' being framed by the two protectorates imposed on Morocco and Tunisia; Italy has seized Libya, even if it is far from having 'pacified' Cyrenaica; Great Britain controls Egypt (and, in condominium with it, Sudan), occupies Aden, and 'protects' the various emirates of the southern coast of the Persian Gulf, from Kuwait to the Trucial Coast of the modern United Arab Emirates. As for Russia, it has gradually incorporated into the Tsarist Empire the immense territories of Turkestan, the eastern Caspian Sea, and, above all, the Caucasus, from which it has largely expelled the Muslim populations. In this sequence of colonial expansion, this is the only case of a

---

[19] In November 1911, the Italian air force carried out the first aerial bombardment in history, against an oasis near Tripoli.

massive expulsion of 'natives' from the conquered territory, since the very significant displacements of population to which the French conquest of Algeria gave rise took place within the three 'departments' thus annexed. The Ottoman Sultanate no longer exercises its effective sovereignty in the Middle East except over Bilad al-Sham, Mesopotamia, and the Hejaz, while central Arabia is experiencing a resurgence of Wahhabi dissidence and the Yemeni imamate is consolidating its autonomy, thanks to the Italian invasion of Libya.

In 1907, the British and Russians defined their respective zones of influence in Persia, to the south and the north respectively. Neither of them sought the break-up of the Qajar regime, knowing that this would be fraught with conflict and threaten their considerable interests there. The same logic now seemed to prevail within the Ottoman Empire, whose remains were being digested by the Russians, French, and British, while Germany was laying plans for the future. The link between financial imperialism and territorial delimitation was particularly visible in the field of oil and railway lines, sometimes combined. This was how, during the construction of the *Bagdadbahn*, German investors obtained the mining and oil exploitation rights for the 20 kilometres either side of the railway line. But Paris and Berlin agreed to recognize France's economic zone of influence south of the Latakia–Homs line, i.e. around Beirut and Damascus. And the British ensured that the last stretch of the railway line, linking Baghdad to the port of Basra on the Persian Gulf, was reserved for them. The Ottomans retained only the administration of the Hejaz railway, essential for the symbolic and logistical management of the pilgrimage from Damascus to Medina, which then continued by caravan to Mecca.

The Western question

Colonial expansion in the Middle East was, as we have seen, part of wider plans, covering, clockwise, the Caucasus, Central Asia, India, East Africa, and the Maghreb. The triangular dynamic between Egypt, Syria, and Iraq, muted by centuries of Ottoman rule, was only temporarily revived by Western intervention. For a few decades, Bonaparte's expedition restored to Egypt the influence it had under the Mamluks from 1250 to 1517. It even nourished Egypt's ambitions in Syria, occupied from 1831 to 1841, before the Eastern question imposed its European priorities on regional dynamics. Egypt, finally neutralized in 1882 under British occupation, then served as a British stepping stone, no longer towards the Levant, but towards Africa. And it was the routes of the railways in Syria and Iraq which henceforth delimited the zones of influence of all those involved. As for Palestine, the stake in the standoff between Syria and Egypt during the counter-Crusade of Nur ad-Din and Saladin, imperialist expansion meant that it gained the status of a 'promised land', both for Anglo-Saxon millenarianism and for Zionist activism.

When, in 1921, the British historian Arnold Toynbee discovered the ravages of the wars in Anatolia, he was struck by the fact that all the parties, even the most opposed, agreed that their destiny depended on decisions taken in European capitals. This shared vision of a great superior and Western design relativized the room for manoeuvre and even the autonomy of action of the Middle Eastern protagonists, who therefore aspired to manipulate these foreign interferences for their own benefit, rather than to develop their own dynamics. This vision still fuels conspiracy theories in the Middle East – from whence they often stem – that are as far-fetched as they are coherent. This is how a certain Christian propaganda at the time caricatured the Lebanese Druze as mere instruments of a British 'plot' and how Abdul Hamid II came to regard his Armenian subjects as a 'fifth column' for European plans. This focus on foreign interference ascribed an often artificial cohesion to imperialist policies. It also resulted in exonerating the Middle Eastern forces of their proven responsibility for the misfortunes of the region.

This was why Toynbee reversed the dominant discourse by speaking of the 'Western question' rather than the Eastern question. The Western question was to be understood, in his view, in the twofold sense of the rivalries of Western powers in the East and of the resulting 'Westernization' of Eastern societies. Toynbee thought that this Westernization was based on the construction of a state that was more imported than 'modern' and on the consecration of the principle of nationalities, also imported. This emergence of nationalisms was accompanied, in the European part of the Ottoman Empire, by the horrors of the Balkan wars. It was encouraged by two empires, themselves multinational, Austro-Hungary and Russia, which thus undermined the multinational character of the Ottoman structure. The following chapter will describe how this process of 'national' fragmentation profoundly affected the Middle East in the nineteenth century. The sectarian dimension of this fragmentation was aggravated by foreign intervention, with its notorious defence of 'minorities'. However, we will see that the original forms of 'living together' that the societies of the region forged were all antidotes to this breakdown of their communities, and comprised many possible paths towards an alternative future.

Chronology

July 1798	Beginning of Napoleon Bonaparte's Egyptian campaign.
February–June 1799	French intervention in Palestine.
May 1801	Dispatch of an American squadron against Libya.
August 1801	Capitulation of Abdullah Menou in Egypt.
August 1804	American bombardment of Tripoli, Libya.
July 1805–March 1848	Muhammad Ali ruler of Egypt.
July 1827	Franco-Anglo-Russian Treaty on Greece.
January 1829	Anti-Russian riot in Tehran.
June 1830	French landing in Algeria.
October 1831	Beginning of the Egyptian campaign in Syria.
January 1835	Coronation in Tehran of Muhammad Shah.
January 1839	British landing in Aden.
February 1840	Anti-Semitic affair in Damascus.
January 1841	Withdrawal of the Egyptian contingent from Syria.
December 1847	Surrender of Emir Abdelkader in Algeria.
December 1848	Official annexation of 'French Algeria'.
February 1852	Ottoman definition of the status quo in Jerusalem.
October 1853–March 1856	Crimean War.
August 1859	Surrender of Imam Shamil in the Caucasus.
May 1860	Foundation in Paris of the Alliance Israélite Universelle.
July 1860	Massacre of Christians in Damascus.
June 1861	Special status of Mount Lebanon.
November 1869	Inauguration of the Suez Canal.
June–July 1878	Congress of Berlin.
September 1879	Anti-British uprising in Kabul.
May 1881	French protectorate over Tunisia.
August 1882	British landing in Egypt.

January 1885	Victory of Mahdi's supporters in Khartoum.
August 1897	First Zionist Congress in Basel.
September 1898	British reconquest of Khartoum.
October 1898	Wilhelm II in Constantinople, Damascus, and Jerusalem.
January 1899	British protectorate over Kuwait.
March 1905	Wilhelm II in Tangier.
May 1906	Anglo-Ottoman agreement on the Sinai border.
August 1907	Anglo-Russian partition of areas of influence in Persia.
September 1908	'Hejaz Railway' to Medina.
April 1909	Foundation of Tel Aviv.
October 1911	Beginning of the Italian invasion of Libya.
March 1912	French protectorate over Morocco.
October 1912	Italo-Ottoman Treaty on Libya.

Further reading

Birdal, Murad, *The political economy of Ottoman public debt* (London: I.B. Tauris, 2010).

Burton, Richard, *The pilgrimage to Mecca* (Stroud: Amberley, 2015).

Cole, Juan, *Napoleon's Egypt: invading the Middle East* (New York: St Martin's Griffin, 2007).

Churchill, Winston, *The river war: the Sudan, 1898* (Sevenoaks: Sceptre, 1987).

Hanioglu, M. Sükrü, *A brief history of the late Ottoman Empire* (Princeton, NJ: Princeton University Press, 2008).

Herzl, Theodor, *The Jewish State* (London: Penguin Books, 2010).

Laqueur, Walter, *A history of Zionism, from the French Revolution to the establishment of the state of Israel* (New York: Schocken Books, 2003).

Said, Edward, *Orientalism* (London: Penguin Books, 2019).

Shahnavaz, Shahbaz, *British imperialism in Southwestern Persia, 1880–1914* (London: Routledge, 2005).

Todd, David, *A velvet empire: French informal imperialism in the nineteenth century* (Princeton, NJ: Princeton University Press, 2021).

SEVEN

Reforms, renaissance, and revolutions (1798–1914)

This chapter, like the previous one, opens in 1798, with the French expedition to Egypt. But this time, we will follow, across the 'long nineteenth century', the internal dynamics of the regimes and societies of the Middle East. The processes of modernization that ran through them had their own logic, sometimes encouraged by external pressure, but often restrained or even ruined by colonial blindness. The French upheaval of 1798–1801 fuelled a profound movement of Arab emancipation, which was soon being referred to as the 'Nahda', literally 'Renaissance'. This Arab equivalent of the European Enlightenment was carried out by the 'enlightened' despotism of the masters of Cairo, and then by the pioneering constitutionalism of the beys of Tunis. So we need to reverse the overall sense of a unilinear continuity and its illusion of a modernity that was exported by Europe to the heart of the Ottoman Empire before being diffused to the Arab provinces. On the contrary, it was in Egypt that the first Middle Eastern project of 'civilization' was consolidated, to use the terminology of revolutionary France. And it was under the threat of this expansive Egypt that the Ottoman Empire embarked in 1839 on the adventure of the Tanzimat, or 'reforms' (the word literally means something more like 'institutionalization'). The Ottoman constitution of 1876, however, came fifteen years later than the first constitution of the Muslim world, adopted in a Tunisia that had become autonomous from the Sublime Porte a century before Egypt.

Invalidating the cliché of a modernity 'imported' from Europe by the Ottomans, who then transmitted it to the Arabs, should not lead to the opposite excess of an Arab vanguardism in the Middle Eastern Enlightenment. It must first be remembered that Arab identity would assert itself only very gradually, thanks to the Nahda, as well as the inability of the Ottoman regime to find a new multinational basis for the benefit of all its subjects. Furthermore, it was an Arab insurrection, aggressive in its puritanism, that was to mark the very beginning of the nineteenth century with its devastating expansionism: the Wahhabi emirate which the Saud family had established in central Arabia extended towards the southern shore of the Persian Gulf, subjugated Qatar and then Bahrain, before beginning a cycle of anti-Shiite raids in the south of Iraq in 1801. Karbala was sacked twice and Najaf was the target of repeated sieges, while massacres and exactions against Shiite 'heretics' followed each other in rapid succession. The Sauds then launched an assault on the Hejaz, where they occupied Mecca for two months in 1803, with the destruction of the graves of the Prophet's relatives. Then, in 1805, it was the turn of Medina, where the mausoleum of Muhammad himself was looted. The Wahhabis justified this sacrilege by their relentless struggle against the 'idolatry' represented by the pilgrimage to the tombs of holy men. The invaders imposed a very strict moral order, punishing breaches of any one of the five daily prayers and repressing the consumption of tobacco.[1] The sharif of Mecca, who governed the Hejaz in the name of the Sublime Porte, came under the tutelage of the Sauds, subjecting the conduct of the *hajj* to their discretion. Wahhabi troops continued their incursions into southern Iraq, as well as Oman, Yemen, and even Syria, reaching as far as Damascus in 1810.

Eventually, it proved too much for the Ottomans, who, unable to react directly, turned to Muhammad Ali. The governor of Egypt dispatched one of his sons, Tusun, at the head of an expeditionary force, which, landing in 1811, took more than a year to regain control of the Hejaz.[2] Muhammad Ali led the pilgrimage caravan himself in 1813 and symbolically sent the keys of Mecca to the Ottoman sultan. But in 1815, Tusun, appointed pasha of Jeddah, was obliged to conclude a pact with the Sauds, who were still the masters of central Arabia. Hostilities resumed the following year on the death of Tusun and his replacement by his brother Ibrahim. This time Cairo was sent instructions from the Sublime Porte to liquidate the Wahhabi emirate, whose capital, the oasis of Diriyah, was besieged, then destroyed in 1818. The leader of the insurgents and his relatives were transferred to Constantinople and there beheaded. This first experience of Wahhabi theocracy tarnished

[1] The Ottoman ulama had legalized tobacco as early as 1652.
[2] Tusun's chief of staff was so fierce that he was nicknamed 'Bonaparte'.

the Ottoman title of Custodian of the Two Holy Cities. The fragility of imperial authority throughout the Arabian Peninsula, even in Iraq and Syria, was unprecedented. On the other hand, Egypt asserted itself as a full power, de facto if not de jure. This was the beginning of a cycle where each request from Constantinople to Cairo avoided a situation where the sultan was humiliated only by Muhammad Ali being given greater autonomy.

The influence of Egypt

Nothing predisposed Muhammad Ali to embody, for nearly half a century, the most authoritarian version of the Arab Enlightenment. Born in Ottoman Macedonia, he was the deputy head of the Albanian militiamen sent in 1801 to restore the authority of Sultan Selim III in Egypt. The power struggles that shook the country after the French withdrawal enabled him not only to play the different parties against each other, but above all to cultivate his local base. In 1805, he became the first governor of Egypt to be supported by popular demand, even if his appointment was technically in the sultan's hands alone. In 1807, he drove back the English contingent that had landed in Alexandria, the first and last attempt at foreign intervention in his reign. In 1811, he massacred hundreds of Mamluks in an ambush at the citadel of Cairo, thus eliminating any challenge to his hold on Egypt. In the process, he abolished the tax lease, providing his administration with substantial resources; but they were deducted in kind, which led him to establish a whole series of public monopolies on the sale and export of these agricultural products.

The contingent that Muhammad Ali commanded in Arabia in 1813 was still Ottoman in its recruitment and doctrine. Ten years later, the introduction of conscription allowed a rapid increase in numbers, guaranteed by the massive enlistment of the Egyptian peasantry. This model of a 'national' army aroused strong resistance because of the harshness of its discipline, but it did establish an unprecedented relationship between the population and the nascent state. It was reinforced by new officer schools, armament industries, and military arsenals. State-run proactivism extended to the civil domain, with ambitious urban projects, in Alexandria even more than in Cairo, and the digging of canals aimed at extending the cultivable area. Cotton production increased very significantly, even if it benefited export to British factories more than the local textile industry. This forced modernization was accompanied, with the establishment of a public printing press in 1822, by an intensive training programme for Egyptian executives, either in Arabic in situ or for a period of several years abroad. This was how, from 1826 to 1831, Imam Rifa'a at-Tahtawi, trained at Al-Azhar in the image of the traditional elite, supervised around forty Egyptian scholarship holders in France. On his return to Cairo, he founded the school of translation there and published *L'Or de Paris* (*The Gold of Paris*), a vibrant plea in favour of shared values between French and Arabs.

Indeed, it was on Paris that Muhammad Ali was resolutely wagering in his work of 'civilization', once the obscurantist emirate of Saud had been dismantled under his assaults. The Arabic term 'Nahda' was increasingly becoming used to designate this multifaceted process of 'rebirth'. French advisers, military and civilian, often chose to embark on this Egyptian venture themselves, not hesitating to convert to Islam, as had the last French governor of the country. Of an entirely different nature was the support that the sovereigns of the Restoration, then of the July Monarchy, consistently granted to the ambitions of the ruler of Cairo. The latter testified to his gratitude by offering to France, in 1830, two obelisks from Luxor, one remaining in situ, the other being finally erected in 1836 on the Place de la Concorde, at the very location of Louis XVI's execution. In the meantime, as we have seen, Paris supported the Egyptian offensive of 1831 in Syria, where Ibrahim Pasha, on the strength of his 1818 victory over the Wahhabis, strove to contain and then repel the Bedouin raids which threatened the valleys of the Orontes and the Euphrates. He sought to be as much a liberator of the Arabs against the 'Turks' as a peacemaker and a modernizer. The councils involving Muslim and minority notables in urban centres were undeniably representative. But the Egyptian model of military conscription and individual taxation struggled to take hold over time, as Ottoman propaganda and British intrigue were both directed against it. Ibrahim Pasha's retreat to Egypt in 1841 closed what was henceforth but a parenthesis in the history of Syria, while the authority of the Sublime Porte over Mecca and Medina was fully restored.

The Tanzimat era

The Ottoman sultans, whose legitimacy as caliphs was recognized by international treaty in 1774, endeavoured to manage the 'Eastern question' at the lowest possible expense. The neutralization of Russia's undermining activity was accompanied by support for Great Britain against France, both engaged in a struggle for influence in the Middle East, and by encouragement for the mediation of Austria. But the European powers agreed to support the Greek independence movement, which further accentuated the dependence of the Sublime Porte on Egypt. Selim III's military modernization programme was ambitious, mobilizing foreign advisers and converts, relying on heavy industry to expand the artillery, and establishing a course of military academies, but he still came up against the tenacious opposition of the janissaries, who even overthrew the sultan in 1807. Ascending to the throne the following year, Mahmud II had to spend a long time keeping the janissaries in check; he waited until 1826 to finally massacre them in the tens of thousands.[3] It was significant that this ruthless liquidation took place fifteen years after the elimination of the Mamluks by Muhammad Ali, who was more coherent and forward-looking in his modernizing plans. It was in any case too late to avoid the twofold humiliation in 1827 of the loss of Greece and the destruction of the Ottoman fleet.

In 1831, Mahmud II completed the overhaul of his military by removing the feudal foundation of the cavalry, which was now professionalized. He also endeavoured to rationalize both the civil bureaucracy under the authority of the grand vizier and the religious hierarchy under the authority of the *sheikholeslam*. This levelling nevertheless appeared very timid in the face of the proactive stance that Egypt was demonstrating in Syria at the same time. And shortly after a resounding victory by Ibrahim Pasha in southeastern Anatolia, in 1839, Mahmud II died, leaving the throne to his sixteen-year-old son Abdulmejid. The young

---

[3] The elimination of the janissaries was accompanied by the persecution of the Sufi brotherhood of the Bektashis, which was organically linked to them (see above, p. 167). In the face of this repression, the Bektashis drew closer to the Alevis, whose esotericism and syncretism they shared – so much so that these two currents have merged in the Alevism of modern Turkey.

sultan initiated, with the edict of Gülhane, an era of reforms, designated under the generic term of 'Tanzimat'.[4] Full-fledged ministries were created, as well as a Council supposed to limit the arbitrary rule of the sultan. The tax lease was officially abolished in favour of a tax levy by the Ottoman administration alone. The principle of military conscription was laid down, with a service fixed later at five years, followed by seven years in the reserve. The guarantee of the rights of subjects, without distinction of religion, was formalized. Secular courts, quite distinct from religious courts, whether Islamic, Christian, or Jewish, were established, particularly for commercial disputes. This was in response to a strong demand from the European powers, within which Great Britain was soon leading an anti-French front; in 1841, Muhammad Ali was forced to withdraw his troops solely to Egypt.

Abdulmejid's reformist trends were reinforced by the restoration of Ottoman authority in Syria. But the implementation of the Tanzimat proved laborious, and above all very uneven depending on the provinces. Only the Anatolian heart of the empire was more or less pliable, thanks to the discipline of conscription, which recurring revolts made impracticable in Bosnia and Albania. A system of recruitment by lot eventually prevailed in Syria and the tax lease remained in force in many regions where the weakness of the Ottoman administration in the face of local notables persisted. Communal riots sometimes broke out, as in Aleppo in 1850, when the urban masses and the traditional elites united to denounce the favouritism allegedly shown to Christians. The demographic dynamism of Eastern Christians contrasted with the stagnation of their Muslim neighbours, a phenomenon stemming as much from the rise in the Christian birth rate as from the fall in mortality, both favoured by missionary activities. This led to wealthy Christians emigrating due to the increasing population density in mountainous areas, while the Muslim immigration towards the empire resulted from the fierce conflicts in the Balkans and the Caucasus, with the expulsion of a large part of the conquered populations.

---

[4] The edict, also called 'imperial rescript', or even 'decree' or 'charter' (in Turkish *Hatt-i sharif*), was signed in the 'Palace of Roses' (Gülhane) in Constantinople. The Tanzimat refer to the Ottoman plans of the *Nizam-i Cedid* ('New Order'), of which they were the implementation.

The Tanzimat aspired to rebuild a modern state on the basis of a 'nation' which would finally be Ottoman and would absorb into its midst the different communities, i.e. the *millets*, the 'nations' invoked in the Eastern question. In 1844, the empire had some 32 million subjects, with 18 million Muslims and 14 million Christians. Catholics numbered less than a million, two-thirds of them settled in Europe, and the 150,000 Jews (still according to Ottoman statistics) were slightly more numerous in Asia. Just over half of the Ottoman subjects lived in the Middle East, whose population was four-fifths Muslim. The challenge of the reforms therefore lay in the universality of the principles that governed them, a universality repeatedly undermined in the name of local particularisms and acquired privileges. In 1856, Sultan Abdulmejid promulgated an emancipation edict[5] for his Christian and Jewish subjects, whose equal rights were guaranteed as *millets* rather than as individuals. But all administrative functions were now open to non-Muslims. This major advance, announced at the end of the Crimean War, was validated by the concert of Europe in the Treaty of Paris which settled the conflict. It was supplemented, in 1858, by a new land code which favoured the Ottoman administration and its latifundia at the expense of the customary use of the land. The adoption of a penal code, followed by the formalization of a civil code, reinforced secular justice in its competences and jurisprudence, while religious courts were increasingly confined to cases relating to personal status.

In Paris in 1856, the European powers remained silent about the emancipation of the Ottoman Jews, since equality of rights was guaranteed to the Jews only in very few European countries. On the other hand, they emphatically welcomed the end of state discrimination against Eastern Christians, in particular with the authorization of the building of new churches. This justification of foreign interference on the basis of the need to defend 'minorities' in turn fuelled internal opposition to Ottoman reforms, leading in 1860 to the massacres of Christians in Lebanon and Damascus. But, instead of promoting equal rights among all Ottoman subjects, we have already seen that the autonomy of Mount Lebanon, imposed under European pressure after this crisis, increased the fragmentation of communities, including among the different

---

[5] This edict took the form of an 'imperial rescript' (*Hatt-i Humayun*).

Christian persuasions. Sultan Abdulaziz, brother of Abdulmejid and son of Mahmud II, ascended to the throne in 1861 to extend and deepen the reforms. He was the first Ottoman ruler to visit his European peers, in 1867, with a tour of Paris, London, Brussels, Berlin, and Vienna. However, he did not manage to stop the continuing decomposition of his empire in Europe, with uprisings in Crete in 1866, Bosnia in 1875, and Bulgaria in 1876. The army accused Abdulaziz of culpable weakness towards Russia and compelled him to abdicate. The sultan was found dead with his veins open shortly afterwards, though whether this was suicide or murder is still contested. His successor, Murad V, was quickly dismissed due to poor mental health.

It was in these tragic circumstances that Abdul Hamid II, son of Abdulmejid and nephew of Abdulaziz, ascended to the throne. Upon taking power in 1839, his father had opened the era of the Tanzimat; he himself immediately embarked on a new constitutional venture. In 1861, as noted above, the beys of Tunis, autonomous from the Sublime Porte since 1701, had already adopted the first constitution of the Islamic world. This experiment had nevertheless only lasted three years, due to a peasant's revolt opposed to military conscription. But Abdul Hamid wagered that a constitution would strengthen him both against the autocratic trend, whose tsarist sympathies weakened the empire at the borders, and against the supporters of the liberal option, strongly supported by Great Britain. A commission of twenty-eight members, including ten ulama and six Christians, drafted the constitution, promulgated after four months of the new reign. Two assemblies, representative of the diversity of the empire,[6] because they were elected by the provincial councils, met successively in 1877. They tried to embody a form of counter-power, against the background of the war launched and successfully prosecuted by Russia. Abdul Hamid drew on this external danger to suspend the constitution at the very beginning of 1878, barely a year after it had come into force.

[6] The first 'assembly of deputies' had 71 Muslims, 44 Christians, and 4 Jews. In the second, there were 70 Muslims out of 120. The diversity of the provinces was also very pronounced. This was not the case in the Senate, whose members were appointed for life by the sultan.

The Persia of Naser al-Din Shah

The exceptional longevity of Naser al-Din Shah[7] on the Qajar throne, from 1848 to 1896, naturally gave him a major importance in the history of Persia. The beginning of his era was marked by the reforming zeal of Prime Minister Amir Kabir, with a reorganization of the army, the establishment of an embryonic university, and the distribution of the first printed newspaper. The country was at the time witnessing the messianic movement of the Bábi Faith, which literally claimed to be the 'gate' of a new prophecy. The leader of the movement, Báb, after declaring himself Mahdi, severed all ties with Islam, encouraging his followers to engage in public violations of sharia law. These provocations fuelled a violent campaign against them by the Shiite clergy, who had Báb executed in Tabriz in 1850. A Bábist plot to assassinate the shah in 1852 led to a bloody repression of the sect, whose survivors were exiled to Ottoman Iraq, there again to be the target of the hostility of the Shiite ulama.[8] This turmoil radicalized the opposition of the religious hierarchy to the desire for openness. The Qajar ruler knew that his legitimacy was very fragile in the face of Shiite piety, with ayatollahs who had become the sole interpreters of the will of the Hidden Imam. He sacrificed Amir Kabir to them; the latter was executed in 1852.

Thus, Naser al-Din Shah had neither the methodical constancy of a Muhammad Ali in Egypt, nor the reforming ambition of the sultans of the Tanzimat. His half-century of reign was an erratic succession of advances and setbacks; he would dismiss modernizing ministers in disgrace so as to pacify the fervour of the clergy. The Great Game between Britain and Russia, moreover, was punctuated by brutal interference at the court of Tehran; this limited the sovereign's room for manoeuvre, as he was reduced to playing the antagonists against one another. The development of the telegraph between 1861 and 1865 allowed the beginnings of centralization of this vast empire which was de facto multinational. But in 1872, the shah decided to subcontract to the British Baron Reuter

---

[7] His name means 'the Victor [in the name] of religion'.
[8] Báb was buried in Acre, while Baha'u'llah, his successor, who was to be exiled and buried in Haifa, chose a resolutely pacifist path, which has become present-day Bahaism.

most of the country's development. He granted him very substantial concessions in the railways, customs, and infrastructure. The sovereign claimed that he was preserving national independence by transferring the risk of these investments to a foreign company, but there was a general outcry against such submission to the 'infidels'. The ulama were joined in their campaign against Reuter by the bazaaris[9] of the merchant class, who opposed such unfair competition. In 1873, the shah finally gave in, thus opening a lasting dispute with Reuter, supported by British power. In 1878, he set up a Cossack guard, commanded by Russian officers and dedicated to his own protection, just as the Safavid ruler of Isfahan had recruited his imperial guard from Armenians and Georgians rather than Persians.

The ulama of the holy cities of Iraq were all the more indomitable in their resistance to the shah as, residing in Ottoman territory, they were sheltered from the arbitrary aspects of Qajar rule. Ayatollah Hasan Shirazi distinguished himself in 1870 by refusing to welcome Naser al-Din Shah on a visit to Najaf, which reinforced his status as a *marja*, or spiritual 'authority to be followed'. It fell to an indefatigable Persian militant, Jamal al-Din al-Afghani,[10] to give a pan-Islamic dimension to this clerical agitation. The tobacco monopoly, granted by the Qajar ruler to a British company in 1890, allowed this external Shiite opposition to encourage an internal boycott campaign. The bazaaris, at the forefront of the protest, were galvanized by the anti-tobacco fatwa issued from Iraq in 1891 by Ayatollah Shirazi. The local tobacco industry workers, laid off by the British concession, were then joined by a large number of their compatriots, the consumption of tobacco being considered an offence against the Hidden Imam. It only took a few weeks for the shah to give in to such pressure and repeal the tobacco monopoly, Shirazi in return lifting his prohibition. This cruel admission of weakness fuelled revolutionary subversion, until the assassination of Naser al-Din by a supporter of Afghani in 1896. Constantinople agreed to hand over three

---

[9] The bazaar/market was the Persian equivalent of the Arab souk; the Persian word '*bazaari*' refers to the class of merchants.

[10] Skilled at covering his tracks, Jamal al-Din chose the name of Al-Afghani, 'the Afghan', to conceal the fact that he had been born in the Persian province of Hamadan.

Iraqi ayatollahs, who, deemed to be accomplices in the regicide, were executed in Tabriz.

The diversity of the Nahda

The fact that the Arabic language was now widespread in print was decisive in the process of the Arab Enlightenment, described by those concerned as Nahda/Renaissance. It promoted the emergence of a new type of public sphere, where Arab intellectuals could exchange views in Arabic from one end of the Mediterranean to the other. These exchanges were enriched by dialogue with expatriates who were studying in Europe or had settled permanently abroad. This circulation of ideas, obviously constrained by state censorship, was nonetheless of unprecedented fluidity and density. It transcended sectarian barriers with, in 1860 in Beirut, the celebration of the homeland (*watan*) by Butrus al-Bustani, a Maronite convert to Protestantism, who opposed the idea that one was inevitably constrained by one's community in the midst of the crisis in Mount Lebanon. In 1876, Sami and Bishara Takla, two Greek Catholic brothers, founded in Alexandria the first Arabic daily, *Al-Ahram* (*The Pyramids*), which continues to be published to this day. The Greek Orthodox Jurji Zaydan, expelled from the University of Beirut for advocating Darwinism, moved to Cairo in 1882. There he produced a monumental work, including a fictionalized history of Arab civilization since the pre-Islamic period. Such Christian intellectuals gladly hailed the Prophet Muhammad as a pioneer of Arab nationalism, of which the Umayyad Caliphate represented, in their view, a first consecration.

The British occupation of Egypt in 1882 marked the end of the enlightened despotism of the khedives, while Abdul Hamid had closed the era of the Ottoman Tanzimat. The Nahda gained in creative autonomy what it lost in state tolerance, developing horizontally and interacting with the diaspora. The career of the Egyptian Muhammad Abduh is revealing in this respect: trained at Al-Azhar, he collaborated with *Al-Ahram*, battled against corruption, and advocated compatibility between Islam and parliamentarism; exiled to Lebanon in 1882, he joined Afghani in Paris, two years later, to found with him the review *Al-Urwa al-wuthqa* (*The Firmest Bond*), a veritable platform for Islamic reformism; returning to Cairo in 1888, he drew up a project for the modernization of Al-Azhar, then a treatise on theological popularization, in order to reconcile the rationalist and dogmatic approaches; and appointed mufti in 1899, he distinguished himself by what for the time were audacious fatwas on social issues. It was also in 1899 that the magistrate Qasim Amin, the Paris comrade of Abduh and Afghani, published in Cairo *The Liberation of Woman*, a manifesto for a feminism that would be implemented less by state activism than by progressive trends in society.

In the effervescence of the Nahda, inspirations that we would today describe as 'nationalist' and 'Islamist'[11] contributed with their own sensibilities to the same assertion of Arab identity and rights. This was in fact more a question of register than of priority: the 'nationalists' opposed the European imperialists by emphasizing the theme and the triptych of the 'right of the peoples', claiming for the Arabs, constituted as a 'people' and speaking their 'language', the 'land' in which to exercise their sovereignty; as for the 'Islamists', they defied Ottoman power, which they accused of having plunged Islam into decadence, basically because the caliphate had been usurped by the Turks at the expense of the Arabs. These two militant registers were all the more compatible in that they were accompanied by a shared requirement to return to the sources: the sources of Arab civilization for the 'nationalists'; the sources of a religion freed from its successive deviations for the 'Islamists'. These two currents of the Nahda could even converge in the work of a single personality, like the Aleppo sheikh Abd al-Rahman al-Kawakibi. As a resolute opponent of Ottoman arbitrary rule, whose abuses against the Arabs he denounced in Arabic, he advocated in the same spirit both the constitutional separation between politics and religion, and the refoundation of the caliphate on an elective basis.

Hamidian absolutism

The suspension of the Ottoman constitution in 1878 marked the end of the four decades of the Tanzimat. Abdul Hamid, who arrived on the throne as the most daring of the reformists, would mark the next three

---

[11] These two terms, in their current meaning, were not used at the time. The 'Islamists' of the Nahda called themselves 'reformists' or 'Salafists' (a term derived from *salafi* 'ancestors', in reference to the very first Muslims, the 'pious ancestors').

decades with an absolutism so closely identified with his person that it was described as 'Hamidian'. He thus earned the sinister reputation of being a 'Red Sultan', the colour of the blood he was accused of loving to shed. His very long reign was nevertheless distinguished, with the exception of the Crete crisis in 1897–1898, by the absence of the conflicts which had so undermined the actions of his predecessors. Where the Tanzimat had failed to stop the disintegration of the empire, the restoration led by Abdul Hamid consolidated what were now stabilized borders. But the horrors of the war inflicted by Russia in 1877–1878 completed, through the massive expulsion of the defeated populations, the demographic change in the Ottoman area, now more than three-quarters Muslim, giving it an unprecedented influence in the Middle East. The sultan was convinced that the European powers would not hesitate to 'balkanize' Anatolia and that the Muslim 'nation' was being fundamentally targeted by this multifaceted aggression. It was a question, therefore, no longer of promoting an Ottoman *millet* by a synthesis of the different communities of the empire, but rather of defending this Islamic entity against a coalition of external dangers.

Abdul Hamid therefore rejected the view that conscription be extended to Eastern Christians. The poll tax that the minority had to pay before the Tanzimat was merely replaced by the tax for exemption from military service. Muslim populations in Constantinople, the Hejaz, and Yemen were also exempt from these obligations. The agitation of the Kurdish tribes, endemic in previous years, culminated with the uprising of 1880, which the sultan suppressed by first diverting the rebels against Persia, before taking them in a pincer movement. Abdul Hamid nevertheless refrained from executing the leader of the insurgents, preferring to transfer him to the capital in 1881. The sultan more generally developed a policy of neutralizing tribal, Arab, Kurdish, or Turkmen notables, whose relatives were 'invited' to stay in the luxurious prison within the imperial palace. The institution in 1891 of a Kurdish cavalry, known as 'Hamidian' (*hamidiye*), was a way of incorporating this tribal component as a supplement, on the Cossack model. The process was completed the following year by the establishment in Constantinople of a 'school of the tribes', inaugurated on the anniversary of the birth of the Prophet.

Abdul Hamid would leave his Yildiz palace, on the heights of the capital, only to attend Friday prayers at the nearby mosque, which bears his name, or to renew the allegiance of his subjects during the two main festivals of the Islamic calendar.[12] The three pillars of his administration were the grand vizier, for civil administration, the *serasker* (Minister of War), for military affairs, and the *sheikholeslam*, for religious matters.[13] Friday prayers were said everywhere in the name of the sultan-caliph, even in Bosnia, which had been occupied by Austria-Hungary since 1878.[14] It would, however, be excessive to speak of Hamidian 'pan-Islamism', a term coined by a French journalist in 1881, on the model of pan-Slavism and pan-Germanism. The symbol of the caliphate was actually mobilized in a dynamic of internal consolidation rather than external expansion. The sovereign's Sunnism was also militant, with brutal conversion campaigns carried out among the Shiites of Iraq, even among the Alevis of Anatolia and the Alawites of Syria. These campaigns were quickly abandoned because of the atrocities of the soldiery. Even more violent was the attempt in 1892 to 'Islamize' the Yazidis[15] of Iraq, with the ransacking of their sanctuary of Lalish, north of Mosul.

The Armenian crisis

While the overwhelming majority of Armenians resided in the countryside of Anatolia and Cilicia, Abdul Hamid increasingly came to see them as a fifth column in the service of a European-style 'balkanization'. The pressure on the lands of the Caucasians exiled in 1878 meant never-ending and insoluble disputes. As for Kurdish loyalty, it was often pledged to the oppression of Armenian peasants, subject to twofold taxation, by the empire and by the tribes. This systematic discrimination gave rise, in line with Russian populism, to the organization of Armenian parties in

[12] These two Eids, marking the end of Ramadan and the end of the pilgrimage, are called *Bayram* in Turkish.

[13] Haunted by the precedent of the abdication of his uncle Abdulaziz in 1876, Abdul Hamid II demanded from the *sheikholeslam* a fatwa abrogating the one that had justified this dismissal.

[14] It was the same symbolic compensation that had led to the reactivation of the caliphate after the loss of Crimea in 1774 (see above, p. 166).

[15] The somewhat esoteric Yazidi religion amalgamates Muslim, Christian, and Mazdean elements in an original doctrine, implanted among the Kurds of Upper Mesopotamia from the twelfth century onwards.

the diaspora, first the Social Democrat Hunchakian Party, in Geneva in 1887, then the Armenian Revolutionary Federation, known as Dashnak, in Georgia in 1890. The first 'Armenian crisis' broke out in 1894 in south-eastern Anatolia, where the suppression of a supposed 'uprising', in fact a refusal to pay for Kurdish 'protection', justified the killings perpetrated by local militiamen. Armenian groups organized the defence of the populace and took the name of 'fedayeen', a term derived from mediaeval Islam, designating fighters ready to die for their faith (*fida'*). But such militants were more inspired by the comitadjis, Macedonian nationalists whose terrorist activities compensated for a very unfavourable balance of power, providing substantial press coverage.

From their base in Constantinople, the Armenian parties strove to mobilize Western diplomats and European opinions. This proactive strategy of internationalization in turn fed into Hamidian obsessions with the 'enemy within'. In September 1895, a Hunchakian demonstration in the capital, harshly repressed, revived the massacres in the interior provinces. In August 1896, Dashnak gambled by seizing the Constantinople headquarters of the Ottoman Bank, which it threatened to blow up along with the employees and customers it had taken hostage. This terrorist extremism aimed to test the limits and make European intervention inevitable. The commando in charge of the raid was finally evacuated on the yacht of the British ambassador, while the Armenians were subjected to veritable pogroms throughout the city. The carnage continued for a few more weeks in Anatolia, despite the international outcry against the 'Red Sultan'.[16] The final toll of this Armenian crisis has been estimated at between tens of thousands and 200,000, even 300,000, victims, an imprecision linked to the lack of reliable data as well as the extent of deaths induced by cold and hunger. Such quarrels over figures, fuelled by opposing propaganda, had already raged during the various Balkan conflicts and cannot be definitively settled.

European hostility drove Abdul Hamid to seek a rapprochement with Mozaffar ad-Din Shah, who, in 1896, succeeded his assassinated father on the Persian throne. The Ottoman sultan had already handed over to Tehran the Iraqi ayatollahs accused of having inspired the regicide. He went further by definitively shelving the plans to convert his Shiite

---

[16] In France's Chamber of Deputies, Jean Jaurès denounced a 'war of extermination'.

subjects to Sunnism, and obtained in return a Persian commitment not to support Armenian militancy. This convergence of absolutisms, which had been completely separate before the terrorist threat, has very contemporary echoes today. It should also be noted that terrorism, in its modern and high-profile manifestation, was introduced into the Middle East by Christian groups, modelled on European vanguard movements. These Armenian formations were also decidedly on the left, politically speaking, as would be the Palestinian groups of the first hijackings of airliners in 1970. Thus, neither the Middle East nor Islam as such constituted a breeding ground historically favourable to terrorism. As for Abdul Hamid, in 1905 he escaped the explosion of an 'infernal machine', in the terminology of the time, which killed twenty-six people as he was leaving Friday prayers. The author of the attack, a Belgian anarchist supporting the Armenian cause, was spared on the orders of the sultan and probably 'turned' by the Ottoman police.

The reign of Abdul Hamid is rarely compared to the contemporary experience of the Meiji era in Japan, though these two monarchies by divine right shared the same determination to modernize their country without Westernizing it. In both cases, an exacerbated nationalism, nourished by the sacralization of the sovereign, conceived modernization as the surest bulwark against imperialist aims. The development of Ottoman infrastructure was spectacular, especially in the railway sector,[17] and it was accompanied by a very significant increase in agricultural production. The main export crops were cotton from Cilicia, tobacco from Syria, and citrus fruits from Palestine. Admittedly, at the beginning of the twentieth century, the empire appeared largely underpopulated, with fewer than 25 million inhabitants,[18] including 1 million in Constantinople alone.[19] But the settlement of Caucasian immigrants on the pilgrimage route from Damascus to Medina made it possible to overcome the Bedouin obstacle on this major axis of Ottoman power, well before the construction of the Hejaz railway. From 100,000 to

---

[17] At the beginning of the twentieth century, the Ottoman Empire had 6,500 kilometres of railways, which transported 16 million people each year.

[18] By way of comparison, the Russian Empire was five times and the German Empire three times more populous.

[19] Cairo, Alexandria, Izmir, and Tehran were then respectively two, three, four, and five times less populated.

200,000 pilgrims were now received each year in Mecca, both by the port of Jeddah and by land. And, despite the bankruptcy proclaimed at the beginning of his reign, the sultan managed to restore public finances, relatively speaking, where the Egyptian khedive had been unable to avoid being put under financial supervision. The fact remains, however, that his modernization was juxtaposed, for example in education, with traditional institutions that he refrained from changing. Only the army was genuinely brought up to date, and it was from the army that the final blow to the sultanate would come.

Persian constitutionalism

Mozaffar ad-Din Shah forged, as we have seen, a solid absolutist partnership with the Ottoman sovereign. He was further encouraged in his despotic tendencies by the multifaceted support of Russia, the main backer of his lavish spending. He was, however, a weak personality, taunted as 'Mauvaise-affaire-eddine'[20] by French diplomats. Fascinated by Europe, where he spent three official visits, he entrusted the reorganization of Persian finances to Belgian advisers, led by a former customs officer. Resistance to the monarch, fuelled by rebellion in the bazaars and the sermons of the ayatollahs, denounced these concessions to foreigners, echoing previous mobilizations against British 'monopolies'. In 1905, liberal opinion was galvanized by the humiliations inflicted on the Russian protector, defeated by the Japanese army, then destabilized by a general strike and the Moscow insurrection. In January 1906, the demand for a 'court of justice' brought the different tendencies of the opposition together in the form of the occupation (*bast*) of the mosques by the protesters. The repression of demonstrators in Tehran led to the collective departure of a thousand leading religious figures for Qom in July 1906. The shah yielded to this challenge from the Shiite hierarchy and agreed to convene a 'national consultative assembly',[21] whose 156 deputies, elected by secret ballot by men over the age of twenty-five,

---

[20] 'Bad-business-eddine', playing on the Shah's name in French, 'Mozaffareddine Shah'. (Translator's note.)

[21] In Persian, as in Turkish, the word *millet* is used for 'nation' (see above, p. 137), and *milli* (sometimes transcribed *melli*) is the word used to translate 'national'.

met in the autumn. This first Parliament worked from the outset on the drafting of a constitution which would submit any international agreement to the prior authorization of the chamber. The law was signed into effect by a Mozaffar ad-Din greatly diminished by the illness which killed him shortly afterwards.

His son Muhammad Ali Shah succeeded him in January 1907, with the firm intention of curbing the constitutionalist momentum. He could count on Ayatollah Fazlullah Nouri, who sought to subordinate these brand new freedoms to the prescriptions of Shiism. The religious hierarchy was divided over the matter, in Persia as in Iraq, between the supporters of the primacy of religion (*mashru'a*)[22] and the partisans of constitutional principles (*mashruta*), led by Ayatollah Akhund Khurasani of Najaf, a disciple of Shirazi. An amendment to the constitution in October 1907, in the form of a 'fundamental law', made Shiism an official religion and required the approval of five ayatollahs to validate each legislative text. This committee would never meet, however, due to tensions within the clerical hierarchy, but also to the revival of revolutionary agitation. The unrest in Azerbaijan, intensified by the immigration of Russian revolutionaries from the Caucasus, cast its shadow even in the capital, where calls for the dismissal of the sovereign were raised. It was in this context that Russia and Great Britain agreed, in August 1907, to a north–south division of their areas of influence in Persia, a division based on their joint support for the Qajar regime.

Thus reinforced by the two European rivals, Muhammad Ali Shah resorted to increasingly heavy-handed behaviour, even having the Parliament occupied by his Cossack guard in June 1908. The period of the 'little tyranny' which then began – so called because it lasted for just one year – was marked by fierce repression. However, the revolutionaries held firm in Tabriz, seized Isfahan in January 1909, and moved on Tehran in May. The belated attempt to restore the constitution did not save the Qajar sovereign, who in July was forced to take refuge in the Russian embassy. The capital was in the hands of the insurgents, who sentenced Ayatollah Nouri to be hanged in public. A thirteen-year-old crown prince, Ahmad Shah, was placed on the throne, under the authority of a regent with close ties to Russia. Quick elections allowed a second

---

[22] The term '*mashru'a*' is derived from 'shari'a'.

Parliament to meet in November 1909. But the majority of the deputies were notables, and they soon came into conflict with the revolutionary elected officials, against a background of tensions in the provinces. The use of an American mission to reorganize the state budget was all the less effective as it was opposed by the British and the Russians. The former intervened in Shiraz and Isfahan, while in December 1911, the latter, already very aggressive in Azerbaijan, ended up imposing the pure and simple dissolution of the Parliament in Tehran.

Thus came to a close a five-year constitutional experiment, which would have many echoes in modern Iran, including during the Islamic Revolution of 1978–1979. The constitutionalist aspiration would henceforth be intimately linked to the nationalist desire to finally emancipate the country from foreign interference. From this stemmed the anti-imperialist dimension of the popular uprising of 1978, when the slogans 'Down with the shah' and 'Down with America' would be chanted together. The coalition that then overthrew the monarch was just as heterogeneous as that which defeated the 'little tyranny' in 1909. It rallied to the charismatic Ayatollah Khomeini, who, exiled in Najaf like Shirazi and Khurasani when they opposed the Qajars, tirelessly preached resistance to the despot. But no sooner had the shah been overthrown than Khomeini would pretend to reconnect with the constitutional heritage of the *mashruta* only to better promote the theocratic legitimacy of the *mashru'a*. The Constitution of the Islamic Republic, approved by referendum, consolidated the supreme authority of Khomeini via a system formally governed by election. As for the Iranian Revolution of 1979, it would have long-standing repercussions for the Middle East, while the Persian experience of 1906–1911 affected only the holy cities of Iraq.

The Young Turk Revolution

The Young Turks[23] movement, which, in 1908, took control of the Ottoman Empire, already had two decades of history behind it. The different groups who recognized themselves in this generic term militated

---

[23] Their French inspiration appears in their Turkish name *Jön-Turk*, transcribed phonetically from the French *Jeunes Turcs*.

for the restoration of the 1876 constitution. For a long time, their publications abroad and their more or less underground activities were met with little success, especially as in 1897 Abdul Hamid negotiated the allegiance of some of their leaders. The Young Turks Congress in Paris in 1902 saw the exclusion of decentralizing tendencies in favour of the Committee of Union and Progress (CUP), deeply marked by the Balkan tragedies. In 1907, in Thessaloniki, this Committee joined the revolutionaries who had infiltrated the army of Macedonia. The Young Turks made a pact with the Armenian Dashnak, despite the latter being responsible for the 1896 attack on the Ottoman Bank, forming a common front against the despotism of the Sublime Porte. The support of the army of Anatolia brought them to power in July 1908. The ultimatum issued by the insurgents to the 'illegitimate government' called for constitutional reconciliation between 'the nation and the sultan'. Abdul Hamid had no choice but to endorse this movement which had so emphatically appealed to him, even if it was so as to strip him of most of the powers accumulated in three decades.

This transition, suffused with lyricism, took the name of the 'Proclamation of Freedom'. The sultan agreed to restore the constitution and to organize a parliamentary vote throughout the empire. Freedom of the press and assembly were now guaranteed, and an extraordinary cultural and political flowering ensued. The number of members of the CUP multiplied a hundredfold, from 3,000 to 300,000 – an increase largely facilitated by the compulsory affiliation of the military. The annexation of Bosnia-Herzegovina by Austria-Hungary in October 1908 fuelled tensions, without, however, compromising the holding of elections the following month. The new assembly had 288 deputies, including 147 Turks (a slight majority) but also 60 Arabs, 27 Albanians, 26 Greeks, 14 Armenians, 10 Slavs, and 4 Jews. Ahmed Riza, the CUP President of Parliament, came to an accommodation with the provincial notables to consolidate the relative majority of his party in the chamber. But this intellectual, steeped in religious positivism, was soon marginalized by the dynamics of military intrigue. In April 1909, the Constantinople garrison rose up against the young Unionist/CUP officers, who were accused of atheism. The sultan did not intervene, although nothing proves that he himself fuelled this paradoxical insurrection of the centre against the provinces. His reign, however, did not survive this period of unrest, in which the Armenians were again the target of massacres, this time in Cilicia.

The capital was reconquered by an 'army of action' raised by the Young Turks in the Balkans, alongside units recruited from minority communities. A fatwa from the *sheikholeslam* legalized the dismissal of Abdul Hamid, who, exiled to Salonika, was dispossessed of his immense fortune. He was replaced on the throne by one of his cousins, the weakling Mehmed V. The constitution was amended so that the government was at last responsible to Parliament. But real power was taken over by hard-core Unionists, who became all the more authoritarian since they had narrowly escaped their downfall. It was no longer a time for the celebration of human rights, but for the exaltation of 'order and discipline' (*zapt-u-rapt*). The shift towards a centralizing militarism was brutally conducted in the name of the fight against separatism and obscurantism. The conscription of Christians now involved their integration into the corps of troops and the dissolution of sectarian auxiliaries.[24] The CUP was evolving into an increasingly intolerant form of party-state. The April 1912 elections, marred by numerous incidents, gave it 269 out of the 275 deputies. Ziya Gökalp, although of Kurdish origin, stood out as the main ideologue of the party, with a reading of Durkheim heavily inflected towards social Darwinism. While the Persian progressives still based their activities on class struggle, the Unionists ended up positioning the Turks themselves as collective victims of oppression, thus justifying their thirst for revenge.

Such fateful tendencies were made worse by external disasters. We saw in the previous chapter how the officer Mustafa Kemal distinguish himself by his courage during the Italian invasion of Libya in 1911. Isma'il Enver, one of the mainstays of the 1908 revolution as well as of the 1909 Unionist uprising, organized resistance to this African débâcle in vain. But it was the two Balkan wars of 1912–1913 that sealed the fate of the empire, against a backdrop of the displacement of between 200,000 and 400,000 Muslims to territory that was still Ottoman. The first of these wars, from October 1912 to May 1913, saw Serbia, Montenegro, Greece, and Bulgaria join forces to annihilate the Ottoman presence in Europe.

---

[24] In 1910, the War School opened to minorities; in this year when 394 officers started their studies, there were only 4 Armenians, 3 Greeks, and 1 Jew.

The second of these conflicts, in June–July 1913, set Bulgaria against its former allies, allowing Enver, appointed pasha, to reconquer Edirne, capital of the Ottomans until 1453, and to symbolically regain a foothold in Europe. The rise of the most intransigent of the Young Turks took place in two stages: in January 1913, the Minister of War was assassinated for not having prevented the fall of Edirne; in June, it was the Prime Minister who was assassinated in retaliation. Thanks to this chaotic bloodshed, a triumvirate established a de facto dictatorship. These were the 'three Pashas': Enver, the Minister of War; Djemal, Minister for the Navy; and Talaat, Interior Minister. Despite their anticlerical leanings, these three leaders sought to use the influence of the caliph to their advantage, now that they had stripped the sultan of all real power. Their vision of the world, militaristic and pessimistic, was based on an exaltation of strength and the Turkish nation, even of a hypothetical Turkish 'race'. They put their country on a veritable war economy, driving into exile nearly 200,000 Greeks living on the Aegean coast. Their pan-Turanism was an echo of pan-Germanism, which could only strengthen their ties with Berlin.

A Middle Eastern cohabitation

The 'long nineteenth century' saw the Ottoman Empire gradually but inexorably pushed out of the European continent. This process, which the Tanzimat struggled to stop and which Hamidian absolutism managed to contain for a generation, was completed after the Young Turk Revolution, though the latter was born in the Macedonian army. A quarter of the Muslim population of the Balkans are said to have perished during this cycle of conflict, while a third took refuge under the authority of the sultan. Such figures, debatable as ever, give some idea of the order of magnitude of this human catastrophe, aggravated by the parallel exodus of Muslims driven out of the Caucasus by Russian expansion. Such huge population displacements generated inevitable tensions which contributed to the massacres of the Armenians in 1894–1896, even more than to those of 1909. Another model was the integration of Kurdish dissidence, under Abdul Hamid, then under the Young Turks, carried out by diverting tribal violence against the Christian peasantry. The vision of a multi-community 'Ottoman nation' was abandoned in favour of a withdrawal into a 'Muslim nation' that the three Pashas themselves would irremediably Turkify.

The contrast between this dynamic of bloody exclusion in Anatolia and the emergence of a 'cohabitation' in the rest of the Middle East is striking. Even if we should not idealize this coexistence, it is worth emphasizing the fruitful nature of this management of difference. The traditional *millet* system, with its autonomy of jurisdiction – a system more or less centralized in line with the Christian Churches,[25] and managed locally for the Jewish communities – was considered so protective by the Europeans that they took advantage of it in the context of the capitulations. But the Egyptian interlude in Syria and the era of the Tanzimat undermined its basis, with the gradual abolition of state discrimination in return for the growing interventionism of the Ottoman authorities in community institutions, sometimes to the benefit of the most 'liberal' ones. In general, the Eastern Christians were quite satisfied with their de facto exemption from military service during the reign of Abdul Hamid, despite the violation it represented of the principle of equality between all Ottoman subjects.

As for the minorities within Islam, the Ottoman regime – state Sunnism – forbade them any official recognition. They were also regularly the target of campaigns of repression, carried out more to stifle local dissent than to impose a form of orthodoxy. But, by being outside the law, they were often exempted from conscription, a factor which, throughout the nineteenth century, could only encourage a wave of conversion of the tribes of southern Iraq to Shiism. The proselytism of the ulama of Najaf and Karbala then targeted nomadic groups that were gradually becoming more settled in their way of life. A single tribal confederation even included Sunni and Shiite segments, with customary law prevailing over religious justice. The fluidity of these moves from one Muslim family to another contrasted with the rigidity of the sectarianism instituted, under European pressure, in Mount Lebanon in 1861: not only were representatives obliged to respect a strict proportion between Muslims and Christians, but each denomination was clearly distinguished from

---

[25] The Orthodox and Armenian patriarchates of Constantinople, pioneers of the *millet* (see above, p. 137), were most successful institution here, unlike the relations established on a local basis with the Copts, the Maronites, and the Assyrians.

the others; this applied to the various Christian Churches, but also to the Sunnis, the Druze, and the Shiites. This unusual importance granted to minority groups in Islam stemmed above all from the protection that Britain sought to exercise over the feudal Druze within the framework of its struggle with France, historically a supporter of the Maronites.

The Arab Enlightenment of the Nahda drew a contrast between the model of the *watan*, the nation-homeland, and the *millet*, the nation-community. Boustani described the Mount Lebanon conflict as a 'civil war' and opened a 'national school' (*wataniyya*) in Beirut in 1863, well before the establishment of the modern Ottoman education system. About fifteen years later, it was in Alexandria that Christine Qardahi established a 'national school for girls'. The ports of Beirut and Alexandria became the privileged crucibles of a nationalism that was both secular and elitist, nourished by the Arabic-language press and exchanges with the diaspora, even though the overwhelming majority of the population remained illiterate. The emancipatory dynamic of the Nahda nevertheless spread to British-occupied Egypt and to the Arab provinces of the Ottoman Empire. Muhammad Kurd Ali, born in Damascus to a Kurdish father and a Circassian mother, was one of the most scathing writers of the Arab press: Ottoman censorship forced him to travel back and forth between Syria and Egypt. As for Jamil Sidqi Zahawi, son of the Kurdish mufti of Baghdad, he wrote in Arabic, verse as well as prose, to castigate discrimination against women, Wahhabi obscurantism, and Hamidian despotism.[26] Here again, belonging to an Arab 'nation' stemmed more from patriotic commitment than ethnic fatality. However, such intellectual effervescence was still the preserve of an elite (*khassa*), following the dichotomy between elite and masses (*amma*), inherited from classical Islam and applied in various ways by these notables of the Ottoman Empire.

The Young Turk Revolution of 1908, with its slogan 'Liberty, Equality, Justice', was accompanied by an unprecedented development of the Arab press. The Revolution was celebrated in Jerusalem by demonstrations involving a mixture of Arabs, Armenians, Turks, Greeks, and Jews, to whom access to the Temple Mount was exceptionally granted. The sixty Arabs elected to the Parliament of Constantinople, whether notable or

[26] Notably in his poem 'To a tyrant', published in Baghdad in 1905.

militant, supported the Ottoman perspective of a plural empire. They were all the more disappointed by the growing inflexibility of the CUP, noticeable from 1909 onwards, and the imposition, the following year, of Turkish as the only language to be used in the administration of the provinces. But it was the Italian invasion of Libya in 1911, and the inability of the Young Turks to defend this Arab land, which swung the Arab patriots into opposition to Constantinople. In Palestine, the pressure exerted by Zionist immigration intensified grievances against the CUP, accused of complicity. An 'Arab Congress' was held in Paris in June 1913, with delegates from Syria and Egypt, both Christians and Muslims, without their sectarian affiliation being highlighted. This congress advocated both a stronger association of Arabs in the decisions of the central power, and an advanced decentralization of their provinces, while supporting the 'reformist demands of the Ottoman Armenians'.

The 'long nineteenth century' covered five clearly differentiated areas in the Middle East: Egypt, whose plans for an authoritarian moderniz- ation, extended to Syria from 1831 to 1841, did not survive its being put under colonial tutelage in 1882; Anatolia, traumatized by the fallout from the conflicts with Russia and in the Balkans, against the backdrop of the Armenian crisis that had been ongoing since 1894; Syria and Iraq, where the Nahda had long maintained the dream of a renewed Ottomanism; Persia, abandoned by its sovereigns to an uneven process of development until the revolutionary upheaval of 1906–1911; and finally Arabia, where the theocratic project of the Sauds, crushed in 1818 and again defeated in 1891,[27] was relaunched by the Wahhabi reconquest of Riyadh in 1902. This last event seemed of little importance to contemporaries and did not assume its full significance until much later. It was the rise of nation- alisms that subsequently mobilized attention and energy, as the risks of 'balkanization' seemed serious in Anatolia. This entire chapter has shown how such collective identities were laboriously constructed, with a permanent tension between national self-assertion and community claims, whether ethnic or religious. The Arab Congress of Paris was the last attempt at conciliation between the Young Turks, who were

[27] The Sauds restored a Wahhabi emirate in Riyadh in 1843, but were expelled by a rival clan supported by the Ottomans in 1891, and were forced to take refuge in Kuwait.

increasingly tempted by pan-Turanism, and the Arabs, who were increasingly demanding when it came to their national rights.[28] The First World War would consummate their split, bringing the Middle East into a fundamentally new era.

[28] The secret society *Al-Ahd* ('The Pact'), founded in August 1913, very quickly gained the support of the vast majority of Arab officers in the Ottoman army, under the authority of a former Unionist, a hero of the anti-Italian resistance in Libya.

Chronology

May 1803	First Wahhabi occupation of Mecca.
May 1807	The janissaries overthrow Sultan Selim III.
March 1811	Massacre of the Mamluks in Cairo.
September 1818	Fall of the first Wahhabi emirate.
March 1821	Beginning of the Greek War of Independence.
May 1826	Rifa'a at-Tahtawi and forty-four Egyptian scholars in Paris.
June 1826	Massacre of the janissaries in Constantinople.
July 1839–June 1861	Abdulmejid I, Ottoman sultan.
November 1839	Beginning of the Tanzimat of the Ottoman Empire.
September 1848–May 1896	Naser al-Din, shah of Persia.
January 1852	Execution of the reformist Prime Minister Amir Kabir in Tehran.
February 1856	Edict of emancipation of Ottoman minorities.
April 1861	Constitution of Tunisia (suspended in April 1864).
August 1876–April 1909	Abdul Hamid II, Ottoman sultan.
December 1876	Ottoman constitution (suspended in February 1878).
July 1881	Ottoman victory against the revolt of the Kurdish tribes.
December 1891	Anti-smoking fatwa in Persia.
August 1894–December 1896	Wave of massacres of Armenians.
August 1896	Armenian attack on the Ottoman Bank.
January 1902	Wahhabi capture of Riyadh.
July 1905	Failed attempt to assassinate the Ottoman sultan.
December 1906	Persian constitution, completed in October 1907.
June 1908	Seizure of Parliament in Tehran by the Imperial Guard.
July 1908	The Young Turks seize power in Constantinople.
November 1908	Election of the first Ottoman Parliament.

April 1909	Failure of the counter-revolution in Constantinople.
July 1909	Abdication of the shah of Persia under revolutionary pressure.
December 1911	Dissolution of the Persian Parliament.
October 1912–May 1913	Ottoman rout in the First Balkan War.
June 1913	Arab General Congress in Paris.
June–July 1913	Reconquest of Edirne in the Second Balkan War.

Further reading

Agoston, Gabor, *Guns for the sultan: military power and the weapons industry in the Ottoman Empire* (Cambridge: Cambridge University Press, 2005).

Bodman, Herbert, *Political factions in Aleppo, 1760–1826* (Chapel Hill: University of North Carolina Press, 1963).

Doumani, Beshara, *Rediscovering Palestine: merchants and peasants in Jabal Nablus, 1700–1900* (Berkeley: University of California Press, 1995).

Fahmy, Khaled, *All the Pasha's men: Mehmed Ali, his army and the making of modern Egypt* (Cambridge: Cambridge University Press, 1997).

Hourani, Albert, *Arabic thought in the liberal age, 1798–1939* (Cambridge: Cambridge University Press, 1983).

Kawakibi (al-), Abdul Rahman, *The nature of tyranny and the devastating results of oppression* (London: Hurst, 2021).

Makdisi, Ussama, *Age of coexistence: the ecumenical frame and the making of the modern Arab world* (Berkeley: University of California Press, 2019).

Nakash, Yitzhak, *The Shi'is of Iraq* (Princeton, NJ: Princeton University Press, 1994).

Rogan, Eugene, L., *The Arabs: a history*, third edition (London: Penguin Books, 2018).

Tahtawi, Rifaa, *An Imam in Paris: account of a stay in France by an Egyptian cleric (1826–1831)*, translated by Daniel L. Newman (London: Saqi, 2004).

EIGHT

The time of mandates (1914–1949)

On 2 August 1914, the day after Germany entered the war against Russia, the three Pashas forged a secret alliance with Berlin. They immediately set up a Special Organization (SO),[1] a structure for propaganda and repression with a mandate as obscure as its powers were exorbitant. The repeal of the capitulations on 9 September further widened the gap between Constantinople and the Triple Entente of France, Russia, and Great Britain. On 29 October, the Ottoman fleet attacked the Russians in the Black Sea. Three days later, Russia declared war on the Ottoman Empire, followed the next day by France and Great Britain. On 14 November, the sultan, in his role as caliph, proclaimed jihad against the French, British, and Russian Allies. This declaration, drawn up by German Orientalists and announced by the *sheikholeslam*, was widely disseminated in Turkish, Arabic, Persian, and Urdu by SO agents and Berlin propaganda.[2] Yet it had a negligible impact, especially among the Arabs, whose national self-assertion now supplanted any consideration of Islamic solidarity. London decided, as a precaution, to formalize its protectorate over Egypt, after more than thirty years of occupation. The khedive was deposed in favour of his uncle, granted the title of 'sultan' for the occasion. The British forces suffered the shock of an offensive launched from Damascus by Djemal Pasha and his fourth army, supervised by German advisers; it was halted on the Suez Canal in February 1915, then gradually driven back out of Sinai.

The troops from Great Britain were supplemented by the Army of India and by contingents recruited in Canada, Australia, and New

---

[1] In Turkish, *Teshkilat-i Mahsusa*.
[2] Historians often used the expression 'jihad made in Germany' to describe this operation.

Zealand. The Allied landing at Gallipoli on 25 April 1915[3] was directly aimed at Constantinople, which was saved, nine months later, only after the death of 140,000 soldiers on both sides. In this Battle of the Dardanelles, Mustafa Kemal won both his stripes as a general and a formidable reputation for heroism and efficiency. As for the Army of India, it had a string of successes following its landing in the extreme south of Iraq in November 1914. After Basra, in October 1915 it occupied the strategic position of Kut, a stepping stone to Baghdad along the Tigris. But the British forces' assault on the capital was halted[4] and they were forced to withdraw to Kut, where they were besieged for five months before capitulating in April 1916. This was a severe blow for the Allies, and the German–Turkish camp, already strengthened by the resistance of the Dardanelles, believed itself to be the master of the Middle East. Djemal Pasha hanged some twenty Arab patriots in Damascus and Beirut, including delegates to the 1913 congress in Paris.

The 'Arab revolt'

It was in this context that the British High Commissioner in Cairo, Henry McMahon, and the Ottoman governor of Mecca, Sharif Hussein, negotiated the entry into the war of an Arab contingent alongside the Allies. Hussein was mandated by the Arab nationalists of Damascus, while his Hashemite affiliation with the Prophet Muhammad[5] boosted his claims to a new Arab caliphate. This traditional leader thus became the paradoxical champion of the Nahda in what we would today describe as its 'nationalist' and 'Islamist' aspects. The sharif's uprising also held out the possibility of a rapid takeover of the Hejaz, which would be the first 'liberated' Arab territory. Hussein demanded the establishment in Damascus of an 'Arab kingdom' for the entire region, a demand that

[3] Since then, 25 April has been celebrated as ANZAC (Australia and New Zealand Army Corps) Day. On 26 April 1915, Italy entered the war on the basis of a secret treaty with France and Great Britain, who offered it part of the Mediterranean coast of Turkey.
[4] The decisive battle took place in November 1915 on the site of Ctesiphon, the former capital of the Sassanid Empire (see above, p. 13).
[5] 'Hashemite' is derived from 'Hashim', the great-grandfather of Muhammad (see above, p. 33). The title of 'sharif' refers to this Prophetic ancestry.

McMahon eventually accepted, despite his specious distinction between 'Arabs' of the interior and 'Levantines' of the coast. It was on the basis of these exchanges of letters that the sharif launched his 'Arab revolt' in June 1916. It was in fact a 'revolution' (*thawra*), the first of a long series of 'Arab revolutions' to be disguised as simple 'revolts' in the press of the time and in subsequent historiography, as if the Arabs were only good at revolting, but incapable of carrying out a revolution worthy of the name.

Yet this was indeed a revolutionary process, in which the supporters of Hussein, led by his son Faisal, seized the Hejaz and besieged the Turkish garrison of Medina. Bedouins from local tribes were joined by former Ottoman officers and volunteers galvanized by the prospect of an Arab kingdom. The Allies gave them very limited material support, despite the success of the latter's operations along the railway linking the insurgent territories to Damascus. It would take all the talent of T. E. Lawrence ('of Arabia') to accredit the myth of a European man importing into Arabia the immemorial techniques of the *razzia* (raid). The reality was that the Arab contribution to the Allied war effort was substantial, given the few means the latter provided. To Hussein, who in November 1916 proclaimed himself 'King of the Arabs', London and Paris only granted the title of 'King of Hejaz'. And for good reason: even before the launch of the Arab revolt, the two European powers had secretly concluded a pact to divide the Middle East. Thanks to this 'Sykes–Picot Agreement',[6] France granted itself Cilicia, Lebanon, and the Syrian coast (the 'blue zone'), as well as a 'zone of influence' extending from Damascus and Aleppo to Mosul. Great Britain, for its part, would achieve direct control of the provinces of Baghdad and Basra (the 'red zone'), in addition to a 'zone of influence' extending from the River Jordan to Kirkuk. Palestine was internationalized in a 'brown zone', in order to neutralize the claims of France and Russia to 'protect' Catholics and Orthodox respectively. The resumption by the British of their offensive in Iraq, with the occupation of Baghdad in March 1917, already enabled them to control the red zone that France had recognized for them.

The entry into the war of the United States, in April 1917, had no military impact in the Middle East, but it placed on the agenda the right

---

[6] Named after the two negotiators, Mark Sykes and François Georges-Picot.

of peoples to self-determination, of which President Woodrow Wilson was a strong supporter. The capture of the port of Aqaba by Faisal in July came as British troops were still bogged down at the gates of Gaza. The Arab insurgents crossed the River Jordan, carrying out raids to support the campaign of General Edmund Allenby, to whom the conquest of Gaza, in November, finally opened the way to Palestine. It was then that the British government published the 'Balfour Declaration', in fact a letter addressed by its Foreign Secretary, Arthur Balfour, to the Zionist leadership. He pledged to support 'the establishment in Palestine of a national home for the Jewish people', subject to respect 'for the civil and religious rights of existing non-Jewish communities'. This was a historic victory for the Zionist movement, which, twenty years after its foundation, saw the fulfilment of the hopes it had placed in British imperialism. A Jewish Legion of a few thousand volunteers fought under the British flag in Palestine.[7] For the Arabs, on the other hand, to be reduced in Palestine to 'non-Jewish communities' devoid of national rights came as a severe shock. This was aggravated by the revelation, following the Bolshevik takeover in Moscow, of the content of the Sykes–Picot Agreement. Despite this twofold betrayal of the British promises of an Arab kingdom, however, the faithful supporters of Sharif Hussein had no choice but to continue their struggle for liberation, hoping for US support for their aspirations when the time came.

The Armenian genocide

In January 1915, two months after the start of hostilities, Russia inflicted a resounding defeat, on the Caucasus front, on the third army of Enver Pasha. The military losses amounted to tens of thousands, while the soldiery of both sides sowed terror in the local populations. Enver ordered the disarmament of the Armenian conscripts, who were sent to labour camps and mostly eliminated there. Turkish propaganda took up the obsessions of Abdul Hamid II directed against an Armenian 'enemy within', in which Assyrians of all denominations were included. But

[7] Mobilized by the charismatic Ze'ev Jabotinsky, this Jewish Legion recruited in comparable proportions in the United States, Great Britain, and the Palestinian Yishuv.

where the Armenian crisis of 1894–1896 had proceeded as much from criminal complacency as from the will of the state, this time it was a plan of systematic liquidation that Talaat Pasha, the Minister of the Interior, persuaded the leadership of the CUP to endorse. The threat of an Allied assault on the capital was coupled with the fear of a comparable operation in largely Armenian Cilicia. On 24 April 1915, on the eve of the Gallipoli landing, hundreds of leading Armenian figures were rounded up by the Constantinople police. This was the start of a wave of carnage perpetrated in eastern Anatolia and Cilicia by government units, assisted by often Kurdish militias.[8] On 24 May, France, Great Britain, and Russia denounced the 'crimes against humanity' of which 'the harmless Armenian population was a victim', noting the 'personal responsibility' of all those who were direct or indirect accomplices. But the Turkish authorities retaliated, two days later, by passing a law of 'deportation' for the Armenians; this law was further tightened the following month. As for the SO, the armed wing of the extermination, it eliminated the evidence of its crimes easily, as its action was covered by state secrecy and imposed on sometimes reluctant officials.

The killings were carried out on the spot, with an orgy of rape and looting; immediately afterwards, the surviving Armenians and Assyrians were deported to Syria, either by rail or, more commonly, in what were true 'death marches', decimated by hunger, thirst, exhaustion, and brigand attacks. A smaller flow of deportees was sent to Urfa and Mosul under equally atrocious conditions. Djemal Pasha, faced with the Allied blockade of the Syrian coasts and the withdrawal of his troops from Sinai, confined the deportees in Aleppo, to divert them towards the Euphrates Valley. It was there that concentration camps, in the literal sense of the term, were established in Maskanah, Dipsi, and Raqqa. Privation and illness consumed tens of thousands of the living dead there until April 1916. The same macabre litany unfolded on the course of the Khabur, which flows into the Euphrates south of Deir ez-Zor. In this city, where massacres were still being perpetrated in the autumn of 1916,

---

[8] The governor of Van, a brother-in-law of Enver Pasha, was responsible for the death of approximately 50,000 Armenians during the month of April 1915 alone. Thousands of criminals were also freed from Ottoman jails to be enrolled into the *tchétés*, the auxiliary militias of the SO.

the Turkish commander transformed the Catholic church into a brothel for female Armenian slaves. In general, sexual violence was commonplace and went unpunished. As for cases of Armenians being rescued by the population, more often in Syria than in Anatolia, they were very risky and often accompanied by the conversion of the survivors, who adopted a new identity.

The appalling toll of the Armenian genocide is generally estimated at 1.5 million victims. Armenian sources have validated this by subtracting half a million survivors from an initial population estimated at 2 million Armenians. But even those for whom this tragedy must be put into the perspective of a truly appalling conflict admit a minimum toll of 600,000–850,000 killed. The Assyrian tragedy, referred to by the Syriac term 'Sayfo' ('Sword'), has been less well studied but is believed to have resulted in 250,000 deaths out of a population of 620,000. Whatever the figures used, the desire to exterminate these Christian populations is indisputable. In July 1919, the Ottoman courts condemned to death in absentia the three Pashas, who had fled abroad. Talaat would be assassinated in Berlin, in March 1921, by an Armenian survivor, who was ultimately acquitted. The Polish jurist Raphael Lemkin, present at this trial, coined the term 'genocide' in 1943; the word was validated at Nuremberg, then by the United Nations. Thus, the Armenian genocide was described as such only after more than a generation. Ottoman Turkey, the country of the judgments of 1919, could no doubt have assumed this historical responsibility. But Mustafa Kemal, as we shall see, granted amnesty to the condemned Unionists in 1923 and founded modern Turkey on this basis. This has resulted to this day in a conflict of memories between the Armenian people and the Turkish Republic, symbolized by the clash between the commemorations of 24 April 1915, for the beginning of the Armenian genocide, and 25 April 1915, for the epic Turkish resistance to the invasion.

The peace to end all wars

We left General Allenby, victor in Gaza in November 1917, about to drive Djemal Pasha out of Palestine. The following month, he solemnly entered Jerusalem, where martial law was proclaimed in all the languages of the city. He organized the military administration of hitherto Ottoman territories into Occupied Enemy Territory Administrations.[9] This allowed him to postpone indefinitely the application of his government's contradictory promises to the French, the Arabs, and the Zionists. Damascus fell in September 1918 and Allenby let Faisal and his supporters hold a victory parade there. Their assistance was indeed essential for the next battle, which, in Aleppo, triggered the Turkish capitulation, effective on the Greek island of Moudros, on 31 October. This armistice ended the First World War in the Middle East, eleven days before the end of hostilities in Europe. Syria in the broad sense emerged exhausted from the conflict, in which some 300,000 civilians had probably perished due to the famine induced by the European blockade and aggravated, in 1915, by a terrible invasion of locusts. Different sources estimate the proportion of war victims at a tenth of the Syrian population, or even a third of the population of Mount Lebanon. Iraq had also suffered greatly from the hostilities, even if it was in Anatolia that the losses were the most appalling, even without the genocide of the Armenians and Assyrians.

Europeans are still struggling to grasp the extent of the trauma represented by the First World War in the Middle East, a trauma accentuated by the calamitous legacy of the Paris Peace Conference. Opened in January 1919, it admitted Faisal only as part of the Hejaz delegation, thus denying him any legitimacy to speak on behalf of Arab nationalists. A 'Syrian General Congress' nevertheless met in Damascus in June 1919 and its eighty-four members, elected or co-opted, advocated the inclusion of Palestine and Lebanon in a federal Syria. But the isolationist wave in the United States weakened President Wilson, who failed to gain Senate backing for his League of Nations project. This, the first international organization with a global vocation, was therefore established without the man who had been its most ardent defender, leaving French and British imperialism completely free to bury the right of peoples to self-determination. In January 1920, the League held its first meeting in London, before transferring its headquarters to Geneva. Two months later, the Parliament in Damascus proclaimed the independence of Syria,

[9] There were three OETAs. The South OETA corresponded to Palestine (under British occupation), the North OETA to Lebanon and the Syrian coast (under French occupation), and the East OETA to inland Syria and Transjordan (controlled by Faisal with British posts).

with Faisal as constitutional sovereign. The colonial powers ignored this: at their meeting in San Remo in April 1920, they attributed League of Nations 'mandates' to France (over Syria, including Lebanon) and Great Britain (over Palestine and Iraq). The territorial reconfiguration of the contemporary Middle East, too often wrongly attributed to the Sykes–Picot Agreement of 1916,[10] was well and truly defined only four years later – in San Remo.

This colonial diktat fanned the flames in Palestine, where riots had just rocked Jerusalem. In May 1920, there was an uprising in Iraq, civilian at first and then military. It took many months and probably 10,000 Arab deaths for the British to suppress this new revolution (*thawra*). In July, French troops, leaving Beirut, crushed the Arab nationalists on the road to Damascus, before deploying throughout Syria. In September, 'Greater Lebanon' was proclaimed over a territory that went far beyond Beirut and Mount Lebanon to include predominantly Muslim areas.[11] The French representative carved the rest of Syria into four 'states': Damascus, Aleppo, the 'State of the Druze', and the 'State of the Alawites'. France relied on the Alawites to play the same role as a relay of colonial influence that the Maronites of Lebanon willingly assumed. A large autonomy was also granted to the province of Antioch, called the '*sanjak* of Alexandretta', of which more than a third of the population was Turkish. In return, Mustafa Kemal, with whom this specific status was negotiated, abandoned the anti-French guerrillas of Aleppo and northern Syria.

Community antagonisms were therefore neither spontaneous nor atavistic, nor even inherited from the Ottoman past, but clearly constructed and exacerbated by colonial domination. France established an increasingly rigid system in Lebanon, where each religious denomination had its specific function. In Syria, it relied more on the minorities of Islam than on the Eastern Christians, in order to neutralize the Sunni majority of the population, which was deeply attached to Arab nationalism. As for Great Britain, it brought Faisal, the fallen king of

[10] This agreement was never implemented as such and in San Remo, Palestine, internationalized by Sykes–Picot, came under British mandate.

[11] These were the Beqaa and South Lebanon, i.e. mainly Shiite areas, as well as Tripoli and its hinterland, which were very largely Sunni.

Damascus, under its wing and placed him in August 1921 on the throne of Iraq. This manoeuvre was supported by the organization of a single-question plebiscite, in which 96% of the voters expressed support for Faisal's coronation. While the anti-colonial resistance brought Sunnis and Shiites together, the British rebuilt the Iraqi state around the former officers (all Sunnis) of the Ottoman army. Such an Iraqi construction, dominated from Baghdad by Sunni Arabs, was from the very start fraught with tensions, since it included the governorates of Basra (mostly Shia) and of Mosul (largely Kurdish).[12] This new order was completed in 1922 with the incorporation of the Balfour Declaration into the British Mandate for Palestine, which led to the boycott of the mandatory institutions by the Arab notables and people. London, however, excluded from this mandate the emirate of Transjordan, a buffer state between the River Jordan and Iraq, entrusted to Abdullah, one of Faisal's brothers.[13]

In that same year, 1922, London granted Egypt the first postcolonial independence in the Arab world. This independence remained strictly limited by the prerogatives that the former protector continued to assume over the Suez Canal, military affairs, and the guarantee of foreign interests, significantly linked to the protection of minorities. It was the culmination of three years of protest against the protectorate, which began in March 1919 with the arrest of the delegation (*wafd*) that the nationalists wanted to send to the Paris conference. This humiliation triggered a veritable popular uprising which displayed its non-violence in the face of an over-armed occupier. Civil disobedience, which Gandhi was at the time failing to mobilize in India,[14] inspired British boycotts in Egypt, go-slows and peaceful processions, with the participation of women – this may have been purely symbolic, but it was still

---

[12] In 1925, the League of Nations, under pressure from Turkey, confirmed the integration into Iraq of the former Ottoman province of Mosul. This city was predominantly Arab, unlike the historically Kurdish cities of Erbil and Sulaymaniyah.

[13] This exclusion of Transjordan from the British mandate, accepted by the Zionist movement in return for the incorporation of the Balfour Declaration, led to the so-called 'revisionist' dissidence of the supporters of Jabotinsky, who continued to claim the eastern bank of the Jordan.

[14] The Amritsar massacre in April 1919 put a damper on Gandhi's non-violent campaign; he relaunched it, this time successfully, the following year.

unprecedented. The crescent and the cross were brandished together in an affirmation of national unity, while a Coptic cleric intervened for the first time at the University of Al-Azhar. The wave of protest itself continued for months, despite incurring a thousand or so victims. The pacifist strategy, the multi-sectarian activism, and the feminine dimension of this 1919 revolution would return in the 2011 *thawra* against the dictatorship of Mubarak. Allenby, who had become high commissioner in Cairo, managed to stabilize the country only by scuttling the protectorate. But the 1922 Treaty of Independence granted Great Britain significant capabilities of intervention. Sultan Fuad then assumed the title of 'king of Egypt' in a constitutional framework where political life was now played out between the palace, the nationalists,[15] and the British, who continued to be excessively interventionist.

From Sèvres to Lausanne

At their San Remo conference in April 1920, the European powers decided not only on the fate of the Arab Middle East, but also on that of Ottoman Turkey. The treaty signed on this basis in Sèvres, four months later, involved the dismemberment of the country between Greece, France, and Italy, which were granted the regions of Izmir, Cilicia, and the Dodecanese respectively. Kurdish autonomy, guaranteeing the rights of the Assyrians, was established in the southeast of Anatolia and, in the event of referral to the League of Nations by the local populations, could lead very quickly to an independent Kurdistan. Armenia, led by the Dashnak party in Yerevan, signed the treaty and was obliged to define its border by arbitration with Turkey. Finally, Constantinople and the straits were demilitarized and the capitulations restored. The unconscionable nature of this treaty allowed Mustafa Kemal, seen as a hero after his resistance in the Dardanelles, to raise the standard of resistance in Ankara, where the 'Grand National Assembly' dubbed him supreme leader.[16] In a few months, he routed the Armenian army and

[15] Their party was called the Wafd, echoing the 'delegation' (*wafd*) of 1919.
[16] As during the Young Turk Revolution of 1908 (see above, p. 225), the armed uprising invoked the name of the sultan-caliph so as to fight his government more effectively.

made a pact with the USSR, which itself would absorb the Republic of Armenia. Thus strengthened on his eastern front, Kemal negotiated with Italy and France to better concentrate against the Greek invader, finally driven back in September 1922. The fire in Izmir then symbolized the end of Asian Greece, with the expulsion of 200,000 to 300,000 Greeks from the Aegean coast. In the process, the sultanate was abolished, even if the caliphate still remained in place.[17]

Kemal successfully led the fight for national liberation, the crushing of separatist aims, and the anti-Ottoman revolution. His success was sealed, in July 1923, by the treaty of Lausanne, which replaced that of Sèvres. The full sovereignty of Turkey over its entire territory was recognized by all the signatories, and an exchange of populations with Greece completed the homogenization of Anatolia. A decade of conflict had left the country devastated, but above all stripped of the Ottoman heritage of ethnic and religious pluralism. State denial of the Armenian genocide stemmed from this refounding of Turkish identity through war.[18] As for Kurdish aspirations, they would henceforth be equated with the dark designs of Sèvres and, as such, mercilessly repressed. The republic was proclaimed in October 1923, with Ankara as its capital and Kemal as its President, while Constantinople officially became Istanbul. Nothing therefore stood in the way of the abolition of the caliphate, made effective in March 1924.

The secularism of Mustafa Kemal, imported into Turkish by the neologism *laiklik*, was, however, the complete opposite of the French separation between Church and state. It was a Sunni state dogma, of the Hanafi rite, that a bureaucratized Islam now sought to impose, in line with Ottoman practice and its denial of minority persuasions, whether Alevi, Alawite, or Shiite. The future Atatürk[19] was above all determined to eliminate the slightest rival power: the fight against 'religious reaction' (*irtica*) enabled him, during the same year, 1925, to impose a one-party regime, to repress a Kurdish uprising, to prohibit Sufi brotherhoods, and

[17] The last sultan, Mehmed V, was exiled, replaced as caliph by his cousin Abdulmejid II.

[18] The general amnesty decreed by Kemal in March 1923 repealed the verdicts rendered in 1919 in absentia against those responsible for the Armenian genocide.

[19] This title of 'Father of the Turks' was solemnly granted to him in 1934 by a unanimous vote of the National Assembly.

to ban any other headgear than the hat. This last prohibition, far from being trivial, aroused all the more protests as it marked the intrusion of the modern state into the individual sphere. Education was unified around public service alone, just as justice was now based on nothing but a civil code and a penal code of European inspiration. In 1928, Sunday became a public holiday and the Latin alphabet replaced the Arabic alphabet. In 1929, women obtained the right to vote, shortly after the British, but fifteen years before the French. It was not only in the Middle East that Kemalist modernization appeared to be in the vanguard of progress.

The Saudization of Arabia

A frequent error in the current debate on the Middle East lies in the claim that Muslims are inconsolable 'orphans' of the caliphate, and have been intent ever since 1924 on compensating for this loss. The reality is that the abolition by the Turkish deputies was an act of internal sovereignty, civil and not religious in nature. By 1914, the Ottoman caliphate had already revealed its inability to mobilize Muslims against the Allies, even in the name of jihad. As for the Arab caliphate, it had already been, from 1258 to 1517, nothing but a symbolic guarantee of the reign of the Mamluks. It is true that France and Great Britain, in order to better bind the Muslim populations of their colonies, would gladly push one of their protégés towards claiming the title of caliph. But even though the sultan of Morocco, encouraged by Paris, could indeed claim prophetic ancestry, he occupied too peripheral a position on the regional chessboard. As for the king of Egypt, backed by London, he suffered both from his constitutional status and from the Macedonian origins of his lineage. Sharif Hussein, the ruler of the Hejaz, thus believed the time was ripe to relaunch the 'Islamist' ambitions of his Arab revolt of 1916, now that his 'nationalist' dream had been shattered by the mandate system. In March 1924, he claimed the title 'caliph' of which Atatürk had just deprived the Ottomans. Four months later, he convened an Islamic congress in Mecca, during the *hajj*, in order to consolidate his own caliphate. He already had two sons on the thrones of Baghdad and Amman; now he could transfer the crown of the Hejaz to a third.

This manoeuvre by the patriarch of the Hashemites was countered by an offensive led by Abdelaziz Ibn Saud, the leader of their sworn enemies. As the master of Riyadh since 1902, he fostered the third project of a Wahhabi theocracy, a project which, unlike the two preceding ones, managed to prove enduring in both time and space. Ibn Saud organized the most fanatical of the Bedouins into the shock troops of the *Ikhwan*, literally the 'Brothers'. Thanks to them, in 1913, he seized the predominantly Shiite province of Al-Ahsa, on the eastern coast. In 1915, Great Britain recognized his sovereignty over Najd and Al-Ahsa, but without asking him to contribute to the anti-Ottoman campaign. London could gauge the depth of the hostility of the Wahhabi puritans for the Hashemite masters of Mecca and Medina, who repeatedly prohibited them from performing the *hajj*. Ibn Saud thus saved his resources during the First World War and then consolidated his intransigent emirate. The French destruction of the 'Arab kingdom' of Damascus and the British patronage of the Hashemites reinforced his hand even more vis-à-vis Sharif Hussein, whose caliphal ambitions he decided to wreck.

Ibn Saud seized Mecca in October 1924, before conquering, after a long siege, the strategic port of Jeddah the following year. He then joined the title of 'king of Hejaz' to that of 'sultan of Najd', before being recognized as such by the European powers and by the USSR. Sharif Hussein was forced into exile in Cyprus because London forbade him to settle with his son in Transjordan, which was already frequently the target of Wahhabi raids. Ibn Saud, together with his religious police, kept a close eye to ensure that the strictest respect was paid to an obscurantist morality, but he was confronted with the one-upmanship of the *Ikhwan*, who insisted that expansion by jihad must continue, first towards Iraq. Their dissident movement was shattered in March 1929, with the decisive help of the British air force. Ibn Saud thus overcame the obstacle of his own extremists, just as the Abbasids, Fatimids, and Safavids had done to stabilize their nascent dynasty. The triptych of Ibn Khaldun that had operated in the course of these glorious precedents also sheds light on the rise of Ibn Saud, whose family 'group', inspired by Wahhabi 'preaching', established the 'power' still dominant in Saudi Arabia today, by expanding from the 'periphery' of Najd to the most revered 'centre' of Islam. The proclamation of the 'Kingdom of Saudi Arabia' in September 1932 formalized an unprecedented regime in which one family seized supreme power, with the designation of 'Saudi' subjects being derived from the name of the reigning family.[20]

The kingdom of Ibn Saud and his doctrine from another age imposed themselves on the ruins of the Hashemite plans for an Arab kingdom in Damascus, then for a renovated caliphate in Mecca. The dynamic of the betrayal of the Nahda by Great Britain and France thus resulted in implanting, in the symbolic heart of Islam, the most retrograde version of its dogma. The colonial empires obviously never considered the long-term consequences of this regression, just as their paternalistic, not to say racist, prejudices prevented them from letting the Arabs take their destiny into their own hands. But it was the refusal to treat the Arab allies on an equal footing, at the end of the First World War, which led to handing over Mecca and Medina to the Wahhabis, even though the latter had remained neutral against the Ottomans. Long before the manna represented by oil, control of the two most sacred places in Islam provided the Sauds with a tremendous power of influence. In addition, by eliminating the Hashemite kingdom of the Hejaz, Ibn Saud also eliminated the only post-Ottoman Arab state that, like his own, had never been colonized.[21] At the very beginning of the autumn of 1932, there was a cruel coincidence between the proclamation of Saudi Arabia and the treaty of independence of Iraq – an independence that was severely restrained by Great Britain, as had been that of Egypt ten years earlier. Ibn Saud and his successors would thus be able to base their status as Custodian of the Two Holy Cities[22] on their heritage, untainted by any colonial subjection.

From Persia to Iran

The Qajars officially remained neutral during the First World War, but this neutrality did not spare Persia the ravages of the combined interventions of the Turks against the Russians, the Germans against

---

[20] By way of comparison, nationals of the 'Hashemite Kingdom of Jordan' are called Jordanians, not 'Hashemians'.

[21] The case of the imamate of Yemen was unique because of its autarkic nature, the south of the country having been under British rule for a century.

[22] It was not until 1986 that this title, inherited from the Ottoman Empire (see above, p. 150), was officially assumed by the Saudi monarch.

the British, and the Allies against the Bolsheviks, against a backdrop of tribal anarchy, famine, and epidemic. Ahmad Shah, who ascended to the throne as a teenager in 1909 in the midst of revolutionary turmoil, remained in Tehran in 1915 only under pressure from London: the British were anxious to avoid any further disintegration of his kingdom. The Qajar sovereign, banned from the Paris conference because of 'neutrality', granted exorbitant privileges to Great Britain in 1919. The British negotiators paid their Persian counterparts, including even the shah, handsomely to conclude this agreement. Patriotic indignation was all the more intense in the country, which condemned the agreement to remain a dead letter. Azerbaijan, always at the forefront of the contestation of imperial power, protested under the name of *Azadestan*, 'the Land of the Free'. The unrest was so serious that the people of Tehran welcomed with relative relief the February 1921 coup by Reza Khan, the Persian commander of the Cossack guard.

The new leader treated Ahmad Shah mildly and summoned the Parliament for the first time since 1915. He obtained from the USSR the withdrawal of the Red Army from the north of the country, without, however, attracting hostility from Great Britain. He reduced, one by one, the centres of regional rebellion, consolidating his image as a restorer of the state. While Minister of War, he was appointed head of government in October 1923 by Ahmad Shah, who now preferred to live on the Côte d'Azur. Tempted for a moment by the idea of establishing a republic of which he would be, like Mustafa Kemal in Turkey, the first President, Reza Khan was dissuaded by the resolute opposition of the ayatollahs. In Qom, he came to an agreement with them to preserve the monarchical principle and, as a pledge of goodwill, he launched a campaign against the Bahais, accused of apostasy by the Shiite clergy. The stage was set for the deposition of the Qajar sovereign by Parliament and the election of a Constituent Assembly, which, in December 1925, voted for the advent of a new dynasty, the Pahlavis, headed by Reza, promoted from khan to shah.[23]

The beginning of the Pahlavi era was accompanied by the inauguration of a calendar specific to Persia, in which the solar year began

---

[23] Reza Khan chose this name, which means 'heroic' and refers to the Pahlavi language of the Sassanid Empire, also known as 'Middle Persian'.

with Nowrouz, i.e. the spring equinox, and was dated from 622, or the Prophet's Hijra. Reza Shah, aware of the considerable backwardness of Persia compared to Turkey and Egypt, embarked on a proactive programme of authoritarian modernization. The state monopoly on sugar and tea, the abolition of the capitulations, and the establishment of a national bank made it possible to free up financing for major infrastructure projects, including the north–south railway and the beginning of a road network. A sedentary lifestyle was imposed with extreme violence on the tribal world, and was aimed as much to stabilize the countryside as to prevent dissent. This imperial Jacobinism, inevitably brutal in a country plagued by so many centrifugal tendencies, was fuelled by territorial reorganization, the competitive recruitment of civil servants, and, of course, compulsory conscription (with two years of service, followed by more than twenty years in the reserve). The former Cossack officer, however, proved to be much less effective in this great military endeavour than in the reform of public education, the programmes of which were extended to private and foreign schools in 1928.

Reza Shah had one major advantage over the Shiite clergy: the ayatollahs of Najaf had been obliged to submit to the British Mandate over Iraq and had thus lost their ability to intervene, as in the Qajar era, on the Persian scene; thus, in 1927, the hierarchy in Qom failed to organize protests against the imposition of Western dress, with suit and kepi, on men. This significant defeat was aggravated by the marginalization of the clergy by the very dynamics of the modernization of justice, the ulama gradually losing their judicial and notarial powers as, little by little, the civil code and criminal procedures eliminated any references to sharia. Clerics still benefited from the tithe that the Shiite faithful paid them directly and Reza Shah was unable to proceed with a cavalier bureaucratization of the type pursued by Kemal. But the imperial power continued to grow, invoking the glory of the pre-Islamic heritage of the country, renamed Iran, the 'country of the Aryans', in 1935. That year, a demonstration was bloodily repressed in the very sanctuary of Mashhad. Boosted by this sacrilege, Reza Shah decreed the general prohibition of the veil, a measure before which even Kemal had recoiled. But this diktat was less a mark of the emancipation of Iranian women than an affirmation of state absolutism.

French sectarianism

France's Third Republic, despite the secularism it professed at home, projected a very aggressive sectarianism in the Middle East. It was a question not simply of the policy of 'divide and conquer' that Great Britain happily practised in order to establish its domination, but of an essentialist ideology which established communities in order to set them against one another. Once Syria had been amputated from Greater Lebanon in 1920, it was itself cut up into 'states', each one supposed to correspond to a dominant group. Playing with sectarian fire in this way eventually proved harmful for France, when an uprising that started in the heart of the 'Druze State' in July 1925 reached Damascus and spread throughout the country. The bombardment of the capital in October failed to halt this revolution (*thawra*), whose 'national council' demanded the independence of Syria, with equality between citizens of all origins. The nationalist insurrection was once again caricatured as a 'revolt', or even a 'Druze revolt', to hide its patriotic dimension. The colonial army, augmented by a contingent transferred from Morocco, recruited its auxiliaries from minority populations, playing the Circassians against the Druze, before enlisting Alawites, Kurds, and Armenians under the banner of its 'special troops'. Damascus was placed in a state of siege and its surroundings were methodically scoured. In the middle of the conflict, in January 1926, the French authorities organized an electoral masquerade, which they thought would hoodwink the League of Nations.[24] The uprising continued for several more months, before giving way in the face of an overwhelming balance of power.

France, bogged down in this military adventure in Syria, simply showed even more concern for the 'star pupil' of its mandate, namely Lebanon. The constitution of May 1926 established as a principle of this republic the 'equitable representation of communities' not only in government, but also in the administration. The 'community-proportional' vote combined democratic voting with sectarian quotas. It marked the consecration for Greater Lebanon of the system designed in 1861, at the instigation of France, for Mount Lebanon, within the

---

[24] Bashar al-Assad would stage similar fake elections in 2014 and 2016 to consolidate his legitimacy vis-à-vis the UN.

Ottoman framework. On the other hand, the nationalists in Syria, defeated militarily, continued to win one election after another. The French authorities, refusing to accept the verdict of the polls, were forced to dissolve the Syrian Constituent Assembly and to promulgate, in 1930, the 'organic statutes' of a 'State of Syria', from which the two 'governments' of the Alawites and Druze were excised. The nationalists retaliated by displaying, from 1932, a flag with three stars, two of them symbolizing Damascus and Aleppo, and the third any other component of a unified Syria, beyond regions and sects. This same three-star flag was taken up by the Syrian revolutionaries in 2011 in order to proclaim their demand for national unity, in the face of the flag of the Assad regime and its manoeuvres designed to foster community-based sedition.

The January 1936 general strike in Syria broke a decade of political deadlock by finally launching negotiations for a Franco-Syrian treaty. The wave of the Popular Front brought supporters of Syrian unity to power in Paris, on the basis of which a treaty of alliance with a twenty-five-year term was signed by the French Foreign Ministry in September. The Syrian Parliament soon ratified the treaty and appointed the chief negotiator Hashim al-Atassi as President of the Republic. But the fall of the government of Léon Blum, in June 1937, encouraged the campaign of the conservative right and the colonial lobby against the ratification of this treaty. This lack of ratification ruined a historic opportunity to restore the balance in relations between the French and the Syrians, and more generally the Arabs. Instead, Paris saw neutralizing Turkey's pro-German tendencies as a priority, amid mounting perils in Europe. The treaty concluded with Ankara, in July 1938, authorizing the deployment of Turkish troops in the *sanjak* of Alexandretta. Paris pledged to guarantee Ankara's supporters a majority in a mock local ballot. This was Atatürk's last combat, as he died four months later; his former Prime Minister Ismet Inönü succeeded him as President. In June 1939, the *sanjak* was officially annexed to Turkey under the name of Hatay. Tens of thousands of Arabs and Armenians fled to the Syrian side of the new border. France, not content with working steadily to divide Syria, except during the Blum interlude of 1936–1937, thus abused its mandate to amputate the territory entrusted to it by the League of Nations.

The Palestinian impasse

The British Mandate over Palestine suffered from the outset from an insurmountable internal contradiction. Where the mandates over Iraq, Syria, and Lebanon, despite their colonial hypocrisy, were supposed to lead to the independence of an established people, Great Britain supported in Palestine the establishment of a 'Jewish national home', without recognizing the national rights of the 90% of inhabitants who were Arabs. The prospect of a unified Palestine, with a guarantee of the rights of the Jewish minority, was thus set aside in favour of the tacit alternative between a two-nation Jewish–Arab state, on the one hand, and two states for the two peoples, on the other. It was this trap that the Palestinians rejected by boycotting the mandate's institutions, even as the Zionists were willingly agreeing to participate in it. British officials bypassed this Arab obstacle by transposing their administrative centralization of Palestine into the religious sphere, based in Jerusalem. They created the office of the grand mufti of Jerusalem, with authority over the provincial muftis, and entrusted the position to the ambitious Hajj Amin al-Husseini. They then placed this grand mufti at the head of a Supreme Muslim Council (SMC), which managed the many pious foundations in the country. The elections to the SMC became significant dates in Arab politics, with a majority pro-Husseini and a minority opposed to him. This was how London consciously 'Islamized' the Palestinian question to eliminate its nationalist elements.

In 1923, Husseini launched an international fundraising campaign for the Noble Sanctuary (*Haram al-Sharif*), focusing on Islamic rather than Arab solidarity. This internationalization also fuelled the rivalry between the rulers of Iraq and Arabia, with Husseini playing Ibn Saud against Faisal. Incidents at the Wailing Wall broke out in September 1928, during the celebration of Yom Kippur, denounced by the Arabs as a violation of the Ottoman status quo on the Holy Places. The Zionist Congress of July 1929 set up a Jewish Agency in Palestine and refused to be restrained by the status quo. Riots broke out the following month in Jerusalem, then spread to Hebron and Gaza, which were emptied of Jewish communities that had been settled there for centuries. Even if this unrest claimed as many victims among Arabs as among Jews, the trauma among the latter was much more intense. It drove the Zionist supporters of the two-nation solution, already a minority within the Yishuv, to give way to the proponents of an exclusively Jewish state. This sectarian polarization also marginalized Palestinian Christians, who had nevertheless played a pioneering role in the resistance to Zionism.[25]

From Palestine, Great Britain pursued a true 'Muslim policy' which served its colonial interests, in particular in India. The grand mufti was thus able to convene in Jerusalem, in December 1931, an 'Islamic Congress' of several hundred participants; Ibn Saud had failed to organize such a meeting in Mecca. London exploited the contrast between its imperial benevolence and France's brutality in Syria, not to mention fascist Italy's appalling crackdown on Arab guerrillas in Cyrenaica, where half of the Bedouin population was confined in concentration camps and tens of thousands of civilians died. It was at this exorbitant cost that Rome could, two decades after its invasion of Libya, finally proclaim that it had 'pacified' the country. The Egyptian delegate to the Islamic Congress in Jerusalem denounced the abuses perpetrated in Libya and launched an urgent appeal for an Arab boycott of Italy.

The seizure of power by Adolf Hitler in 1933 led to a massive wave of German Jews leaving for Palestine,[26] the only country where they were welcomed without restriction. In three years, the workforce of the Yishuv doubled, reaching almost 30% of the population of the territory under mandate. This unprecedented migratory pressure was the direct cause of the revolution (*thawra*) of 1936–1939, improperly translated, once again, as 'Arab revolt'. A general strike was proclaimed in April 1936 by an Arab Higher Committee (AHC) formed by the various Palestinian factions, albeit chaired by Mufti Husseini. The movement was harshly repressed by the British, who imposed collective sanctions. The strike also facili-tated the Yishuv's integration of the new wave of migrants, according to the principles of a potentially self-sufficient Jewish economy. In October 1936, the Arab sovereigns, at London's request, pushed for the end of the protest. The heavy toll of Arab losses led the increasingly divided AHC to suspend the general strike. An unprecedented guerrilla warfare, however,

[25] In 1931, the Arab population of Jerusalem was as much Christian as Muslim (20,000 for each community), compared to 50,000 Jews.
[26] Just one agreement concluded in 1933 between the Jewish Agency and the German Foreign Office allowed more than 50,000 Jews to emigrate to Palestine.

continued to develop, adopting as its rallying sign the keffiyeh, the traditional headscarf of the Palestinian peasants. In response, Great Britain
sent reinforcements of 20,000 soldiers against some 2,000 insurgents.

The publication in July 1937 of a British partition plan between a Jewish
state and an Arab state revived the Palestinian uprising. The mandatory
power mobilized veterans of the counter-insurgency forces in Ireland
and enlisted thousands of Jewish auxiliaries. The Zionist movement saw
its gradualist strategy triumph, while its paramilitary branch, Haganah
('Defence'), was strengthened by collaboration with the British. Only
the revisionist dissidents of Irgun ('Organization') refused any dividing
up of the 'land of Israel', distinguishing themselves by the indiscriminate
nature of their anti-Arab attacks. For a time, the repression fostered
recruitment of nationalist guerrillas, who even managed, in October
1938, to temporarily seize the Old City of Jerusalem. But the methodical
character of the British campaign eventually exhausted Arab resistance in
local struggles that were bound to be lost against a much better-equipped
and better-structured enemy. In March 1939, once order was restored to
Palestine, London adopted a White Paper which abandoned the idea
of partition, capped Jewish immigration for five years, and promised
the country's independence within ten years. The Zionists felt betrayed,
although Husseini, a refugee in Lebanon, was no less critical of this text.
In general, the nationalist elite, decimated by executions, imprisonments,
and exile, was unable to mobilize enough to take advantage of the White
Paper. The reality was that the Arabs, crushed as a national movement,
had perhaps already lost Palestine, even before the Second World War.

Kurdish mobilizations

The Hamidian myth of a union between Turks and Kurds under the
Ottoman banner continued, as we have seen, to be fostered by the
Young Turks, even during the perpetration of the Armenian genocide. In
addition, Kurdish intellectuals were able to make their decisive contribution to Unionist ideology and to the Arab Nahda. Finally, the Kurdish
regions remained under the influence of a traditional elite, combining
tribal authority and Sufi charisma. All these factors contributed to
the late emergence of Kurdish nationalism, with the establishment
in 1918 in Istanbul of the Society for the Advancement of Kurdistan.

This committee negotiated with the Armenian delegation to the Paris conference and agreed to share the eastern provinces of Turkey between a Greater Armenia and a future Kurdistan. Great Britain, whose authority France then recognized over Mosul (in return for a share of the area's oil), hoped to divert Kurdish claims in northern Iraq towards Turkey. It was in this context that the 1920 Treaty of Sèvres envisaged an independent Kurdistan in hitherto Ottoman territory.

The Arab kingdom of Damascus was then swept away by the occupying French troops, based on the mandate over Syria granted them by the League of Nations. Nationalist guerrilla warfare, however, persisted in the north of the country, with the support of Mustafa Kemal, who saw it as the best way to weaken French claims on southern Anatolia. This anti-colonial resistance was led by Ibrahim Hanano, a Kurdish notable from the Aleppo region, for whom Syrian patriotism inevitably took precedence over ethno-linguistic affiliations. In return for France's abandonment of Cilicia, Kemal suspended his support for the Syrian insurrection in 1921, which soon collapsed. Hanano, captured by the French army, was sentenced to death in 1922, but pardoned because of his immense popularity. He remained, until his death in 1935, the symbol of an intractable nationalism, which never ceased to demand the unconditional independence of Syria. In 2012, 'Hanano District', one of the modern areas of Aleppo named after him, became a bastion of the Syrian resistance, both Arab and Kurdish, to the Assad regime. In 2016, the entire area was handed over to Russia by Turkey, which repeated its betrayal of Syrian nationalism from one century to the next.

As for the prospect of a Kurdistan, which was opened up in Sèvres in 1920, it was ruined by the crushing of various uprisings between 1922 and 1925: in Iran, Reza Khan subjugated the stronghold that a Kurdish chief, amid the general anarchy, had ruled for four years in the northwest of the country; in Iraq, the 'kingdom of Kurdistan', established in Sulaymaniyah, lasted barely more than a year before falling to the British army; in Turkey, in 1923, Mustafa Kemal obtained the abrogation of the Treaty of Sèvres by the Treaty of Lausanne, which was silent on Kurdish rights; and in 1925 he suppressed a significant Kurdish insurrection in the region of Diyarbakir. Each of these dissidences was neutralized without any genuine Kurdish solidarity manifesting itself across state borders. This did not prevent Kurdish militants from deploring the division of their dream Kurdistan between a Turkish 'North' (*Bakûr*), an Iraqi 'South' (*Bashûr*), an Iranian 'East' (*Rohjelat*), and a Syrian 'West' (*Rojava*).[27] It was not until 1946, and with the decisive support of the USSR, that a 'Kurdish Republic' was proclaimed in the Iranian city of Mahabad, with the reinforcement of thousands of Kurds from Iraq. These volunteers earned the name of *peshmerga*, 'those who go to meet death', now a generic name for Kurdish fighters. But this first experiment in modern separatism collapsed after a few months.

The Second World War

The United Kingdom was the dominant power in the Middle East at the start of the Second World War in September 1939. In accordance with the treaty concluded three years earlier with Egypt, the entire territory of that country was placed at the disposal of the British command, which in June 1940 accepted that Syria and Lebanon came under the authority of Vichy. On the other hand, it mobilized against the Italian breakthrough in eastern Egypt, led from Libya in the autumn of 1940. The British counter-attack routed the fascist troops, who were driven out of Egypt and then, in February 1941, eliminated from Cyrenaica. A pro-Nazi coup in Baghdad two months later was suppressed with the reoccupation of Iraq by the former mandatory power. The use of Syrian airports by the German air force led, in June 1941, to a joint offensive by the United Kingdom and Free France, which replaced the defeated Pétainists in Beirut and Damascus. In the same month of June 1941, Hitler's invasion of the USSR brought the latter into the camp of the Allies and the Trans-Iranian Railway became a major supply route for the Red Army via the Persian Gulf. Meanwhile, the Germanophilia of Reza Shah, under cover of official neutrality, was no longer tolerated by London, which overthrew him in favour of his son Muhammad Reza, leaving Iran to be jointly occupied by the Soviets to the north and the British to the south.

The Zionist leadership, despite its rejection of the British White Paper in Palestine, was firmly committed to the struggle against the Axis powers. In the summer of 1941, David Ben-Gurion, the Labour leader of

---

[27] It was under this name of Rojava that, in 2013, the Kurdish separatists proclaimed their autonomy in the northeast of Syria.

the Yishuv, even brought Haganah into the Anglo-Gaullist campaign in Syria. The Irgun revisionists rallied to this anti-fascist line, which caused the secession of the group known as Lehi,[28] since for them the United Kingdom remained the main enemy. On the Arab side, Mufti Husseini, installed in Baghdad since 1939, actively supported the pro-Nazi junta there. The British reconquest of Iraq drove him into exile again, this time in Germany. Received by the Führer in November 1941, he was responsible for organizing propaganda and the recruitment of Muslims for the Third Reich. But this second 'made in Germany' jihad was no more effective than in 1914, when Berlin had wagered betting on the Ottoman caliph's appeal for jihad against the Allies. Only in Bosnia did Husseini succeed in encouraging the enrolment of his co-religionists into the SS. On the other hand, his efforts in the Arab world failed, despite the deployment of Nazi propaganda. In Palestine itself, the number of volunteers who engaged to fight alongside the British was comparable for Jews and Arabs.

Faced with the failure of the Italian troops in Libya, Berlin sent its own Afrikakorps there, which drove the British back from Cyrenaica in June 1942. Alexandria seemed threatened and panic swept through Cairo.[29] But the United Kingdom regained the initiative and broke the German front at El-Alamein in November. Shortly after, the United States landed in North Africa and its Arabic propaganda presented the fight of the American soldiers as a 'jihad' for freedom. President Franklin Roosevelt depicted his country as an alternative to European colonialism and as a champion of the rights of peoples. This intensified pressure on France's Charles de Gaulle, who in 1941 had considered the independence of Syria and Lebanon before postponing it until after the war. The elections in the summer of 1943 in Damascus and Beirut gave a clear majority to the nationalists, who demanded the dissolution of the mandates. In the autumn, the French authorities tried to suppress the movement, before yielding to Anglo-Saxon pressure.

[28] Lehi was the Hebrew acronym for Fighters for the Freedom of Israel, but British propaganda preferred to use the pejorative term 'Stern group', after its founder.
[29] The future president Anwar Sadat, then a young nationalist officer, was sentenced for spying for the Afrikakorps, as he hoped the latter would put an end to British domination over Egypt.

Gaullist brutality created unanimous resistance on the part of the Syrians and Lebanese, whose independence was negotiated simultaneously, reversing the imposition of the mandates in 1920. In Beirut, an unwritten 'national pact' entrusted the presidency of the Republic to a Maronite and the direction of the government to a Sunni; the Christians undertook to recognize the Arab character of Lebanon, in return for Muslim abandonment of Syrian irredentism. Despite its patriotic overtones, this Lebanese pact resulted in perpetuating political sectarianism, including in the administration.[30] In March 1945 in Cairo, Syria and Lebanon, whose sovereignty was now recognized, took part in the establishment of a 'League of Arab States'. They were the only two republics there, alongside King Farouk's Egypt and Ibn Saud's Arabia, as well as the two Hashemite monarchies of the regent Abd al-Ilah in Iraq and his uncle, the Emir Abdullah, in Transjordan.[31] These six states took part in the founding conference of the United Nations (UN) the following month. De Gaulle failed to recognize this new situation and tried to stem the nationalist wave by bombarding Damascus in May 1945. He was once again repudiated by Washington and London. France was obliged to withdraw all its forces from Syria and Lebanon in 1946, while the United Kingdom maintained most of its military presence in the newly independent countries.

The United States then enjoyed great popularity in the Middle East, where its military power impressed people as much as its anti-colonialist posture seduced them. Roosevelt may not have been convinced by Mahan's 1902 thesis on the Middle East as the key to world hegemony. He nevertheless gauged the importance of Middle Eastern oil for the prosperity of the United States, in the perspective of a potential showdown with the USSR. This was why, in February 1945, just after the Yalta summit with Churchill and Stalin, he flew to Egypt to meet secretly with Ibn Saud. This interview established an informal pact in which the defence of Saudi Arabia by the United States guaranteed the American

[30] This national pact was concluded on the basis of the 1932 census, which gave a slight majority to the Christians in the resident population in Lebanon. No other census has been carried out since, as the institution of sectarianism has politicized the demographic question.

[31] In 1936, Farouk succeeded to the throne of Egypt after his deceased father Fuad. As for Imam Yahya's Yemen, it joined the Arab League in May 1945.

supply of Saudi oil. Roosevelt died the following month, bringing his Vice-President, Harry Truman, to the White House. The new head of state had worked his way up the Democratic Party apparatus, first in Missouri, then at the federal level. Anxious to maintain the sympathies of the Jewish electorate, he was also sensitive to the Bible Belt mentality of the Southern Democrats and the general rejection of a new wave of immigration to the United States. Such political considerations led him to support the Zionist demand for an opening up of Palestine to Jewish immigration – a demand that, with the discovery of the horror of the Holocaust, was charged with the need for urgent moral reparation. As early as 1945, the petro-military pact with Saudi Arabia and – more on domestic than diplomatic grounds – support for Zionism already defined the Middle Eastern policy of the United States.

The founding of Israel

In 1945, Palestine was shaken by a series of anti-British attacks, ascribed to Irgun and Lehi, while Haganah, often associated with this type of terrorism, officially focused on the illegal transfer of Jewish immigrants. The immense plight of Holocaust survivors in Europe fuelled the Zionist propaganda that the establishment of a Jewish state was the only way of ensuring 'Never again'. In 1946, Truman intensified his pressure on a United Kingdom exhausted by the world conflict. In February 1947, London decided to rely on the UN to settle the Palestinian question. The Arabs, with their two-thirds majority in the population, demanded immediate independence. The UN came up with a partition plan between an Arab state and a Jewish state which was allocated more than half of the territory, with Jerusalem having an international status. The Arab side rejected this plan, which was approved by the Zionist movement (with the exception of Irgun and Lehi). Stalin viewed the Marxist progressivism of the Jewish militants of Palestine as the best ally against the British order in the Middle East, of which the Arab regimes were in his eyes merely puppet states. Moscow's move towards favouring the partition plan represented an unexpected convergence with Washington at the start of the Cold War. The partition of Palestine was approved in November 1947 by the required two-thirds majority of the UN General Assembly.

This plan never even started to be implemented because hostilities began immediately between the Zionist militias, attached to ensuring territorial continuity between their different enclaves, and the Arab groups, badly organized and much less well armed. Abdullah of Transjordan secretly negotiated a partitioning of Palestine with the Zionist leaders, in which he would appropriate the territories reserved for the Arab State. In March–April 1948, Palestinian resistance collapsed, especially in the Jerusalem region, which led to the exodus of entire populations. On 14 May, in Tel Aviv, on the eve of the expiry of the British Mandate, Ben-Gurion proclaimed the founding of the State of Israel. The United States and the USSR very quickly granted it their recognition. The conflict, a Jewish–Arab civil war in Palestine, became international: the first Arab–Israeli war. The 20,000 soldiers sent by the Arab States[32] remained, even with the support of the thousands of militiamen involved since the winter, inferior in number to the 30,000–35,000 combatants of the brand-new Israeli army.[33] The latter lacked heavy armament and the harshness of the clashes of the previous months had taken its toll, whereas the troops it faced were still fresh. But it benefited from a unity of command which was sorely lacking in the Arab camp, with Transjordan avoiding the fight against the Israelis, except in Jerusalem, which had remained outside the partition plan.

The UN mediator for Palestine, Folke Bernadotte, managed in June 1948 to negotiate a truce, but he could not avoid the resumption of hostilities. He sought to save the partition plan and encourage the return of Arab refugees, of whom there were already hundreds of thousands. His assassination by Lehi, in September in Jerusalem, meant that the outcome was decided by force of arms alone, and thus the victory fell to Israel.[34] The UN limited itself, from January 1949, to sponsoring a series of armistices between Israel and its Arab neighbours. The conference meeting in Lausanne the following summer failed to reach a

[32] The numbers are estimated at 10,000 Egyptians, 4,500 Transjordanians, 1,500 Syrians, the same number of Iraqis and Saudis, and 1,000 Lebanese.
[33] It was constituted under the name Tsahal (the Hebrew acronym for the Israel Defence Forces/Tzva Haganah Le Israel) by amalgamation with Haganah.
[34] In total, 1% of the population of Mandatory Palestine perished in the conflict, a proportion which was reflected in the Israeli losses (mainly military) and the Palestinian losses (largely civilians).

peace settlement, placing the region in a situation of indefinite ceasefire. Palestine disappeared, divided between Israel, which absorbed 77% of its territory, and Transjordan, which annexed 22%, namely East Jerusalem and the West Bank. This 'union' between the two banks of the River Jordan allowed Abdallah to proclaim himself 'king of Jordan', instead of only Transjordan. As for the Gaza Strip, administered by Egypt, it included, out of 1% of Mandatory Palestine, a quarter of its Arab population. This was the Nakba, literally the 'Catastrophe', for the Arabs of Palestine, the majority of whom were reduced to being nothing more than refugees,[35] for whom the UN created a specific agency, without a mandate to ensure their return to their land.

Israel held its first elections in January 1949, while the conflict was still raging, hence there was a single constituency ballot, with nationwide proportional representation. Ben-Gurion obtained a comfortable majority of 90 deputies out of the 120 in this Knesset (Assembly) for his Labour Party and its allies, while the revisionists of Menachem Begin, former head of Irgun, were marginalized. Parliamentarians elected Chaim Weizmann, the inspiration for the Balfour Declaration and first leader of the Jewish Agency, as President of the State, a largely ceremonial post. Executive power was firmly exercised by the Prime Minister, who, to avoid disputes over the official status of Judaism, chose not to draft a constitution. A default consensus thus brought together secular and religious people in a state that defined itself as both Jewish and democratic. The law on military service, fixed at thirty months for men and twenty-four months for women, established the framework of a Jewish nation in arms, from which Arabs were excluded.[36] The 'Absentee Property' law legalized the transfer to Zionist institutions of the property of Palestinians 'absent' from the UN partition plan. The 'Law of Return'

---

[35] The Arab population of Palestine, estimated at 1.3 million in 1948, was divided, a year later, into four categories: 160,000 who remained in Israel; 80,000 original inhabitants of the Gaza Strip; 300,000 inhabitants who were now 'Jordanians' from East Jerusalem and the West Bank; and at least 750,000 refugees, dispersed between the Gaza Strip, Jordan, Syria, Lebanon, and even beyond (these last two figures are the subject of bitter debates).

[36] Only the Druze are subject to conscription, while Bedouin enlistment was encouraged, but on an individual basis. Martial law was imposed on the predominantly Arab areas of Israel until 1966.

prescribed that 'every Jew has the right to immigrate to Israel', encouraging unprecedented *aliyah*, with the population doubling in three years. This trend involved large Sephardic communities, including from Yemen, transferred by airlift, while until 1948 Zionism recruited mainly from the Ashkenazi populations of Europe. The socialistic system of the new state made it possible to proactively integrate such waves of immigration.

The failure of the Arab elites

The Middle East had been hit very hard by the First World War, but was much less so by the Second. Its population doubled during the first half of the twentieth century, due to the acceleration of demographic growth that had begun in the second half of the previous century. Egypt and Turkey both had around 20 million inhabitants; Cairo, with 2 million people, was twice the size of Istanbul. The Middle Eastern population remained three-quarters rural, even if the growth of urban centres was spectacular, with the development of the ports of Beirut and Alexandria, as well as the new districts of Heliopolis in Cairo and Abu Rummaneh in Damascus. A new middle class was involved in the administration of the nascent states, in the booming liberal professions, and in a globalization very much shaped by colonial priorities.[37] The rural exodus also nurtured new forms of artisans and proletarians, with the resulting social struggles. The army became a formidable social ladder for the most deprived classes, at a time when the stranglehold of the post-Ottoman elites remained very strong on landed property, medium-sized industry, and big business.

The abandonment of the Palestinian people in 1949 sealed the failure of these Arab elites to defend their national rights, first against the colonial powers, then in the face of Zionist dispossession. But it had been two decades since such elites had been held to account by formations constituted on the Bolshevik model. The Muslim Brotherhood, founded in Egypt in 1928 by Hassan al-Banna, was no doubt Islamist,

---

[37] This was the case of the pipeline inaugurated in 1935, transporting Iraqi oil from the fields of Kirkuk to the Palestinian port of Haifa and the Lebanese port of Tripoli.

but its 'supreme guide' had the same authority as the 'general secretary' of the communist parties, the 'advisory council' (*majlis al-shura*) of the former corresponding to the 'political bureau' of the latter, with in both cases a central committee, mass organizations, and a very undemocratic 'centralism'. The Muslim Brotherhood condemned compromises with British imperialism made by parliamentary parties, in the forefront of which was the Wafd. They saw Palestine as the perfect cause over which to mobilize widely in Egypt, in 1935–1936, without directly challenging the authorities. With hundreds of thousands of supporters, they developed subsidiaries in Syria and Jordan, as well as a paramilitary branch, mobilized against Israel in 1948. They publicly attributed the defeat of this 'jihad' in Palestine to King Farouk, whose Prime Minister was assassinated; this led in retaliation to the murder of Banna. The organization now had its emblematic 'martyr', slain by a regime branded as 'impious'.

Many formations advocating radical nationalism at this time shared with the Muslim Brotherhood not only its Leninist-type structure, but also an increasingly virulent hostility towards the liberal order. They also developed secret armed structures, adopting a putschist perspective. This was the case for the Party of National Brotherhood in Iraq, one of whose founders led the pro-Nazi coup d'état of 1941. The Syrian Social Nationalist Party advocated, from Lebanon, the 'greater Syrian' union between that country, Syria, Iraq, Jordan, and Palestine. As much opposed to pan-Arabism as to Lebanese independence, this party attempted a putsch in Beirut in 1949, for which its leader was executed – an act that was then avenged by the death of the Lebanese Prime Minister Riad Al Solh in 1951. The Ba'ath ('Resurgence') Party, established in Damascus in 1947, rallied publicly to a form of 'Arab socialism' in the name of a 'united nation' from Morocco to the Persian Gulf, carrying a 'universal message'. Such 'progressive' formations profited from the discredit into which Stalin's support for Israel had plunged the communist parties of the Arab world. They drove the class protest against the traditional notables – a protest that the Muslim Brotherhood did not neglect: its Syrian branch claimed to embody 'Islamic socialism'. Finally, all these groups questioned, in the name of pan-Arab, 'greater Syrian', or Islamic solidarity, the legitimacy of the borders within which emancipation from colonial rule was achieved.

It is obvious that this emancipation was laborious, uneven, and imperfect, and carried out in an often artificial, always arbitrary territorial framework, where the emergence of an authentic citizenship had to struggle against a more or less established communitarianism. But the Arab elites, so harshly castigated for their numerous shortcomings, maintained, within this constrained environment, a pluralist system with a relatively free press, properly fought elections, and a parliamentary management of the different factions involved. France in Syria and the United Kingdom in Egypt came up against the steadfastness of Arab deputies refusing to betray their voters, at a time when registration chambers were content to offer the 'saviour of the nation' the abolition of the caliphate in Turkey and the overthrow of the Qajars in Iran. This heritage of Arab pluralism was methodically concealed by the dictatorships of the second half of the twentieth century, quick to denounce the 'corruption' of fallen regimes in order to conceal their own turpitude. Supposedly enlightened figures would sing the same refrain in 2011, claiming, in defiance of historical reality, that the absence of parliamentary experience condemned the Arab world to the darkness of authoritarianism. On the contrary, it is important to rehabilitate this liberal past if we wish to understand the full brutality of the shift to despotism. Welcome to the age of the hijacking of Arab independence.

Chronology

2 August 1914	Secret alliance between Ottomans and Germans.
14 November 1914	Ottoman call for jihad against the Allies.
18 December 1914	British protectorate over Egypt.
24 April 1915	Beginning in Constantinople of the Armenian genocide.
July 1915–January 1916	Hussein–McMahon correspondence.
16 May 1916	Franco-British agreement known as 'Sykes–Picot'.
10 June 1916	Launch of the 'Arab revolt' in the Hejaz.
2 November 1917	Balfour Declaration on Palestine.
9 December 1917	British occupation of Jerusalem.
31 October 1918	Armistice of Moudros.
18 January 1919	Opening of the Paris Peace Conference.
9 March 1919	Anti-British 'revolution' in Egypt.
19–26 April 1920	San Remo Conference on the Middle East.
May–October 1920	Anti-British uprising in Iraq.
24 July 1920	French victory over the Syrian nationalists.
10 August 1920	Treaty of Sèvres dismembering Turkey.
1 September 1920	Proclamation of Greater Lebanon.
21 February 1921	Reza Khan's coup in Tehran.
23 August 1921	Faisal, first king of Iraq.
28 February 1922	Formal independence of Egypt.
24 July 1923	Treaty of Lausanne, cancelling that of Sèvres.
3 March 1924	Abolition of the caliphate by the Turkish Parliament.
13 October 1924	Capture of Mecca by Ibn Saud.
18–20 October 1925	French bombardment of Damascus.
12 December 1925	The Qajars supplanted by the Pahlavis.
16 December 1925	Mosul given to Iraq by the League of Nations.
23 May 1926	Constitution of the Republic of Lebanon.
23–29 August 1929	Inter-communal riots in Palestine.
22 September 1932	Official proclamation of Saudi Arabia.
3 October 1932	Formal independence of Iraq.
24 November 1934	Mustafa Kemal proclaimed 'Atatürk'.

19 April 1936	General strike of the Arab population of Palestine.
9 September 1936	Franco-Syrian treaty signed in Paris.
17 March 1939	UK 'White Paper' on Palestine.
21 June 1941	Capture of Damascus by Anglo-Gaullist troops.
16 September 1941	Abdication of Reza Shah in favour of his son.
3 November 1942	British victory at El-Alamein.
22 November 1943	Independence of Lebanon.
14 February 1945	Roosevelt–Ibn Saud summit in Egypt.
22 March 1945	Foundation of the Arab League in Cairo.
17 April 1946	End of the French withdrawal from Syria.
29 November 1947	UN partition plan for Palestine.
14 May 1948	Proclamation of the State of Israel.
17 September 1948	Assassination of Folke Bernadotte in Jerusalem.
25 January 1949	First Israeli elections to the Knesset.
15 September 1949	Failure of the UN conference in Lausanne.

Further reading

Akçam, Taner, *The Young Turks' crime against humanity: the Armenian genocide and ethnic cleansing in the Ottoman Empire* (Princeton, NJ: Princeton University Press, 2012).

Barr, James, *A line in the sand: Britain, France and the struggle for the mastery of the Middle East* (London: Simon & Schuster, 2012).

Cohen, Mitchell, *Zion and state: nation, class, and the shaping of modern Israel* (New York: Columbia University Press 1992).

Fawaz, Leila Tarazi, *A land of aching hearts: the Middle East in the Great War* (Cambridge, MA: Harvard University Press, 2014).

Kassir, Samir, *Beirut*, translated by M. B. DeBevoise (Berkeley: University of California Press, 2010).

Khalidi, Rashid, *Palestinian identity: the construction of modern national consciousness* (New York: Columbia University Press, 2010).

Khoury, Philip S., *Syria and the French Mandate: the politics of Arab nationalism* (Princeton, NJ: Princeton University Press, 1987).

Krämer, Gudrun, *A History of Palestine: from the Ottoman conquest to the founding of the State of Israel* (Princeton, NJ: Princeton University Press, 2008).

Motadel, David, *Islam and Nazi Germany's war* (Cambridge, MA: Harvard University Press, 2014).

Thompson, Elizabeth, *How the West stole democracy from the Arabs: the Syrian Congress of 1920 and the destruction of its historic Liberal–Islamic alliance* (London: Grove Press, 2020).

NINE

The Cold War and the Arab–Israeli conflict (1949–1990)

In 1949, the Middle East settled into a situation of neither war nor peace between Israel and its Arab neighbours. This was also the year in which the Syrian chief of staff, trounced in the recent conflict, took power in Damascus. He established a military-style dictatorship there, where the previous interventions of an Arab army in neighbouring Iraq had preserved the monarchical framework. This coup was itself followed by two other putsches within a few months, at the end of which General Adib al-Shishakli restored the parliamentary regime for two years. In December 1951, Shishakli carried out the fourth coup in independent Syria, suspended the constitution, and banned political parties. Only the Arab Liberation Movement was now legal, which had been created to make him President with officially 99.7% of the vote.[1]

In January 1952, the massacre of Egyptian police by the British army on the Suez Canal caused the 'Cairo fire', i.e. the ransacking of shops, cinemas, and hotels identified with European interests. The Muslim Brotherhood, very much in evidence during these riots, intrigued with a group of conspiratorial officers led by Lieutenant-Colonel Gamal Abdel Nasser, himself a former Muslim Brother. Six months later, these 'Free Officers' overthrew King Farouk, who was soon forced into exile, and proclaimed the 'blessed revolution'.[2] The date of their coup, 23 July, became Egypt's national day, and still is today.

The Free Officers imprisoned the ruling generals, with the exception of the highly popular Muhammad Naguib, who served as their Prime

---

[1] This practice of unanimous referendums was introduced into the Middle East by the British, who, in 1921, had Faisal 'elected' king of Iraq by 96% of the vote (see above, pp. 243–4).

[2] It was Anwar Sadat, sentenced in 1942 for giving intelligence to the Nazis (see above, p. 259, n. 29), who announced this seizure of power.

Minister, but real power was vested in a Revolutionary Command Council (RCC) chaired by Nasser. Naguib, attached to parliamentarism, was supported by the Muslim Brotherhood, convinced that the elections would turn to its advantage. In June 1953, the struggle between the various groups resulted in Naguib becoming President of the brand-new Republic, but against a background of the dissolution of its political formations. In April 1954, the head of state failed to restore pluralism: the Liberation Rally, an offshoot of the RCC, remained the only authorized party and all trade unions were banned. Six months later, an assassination attempt on Nasser, attributed to the Muslim Brotherhood, justified the arrest of 20,000 Islamists, while Naguib was placed under house arrest. Widely publicized trials were carried out against the opposition, associated with the supposedly unfailing alliance between 'imperialism', 'Zionism', and 'reaction', i.e. the deposed monarchy. The transition from putsch to dictatorship was completed in June 1956, with the approval, by 99.8% of the votes, of a new constitution which brought Nasser to the presidency of the Republic.

The half-century of Arab independence ran from 1922, with the formal emancipation of Egypt, to 1971, the year of the admission to the UN of the last four British protectorates in the Gulf.[3] Within this cycle of independence, the twenty years from 1949 to 1969 saw them hijacked by military juntas which damned as 'reactionary' the constitutional regimes established at the time they gained sovereignty. This process of hijacking, initiated in 1949 by the flurry of coups in Syria, continued in Egypt and Iraq, and concluded with the overthrow in 1969 of King Idriss of Libya.[4] The putschists of Tripoli then established an RCC on the Egyptian model, and placed at its head Colonel Muammar Gaddafi, an ardent emulator of Nasser. Gaddafi would later confess that he chose a military career over public service as the former gave him the chance of participating in a coup. Such unbridled lust for power fuelled the momentum of conspiracy long after the constitutional order had been brought down. This Darwinian process therefore favoured the emergence

---

[3] These were the United Arab Emirates, Qatar, Bahrain, and Oman.

[4] As the architect of the independence of a federal Libya in 1951, Idriss centralized the power of this constitutional monarchy in Tripoli in 1963. In 1955, he was the first Arab leader to impose the principle of national sovereignty over oil resources.

of the man who was the most implacable of putschists, in the course of power struggles which divided ruling juntas everywhere.

This militarization of Arab politics fed on the Palestinian 'Catastrophe' and the conflict with Israel, through which the history of this period is generally viewed. But this is to forget that the defeats inflicted by Israel on these 'revolutionary' officers never weakened the dictatorial nature of their power: quite the contrary, they at most simply enabled one clan to eliminate another.[5] And, above all, such a view neglects the instrumentalization of this external conflict for the purposes of internal repression, as any form of protest, even the most peaceful, was viewed as treason and treated as such. This stigmatization of the opposition, whether liberal, progressive, or Islamist, justified its eradication by the various political police forces, to the benefit of the single party. There were indeed several of these forces, designated in Arabic under the generic term of 'mukhabarat',[6] so they did not constitute a counter-power to the current despot. The people were endlessly appealed to by state propaganda, but were actually summoned only to provide unanimous demonstrations of support for the regime, with 'elections' producing almost 100% support.

Nationalism and anti-communism

The Turkey of President Inönü, who succeeded Atatürk in 1938, maintained its policy of neutrality during the Second World War. It declared war on Germany only in February 1945, in order to participate in the founding conference of the UN, and above all to benefit from American support in the face of the Soviet desire to turn the country into a satellite. Truman intensified aid to Turkey from the start of the Cold War, and even brought it into the North Atlantic Treaty Organization (NATO), at the same time (1951) as Greece. The counterpart of this integration into the Western camp was the opening up of the political field, with the creation of a Democratic Party by dissidents of the Kemalist party-state. They won the majority in the 1950 elections and their leader Adnan Menderes became Prime Minister, while Inönü became head of the parliamentary

---

[5] Although the 'Six-Day War' was a disaster for Egypt in 1967 (see below, pp. 279–80), it enabled Nasser to get rid of his main rival, the chief of staff, Mohamed Fawzi.
[6] This Arabic term means 'intelligence services'.

opposition. An 'Atatürk Protection Law', still in force, was passed against the defamation of the founder of modern Turkey. More would have been needed to calm the apprehensions of the Kemalists in the face of economic liberalization and the revival of the brotherhoods. Only a militant anti-communism could resolve such contradictions. It was also in this spirit that Turkey strengthened its ties with Hashemite Iraq and imperial Iran. The three regimes were all the more hostile to the USSR as it welcomed the survivors of the short-lived 'Kurdish Republic' of Mahabad and seemed to be the only state to support Kurdish separatism.

Muhammad Reza, placed on the Pahlavi throne in 1941 by the United Kingdom, was for a long time subjected to intense pressure from Stalin, whose troops did not withdraw from Iran until 1946. This withdrawal consolidated the dominant position of London, which excluded the least concession in the oil sector. Iran's foreign currency resources collapsed due to devaluations of the pound sterling and the refusal of a fair sharing of oil revenues, even though the United States had accepted this in Saudi Arabia.[7] Muhammad Mossadegh, one of the few deputies to have refused the establishment of the new dynasty in 1925, became the champion of anti-British protest. Parliament elected him Prime Minister in April 1951 to implement the nationalization of oil, in a climate of patriotic fervour. London and Washington decided in retaliation to boycott Iranian oil, plunging the country into a serious recession. Although arbitration by the International Court of Justice in July 1952 was favourable to Tehran, it did not suspend the war of attrition led by the United Kingdom, with which Iran, three months later, broke off diplomatic relations. The United States, led by the Republican 'hawk' Dwight Eisenhower, therefore took over the matter of Iran. The CIA branch in Tehran organized a methodical destabilization operation,[8] stigmatizing Mossadegh as a communist puppet and even as an enemy of Islam. The shah fled the country to avoid direct association with the coup d'état which overthrew Mossadegh in August 1953. The CIA deemed the

---

[7] ARAMCO (Arabian American Oil Company) was founded in 1944, shortly before the Roosevelt–Ibn Saud summit (see above, p. 260), while APOC (Anglo-Persian Oil Company), established in 1909, became the AIOC (Anglo-Iranian Oil Company) in 1935 and BP (British Petroleum) in 1955.

[8] CIA documents on this 'Operation Ajax' were declassified in 2000.

operation so successful that it served as a model for the overthrow of the democratic government of Guatemala the following year. Muhammad Reza, upon his return to Tehran, imposed martial law and repressed even liberal opposition in the name of the anti-communist struggle. Like his father thirty years earlier, in 1955 he launched a campaign against the Bahais, once again intended to win the favour of the Shiite clergy for the Pahlavis. It was also in 1955 that Iran joined the 'Baghdad Pact' which united Iraq, Turkey, and Pakistan in resolute opposition to the USSR.

Nasser, an emblematic figure in the emerging 'Third World', posed as a nationalist alternative to the Baghdad Pact. However, he turned to the United States to finance his major dam project on the Nile, at Aswan. It was America's refusal to do so that precipitated Nasser's nationalization of the Suez Canal in July 1956. He proclaimed in a resounding speech that 'poverty is not shameful, it is the exploitation of peoples that is'. The link forged between the control of national resources and the social revenge of the underprivileged transfigured Nasser into a champion of the wretched of the earth, while Mossadegh's nationalization of oil, five years earlier, had had only a limited echo outside Iran. The Nasserist wave took on such magnitude in the Arab world that Israel, the United Kingdom, and France secretly made a pact to bring it down.[9] This was 'Operation Musketeer', launched on 29 October by an Israeli offensive against the Egyptian Sinai Peninsula. Paris and London pretended to intervene between the belligerents so as to occupy the Suez Canal. Nasser's troops fell back everywhere before the invaders. Very quickly, however, this military triumph turned into a political disaster.

Eisenhower was furious at such an eruption of 'gunboat policy' in the middle of the Cold War. The USSR, meanwhile, took advantage of this crisis to crush the anti-communist uprising in Hungary. Washington forced Paris and London to withdraw from the Suez Canal, while Israel was obliged unconditionally to evacuate Sinai and the Gaza Strip. A contingent of UN 'blue helmets'[10] was deployed on the Israeli–Egyptian

[9] The socialist government of Guy Mollet in France was convinced that the independentist insurrection unleashed in 1954 in Algeria would collapse with Nasser.

[10] These peacekeeping forces, the first of their kind for the UN, were urgently equipped with American equipment, whose green helmets were repainted blue for the occasion. Blue helmets were to become emblematic of this type of operation.

border. The two former colonial empires drew divergent lessons from this historic humiliation: the United Kingdom began a gradual process of disengagement 'east of Suez', with the independence of Kuwait in 1961, of South Yemen in 1967, and, finally, of the United Arab Emirates, Qatar, Bahrain, and Oman in 1971; France, on the contrary, embarked on the development of atomic weapons, the technology for which it secretly transferred to Israel, while remaining the latter's main military partner. The Arab capitals, with the exception of Beirut, broke off diplomatic relations with Paris. Nasser may have been saved from disaster by the very same 'imperialism' that he claimed to be fighting, but his aura as a modern Saladin appeared irresistible.

The United Arab Republic

In Syria, the authoritarian parties refused to pursue the parliamentary experiment that was again made possible in 1954 by the fall of Shishakli. They preferred, on the initiative of the Ba'ath, to scuttle the independence of the country in order to offer it to Nasser. Thus, in February 1958, the United Arab Republic (UAR) came into being: its two-star flag, for Egypt and Syria, replaced the three-star flag of Syrian independence in Damascus.[11] This 'union' established a proconsulate of Egyptian officers over the mere 'northern province' that Syria had become. In this context, the whole world saw the overthrow of the Iraqi monarchy in July 1958 as inspired by Nasser. The leader of the putschists, Colonel Abd al-Karim Qasim, however, turned out to be more patriotic than pan-Arab. He refused to join the UAR and relied on progressive formations to counter the aims of Cairo. In addition, this time, the deposed sovereign and his relatives, exiled during the 1952 coup in Egypt, were massacred. This murder, the basis of the new Republic, dragged the history of Iraq into a cycle of unprecedented violence. In any case, it meant the end of the Baghdad Pact, reduced to being no more than a Turkish–Iranian arrangement, supported at arm's length by the United States.

Supporters of the UAR attempted to seize Mosul in March 1959, but their uprising was quickly crushed by the army, supported by communist

---

[11] This flag is still that of the Assad regime in Syria, as the three-star flag was appropriated in 2011 by the revolutionary forces.

and pro-Qasim militias. It should be noted that these militiamen were largely Shiites and Kurds, the Nasserites being mostly Sunnis. Turning this bloodbath into a confrontation between Shiites and Sunnis, or even between Arabs and Kurds, is a step that would be easily taken today. But ideological conflicts were at that time much more virulent than splits between communities, even if the latter aggravated the former. The antagonism between Qasim and Nasser can also be interpreted in the light of the Middle Eastern triangle regularly mentioned in this work, with Iraq resisting the Egyptian hegemony already imposed on Syria. In October 1959, Qasim escaped an assassination attempt perpetrated by a Ba'athist commando unit that took refuge in Damascus.[12] Two months later, the master of Baghdad accused 'three gangsters' of having divided the spoils of Palestine between them in 1948, placing Israel, Jordan, and Egypt on the same level. When, in the summer of 1961, Iraq threatened to invade newly independent Kuwait, Egypt took part in the inter-Arab force dispatched to protect the emirate. Despite this huge split between Nasser and Qasim, the United States continued to treat the opposing tendencies of Arab nationalism with equal suspicion. They preferred, in their showdown with the USSR in the Middle East, to rely more and more on Saudi Arabia and, through it, on political Islam.

The Arab Cold War

The Muslim Brotherhood, persecuted throughout Egypt since 1954, was now also repressed in the Syria of the UAR. It could operate freely only in Jordan, where it supported the annexation of the West Bank by the Hashemite Kingdom. Its members therefore fled in their thousands to Saudi Arabia, which offered them, in addition to political asylum, the opportunity to invest in the country's new 'Islamic' educational and training institutions. The hijacking of Arab independences thus resulted in locking the Nahda and its heirs into a grim alternative between, on the one hand, the nationalism of the military dictatorships and, on the other, the Islamist fusion of Saudi Wahhabism and the exiled Muslim Brotherhood. It meant the end of the fruitful dialogue between these

---

[12] The participation of the young Saddam Hussein in this commando unit would contribute to his militant legend.

two currents of thought which had made the Arab renaissance of the nineteenth century so fertile. The closing of the democratic horizon accelerated this polarization between a militarized nationalism and Saudi Islamism, a polarization that degenerated into a veritable 'Arab Cold War'.[13]

The two tutelary figures of this war were Nasser and Faisal of Arabia.[14] The first round in the contest went to the Saudis, who, in September 1961, celebrated the breakaway from the UAR and the restoration of Syrian sovereignty. The de facto occupation of the 'Northern Province' by Egypt had been so brutal that there was general relief in the country. King Hussein's Jordan was confirmed in its pro-Saudi stance. However, Nasser took his revenge a year later when one of his emulators proclaimed a republic in North Yemen. The overthrown imam was merely wounded in the putsch and, taking refuge in Arabia, he organized the resistance of the monarchist tribes there. The Egyptian contingent, sent to support the new regime, saw its numbers grow inexorably, reaching 70,000 soldiers. But the royalist guerrillas, served by difficult terrain where they were perfectly at home, inflicted heavy losses on the expeditionary force. The Egyptian air force retaliated by striking at the rear bases of the insurgency in Saudi territory. This led Washington, in June 1963, to deploy fighter planes in Arabia, which were enough by their mere presence to dissuade new Egyptian raids.[15]

The putsches that again shook Syria and Iraq in 1963 did not affect the balance of power between Nasser and Faisal. In March, the Ba'athist soldiers who seized power in Damascus restored the two-star flag of the UAR there, even if their ambition was turned towards Iraq, where their party comrades had contributed, a month earlier, to the overthrow of Qasim. The Iraqi Ba'athists were, however, excluded from power in November; each of these reversals in Baghdad was accompanied

---

[13] This expression was coined by American historian Malcolm Kerr, who was assassinated by Hezbollah in Beirut in 1984.

[14] Faisal did not become king of Saudi Arabia until November 1964, but he had long since usurped many prerogatives from Saud, his brother and predecessor.

[15] This operation, suspended after six months, was marked by the Saudi refusal to accept Jewish soldiers; the United States adapted to this by refusing to specify the religion of its troops.

by bloody purges.[16] In order to monopolize the Palestinian question in these times when Arab states were striving to outbid one another, in May 1964 Nasser established a Palestine Liberation Organization (PLO). He entrusted the presidency to a former ambassador of Saudi Arabia at the UN, who had gone over to Egypt and was himself of Palestinian origin. Faisal retaliated by giving his support to Yasser Arafat and his Palestine Liberation Movement, Fatah, whose fedayeen[17] began the 'armed struggle' in January 1965. These infiltrations, described as 'terrorist' in Israel, remained limited, while Cairo's propaganda was unleashed against Fatah, seen as akin to the Muslim Brotherhood and other 'agents of imperialism'. The Palestinians, kept out of the Arab scene since 1949, regained visibility thanks to this twofold instrumentalization: of the PLO by Nasser and of Fatah by Faisal. A new putsch in Damascus, in February 1966, pitted the Ba'athists against each other and worked to the advantage of the leftist proponents of the 'people's war', who granted the fedayeen unprecedented facilities. Israel held the Syrian authorities responsible for these Palestinian infiltrations, leading to rising tensions on the Israeli–Syrian border.

Nasser, obsessed by his rivalry with Faisal, saw Syrian vulnerability as simply an opportunity to regain a foothold in Damascus. In November 1966, a defence pact was announced between Cairo and Damascus. The Egyptian despot was aware that a third of his army was bogged down in Yemen, after four years of conflict, and despite the increasingly frequent use of chemical weapons. But he did not seriously envisage a conflict with Israel; he merely drew on the rhetoric of war to establish his authority in the Arab world. He did not react to an aerial confrontation between Israel and Syria in April 1967, which fuelled the accusations against him in the press in Damascus and Riyadh. As the escalation continued, on 15 May, Nasser demanded that the UN withdraw the blue helmets deployed on the Israeli border since the end of the Suez crisis a decade earlier. On 22 May, he ordered the closure of the Gulf of Aqaba, subjecting the port

---

[16] The overthrow of Qasim led to the recognition by Iraq of the independence of Kuwait, proclaimed two years earlier and guaranteed until then by an inter-Arab force.

[17] This term, popular in mediaeval Islam, but taken up at the end of the nineteenth century by the Armenian militiamen (see above, p. 221), referred to faith (*fida'*) in the struggle, even including the supreme sacrifice.

of Eilat to blockade. Then, four days later, he promised 'the destruction of Israel' in the event of an attack on Egypt or Syria. This boasting seemed to pay off since, on 30 May, King Hussein of Jordan went in person to Cairo to place his army under Egyptian command. Nasser was convinced that he had finally won the Arab Cold War.

The seventh day

The Labour politician Lévy Eshkol succeeded David Ben-Gurion as head of the Israeli government in 1963. He largely deferred in military matters to his chief of staff, Yitzhak Rabin. Their policy of restraint, in the face of repeated provocations by Nasser in May 1967, earned Israel broad support in the Western world, which was convinced that a new Holocaust was brewing. The rallying of Jordan to the Egyptian–Syrian camp led, on 1 June, to the formation of an Israeli government of national unity, in which the 'hawk' Moshe Dayan assumed the defence portfolio. The generals persuaded Eshkol to adopt their pre-emptive strike and went on the offensive in the early hours of 5 June. The Egyptian air force was destroyed on the ground, before the same fate was inflicted on the Jordanian air force. A wave of bombardments against Syria managed, on the very first day of the conflict, to deprive the Arab armies of air cover. On 7 June, the Old City of Jerusalem was conquered. Moshe Dayan and the general staff went to the Wailing Wall,[18] then to the Noble Sanctuary (*Haram al-Sharif*)arHaram Haram. The Jordanian army retreated to the eastern bank of the Jordan, blowing up bridges as it did so. The Egyptian collapse continued and, on 8 June, the Israelis reached the Suez Canal. This 'Six-Day War' ended with a devastating offensive against the Syrian army.

Israel seized not only the West Bank and Gaza, but also the Egyptian Sinai and the Syrian Golan Heights. East Jerusalem was de facto annexed, as part of a 'municipal' unification of the Holy City, with control over the third holiest site in Islam. Masses of Palestinian refugees crossed the Jordan, joining the first wave from 1948 in the camps. After the Nakba, the 'Catastrophe' which had struck the Palestinians at that time, it was

---

[18] The 'Maghrebi quarter', historically inhabited by Muslims of North African origin, was razed on 11 June to establish the current view over the *Kotel*, as the (Wailing) Wall is known in Hebrew.

now the shock of the Naqsa, the 'Reversal', which impacted on all Arabs. Egyptian propaganda, paralysed by this rout, accused the United States of having directly contributed to it. American institutions were targeted by rioters in Arab capitals, who severed relations with Washington as they had done in 1956 with France, when America was being celebrated for its assistance to Nasser. The USSR and its 'socialist' satellites, with the exception of Romania, in turn cut diplomatic ties with Tel Aviv. Never had the polarization between US-allied Israel, on the one hand, and the Arab states backed by the Soviet bloc, on the other, been so strong. While Egypt was obsessed with its showdown with Saudi Arabia, believing it was getting the upper hand in May 1967, the Hebrew state clearly won the Arab–Israeli Cold War. As for Nasser, he soon had to consent to Faisal withdrawing Egyptian troops from Yemen.[19] Thus, even the Arab Cold War ended in an Egyptian defeat.

The Cairo and Damascus dictatorships were too militarized to be seriously shaken. The priority given to the protection of the regimes by their praetorian guard also played a part in the mediocrity of their performance on the battlefield. But pan-Arabism, whether Nasserite or Ba'athist, had lost most of its appeal. The revolution (*thawra*) of the fedayeen became the new goal to aim for; it was all the more idealized by the Arabs as the whole of Palestine had escaped their grasp. Fatah, supported by the Jordanian army, did not abandon its positions in the face of an Israeli assault in March 1968 in the Jordan Valley. This was enough to transform this confrontation on Jordanian soil into the beginning of a 'war of liberation' and the fedayeen into champions of Arab honour. Yet again, Nasser had to bow to the new deal: in February 1969, he allowed Arafat and the armed factions to take control of the PLO and, in November, he forced Lebanon to grant the fedayeen freedom to act from its territory.

The UN, however, continued to consider the Palestinians solely as refugees, and not as a people with strong national rights.[20] The PLO therefore distrusted diplomatic manoeuvres, as it feared paying the price

[19] The conflict continued until the compromise of 1970 when Faisal recognized the 'Arab Republic' of Sanaa, provided that it was conservative, as a buffer state against South Yemen that the USSR would turn into its satellite.

[20] Security Council Resolution 242 of November 1967, the main document on this subject, called on Israel to 'withdraw from territories occupied during the recent conflict', but only mentioned the 'just settlement of the refugee problem'.

for them. It set up bases in Jordan, where half of the population was of Palestinian origin,[21] consolidating its presence in the refugee camps and the Jordan Valley. On top of that, Fatah was challenged on its left by the Popular Front for the Liberation of Palestine (PFLP), which endeavoured to combine anti-Israeli struggle with Arab revolution. In August 1970, the mediation of the United States put an end to the 'war of attrition' between Israel and Egypt on the Suez Canal. Palestinian radicals feared that King Hussein would follow the same logic. In September, the PFLP hijacked Western airliners at a Jordanian airport and destroyed them there in front of the press.[22] This marked the eruption in the Middle East of a declamatory terrorism which struck at civilian targets with no direct link to the current conflict, but were amalgamated into this confrontation in the name of a globalized rhetoric. In an involuntary echo of the capture of the Ottoman Bank by the Armenian fedayeen in 1896, a self-proclaimed and Marxist vanguard wagered on the internationalization of the crisis with a spectacular coup. As then, the reckless terrorist plot backfired on the very cause it was meant to promote.

In the course of this 'Black September', the entire PLO was dragged by the PFLP into a losing battle with troops loyal to King Hussein. The fedayeen could have been saved only by reinforcement from the Syrian armoured vehicles which crossed the border, but Hafez al-Assad, in charge of defence in Damascus, refused to grant them air cover, leaving the Jordanian air force to crush them. Assad preferred to sacrifice part of his own army so as to weaken his Ba'athist rivals, a manoeuvre crowned with success two months later by the putsch which inaugurated his three decades of absolute power over Syria. As for the PLO, it realized its tragic isolation in the face of Arab regimes which came together to neutralize its potential for destabilization. Nasser, on the verge of death, mobilized his last energies in favour of a ceasefire favourable to King Hussein. The fedayeen were forced to retreat to northwestern Jordan, from where they were later expelled to Syria and then Lebanon. The escalation between the Palestinian factions, itself encouraged by the settling of scores

---

[21] After annexing the West Bank in 1949, Jordan did indeed grant citizenship to all of its new subjects, including Palestinian refugees.
[22] The PFLP retained fifty-five hostages, after releasing the crews and the rest of the passengers.

between Arab regimes, fed into the terrorist spiral. A group dubbed 'Black September' led a bloody Israeli hostage-taking in September 1972 at the Munich Olympics. Israeli reprisals, initially against the Palestinian camps in Lebanon, were even more deadly than usual.

The 1967 triumph put Israel in control of a vast swathe of Arab territory and consolidated the reverse partnerships forged with the Iran of Muhammad Reza and, to a lesser extent, with a Turkey under military tutelage.[23] This dominant position and the mastery of nuclear weapons meant that King Hussein's overtures were not followed up, despite his numerous secret interviews with Israeli leaders. Nor did the expulsion of thousands of Soviet advisers by Anwar Sadat, Nasser's successor, lead Israel to amend its intransigent line towards Egypt. It is true that, in East Jerusalem and the West Bank, the Jewish state, intoxicated by its military supremacy, was reviving the religious language of attachment to *Eretz Israel*.[24] Even if the colonization of the West Bank was limited, and mainly meant to ensure security, Hebron, from where the Jews had been driven out in 1929, saw the first settlement of a messianic type. In addition, the repercussions of Arab independence and conflicts with Israel had led to the gradual disappearance of Sephardic communities in the Middle East. These 'Eastern' Jews, whose proportion continued to grow in Israel itself, felt they were discriminated against by the largely Ashkenazi Labour establishment. Having broken away from their original society also meant that they doubted any chances of reconciliation between their new state and its Arab neighbours.

The oil shock

Both Sadat and Assad took power in the autumn of 1970 and imposed a policy of 'rectification' of past mistakes, which allowed them to eliminate their rivals. Each forged a solid cooperation with Faisal, against a backdrop of economic liberalization, repression of the left, and overtures to the United States. Any real radical impetus now came from Iraqi general Ahmed Hasan al-Bakr, who finally installed the Ba'ath in power

[23] In 1960 and 1971, two coups were meant to restore the Kemalist 'order' in Ankara.
[24] This Hebrew translation of the 'Land of Israel' was sometimes seen as implying a 'Greater Israel' over all of former Mandate Palestine.

in 1968, with a distant relative, Saddam Hussein, as his deputy. The nationalization of oil in 1972, two decades after the failed attempt in Iran, enabled Baghdad to position itself as the spearhead of a combative Third Worldism. As with Qasim's resistance to the UAR, Bakr and Saddam flaunted the independence of Iraq against the Sadat–Assad tandem. In the fool's game of Arab despotism, the fact that Damascus and Baghdad were of the same party did not bring them any closer, but in fact widened the gap between the two pan-Arab Ba'ath leaderships; each claimed to be the only legitimate one, the Syrian party having an Iraqi branch, illegal in Iraq, and vice versa. Added to this was an underlying community antagonism, which deserves explanation in a party claiming to be secularist.

As we have seen, in 1959, an uprising in the Sunni city of Mosul was crushed by mainly Shiite and Kurdish militiamen. The Iraqi Ba'ath, in its opposition to Qasim and communism, attracted many Sunni militants, whom a decade of struggles and intrigues united around Bakr. In Syria, before and after the victorious putsch of 1963, the Ba'athist officers tended to be from minorities of Islam; successive purges had reinforced their local solidarity. Assad the Alawite, in his march to personal power, first eliminated his Druze and Isma'ili rivals before opposing and triumphing over other Alawite generals in 1970. In Damascus as in Baghdad, a dynamic of conspiracy, by definition anti-democratic, led Assad and Bakr, once they had become presidents, to privilege their immediate entourage, Alawite in the case of the former and Sunni in the case of the latter. These contradictions, aggravated by the showdown between the two Ba'aths, did not, however, disturb the relationship between Assad and Sadat, who were not separated by any ideological competition and who were brought closer by their shared interests.

The Egyptian and Syrian dictators both sought to wipe out the humiliation of 1967 in order to consolidate their 'rectified' regimes. They planned a joint offensive in Sinai and the Golan Heights to force Israel to negotiate a withdrawal. Their coordinated assault, on 6 October 1973, took the Jewish state by surprise,[25] before a vigorous counter-attack

[25] The Israeli reaction was, moreover, slowed down by the Yom Kippur holiday. This war began during the month of Ramadan, and is thus known as the 'Yom Kippur War' in Israel and the 'Ramadan War' in the Arab world, while the term 'October War' is favoured by historians.

enabled Israel, after ten days, to establish a bridgehead on the western bank of the Suez Canal and threaten the suburbs of Damascus. The airlift that the United States organized for the benefit of the Israeli army was crucial in this reversal. In the view of King Faisal, there was indeed co-belligerence this time. In retaliation, on 20 October, he announced an oil embargo against the United States. The other Arab producers followed suit, which led to a quadrupling of barrel prices in a few weeks. Israel, requested by the UN Security Council to accept a ceasefire on 22 October, did not comply until two days later.

This oil shock generated colossal resources for the Gulf monarchies. The former British protectorates, emancipated two years earlier to general indifference, were now courted on all sides. The United Arab Emirates, Kuwait, and, of course, Saudi Arabia attracted millions of immigrants, primarily from the rest of the Middle East. Their transfers in foreign currency quickly had a major impact on the economies of Egypt, Yemen, and Jordan. Proud of their social success, they accepted, in their country of origin, hitherto unknown social and religious practices. Supposedly 'Islamic' behaviour in dress, family, and prayer soon became widespread, in imitation of the Gulf. Saudi Arabia also invested a substantial part of the oil windfall in its institutions and its networks for international proselytism. This is how the Islamist synthesis between Wahhabi preachers and the Muslim Brotherhood spread with unparalleled vigour. So we need to date this fundamentalist wave in the Middle East to the oil shock of 1973, even though it is too often associated with the débâcle of 1967, as if Islamism had automatically occupied a ground left vacant by pan-Arabism. The windfall from oil allowed the Sauds to accentuate the patrimonial ruling of the country that bore their name, while the most fanatical of their supporters saw this tremendous wealth as the very proof of the virtues of the reigning family.

In 1973, Faisal, who had protected Arafat so much against Nasser during the Arab Cold War, granted signal support to the leader of the PLO, who in his eyes was the best bulwark against the leftist excesses of some Palestinian factions. Saudi generosity was coupled with substantial transfers from Palestinians settled in the Gulf, and the PLO benefited likewise from a tithe on the community of Kuwait.[26] Arafat, who

---

[26] It was in Kuwait that Fatah, the majority in the PLO, was founded in 1959.

personally controlled the finances of his organization, used this financial leverage to stem the terrorist escalation of the fedayeen groups. In June 1974, he had the PLO endorse the principle of a 'Palestinian Authority' over 'every portion of the liberated territory'. The PFLP retaliated by forming a 'Rejectionist Front' made up of factions attached to the 'liberation of all Palestine'. Arafat took the risk of breaking the default consensus within a politically fragmented and geographically dispersed movement. His reward for this, in October, was the admission of Palestine as a full member of the Arab League, to the great displeasure of Jordan. He was invited the following month to the UN General Assembly, where the Palestinian cause received support in principle from the recently decolonized countries. The PLO henceforth enjoyed a financial base and diplomatic support rare for a liberation movement. Arafat consolidated the new 'state within a state' he had established in Lebanon and travelled the world to plead the cause of his people. But, absorbed as he was by his activities on the Arab and international scenes, he increasingly struggled to grasp the daily reality of his compatriots under Israeli occupation.

The Pax Americana

In October 1973, the United States faced a major crisis in its Middle Eastern system, its alignment with Israel having compromised its pact with Saudi Arabia – hence the oil shock. Republican President Richard Nixon instructed his chief diplomat, Henry Kissinger, to apply a simple doctrine: no war in the Middle East could be won thanks to the USSR; no peace could be concluded there without the United States. The airlift of the October war had already enabled Israel to sweep away the achievements of the Arab armies supported by Moscow. Now it was necessary to lay the foundations of a *Pax Americana* which would be fostered under the exclusive aegis of the United States. Both Assad and Sadat sought such a sponsorship, from which they expected an American guarantee of the sustainability of their respective regimes. Syria's boycott of the UN peace conference, held in Geneva in December 1973, was decisive in the launch of Kissinger's shuttles between Israel and Egypt, on the one hand, and between Israel and Syria, on the other. At the beginning of 1974, these activities culminated in two parallel agreements to disengage in Sinai and the Golan Heights – Israel continued to occupy a majority of both territories. The oil embargo imposed by Arab countries on the United States was lifted after five months.

Kissinger thus managed to break the common front between Egypt and Syria, as well as to restore the Washington–Riyadh axis, without asking anything from Israel other than going 'step by step'. Despite its major investment in the Middle East, the USSR was obliged to endorse an American-brokered Israeli–Syrian agreement at the UN. For a quarter of a century, Assad would scrupulously respect the ceasefire established with Israel on the occupied Golan Heights. The PLO's diplomatic campaign in 1974 ran counter to this dynamic with, as we have just seen, some success. Arafat was all the more reluctant to involve his forces in the civil war that broke out in April 1975 in Lebanon. While the Christian right of the Phalangists denounced the Palestinian 'occupation' of the country, for a long time it fought only the Lebanese National Movement (LNM), a coalition of progressive and Muslim militias. The clashes were particularly violent in the centre of Beirut, with the dissemination of snipers who targeted the civilians of the opposing camp indiscriminately. Similarly, kidnappings based on identity cards, which mentioned a person's religious affiliation, became commonplace in all their horror.

It was not until January 1976 that the Phalangists carried out a massacre in a Beirut slum with a large Palestinian population, leading to the participation of the PLO in the liquidation of a Maronite locality north of Sidon. These killings and counter-killings widened the sectarian gap between militias in Lebanon, while the capital was divided between a 'Christian' East and a 'Palestinian-Islamo-progressive' West. The intervention of the PLO enabled the LNM to successfully go on the offensive, which prompted Assad to invade Lebanon in June 1976, fearing that a pro-Palestinian Lebanon would compromise his own arrangements with Israel on the Golan Heights. Assad was taking advantage of the call for help from the Lebanese President, Élias Sarkis, himself a Maronite – a call relayed by the Falangist leaders. Israel supported the intervention of the Syrian army against the PLO and the LNM, but prohibited it from deploying south of Sidon, leaving the fedayeen in de facto control of southern Lebanon. Saudi Arabia, where King Khalid had succeeded

Faisal[27] a year earlier, endorsed Assad's victory over Arafat. The Damascus troops were presented as an 'Arab deterrent force', dedicated to bringing calm to the country. The Syrian occupation of Lebanon would last nearly thirty years.

Democrat Jimmy Carter, who entered the White House in January 1977, drew on his Baptist faith to nurse his ambition to reconcile the 'sons of Abraham'. He recognized both Israel's right to 'defensible borders' and the Palestinians' right to a 'homeland'. His pacifist commitment was thwarted in May, however, with the defeat in the Israeli elections of the Labour Party, in power since independence in 1948. Menachem Begin, the new Prime Minister, was a significant revisionist for whom the abandonment of Jordan already represented a painful concession on the part of Zionism. His party, the Likud, relaunched the colonization of Gaza and the West Bank, described as 'Judea and Samaria', and proclaimed the indivisibility of *Eretz Israel*, the 'Land of Israel'. Sadat thought he could solve this impasse by going in person to Jerusalem in November to advocate peace in a vibrant speech to the Knesset, but Begin remained inflexible. Meanwhile, Arafat, who had hesitated to accompany Sadat to Jerusalem, tried a military manoeuvre to return to the centre of the stage, launching a major attack by Fatah in Israel in March 1978. This led to the occupation of southern Lebanon by Israeli troops, whose withdrawal Carter demanded, and subsequently obtained.[28]

With the PLO having excluded itself from the ongoing diplomatic process in the American President's eyes, he focused on peace between Israel and Egypt, welcoming Begin and Sadat to his residence in Camp David, north of Washington, in September 1978. This summit lasted thirteen days, during which the three leaders were cut off from the world. It led to two agreements. The first constituted the basis of an Israeli–Egyptian treaty, with the dismantling of Israeli colonies in the Sinai and evacuation from this Egyptian territory spread over three

---

[27] Faisal was killed in Riyadh in March 1975 by one of his nephews. The wildest conspiracy theories have been put forward to explain this murder, but it was just the work of a mentally unbalanced man.

[28] The Israeli army, however, continued to control, on its northern border, a 'security belt' managed by a militia of Lebanese auxiliaries.

years. The second dealt with 'peace in the Middle East' and provided for the association of Jordan and 'representatives of the Palestinian people' in the establishment of transitional autonomy for the West Bank and Gaza. Begin's refusal to make any concessions in 'Judea and Samaria' convinced King Hussein, despite pressure from Carter, not to endorse this process, which was itself condemned by the PLO. Thus, the Palestinian component of Camp David was stillborn, and with it Carter's grand design for a Middle East peace. The Israeli–Egyptian treaty of March 1979 earned its two signatories the Nobel Peace Prize, but it did not prevent Egypt from being excluded from the Arab world; exceptionally generous American aid could not make up for this. The Arab League left Cairo and set up its headquarters in Tunis. In the West Bank and Gaza, Israeli secret service forces encouraged Islamist networks in order to neutralize PLO supporters. In Libya, meanwhile, Gaddafi consolidated the absolute power of his 'Jamahiriya', literally his 'massocracy' or 'state of the masses', whose totalitarian tendencies sought to liquidate any form of intermediate body.

The Islamic Revolution

Muhammad Reza, proclaimed 'king-of-kings, sun of the Aryans', organized sumptuous ceremonies in Persepolis in 1971, a year supposed to mark the 2,500th anniversary of the Achaemenid Empire. His political police, the Savak, trained by the CIA, muzzled the various tendencies of the opposition, while the Shiite clergy endured in silence the official exaltation of the pre-Islamic past. The surge in oil prices allowed the shah to buy social peace; he also equipped himself with an arsenal worthy of his ambition – encouraged by the United States – to be the 'policeman of the Gulf'. In 1971, he seized three strategic islands guarding the entrance to the Strait of Hormuz,[29] but recognized the sovereignty of Bahrain, long claimed by his predecessors. In 1973, he intervened directly in Oman to protect the sultanate from a Marxist insurrection supported by its southern Yemeni neighbour. He also supported a Kurdish uprising in Iraq in 1974, before abandoning it the following year, in exchange for a

[29] These three islands were occupied by Iran a few days before the admission to the UN of the United Arab Emirates, which still demands their return.

settlement in his favour of the border dispute on the Shatt al-Arab, the common estuary to the Tigris and the Euphrates.[30]

Muhammad Reza was very close to Sadat, and supported the latter's overtures for peace with Israel, itself a key partner of Iran. The shah thought he had neutralized religious opposition by exiling, in 1964, its most virulent figure, Ayatollah Khomeini. He cared little for the diatribes of the prickly cleric against the corruption of the imperial regime, his submissiveness towards Washington, and his compromises with Israel. In the holy city of Najaf, in Iraq, Khomeini then developed the theocratic project of a 'government of the religious judge' (*velayat-e faqih*). He deliberately projected himself into this supreme role, thereby breaking with the tradition of Shiite quietism. For him, it was a question no longer of critiquing the failures of the sovereign in the name of the Hidden Imam, but rather of seizing power and exercising it. The unprecedented nature of this vision was paradoxically not realized by the overwhelming majority of observers, even activists, in those times that were so imbued with a Third-Worldist rhetoric. As for the Iraqi leaders, they mainly viewed Khomeini as a highly convenient means of putting pressure on their powerful neighbour.

The 'Tehran Spring' blossomed in 1977 thanks to the unprecedented tolerance of the imperial regime, at the promptings of the Carter administration. A space seemed to be opening up for a liberal and progressive challenge to the shah that would curb his megalomania. But in January 1978, the publication by Savak of calumnies against Khomeini provoked a riot in Qom, which was harshly repressed by the police. The demonstrations paying tribute to the victims, forty days later,[31] were themselves repressed, feeding from one fortieth day to another into a cycle of radicalization, up until the 'Black Friday' of 8 September, marked by the bloody intervention of the army. The Iraqi Ba'ath, worried by the echoes of this unrest among its predominantly Shiite population, asked France to take in Khomeini, who left Najaf for the Parisian suburb

---

[30] The Iraqi–Iranian border, fixed before 1975 on the eastern bank of the estuary, was now drawn through the middle.

[31] The forty-day period of mourning is very popular in Shia piety, where a specific feast marks the fortieth day following the death of Hussein each year (see above, p. 48).

of Neauphle-le-Château. The incendiary sermons of the man who now called himself 'imam' circulated on cassettes throughout Iran. In December, for two days in a row, the commemoration of the martyrdom of Imam Hussein attracted more than a million people in Tehran, from whose streets the army withdrew its armoured vehicles. In addition, the protest strike in the oil sector led to the suspension of exports. The bourgeoisie of the trading sector, hitherto only patchily mobilized, joined the movement, paralysing the country.

In January 1979, Muhammad Reza left Iran for Egypt. Two weeks later, a vast throng of millions of people welcomed Khomeini, back from exile on a special Air France flight. The gallant last stand of the Imperial Guard could no longer prevent, on 11 February, the overthrow of the Pahlavis by the first 'Islamic Revolution' in history. Anti-imperialism filled the air with cries of 'Down with America!', and the Israeli embassy, promptly evacuated, was handed over to Arafat himself, becoming the embassy of Palestine. The coalition of opposition to the shah, who had seen Khomeini as merely a tutelary figure, now discovered that he was the founder of a new regime. The imam had the 'Islamic Republic' approved by referendum with 98% of the votes, a credible score for once, unlike the plebiscites of the Arab dictatorships. He set up the 'Guardians of the Islamic Revolution', the Pasdaran, the Khomeini equivalent of the Imperial Guard, a Party of the Islamic Republic, and networks of 'committees' of unconditional supporters supervised by the clergy. Revolutionary courts handed down ever more death sentences, especially in the Kurdish provinces, even though the Peshmerga there, already rebelling against the shah, were merely claiming a form of autonomy.

The asylum given to the deposed sovereign in the United States, in November 1979, provided the pretext for the seizure of the American embassy in Tehran, where dozens of agents were held hostage for 444 days. This coup enabled Khomeini to raise the spectre of the overthrow of Mossadegh by the CIA in 1953, and to accuse all of his own adversaries of being linked with the American 'Great Satan'. In December, a new referendum ratified the Constitution of the Islamic Republic, with a unanimous vote much more questionable than in the spring. In line with the ideas Khomeini had propounded in Najaf, a two-tier system of legitimacy was instituted, with the electoral legitimacy of the President and Parliament subject to the theocratic legitimacy of the 'Guide of the Revolution', explicitly derived from the Hidden Imam. Most of the ayatollahs denounced this hijacking of centuries of Shiite dogmatics, but their protests were quickly repressed in Qom and Tabriz. The clerics loyal to Khomeini, on the other hand, benefited from annuities in the various religious foundations, the most powerful of which, the Astan Quds (the 'Sacred Threshold'), extended its hold throughout Mashhad. There were mass nationalizations, de facto or de jure, with an increase from 40% to 70% of the state's share in industry.

The Gulf War

Saddam Hussein, whose devouring ambition did not fit well with a mere vice-presidency, dismissed Bakr in July 1979. Despite his lack of military experience, he had already given himself the rank of general. He now combined the posts of head of state and Prime Minister, entrusting the management of the intelligence services to close relatives. He himself assassinated several of his Ba'athist rivals, accused of giving intelligence to Syria. He established a Republican Guard, to protect himself alone, but he was mainly faced by the challenge of Shiite protest, led by Ayatollah Baqir al-Sadr from Najaf and galvanized by the revolution in Tehran. Sadr had welcomed Khomeini during his Iraqi exile, and contributed to the drafting of the new Iranian constitution. Saddam ordered his execution by hanging in April 1980, transforming him into a martyr of a movement that simply drew fresh impetus from it. By striking Iran, Saddam hoped not only to take advantage of the intense unrest in the Islamic Republic, but also to extinguish the source of inspiration for Shiite dissent in Iraq. In September 1980, on live television, he tore up the border agreement concluded between Bakr and the shah. His troops invaded Iran, where they came up against fierce resistance fuelled, including in the Arabic-speaking province in the southwest of the country, by a general burst of enthusiasm for the sacred union. In believing that he could topple Khomeini, Saddam probably offered the Islamic Republic the chance to regenerate itself as the embodiment of Persian nationalism.

This major conflict profoundly restructured the Middle East, where the neutralization of Egypt and the fall of the shah aggravated the struggle between the two Ba'aths for regional leadership. The Assad regime decided to side with the Islamic Republic, out of shared hostility towards Saddam and in the name of 'resistance' to Israel. By contrast, the other Arab countries and the PLO rallied to Baghdad, whose campaign was largely financed by the oil monarchies. The Iraqi offensive claimed to be a modern repeat of that at Al-Qadisiyyah in 637, which saw the victory of the Arabs over the Persians, but also of Islam over Mazdaism. Iranian propaganda was no less excessive in equating, for example, Saddam with the caliph who had Hussein executed in 680. This appeal to the epic of the first century of Islam paradoxically proved that the split between Sunnis and Shiites, far from being spontaneous, needed to be dug out methodically by the war machine of the two despotisms of Iraq and Iran. The sacred union which saved the Islamic Republic in the name of Persian nationalism also held, albeit in a more attenuated mode, in Iraq, where the infantrymen, largely Shiites, remained loyal and combative.

Assad chose to ally himself with Khomeini, in defiance of the Arab world, for equally domestic reasons. Since 1979, he had been confronted with a wave of political and trade union protests, while an armed fraction of the Muslim Brotherhood continued its attacks. These Islamist insurgents took up the anathema launched, in the fourteenth century, by Ibn Taymiyyahh against the Alawites, accused of collaborating with Israel now as they allegedly collaborated with the Crusaders then. This stigma fed into anti-Alawi terrorism and allowed Assad to strengthen his still failing grip on his home community. Following a process already observed in Lebanon and Iraq, sectarian polarization maintained its own cumulative dynamic. The indiscriminate liquidations of Sunni civilians by the Ba'athist forces culminated in March 1982 in the slaughter at Hama.[32] Saddam's support for the Syrian Muslim Brotherhood in turn justified Assad's aid to Shia opponents in Iraq and, of course, the historic pact with Khomeini. But the Assad regime, contrary to an all too widespread cliché, did not act as a 'Shiite' state, firstly because the Alawites are precisely not Shias,[33]

---

[32] At least 10,000 people were killed by the Assad regime during the crushing of this city in central Syria, which had come under Islamist control in the previous month.
[33] Hafez al-Assad also took advantage of his occupation of Lebanon to impose official recognition of an Alawite community there, quite distinct from the Shia.

and secondly because this 'state of barbarism'[34] cannot be reduced to a sectarian structure.

The invasion of Lebanon

Menachem Begin and his Defence Minister, Ariel Sharon, taken aback by the fall of the shah, were glad to see Saddam launch the best equipped of the Arab armies towards the east. Israel secretly offered the Islamic Republic its military assistance in the face of the Iraqi invasion. Despite its outbursts against the 'Little Satan', Tehran gladly accepted this support, which was crucial for the spare parts of the American matériel acquired under the shah.[35] Complex circuits to supply Israel with oil from Iran were set up; at the same time, two-thirds of the Iranian Jewish community emigrated. In June 1981, the Israeli air force bombed the Osirak power plant, the heart of Saddam's nuclear programme.[36] This raid, with a range of 1,600 kilometres, carried out via Saudi Arabian airspace, preserved Israel's monopoly over atomic weapons in the region. The shock of Sadat's assassination three months later was quickly absorbed by the crushing of an Islamist uprising in Upper Egypt and the appointment of the designated successor, Hosni Mubarak, as President. Israel could therefore complete its withdrawal from Sinai in April 1982, in accordance with the peace treaty. This neutralization of Egypt left Israel free to attack Syria and the PLO on its northern border.

The hostage crisis in Iran tarnished the last year of Carter's presidency before he was succeeded by Republican Ronald Reagan. As a neo-cold-warrior, the new President was inclined to consider Assad and Arafat as mere pawns of the USSR. This was why he subscribed to the Israeli invasion of Lebanon in June 1982, even if it very quickly exceeded the limit of 40 kilometres initially set to rid Israel of the 'terrorist' threat on its northern border. Begin and Sharon were in fact determined to install in power in Beirut their Phalangist ally Bashir Gemayel, a bitter enemy of

---

[34] This is the definition given by Michel Seurat, who died at the hands of Hezbollah in 1986; he applied Ibn Khaldun's triptych to the conquest of the Syrian 'centre' by the 'group' of Assad, carried from the coastal 'periphery' by Ba'athist 'preaching'.
[35] The bringing down of a cargo aircraft in Soviet Armenia in July 1981 revealed the extent of this air traffic.
[36] An Iranian raid on Osirak had failed in September 1980.

the PLO and Syria. Assad concluded a ceasefire which gave the invaders access to Beirut. The Israeli army, welcomed as a liberator in the east of the city, besieged the west and its half-million civilians. Arafat posed as the leader of resistance to this blockade of an Arab capital, in the face of which all the Arab regimes and their armies remained passive. The siege, punctuated by intensive bombardments of densely populated areas, lasted two and a half months. Begin demanded a PLO capitulation, Sharon endeavoured to liquidate its leaders, while François Mitterrand, on the strength of his historic visit to Israel in March 1982 – the first by a French head of state – spared no effort to avoid a bloodbath.

At the very end of August 1982, the evacuation of Arafat and his thousands of fighters took place under the aegis of a Franco-American–Italian 'Multinational Force'. But a new escalation occurred in mid-September. Bashir Gemayel, just elected President of the Republic, perished in a terror attack orchestrated from Damascus. West Beirut was occupied by Israel, which allowed groups of Christian militiamen to enter the refugee camps of Sabra and Shatila. Here, a massacre of Palestinian civilians was perpetrated over two long days. The discovery of the horror led, in Beirut, to the return of the Multinational Force and, in Tel Aviv, to huge protest demonstrations. Sharon, personally implicated in the tragedy, lost the defence portfolio. Amin Gemayel was propelled to the Lebanese presidency, in place of his murdered brother. In May 1983, pressure from Reagan forced him to sign a peace treaty with Israel, the clauses of which were so draconian that Syria could now sponsor a rejectionist front against it.

Assad, whom Israel believed it had marginalized a year earlier, had only allowed Begin to finish in Beirut the process of liquidating the PLO which he himself had begun in Lebanon in 1976. He also turned against Reagan the logic of the Cold War and obtained massive support from the USSR to not only restore, but also to double Syria's military capabilities. Finally, he exploited his alliance with Khomeini to establish in Lebanon, under the auspices of the Syrian and Iranian intelligence services, a 'Party of God' (Hezbollah), whose suicide operations changed the balance of power.[37] This led to devastating attacks: in

[37] Hezbollah, established in Lebanon in 1982, did not announce its official foundation until three years later, so as not to have to assume responsibility for these terrorist carnages.

November 1982 on the Israeli command in Tyre (76 dead); in April 1983 on the American embassy in Beirut (63 dead); and in October on the barracks of the American and French contingents of the Multinational Force (241 marines and 58 paratroopers were killed). When pro-Syrian militias seized West Beirut in February 1984, the United States left the country in a hurry. France waited an additional month to withdraw its contingent, failing to secure its replacement by the UN. The peace treaty with Israel was abrogated by Lebanon, once again under the influence of Damascus. In the south of the country, the Israeli occupation elimi-nated the challenge of the PLO only to find itself faced with the 'Islamic resistance' of Hezbollah.

The Iranian turnaround

The Iraqi offensive of September 1980 quickly got bogged down. After three months, it had taken control of only 1% of enemy territory and only one city, the port of Khorramshahr. Saddam then decided to support the Iranian Peshmerga, who took revenge for the repression ordered in 1979 by Khomeini and succeeded in 'liberating' the Kurdish provinces in the spring of 1981. In the summer, as a result of plots probably woven in Baghdad, attacks liquidated the heads of the presi-dency and the government of Iran. In October, *hojatoleslam*[38] Ali Khamenei, until then a political commissar of the Revolutionary Guards, became President of the Islamic Republic. This rise was a reward for his absolute loyalty to the 'Guide' Khomeini, a loyalty that had already earned him an assassination attempt. The following month, the Al-Quds (Jerusalem) counter-offensive mobilized waves of infantry for the first time, fanaticized by the prospect of liberating not only their territory, but the Holy City itself. The propaganda of the two belligerents stigmatized the 'Zionism' of the opposing camp, while, in April 1982, Assad decided to close his border with Iraq, as well as the oil pipeline which crossed his territory. This was a severe blow for Saddam and transformed the Jordanian port of Aqaba into the main outlet for Iraq, with long lines of trucks to ensure supplies.

---

[38] This title is inferior to that of 'ayatollah' in the clerical hierarchy of Shiism (see above, p. 171).

In May 1982, the Revolutionary Guards, after driving the Peshmerga out of the Kurdish towns, entered liberated Khorramshahr. In June, Saddam withdrew all of his forces from Iranian territory and declared a unilateral ceasefire. Saudi Arabia accompanied this peace overture with an offer of $50 billion in war reparations to Iran. The Israeli siege of Beirut publicly justified these gestures of appeasement in the name of an imperative of Islamic solidarity. But Khomeini brushed aside these proposals, determined as he was to chastise Saddam and overthrow his regime. In July, he launched his troops against Iraq, with the declared objective of Basra, the country's second city. This invasion aroused in Iraq, albeit in an attenuated form, a groundswell of patriotism comparable to that which had united the Iranian population in the autumn of 1980. However, Khomeini had now compromised the determined dynamic of mobilization of his compatriots against the Arab 'aggressor'. The UN, which had reacted weakly to the opening of hostilities by Baghdad, this time designated Iran as solely responsible for the continuation of the conflict. The USSR suspended its significant military cooperation with Tehran and intensified its support for Iraq. The Iranian Communist Party, so far spared by the general repression, bore the brunt of this Soviet abandonment. This marked the end in the Middle East of a communist movement which, already greatly weakened in the Arab world, had survived only by making pacts with the worst dictatorships. In addition, pro-Iranian Hezbollah targeted Lebanese progressives to monopolize resistance against the Israeli occupation.

The Arab world, with the exception of Syria, then lined up behind Iraq and lived in fear of an Iranian breakthrough. Mubarak played on this Arab solidarity to bring Egypt out of its isolation, with rotations of officers going to serve in Iraq as 'advisers' on the front. Ali Abdullah Saleh, who had ruled North Yemen since 1978, sent thousands of 'volunteers' recruited from the tribes to Iraq. Saudi Arabia and the Gulf Emirates massively funded Saddam's war effort and enjoined their allies to deliver the most advanced military technology to Baghdad. The United States did likewise, but it was Mitterrand's France that was most committed to Baghdad. Tehran took revenge on these two countries with spectacular attacks in Beirut, coordinated with Assad's help. The Iranian offensives stalled and, in the summer of 1983, Khomeini launched a campaign to support a Kurdish uprising in Iraq, mirroring Saddam's manoeuvre two years earlier. It had limited impact. Not only did the Iranian Kurds, abandoned by their compatriots in Iraq, turn against them, but the two Kurdish parties in Iraq were divided: the Kurdistan Democratic Party integrated itself into the Iranian system, while the Patriotic Union of Kurdistan negotiated its neutrality with Saddam.[39]

Saddam's gas warfare

The Iranian–Iraqi front stretched for over 1,200 kilometres, but it was in the marsh zone in its far south that Khomeini ordered a major offensive in February 1984. It was repelled by Saddam only at the cost of an unprecedented use of chemical weapons,[40] with high-voltage lines being connected to the swamps to electrocute the invaders. The Islamic Republic celebrated with fervour the cult of the 'martyrs', built a 'fountain of blood' where the reddened water of their sacrifice flowed in Tehran, and recruited from the age of twelve 'volunteers' (*bassij*), sent to the front with the 'key' to paradise hanging from their necks. Hundreds of thousands of Iranians fled, usually via Turkey, to escape both the moral order and the risks of conscription. This exodus of part of the middle class radicalized the populist discourse of the regime in favour of the 'underprivileged'. In Iraq, Saddam organized his own personality cult to megalomaniac proportions. However, he was careful to limit the impact of the conflict on the country, while ensuring the loyalty of the army through regular purges. The Republican Guard, generously endowed, became the backbone of the regime. Baghdad also benefited from its rapprochement with Ankara, whose army was authorized to pursue the Turkish peshmerga of the Kurdistan Workers' Party (PKK) in the far north of Iraq. This new group, whose intransigent Marxism combated traditional hierarchies, further aggravated divisions among the Kurds.

In March 1985, Khomeini launched the second battle of the marshes. Though his soldiers were now equipped with gas masks and atropine

---

[39] The KDP leader was Masoud Barzani, whose father had led the 1961–1970 and 1974–1975 uprisings against Baghdad. Jalal Talabani's PUK split from the KDP after the shah abandoned the Kurdish guerrillas in 1975.

[40] These were tabun, sprayed from aircraft, and mustard gas, fired by shells. The Egyptian army had already used gas occasionally in Yemen in 1965–1967 (see above, p. 278).

syringes, they were turned back by the Republican Guard and the Iraqi army, which once again resorted to chemical weapons. These fierce fights, sometimes hand-to-hand, recalled the Dantesque images of the First World War in Europe. They were accompanied by a 'war of the cities', where the two countries indiscriminately launched ballistic missiles against their respective urban centres. The Iraqi air force decreed a no-fly zone over all Iranian territory and carried out indiscriminate bombings as far as Tehran. The truce, concluded in June 1985 under the aegis of the UN, concerned only this war of the cities, as hostilities continued on two fronts, in the marshes and Kurdistan. Two months later, Ali Khamenei was re-elected president with 88% of the vote, Iranian propaganda having succeeded in covering up the scandal of his sister's defection to Iraq. In February 1986, Iran seized the Iraqi peninsula of Al-Faw, at the mouth of the Shatt al-Arab. Saudi Arabia responded to this breakthrough by doubling its oil production, which caused prices to collapse. Iraq, unlike Iran, was able to make up for this brutal cut in its revenues through the generosity of its Gulf allies. The Reagan administration encouraged this oil 'counter-shock' to weaken Mikhail Gorbachev's USSR.

Tehran managed to reconcile under its aegis the Kurdish parties of Iraq, which launched coordinated operations involving both Peshmerga and Islamic Revolutionary Guard Corps in the north of the country. Saddam retaliated in the spring of 1987 with a scorched earth campaign, involving forced Arabization and the deportation of populations. A new Iranian offensive in March 1988 seized the Kurdish town of Halabja. Saddam ordered it to be carpet-bombed with napalm, followed by the spreading of lethal gases. Thousands of civilians were killed in this carnage, which halted the Iranian advance. In April, the Republican Guard won the battle for the reconquest of Fao,[41] following which Saddam made a highly publicized thanksgiving pilgrimage to Mecca. Iraq gradually managed to expel Iranian forces from the territories they continued to occupy. In July, Khomeini finally agreed, in his own words, to 'swallow the poison' of a ceasefire, effective the following month. Both countries were ruined and exhausted, with approximately 200,000 dead on the Iraqi side and 500,000 on the Iranian side, which corresponds to

---

[41] In the same month, April 1988, the Iranian navy was hit hard by the United States, in the name of guaranteeing freedom of movement throughout the Persian Gulf.

the ratio between the populations of the two countries. These losses were overwhelmingly military, despite the war of the cities and the massacres of the Kurds in 1987–1988 in Iraq. Saddam swaggered, even if he had to recognize the border with Iran which he had justly denounced in 1980. As for Khomeini, he died in June 1989, bequeathing his title of 'Guide' to Khamenei, promoted to ayatollah for the occasion.

The survival of the Islamic Republic was thus ensured by political allegiance rather than by religious legitimacy, a paradox that is not emphasized enough for this theocratically inspired system. Khamenei may have been hastily appointed 'ayatollah', but unlike Khomeini, who could combine the two legitimacies of religious charisma and political power, he was quite unable to claim to be a *marja*, a spiritual authority to be followed by faithful Shiites. Thus when he did indeed claim this title in 1994, following the deaths of highly respected ayatollahs in Iraq and Iran, resistance to this coup was so strong in Iran itself that he was obliged to restrict his claims to Shiites living outside Iran. In this way, the Lebanese Hezbollah, by choosing Khamenei as both a political and religious guide, comprised the big battalions of his followers abroad. But the ayatollahs of Najaf continued to be the most popular in Iraq as well as in Iran. This pre-eminence was based on the desire of the Shiite hierarchy, supported by the vast majority of the faithful, to dissociate the political domain from the religious domain, contrary to the very principle of the Islamic Republic. Such tensions at the very heart of the Shiite clergy once again invalidate sectarian generalizations.

The first intifada

Yitzhak Shamir, former military leader of Lehi, succeeded Menachem Begin in 1983 as head of Likud and the Israeli government. The following year, he brought the Labour Party into a government of national unity, of which he assumed the leadership alternately with Shimon Peres, Yitzhak Rabin holding the defence portfolio. The policy of the 'iron fist' in southern Lebanon failed to stem the rise of a resistance that Hezbollah now took over. As for the PLO, it had to follow the Arab League, settling in Tunis, where its headquarters were bombed in October 1985 by the Israeli air force. Arafat, who emerged unscathed from this raid, resumed his diplomatic tours to promote the Palestinian cause. But a new generation was emerging in the West Bank and Gaza, driven by the urgent need to end an increasingly oppressive occupation and colonization. This generation recognized itself in the PLO, while reproaching its exiled leadership for having lost the sense of the realities of the 'interior' of Palestine.[42] Anti-Israeli riots began in a refugee camp in the Gaza Strip in December 1987, and soon extended to all the occupied territories. Even in East Jerusalem, the unrest reactivated the 'Green Line' that separated Israel from Jordan before 1967.

This marked the beginning of an 'intifada', literally an uprising, whose refusal of armed struggle reconnected with the general strike of 1936 in Palestine, as well as with the non-violent 'revolution' of the Egyptian people against the British occupation in 1919. Where we have seen so many Arab peoples dragged by their despots into bloody conflicts, this 'stone revolution' faced the PLO with the historical responsibility of limiting the 'liberation of Palestine' to territories occupied in 1967. King Hussein of Jordan accepted the new deal in July 1988, and publicly renounced any claim to the West Bank. The next step was taken in November in Algiers, where the PLO National Council met. Despite the opposition of the PFLP, the State of Palestine was proclaimed on the basis of UN resolutions and, therefore, of the recognition of Israel. The following month, the United States finally agreed to enter into dialogue with the PLO. This diplomatic breakthrough was, however, limited to the level of the American ambassador in Tunis, while Shamir refused the slightest concession to the 'terrorists'. This obstacle played into the hands of Palestinian Islamists, who, long encouraged by Israel, had formed Hamas, the acronym for the Islamic Resistance Movement. Supported by Damascus and Tehran, they took up the demand for the 'liberation of all Palestine', a demand abandoned by the PLO, and henceforth Islamized.

The Afghan blindspot

While all these upheavals were shaking the Middle East, no one paid any attention to the journey of a phalanx of Arab extremists on the borders of Afghanistan. In the very last days of 1979, the quarrels tearing the

---

[42] In Arabic *dakhil*, opposed to *kharij*, the 'outside' of exile.

local Communist Party apart forced the Red Army into direct intervention. For the USSR, it was a matter of preserving in Kabul the only 'Democratic Republic' on its southern border. The invaders initially limited themselves to controlling the urban centres and the strategic axes, but the generalized insurrection quickly led them to deepen their commitment. The Afghan uprising in the name of jihad was part of a trend, lasting a century and a half, of national resistance pursued in Islamic terms, since Abdelkader in Algeria and Shamil in the Caucasus. The very strong local roots of the combatant groups enabled them to hold their own against the ferocity of the invasion, but it prevented them from forming a coalition on a national scale. Of the 15 million Afghans, around 2 million took refuge in Iran and 3 million in Pakistan, where their camps were often set up in 'tribal areas'. These spaces of lawlessness had been established at the time of the Indian Empire, as a way of protecting itself already from unrest in Afghanistan. The system was given a new lease of life by independent Pakistan as a veritable tribal buffer zone against Afghan irredentism.[43]

Saudi Arabia saw Afghanistan as the ideal Islamic cause for it to go beyond the Arab framework of its ambitions and to counter the 'exporting' of the Iranian revolution. Tehran then focused on helping the insurgents in the border province of Herat and on the predominantly Shiite central plateau. The Islamist generals in power in Pakistan were promoted to Washington's strategic partners in this new episode of the Cold War. The Saudi services concluded an agreement with the CIA for equal funding of anti-Soviet groups. Billions of dollars were poured out in ten years, mainly in the tribal areas where Wahhabi preachers were ubiquitous. It was in this context that a 'Services Bureau' was established in 1984 in Pakistan to channel Arab candidates towards the Afghan jihad. This office was headed by two former members of the Muslim Brotherhood, disavowed by their organization. Sheikh Abdullah Azzam, a Jordanian of Palestinian origin, developed the argument of a 'global jihad' in which every Muslim throughout the world had the imperative

---

[43] Afghanistan had been contesting its border with Pakistan since 1949, a border drawn in 1893 by London. Eastern Afghani tribes and Pakistani tribal areas are part of the same Pashtun ethnic group, which has historically held power in Kabul, due to its relative majority in the population.

obligation to come and fight in Afghanistan. This marked a break with fourteen centuries of Sunni theology, according to which jihad, whether defensive or offensive, was always linked to a population and a territory. His deputy, Osama bin Laden, was the son of the richest Saudi public works contractor. Contrary to a widespread assertion, Bin Laden did not need the support of the CIA as his Saudi resources were plentiful. On the other hand, Azzam conducted recruitment tours for his Services Bureau as far as the United States.

Thousands of Arab volunteers thus moved towards the tribal areas of Pakistan, even if only a small part of them crossed the border to actually fight in Afghanistan. Bin Laden himself only took part in fighting against the Red Army for ten days in 1986. He nevertheless built up his militant legend, using the medium of the video cassette, just as Khomeini had broadcast his revolutionary message in audio format in 1978. In general, the contribution of Arab militants to the conflict was negligible, with a few tens of deaths for hundreds of thousands of Afghan victims of the Soviet occupation. But the tribal areas had become a veritable incubator for Arab extremism. Military training there was less intended for the Afghan jihad than for a violent subversion of the countries of origin. The USSR began its withdrawal from Afghanistan in May 1988, rendering the Services Bureau obsolete. Bin Laden, emancipated from his mentor Azzam, then established his own 'jihadist' organization, since it was dedicated to global jihad. This was Al-Qaeda, 'the Base', founded in Pakistan in the greatest secrecy, on the very day of the ceasefire between Iran and Iraq. Bin Laden, back in Arabia, was celebrated there as a hero, while the Saudi intelligence services, unaware of the existence of Al-Qaeda, mobilized its supporters for operations to destabilize communist South Yemen.

Reversed fronts

The Middle East has been, since 1945, a fertile ground for reversals of alliances and reversed fronts, in addition to unholy wars waged under cover of open conflicts. This was how Transjordan, officially at war with the Jewish state in 1948, shared out Palestinian territory with it. And how anti-Zionist Syria made a pact with Israel in 1976 to defeat the PLO in Lebanon. As for Nasser, the priority he gave to his war against Saudi Arabia in Yemen made him lose sight, in 1967, of the reality of the conflict with Israel, into which he rushed without serious preparation. The different branches of Arab nationalism were constantly tearing each other apart, instead of opposing a unified front to the supposedly common enemy. The contradictions were even more violent between the two Ba'aths, to the point of leading Saddam to support the Muslim Brotherhood in Syria while, on the other hand, Assad broke Arab solidarity by allying himself with Khomeini. Israel was no more consistent in its official doctrine when it wagered on the Islamists to divide the Palestinian camp, or when it secretly re-established with revolutionary Iran the reverse partnership in force under the shah.

The cliché that 'the enemy of my enemy is my friend' is valid only if the main objective of each of the actors in these often intertwined conflicts is identified. Another problem is that, all too frequently, there is a confusion between 'reason of state', the cornerstone of the Westphalian vision of international relations, and 'reason of the regime', the compass of authoritarianisms that disguised their factional interests as national priorities. Israel, established and experienced as a Jewish and democratic state, stands out by its ability to mobilize in the name of a higher interest, admittedly at the cost of the exclusion of its Arab minority from this patriotic dynamic. The military hierarchy in Turkey claimed to embody a reason of state, identified with the Kemalist heritage, and in its name carried out the three putsches of 1960, 1971, and 1980, each time followed by a laborious restoration of the party system. As for the Islamic Republic of Iran, it managed to survive, first through the sacred union that Iraq's aggression provoked, then through the 'revolutionary' prolongation of the conflict, a prolongation which was just as disastrous for the country as it was beneficial to the regime.

The failure of the elites which emerged from the Nahda sealed, in the Arab world, the impossibility of an authentic reason of state, and a fortiori of a policy carried out according to the general interest. Everywhere, the rulers, and they alone, impose their priorities in the name of a nation reduced to silence. Once the independence-negotiating dynasties in Egypt, Iraq, and Libya had been eliminated by coups, the surviving monarchies relied on patrimonial legitimacy, the reigning family having literally built the country around it, in Arabia, Jordan, and the Gulf emirates. Dictatorial republics, on the other hand, have struggled to anchor their legitimacy in anything other than repression, despite agrarian reforms, nationalizations, major infrastructure projects, and, of course, investment in education and health. The focus on the 'masses' was in fact accompanied by a ban on access to citizenship, with people being taken hostage by the 'reason of the regime' in power. The sectarian republic of Lebanon is a very special case, but the sectarian 'reason of the regimes' was decisive in the descent into hell where the militiamen held sway. In this respect, the defeat of the PLO in 1976 against Syria was also the defeat of the Lebanese left and its project of secularization.

Let us experiment with an iconoclastic transposition of Ibn Khaldun's triptych to the case of Israel. The Jewish 'group', bearer of Zionist 'preaching', succeeded, from the world's periphery, in conquering the Palestinian 'centre'. Settler colonization and support from the diaspora as well as from the United States, it will be objected, make such a transposition questionable. But it is indisputable that the Arab Middle East, split under the blows of the Nakba of 1948 and the Naqsa of 1967, was exhausted in a spiral of conflicts between Cairo and Riyadh, Cairo and Baghdad, Damascus and Baghdad, not to mention the conflicts that were settled by proxy in Beirut. Nationalist 'preaching' sounds more and more hollow, just as the ideological substance of party-states evaporates, which little by little deprives the dominant 'group' of any solidarity other than a community-based one. This is how the Ba'ath dropped the mask of the reign, in Damascus, of an Alawite clan over a Sunni majority and, in Baghdad, of a Sunni clan over a Shiite majority. Republican dictatorships, driven solely by 'reason of the regime', thus fuel a sectarian dynamic that only a real process of national emancipation could have stopped.

Saudi Arabia is free of such contradictions since its state-building process was literally 'Saudi', therefore identified with the ruling family, and state Wahhabism excludes only the Shiite minority on the eastern coast. The oil crisis of 1973 also offered fabulous resources to fundamentalist preaching, in the Middle East and beyond. But the Khomeini victory of 1979 marked the emergence of a revolutionary alternative to the Islamist model hitherto associated with Riyadh. The Islamic Republic of Iran, despite its universalist pretensions, nevertheless inscribed its Shiite particularism in the very text of its constitution and concentrated the 'exporting' of its revolution to Shiite communities alone. The Islamist dynamic, far from being uniform, thus led, like the nationalist dynamic before it, to new fault lines in the Middle East. The antagonism between Sunnis and Shiites, far from being a timeless given, has never been so accentuated as since the confrontation between two regimes of theocratic inspiration in Tehran and Riyadh. Despotisms, whether nationalist or Islamist, have indeed been the main factors of sectarian polarization in the Middle East. But it was the United States, more out of imperial blindness than out of calculating cynicism, that would contribute decisively to this process of decomposition and fragmentation, a process that has continued until the present day.

Chronology

30 March 1949	First of three putsches in eight months in Syria.
29 April 1951	Muhammad Mossadegh, Prime Minister in Iran.
22 October 1951	Turkey joins NATO.
24 December 1951	Independence of the 'United Kingdom' of Libya.
23 July 1952	'Free Officers' coup in Egypt.
19 August 1953	CIA coup against Mossadegh in Iran.
24 February 1955	'Baghdad Pact' against the USSR.
26 July 1956	Nationalization of the Suez Canal by Nasser.
29 October 1956	Franco-Anglo-Israeli attack on Egypt.
2 February 1958	Egyptian–Syrian United Arab Republic (UAR).
14 July 1958	Overthrow of the Iraqi monarchy.
28 September 1961	Syrian withdrawal from the UAR.
26 September 1962	Yemen Arab Republic in Sanaa.
8 March 1963	Ba'ath takeover of Syria.
21 June 1963	Lévy Eshkol, Prime Minister of Israel.
2 November 1964	Faisal, king of Saudi Arabia.
1 January 1965	Fatah's first anti-Israeli attack.
5–10 June 1967	Arab–Israeli 'Six-Day War'.
30 November 1967	People's Republic of Yemen in Aden.
17 July 1968	Ba'ath takeover of Iraq.
4 February 1969	Yasser Arafat, leader of the PLO.
1 September 1969	Muammar Gaddafi's putsch in Libya.
6–27 September 1970	'Black September' crisis in Jordan.
28 September 1970	Death of Nasser, replaced by Anwar Sadat.
17 November 1970	Hafez al-Assad seizes power in Syria.
1 June 1972	Nationalization of Iraqi oil.
6–24 October 1973	Yom Kippur/Ramadan Arab–Israeli War.
20 October 1973	Saudi Arabia oil embargo against the United States.
21 December 1973	UN Peace Conference in Geneva.
13 April 1975	Beginning of the 'civil war' in Lebanon.

1 June 1976	Syrian intervention in Lebanon.
17 May 1977	Victory of the Likud in the Israeli elections.
19 November 1977	Visit of President Sadat to Jerusalem.
5–17 September 1978	Israeli–Egyptian summit at Camp David.
11 February 1979	Islamic Revolution in Iran.
26 March 1979	Israeli–Egyptian peace treaty in Washington.
16 July 1979	Saddam Hussein absolute master of Iraq.
4 November 1979	Capture of the US embassy in Iran.
27 December 1979	Soviet invasion of Afghanistan.
22 September 1980	Iraq invades Iran.
6 October 1981	Sadat assassinated in Cairo.
6 June 1982	Israeli invasion of Lebanon.
13 July 1982	Iranian counter-offensive in Iraq.
16–18 September 1982	Massacre in Sabra and Chatila.
18 April 1983	Attack on the American embassy in Beirut.
15 August 1984	Beginning of PKK insurgency in Turkey.
9 December 1987	Beginning of the first Palestinian intifada.
16 March 1988	Chemical attack on Iraqi Kurds.
15 May 1988	Beginning of the Soviet withdrawal from Afghanistan.
20 August 1988	Ceasefire between Iraq and Iran.
15 November 1988	Proclamation of the State of Palestine in Algiers.
3 June 1989	Death of Khomeini.

Further reading

Adib-Moghaddam, Arshin (ed.), *A critical introduction to Khomeini* (New York: Cambridge University Press, 2014).

Batatu, Hanna, *Syria's peasantry, the descendants of its lesser notables, and their politics* (Princeton, NJ: Princeton University Press, 1999).

Hegghammer, Thomas, *The caravan: Abdallah Azzam and the rise of global jihad* (New York: Cambridge University Press, 2020).

Kandil, Hazem, *Soldiers, spies and statesmen: Egypt's road to revolt* (London and New York: Verso, 2012).

Kerr, Malcolm, *The Arab Cold War: Gamal Abd al-Nasir and his rivals, 1958–70* (Oxford: Oxford University Press, 2003).

Razoux, Pierre, *The Iran–Iraq war*, translated by Nicholas Elliott (Cambridge, MA: Harvard University Press, 2015).

Sacco, Joe, *Footnotes in Gaza* (London: Jonathan Cape, 2009).

Seale, Patrick, *The Struggle for Syria: a study of post-war Arab politics, 1945–58* (New Haven, CT: Yale University Press, 1987).

Segev, Tom, *1967: Israel, the war, and the year that transformed the Middle East*, translated by Jessica Cohen (New York: Metropolitan Books, 2007).

Trabulsi, Fawwaz, *A history of modern Lebanon* (London: Pluto Press, 2007).

TEN

The life and death of the American Middle East (1990–2020)

When Alfred Mahan conceptualized the Middle East in 1902 as the key to global hegemony, his discourse was addressed to the dominant maritime power of the moment, Great Britain. It was not until 1945 that Roosevelt, by forging the American–Saudi pact, and Truman, by siding with the Zionist camp, established the two pillars of American policy in the Middle East. It was in this region that, in 1956, Eisenhower triggered the end of the colonial empires of France and the United Kingdom. In 1967, the military triumph of Israel sealed American pre-eminence, as did the victory of Saudi Arabia in its 'Arab Cold War' against Egypt. It was in the Middle East that the United States compensated in 1973 for its setbacks in Vietnam by initiating a negotiated process that dissociated Egypt, even more than Syria, from its Soviet sponsor. But the oil shock then demonstrated the vulnerability of the United States to Middle Eastern unrest, even on the part of its closest allies. Faisal's Saudi Arabia was no more an American pawn than was Begin's Israel. This ruined Carter's 1978 plan for a *Pax Americana* on a regional scale, and in 1982 it led to Reagan's venture in Lebanon, from which the United States emerged humiliated two years later. Yet, in 1990, it was in the Middle East that Washington was to lay the foundations of a post-Soviet 'new world order'.

'Desert Storm'

When George H. W. Bush, Reagan's Vice-President, succeeded him in the White House in 1989, the new Cold War cycle, fuelled by Republican administrations, had ended in triumph for the United States, while the USSR, exhausted by the arms race and the oil 'counter-shock', was withdrawing its troops from Afghanistan. From the vantage point of Washington, the conflict between Iran and Iraq made it possible to neutralize the two belligerents and their desire to export their respective models. But Saddam waged his war on credit; he was financed by the Gulf monarchies, and he aimed to make them pay the colossal bill for the reconstruction of Iraq. Tensions rose between Baghdad and its donors, who were increasingly reluctant to renew their generosity. These tensions were aggravated by the restoration of the border status quo on the Shatt al-Arab, which left Baghdad with only half of this estuary as its sole outlet into the Persian Gulf. Hamstrung by the ceasefire on the Iranian side, Saddam stepped up the pressure on his Kuwaiti neighbour to expand his maritime access. In this way, he reconnected with Ottoman claims on Kuwait and Baghdad's challenge in 1961 to the independence of the emirate.

On 2 August 1990, Iraqi troops invaded Kuwait and wiped out the army within hours. Bush took the lead in the international mobilization against this show of force in order to dissuade Saddam from continuing his offensive towards Saudi Arabia. On 6 August, American troops set up their 'Desert Shield' in the heart of the oil zone, on the eastern coast of the kingdom. Two days later, Saddam reacted by decreeing the pure and simple annexation of Kuwait. The closure of Iraq's borders led to the taking of thousands of Westerners as hostages, then their release in instalments following the whims of Baghdad. In the Arab world, demonstrations celebrated Saddam as the new Saladin, equating the oil monarchies with Western imperialism, and even with Israel. Indeed, Baghdad said it would withdraw from Kuwait only in return for Israel's evacuation of all the occupied Arab territories. Jordan and Yemen, already committed to Iraq in its conflict with Iran, once again rallied to it. The PLO was caught up in this escalation of nationalism against the backdrop of the deadlock of the intifada in the West Bank and Gaza.

Pro-Saddam fever also swept over the Muslim Brotherhood, which took the risk of a confrontation with its Saudi patron so as not to cut itself off from its popular base. Riyadh retaliated by expelling the Islamist brotherhood from its positions of responsibility and replacing it with supporters of a literalist approach to dogma. This represented the victory of the 'Salafist' current, with proven loyalty to the power in place, over the 'idolatry' that, in its view, political activism represented. Salafism and its rigorous moral order now controlled the proselytizing network of Saudi Arabia and, in lieu of the Muslim Brotherhood, benefited from these formidable resources. But what was at the time an ultra-minority tendency refused to choose between support for Baghdad and endorsement of the American deployment. Osama bin Laden, placed under house arrest before being expelled to Pakistan, would embody this jihadist extremism. While international attention focused on the Saudi–Kuwaiti border, there was a split between the activism of the Muslim Brotherhood, the herd mentality of the Salafists, and the extremism of the jihadists. Qatar, another Wahhabi emirate, would take many years to become the official patron of the Muslim Brotherhood, a way to emerge from the shadow of Saudi Arabia and assert itself on the international scene.

As summer of 1990 ended, it was time to mobilize against Saddam. The United States was methodically building up a coalition whose Arab component, though militarily weak, was politically essential. Mubarak's Egypt placed at the service of Saudi Arabia the same officers who had acted as Saddam's 'advisers' against Iran. Assad's Syria traded its participation against the American blank cheque in return for the crushing of the last patriotic redoubt in Beirut, thus pocketing the fruit of fourteen years of occupation of Lebanon. Assad was wise enough, in his expansionist aims, to be more patient and less provocative than his Ba'athist counterpart in Baghdad, Saddam. On 29 November 1990, American diplomacy, after months of negotiations, ensured that the UN Security Council passed resolution 678, which gave Iraq until 15 January 1991 to evacuate Kuwait; if it failed to do so, the resolution legitimized the use of force. At this time, 500,000 American soldiers, supported in Saudi Arabia by a coalition of thirty-four nations, faced a comparable number of Iraqi soldiers. However, this equivalence existed only on paper, while Washington had obtained a UN mandate to wage the war as it pleased.

On 16 January 1991, Bush launched 'Desert Storm', a six-week campaign that involved shelling Iraqi targets, both military and civilian.[1] The technological superiority of the United States was overwhelming and world opinion discovered the spectacular effectiveness of the Pentagon in real time, thanks to CNN.[2] Saddam tried to widen the conflict by

---

[1] This campaign, launched by the White House on the evening of 16 January 1991, began, due to the time difference, in the early hours of 17 January in the Middle East.

[2] In addition to being accredited to the coalition, this American non-stop news channel had the only Western correspondent in Baghdad.

firing forty missiles into Israel, where the risk of a chemical strike was taken very seriously. But these missiles carried conventional loads and ultimately killed only three Israelis. Bush deployed batteries of inter-ceptor missiles and prohibited Israel from any form of retaliation. The ground offensive, launched on 24 February, lasted just one hundred hours. Washington highlighted the role played by Arab contingents in the liberation of Kuwait. The lack of resistance surprised even the most optimistic of American planners. In fact, the Iraqi army had fallen apart, while the Republican Guard protected Saddam and the capital. The United States lost only 154 soldiers in combat during the entire campaign, while Iraqi losses were at least a hundred times higher: a combined Iraqi civilian/military death toll of tens of thousands cannot be ruled out. This imprecision, due to the chaos then prevailing in Iraq, was aggravated by the overlapping of conflicts with a vast anti-Saddam insurrection as soon as Kuwait was liberated.

The new order

On 2 March 1991, rebellion broke out in Basra and spread to the holy cities of Najaf and Karbala before reaching the Shiite neighbourhoods of Baghdad. Thousands of deserters took to guerrilla warfare, convinced that the United States, after weeks of encouraging them to insubordi-nation, would give them support. On 5 March, the Kurdish provinces rose up in turn. The regime accepted all American conditions for a ceasefire and could thus concentrate its forces on the home front. The Bush administration, fearing that Iran would profit from the unrest, tolerated the deployment of helicopters and the use of napalm against insurgent cities. Once the Shiite revolt was crushed, Saddam turned to the Kurdish north, from where waves of people fled to Turkey. On 6 April, a no-fly zone was finally imposed by the United States, the United Kingdom, and France north of the 36th parallel, allowing the population to take refuge there without leaving Iraq.[3] But Saddam got

[3] The Kurdistan Democratic Party (KDP) and the Patriotic Union of Kurdistan (PUK) managed this de facto autonomy of Iraqi Kurdistan, before tearing each other apart from 1994 to 1997, the year in which the area was divided between the two parties, with the KDP in Erbil and the PUK in Sulaymaniyah.

through the ordeal, at the cost of slaughtering tens of thousands of civilians and ransacking holy Shiite cities. The carnage took place behind closed doors, with the foreign press considering the crisis to have ended with the liberation of Kuwait. The regime even took advantage of very harsh international sanctions and generalized rationing to strengthen its grip on a population that was now at its mercy.

Bush declared, as early as September 1990, that the restoration of Kuwait's sovereignty was only the first step towards the establishment of a 'new world order'. Ordinary citizens, however, celebrated in Europe for the fall of the Berlin Wall and the collapse of the socialist bloc, had no place in this new order in the Middle East. The Iraqi population made this cruel discovery in March 1991, when it was abandoned to the savagery of Saddam. A historic opportunity to rebuild a plural Iraq, even if not one that would have been democratic from the outset, was thus lost. This mattered little to American strategists, for whom only the ruling powers in these respective states counted. The manoeuvres were both intelligent and brutal, and based on the imperative to defend Saudi Arabia, with the assistance of Egypt and Syria, while Israel was, for the first time, obliged to suffer being bombed without reacting. This reconfiguration of the Middle East wrecked the triangular relationship between the structuring poles of the region. It was accompanied by an embargo on Iraq, to the great satisfaction of Iran, which was finally rid of the Ba'athist challenge on its border. As for Turkey, its strategic role in NATO, far from disappearing with the Soviet threat, justified the creation of a buffer zone on its southeastern border, in Iraqi territory.

This great imperial endeavour was notably coherent; meanwhile, the USSR, reduced to impotence, could only endorse Washington's designs. This 'new order' was nevertheless limited, in the Middle East, to recycling the arrangements of the old order, with its arbitrariness and its brutality merely intensified. It was closely based on the sanctuarization of the Saudi regime, reinforced by a hardening of Salafist trends in their most regressive aspects. So much for those naïve souls who believed that the deployment of half a million Western soldiers should have automatically led to the reform of the Wahhabi kingdom. The United States and its allies, by agreeing to be defrayed for their commitment, became less the protectors of the oil monarchies than indebted to them, as they competed for their favours and contracts. Jordanian, Palestinian, and

Yemeni immigrants from the Gulf, on the other hand, were deprived of their transfers in foreign currency and paid for the alignment of their leaders with Saddam by being expelled en masse to their countries of origin. They were replaced by Indians, Pakistanis, Bangladeshis, and Filipinos, who were reputed to be more docile. The gap between the poorest and the richest Arabs was still widening. But it was undoubtedly the regressive Salafist trend that represented the most fatal legacy of this crisis. And the West, by intervening unconditionally to save threatened Saudi Arabia, made a powerful contribution to such a trend.

The peace process

Bush convened a peace conference in Madrid in October 1991, the fundamental objective of which was to consecrate American hegemony in the Middle East. Mikhail Gorbachev assumed a symbolic co-presidency shortly before the official disappearance of the USSR. The UN and the twelve members of the European Union had just one observer's seat each. American diplomats negotiated with Israel, Syria, and Lebanon over the conditions of their presence. They also saw to the constitution of a Jordanian–Palestinian delegation, from which the PLO was excluded, as were the residents of East Jerusalem and the refugees – at Shamir's insistence. The conference broke up after two days to let Israel negotiate bilaterally, in Washington, with each of the Arab parties. This was the beginning of the 'peace process', the unfolding of which guaranteed the pre-eminence of the United States, with no deadline for a result. The American recourse to 'constructive ambiguity', supposed to smooth out the differences, confused the issue even more.

The continuation of the Palestinian intifada gave rise in Israel to a 'peace camp' favourable to a withdrawal from the occupied territories, and especially from the Gaza Strip. In June 1992, Labour won its first electoral victory since 1973 and Yitzhak Rabin, who had become Prime Minister, could even boast of a 'Jewish majority' for peace.[4] But he thought that American mediation was too laborious, especially as it

---

[4] The Rabin government actually had a majority in the Knesset without the support of the 'Arab' parties, so called since they came from the 20% of the population who were Arabs.

excluded the PLO. This was why Rabin, eager to succeed, established a secret negotiation channel with Arafat, under the auspices of Norway. These 'Oslo Accords', concluded in September 1993, amounted to mutual recognition between Israel and the PLO. A 'Palestinian Authority' would take control of the territories gradually evacuated by Israel. The Israeli right accused Rabin of having made a pact with the 'terrorists'. Arafat was also widely criticized in his camp for postponing the settlement of issues related to Jerusalem, borders, colonization, and refugees until after a five-year transition period. But this diplomatic breakthrough aroused such international enthusiasm that the United States, although absent from Oslo, sponsored the signing of these agreements at the White House. Democratic President Bill Clinton, who had succeeded Bush eight months earlier, could thus pose as a paradoxical 'peacemaker'.

The reality was that American diplomats ensured the implementation of agreements negotiated without them. Hence the tensions and frustrations that led, in May 1994, to an Israeli withdrawal limited to two-thirds of the Gaza Strip and, in the West Bank, to the city of Jericho alone. Even though Arafat was greeted by jubilant crowds when he returned to Gaza two months later, each new Israeli evacuation remained conditional on the Authority's performance in the fight against terrorism. The repression of Hamas and the PFLP by Arafat's services fuelled Palestinian dissension. This stalemate convinced King Hussein to carry out his own secret negotiations with Rabin. The peace treaty between Israel and Jordan, signed in October 1994, was once again the fruit of bilateral talks conducted away from the Americans. Meanwhile, in Washington in September 1995, the peace process finally led to an agreement about the West Bank. This territory was divided into zone A of the Palestinian Authority (3%), zone C under the exclusive control of Israel (72%), and zone B, where the Palestinian administration coexisted with the Israeli security forces (25%). The Palestinian population largely came under the complete or partial control of the Authority.

There was a new outcry within the PLO, where Arafat was accused of having sold off the land of Palestine to transform his Authority into an agent of collaboration with Israel. The denunciation was even more virulent in Israel, where Rabin was caricatured as a member of the SS in rallies led by Benyamin Netanyahu, who had succeeded Shamir as the head of Likud. In November 1995, Rabin was assassinated while

leaving a peace rally in Tel Aviv; his killer was a Jewish extremist linked
to messianic settlers. Shimon Peres succeeded him at the head of the
Labour government, while Arafat was elected President of the Palestinian
Authority in January 1996 with 87% of the vote. This election, conducted
under international supervision, contrasted with the masquerades of the
Arab regimes. Arafat now combined this title with the leadership of the
PLO and Fatah, drawing on these three levels of legitimacy. But Peres
faced Netanyahu in a ballot overshadowed by a wave of Hamas suicide
bombings. In May, the Likud leader narrowly won the election. As head
of the Israeli government, he proceeded to bury the Oslo agreements,
which he had condemned from the start.

The collapse of the process

Clinton, who had wagered everything on the election of Peres, maintained
icy relations with Netanyahu. The latter, familiar with the United States,
where he had lived half his life, fostered his relations with the Republican
Party, which had a majority in both chambers of Congress. On the
American right, he could count on the support of the 'Christian Zionists',
those fundamentalists for whom the 'return' of the Jewish people to their
land, including on the occupied West Bank, was part of the fulfilment
of the prophecies. Archaeological excavations under the Noble Sanctuary
(*Haram al-Sharif*) in Jerusalem led in September 1996 to an outbreak of
violence between Israelis and Palestinians. A year later, the extraordinary
assassination attempt on Khaled Mashal, a Hamas leader in Amman,
turned into a humiliation for Netanyahu,[5] forced as he was to release
Ahmed Yassin, the founder of the Islamist movement, who was soon
back in Gaza. The growing power of Hamas could not, however, fail to
weaken Arafat, whose autocratic rule undermined the legitimacy and
effectiveness of the Palestinian Authority. In general, the peace process
was losing its appeal for both populations: for the Israelis because of the

---

[5] The Mossad commando unit tasked with injecting a slow-acting poison into
Mashal, the leader of the Hamas Political Bureau, was intercepted by the Jordanian
intelligence services, who only agreed to release him in exchange for the antidote,
and also seventy-four Palestinians and Jordanians detained in Israel, including
Yassin.

continuation of Hamas attacks, even though there were fewer of them, and for the Palestinians because of the Israeli blockages and increased colonization. The Clinton administration bore a heavy responsibility for this disaffection, since the only agreement concluded under its aegis, in January 1997, divided Hebron between the two parties,[6] adding an additional zone of friction to the Israeli–Palestinian equation.

Washington thought it would find room for manoeuvre in May 1999 with the electoral defeat of Netanyahu, replaced at the head of the government by the Labour leader Ehud Barak, former chief of staff, while Ariel Sharon assumed the leadership of Likud. The Knesset was the most divided in Israeli history, forcing Barak to rely on a coalition of seven parties. The new Prime Minister favoured talks with Syria over negotiations with the PLO. But the so-called 'constructive' ambiguity of the Clinton administration proved counterproductive in the face of the implacable Assad. A dispute over a residual portion of the Golan Heights, even though Israel agreed to evacuate 99% of them, was enough to derail the American–Syrian summit in Geneva in March 2000. Such a failure convinced Barak, two months later, to decide on the unilateral withdrawal of Israeli troops from Lebanon. Hezbollah celebrated the end of twenty-two years of Israeli occupation,[7] which it attributed solely to its 'Islamic resistance'. This was the last battle of Hafez al-Assad, who died in June 2000 in Damascus. His son Bashar inherited, with absolute power, his titles of 'President of the Republic', 'Secretary General of the Ba'ath', and 'Head of the Armed Forces'. For the first time, an Arab republic ensured that its dictators followed one another in a dynasty. Clinton summoned Barak and Arafat to Camp David in July 2000, hoping to repeat Carter's successful mediation in 1978 between Begin and Sadat. But this tripartite summit was much less well prepared, with an American President at the end of his second and final term. It would take many months for the 'Clinton parameters' to propose an overall settlement, with the establishment of a demilitarized Palestinian state in

---

[6] A thousand Israeli soldiers protected a few hundred settlers in a still predominantly Arab part of Hebron, with the rest of the city and its population falling to the Palestinian Authority

[7] Israel had controlled a 'security belt' in southern Lebanon since 1978 (see above, p. 287, n. 28), long before its 1982 invasion.

the Gaza Strip and almost all of the West Bank. Jerusalem was to be the capital of the two states, and territorial exchanges allowed Israel to annex the settlement blocs and, finally, limit refugees' 'right of return' to the Palestinian state alone. The contours of this two-state solution were still unclear at Camp David, a summit that was a failure due to Clinton's far from 'constructive' ambiguity. Barak accused Arafat of having refused the most generous offer ever made to the Palestinians, even though such an offer was not formalized at Camp David and would not be so until five months later.[8] The PLO, for its part, was under intense pressure from Hamas, for whom the Israeli withdrawal from Lebanon demonstrated the futility of diplomatic means and the virtue of 'Islamic resistance' alone.

The visit of Sharon and a Likud delegation to the Noble Sanctuary in September 2000 was the last straw. Palestinian riots spread to Arab areas of Israel and were harshly suppressed. This was the beginning of the second intifada, associated with 'Al-Aqsa', in celebration of the sacredness of Jerusalem, and in sharp contrast with the peaceful uprising of 1987, due to its Islamic language and its recourse to armed struggle. Indeed, all factions resorted to suicide bombings, a mirror escalation of Israel's use of its air force and artillery in the West Bank and Gaza for the first time since the occupation had begun in 1967. This push to extremes deprived of their substance the talks that Clinton finally conducted with rigour. In January 2001, George W. Bush, the son of Clinton's predecessor, moved into the White House. Shortly after, Sharon was brought to power in Israel in a landslide victory. This closed the cycle of the peace process.

Global wars

Bin Laden, expelled from Saudi Arabia in 1991, was stripped of his nationality three years later. He then wove the web of Al-Qaeda from Sudan, where the military-Islamist dictatorship welcomed him until 1996, when he settled in Afghanistan, where he placed himself under the protection of the Taliban, literally the 'seminarians'. This ultra-conservative militia had imposed its 'Islamic Emirate' in the chaos that followed the withdrawal

[8] In December 2000, the Clinton parameters for a two-state solution were presented at the White House to the Israeli and Palestinian delegations. They were non-negotiable, and they were endorsed by Barak and Arafat in the following days.

of the Red Army and the fall of the communist regime in 1992. Bin Laden declared 'global jihad' against the United States, calling for attacks against its nationals and its interests throughout the world, as long as its 'occupation' of Saudi Arabia lasted. In August 1998, Bin Laden ordered a double suicide attack on the US embassies in Kenya and Tanzania (224 dead, including 12 Americans).[9] Clinton responded by firing missiles at an Al-Qaeda base in Afghanistan, from which Bin Laden emerged unscathed. After this US strike on their territory, the Taliban consolidated their pact with the jihadists. In June 1999, the FBI declared Bin Laden public enemy number one and placed a $5 million bounty on his head. US propaganda thus ensured the worldwide notoriety of Al-Qaeda, whose training camps welcomed ever more volunteers. Bin Laden then embarked on the planning of an attack of an unprecedented scale on American soil.

On 11 September 2001, two planes hijacked by Al-Qaeda crashed into the twin towers of the World Trade Center in New York, while a third destroyed part of the Pentagon in Washington. A fourth plane, which crashed in the middle of the countryside thanks to the self-sacrificing intervention of its passengers, was aimed at the Capitol, perhaps even the White House. Nearly 3,000 people were killed in these attacks, for which Bin Laden was careful not to claim responsibility, so that he could pose as the leader of the 'resistance' to the inevitable American response. The UN supported the ultimatum of the United States against the Taliban, who nevertheless refused to hand over Bin Laden. About forty countries, in various capacities, joined in the offensive launched in October by Washington against the Islamic Emirate. The jihadists were convinced that their adversaries would get bogged down in Afghanistan like the Red Army before them. But the Bush administration skilfully allowed the Afghan militias of the 'Northern Alliance', opposed to the Taliban, to prosecute the fighting on the ground. US air, artillery, and intelligence support was critical, but it was Afghans, not invaders, who overthrew the Islamic Emirate. Two-thirds of Al-Qaeda members were killed or imprisoned. Bin Laden fled to Pakistan.

Instead of being content with this resounding victory, George W. Bush launched the 'global war on terror'. American power thus fell into

[9] This carnage was meant to mark the eighth anniversary of the start of 'Desert Shield', and therefore of the so-called US 'occupation' of Saudi territory.

the jihadist trap by 'globalizing' the confrontation that Al-Qaeda itself sought to extend to the whole planet. The Arab dictatorships willingly offered their collaboration, both to curry favour with Washington and to brand those who opposed them on the domestic front as 'terrorists'. While the Cold War Arab despots liquidated their dissidents in the name of fighting 'reaction', Zionism, and imperialism, their 'global war' successors justified the ferocity of their repression in the name of 'counter-terrorism'. In Israel, Sharon equated Arafat with Bin Laden in order to combat the second intifada ever more harshly. In March 2002, the Israeli army again occupied the entire West Bank. Arafat, besieged in the offices of his presidency, would not emerge for two and a half years. The Authority was in a shambles and the dream of a Palestinian state had come to an end.

The ideologues of the Bush administration continued to drive home their advantage. Improperly called 'neo-conservatives', they actually advocated a revolutionary reshaping of the Middle East, committed to regime change in Baghdad. The fall of Saddam was supposed to open a virtuous circle of democratization in Iraq; democracy would then spread to the other Arab countries, thus inevitably leading to peace with Israel, since two democracies cannot go to war. The paternalistic prejudices of the neo-conservatives were aggravated by the messianic fever of the Christian Zionists, determined to defeat the Muslim Antichrist. In January 2002, Bush solemnly denounced an 'axis of evil' that included Iraq, Iran, and North Korea. The disinformation campaign was such that a majority of Americans now thought Saddam was guilty for 9/11. The day after the first anniversary of these attacks, Bush denounced in the UN the threat that, he claimed, Iraq represented for world peace. In February 2003, Colin Powell, the US Secretary of State, insisted at the Security Council that Saddam had 'weapons of mass destruction' and was collaborating with Al-Qaeda. The plea of his French counterpart for a 'disarmament in peace' was warmly applauded, but it was too late to stem the warmongering of the United States.

The occupation of Iraq

On 20 March 2003, a deluge of missiles fell on Iraq. This was the 'shock and awe' destined to paralyse the enemy under an overwhelming balance of power. In fact, the 150,000 American soldiers took only three weeks to conquer southern Iraq and reach the capital. On 9 April, the toppling of a statue of Saddam was staged in Baghdad, in what purported to be an Arab remake of the fall of the Berlin Wall. But chaos reigned in the country. The arms depots were stormed by various militias. The Baghdad museum was looted, as were many archaeological sites. The occupying forces refused to maintain order, contenting themselves with guarding certain strategic positions, including the Ministry of Petroleum. The first two decisions of the American proconsul[10] were the demobilization of the army and the purging of Ba'ath members. Thus tens of thousands of laid-off soldiers returned to their homes with their personal weapons, while the mass of civil servants, forced by the dictatorship to join the Ba'ath, were excluded from public service. In a short time, the entire Iraqi state collapsed. On 1 May, from the deck of an aircraft carrier cruising in the Persian Gulf, Bush announced 'mission accomplished'.[11] Yet not a single trace of the 'weapons of mass destruction' had been found.

American troops in Iraq were supported by some 20,000 soldiers from a disparate coalition. But where the coalitions of 1990 and 2001 had gathered around the United States, the 2003 coalition proved divisive, particularly in Europe: the United Kingdom, Spain, and Italy committed to the US, while France and Germany were critical. These differences between European governments contrasted with the massive opposition of all European peoples to the invasion of Iraq. The occupation authorities set up their headquarters in Baghdad in the same 'green zone' from which Saddam and his clique had already ruled the country. They used the same prisons to inflict inhumane treatment, the images of which would cause an outcry.[12] Only the target of the mass repression changed: previously it had been the opponents of the Ba'ath, now it was the 'terrorists', the vast majority of whom were Sunnis. The Shiite and Kurdish militias fighting alongside the United States accentuated

[10] His official title was 'provisional administrator of the coalition'.
[11] The invasion of Iraq in 2003 is often called, from a Western point of view, the 'Second Gulf War', the first having been the liberation of Kuwait in 1991. But it was the Iran–Iraq conflict of 1980–1988 which historically represented the first of these three 'Gulf Wars'.
[12] This was the revelation, in the spring of 2004, of the torture filmed in Abu Ghraib prison by American jailers.

this community bias, while the proconsul surrounded himself with former exiles, who were portrayed as heroes thanks to their resistance to Saddam, but who were ignorant of everything to do with the generation that had grown up under the embargo.

In April 2004, the blindness of the United States led it to face both a Shiite uprising and a Sunni guerrilla war. They involved a heterogeneous gathering of authentic patriots, those nostalgic for Saddam, and Islamists of different persuasions. American propaganda exaggerated the role of Abu Musab al-Zarqawi, a Jordanian jihadist, in order to conceal the Iraqi dimension of this insurrection. But this manoeuvre actually resulted in increasing Zarqawi's prestige as a militant, and therefore his recruitment and financing capacities. On the Shia side, Muqtada al-Sadr, the great-nephew of Baqir al-Sadr, hanged on Saddam's orders in 1980, and the son of an ayatollah himself assassinated by the dictatorship, deployed Islamic language to raise a 'Mahdi's army' against the occupier. This time, the United States could not accuse the insurgents of Ba'athist sympathies. They accelerated the establishment of an Iraqi government responsible, in June 2004, for organizing elections. But the American army continued to control the country, and two months later it besieged Muqtada al-Sadr in the mausoleum of Ali in Najaf. After bloody clashes in the holy city, the head of the Mahdi army agreed to withdraw with his supporters to the Shiite suburbs of Baghdad. As for Zarqawi, Bin Laden appointed him leader of the Iraqi branch of Al-Qaeda.

The American invasion of Iraq thus enabled the jihadists, hitherto confined to the Afghan periphery, to gain a foothold in the heart of the Middle East. Resistance to 'Crusader aggression', to use Al-Qaeda's rhetoric, also favoured a revival, this time in Europe, of anti-Western terrorism, with the attacks in Madrid in March 2004 and in London in July 2005. In Iraq itself, the Sunni boycott of the January 2005 elections to the Constituent Assembly led to a federal-type project favourable to the Kurdish and Shiite provinces which held oil resources in the north and south. The new constitution, massively rejected by the Sunnis, widened the gap between the communities. The United States, eager to exit from the Iraqi quagmire, refounded the country on a tripartite pact which amalgamated elements of the British Mandate of 1920–1932 and the sectarianism instituted by France in Lebanon. This combination offered real power to a Shia Prime Minister, with Kurds holding the presidency of the state and the Sunnis the presidency of Parliament. But the Kurds, whose language acquired the same status as Arabic, enjoyed the highly advanced autonomy of their 'regional government' in Erbil. Sunnis had no such compensation for their exclusion from central power.

Worse still, because of the security imperative of the United States, the new institutions favoured the parties backed by powerful militias. Such a militarization of the sectarian dynamic, with increasingly brutal leaders, aggravated the discrimination against minorities who lacked such armed groups. This was obviously the case for the Christians, whose population, due to emigration, had halved in a few years, but also for the Yazidis, despite their being of Kurdish ethnicity. The Turkmen now looked to Ankara to assert their rights and arm their activists. The Bush administration thus set in motion an infernal mechanism that led to the 2006 civil war between Shiite and Sunni militias. In the once multi-sectarian capital, walls sprang up between neighbourhoods that had become homogeneous, and there was an exodus of Sunni and Christian populations. Not only was the country militarized, it was also looted by parties organized into veritable mafias. As for Iran, it took advantage of this disintegration to develop its networks and promote its own interests.

The axis of resistance

Bush not only offered the Islamic Republic the head of Saddam[13] and the dismantling of his regime, it also allowed Iran to free itself from the border which had been drawn in 1639 between the Ottomans and the Safavids, and had since separated the Arabs from the Persians. What Khomeini was unable to achieve by prolonging the terrible war with Iraq from 1982 to 1988, Khamenei achieved without firing a shot, leaving the United States to liquidate the Ba'athist enemy itself. This regional change was accompanied by a reversal of the balance of power within the Shiite clergy. The ayatollahs of Najaf and Karbala had, for two centuries, fostered a clerical autonomy which conferred on them a decisive influence on the future of Iran. The dramatic changes of 2003 reversed this relationship to the benefit of Khomeinist Iran and of the

---

[13] Captured in December 2003 by Kurdish militiamen, the ousted dictator was hanged three years later, cursed by the Shiites, after a highly controversial trial.

ayatollahs of Qom, who invaded Najaf to impose their very specific vision of Shiism. The Gulf monarchies, initially favourable to the overthrow of Saddam, were paralysed by this irruption of Iran onto Arab soil and reacted by supporting the Sunni guerrillas in Iraq. As for Bashar al-Assad, he also supported this guerrilla war, as it would bog down the United States in Iraq and divert it from a possible intervention in Syria. In this Middle East which was so fond of swapping sides, the protégés of the United States in the Arabian Peninsula ended up financing an anti-American insurgency on their doorstep, while Syria, the ally of the Islamic Republic, fuelled Sunni violence against the supporters of Tehran in Iraq.

Iran's growing power in Iraq and the region made it less urgent for Khamenei to pursue his country's nuclear programme. From 1987 to 1992, the Islamic Republic signed cooperation agreements with Pakistan, China, and Russia in the nuclear field. But it was a mafia network based in Dubai which allowed Tehran to acquire its first centrifuges. In October 2003, the mediation of France, the United Kingdom, and Germany convinced Iran to suspend its uranium enrichment activities. A formal agreement was concluded to this effect a year later, giving this suspension the potential prospect of a lasting settlement. This virtuous process collapsed in the summer of 2005, with the election of Mahmoud Ahmadinejad as Iranian President. This was the first time that a non-cleric had occupied this post: Ahmadinejad had spent his career in the Revolutionary Guards, particularly during the conflict with Iraq. The new Iranian President also espoused a messianic ideology and was convinced of the imminence of the return of the Mahdi. So he indulged in repeated international provocations and publicly threatened to destroy Israel. Despite these sinister gestures, the Bush administration concluded in December 2007 that Iran had probably not resumed its military programme.

Bashar al-Assad, who in 2000 inherited absolute power over Syria from his father, could count on the diplomatic support of France's President Jacques Chirac. France no longer questioned the Syrian protectorate over Lebanon, because it was wagering on its own cooperation with Damascus to make this protectorate more benevolent. The great beneficiary of this new situation was the Lebanese Prime Minister, Rafic Hariri, who was closely linked to Chirac and Saudi Arabia. But the US occupation of

Iraq caused Assad once again to tighten his grip on Lebanon. Hariri, ousted from the presidency of the government in 2004, died in February 2005 in an attack attributed to Hezbollah. Huge demonstrations shook the country the following month, polarizing opponents and supporters of Syria. Assad decided to withdraw his troops after twenty-nine years of occupation, but a campaign of assassinations of anti-Syrian figures soon revealed that the domination of Damascus, while being less direct, was no less brutal. This 'Cedar Revolution' of 2005 widened the gap between Sunnis and Shiites in Lebanon, divided Christians between these two antagonistic camps, and, finally, established the pre-eminence of Hezbollah, which was better equipped than the army itself.

The Islamic Republic proclaimed the solidity of this 'axis of resistance', which, from Tehran to Damascus and Beirut, would stand up to American plans in the Middle East. The Arab dictatorships in return lambasted the 'Shiite crescent' which had thus been consolidated, hoping to mobilize against this threat their American sponsors, who were themselves responsible for Iranian expansion in Iraq. Hamas was a prickly Sunnist body, but it joined this 'axis' in the name of the 'Islamic resistance' it shared with Hezbollah. The death of Arafat[14] left the PLO and the Palestinian Authority, in 2005, in the hands of Mahmoud Abbas, a declared opponent of the militarization of the intifada. Sharon, however, refused to coordinate with him the Israeli withdrawal from the Gaza Strip, which played into the hands of the Islamist militias. Hamas won the Palestinian elections in January 2006 and, in June, came into conflict with Israel in Gaza. In the name of 'resistance' solidarity, Hezbollah opened a second front in northern Israel, leading to a 'thirty-three-day war' that was devastating for Lebanon, but also an ordeal for the Jewish state.[15] Hezbollah claimed a 'divine victory' that was celebrated by Ahmadinejad and Iranian propaganda. In June 2007, Hamas took military control of the Gaza Strip, from which the PLO was expelled.

[14] The leader of the PLO, besieged since 2002 in the Palestinian presidency, was evacuated in October 2004 while he was extremely ill; he died shortly afterwards in a hospital in the Paris suburbs.

[15] The civilian losses in Israel, some 120 dead, represented only one-tenth of the civilian losses in Lebanon, but were equivalent to the military losses in Israel due to the hundreds of rockets fired by Hezbollah on the north of the country.

The conflict between the 'Palestinian Authorities' of Ramallah and Gaza[16] further weakened the two-state solution, which encouraged both the Israeli 'hawks' and the supporters of the 'axis of resistance'.

This disintegration of the Arab Middle East was intensified by the remarkable return of Turkey, which had kept its head down in the region ever since the annexation in 1939 of the Syrian province of Antioch. Recep Tayyip Erdoğan, whose Islamo-conservative AK Party[17] won the 2002 elections, became Prime Minister the following year and saw the Middle East as the 'strategic depth' of his country. He set out to develop mutually beneficial cooperation with all his neighbours, which led him to refuse the use of Turkey as a rear base for the American invasion of Iraq. Even if the Pentagon thereafter harboured a lasting distrust of its Turkish ally in NATO, this demonstration of sovereignty allowed Erdoğan to develop his relations with Ahmadinejad, and especially Assad. The free movement agreement he signed with the latter in 2007 was very beneficial to the border provinces of Gaziantep in Turkey and Aleppo in Syria. Ankara also guaranteed the trade, in particular the oil trade, of the Kurdish government in northern Iraq, in return for tolerance for Turkish raids against the PKK.[18] Finally, the AK Party, a minority component of which came from the Muslim Brotherhood, became the rallying point for the different branches of the brotherhood, banished from Saudi Arabia and targeted by the United Arab Emirates. In 2008, Erdoğan even sponsored secret talks between Israel and Syria, both of which had until then refused any other mediation than that of America.

The Cairo speech

The American hegemony over the Middle East that was sealed during the mandate of Bush Sr had already been undermined by Clinton's

[16] Since its election victory in January 2006, Hamas had claimed to be the only legitimate 'Palestinian Authority'.
[17] The AK Party (or AKP) is the English abbreviation used to refer to the Justice and Development Party in Turkey.
[18] The KDP in power in Erbil was historically opposed to the Marxist PKK, whose Turkish Peshmerga were conducting guerrilla warfare from the mountains in the far north of Iraq. Saddam Hussein had already tolerated Ankara's raids against the PKK on his territory (see above, p. 297).

calamitous mishandling of the peace process. But it was Bush Jr who destroyed his father's great work by yielding to the neo-conservative folly of the invasion of Iraq. The hundreds of billions of dollars swallowed up in this adventure, not to mention the loss of thousands of American service personnel, should have been enough to invalidate the conspiratorial visions of an omniscient and Machiavellian America. The reality was a disaster – obviously so for societies in the Middle East, but also for the interests of the United States. With Vladimir Putin, Russia (marginalized in the region since the collapse of the USSR) was beginning to stage a return as patient as it was methodical, cultivating its relationship with Iran and its allies, albeit without ruling out other military and oil partnerships. While the defence of Saudi Arabia had been the pillar of the 'new order' of 1991, Bush Jr permanently weakened his Saudi partner by opening Iraq to the multifaceted influence of Iran, bringing the jihadist threat into the region,[19] and burying the Arab–Israeli peace process. The 'Abdullah plan', endorsed in 2002 by the Arab League on the initiative of the crown prince of Arabia, who became king three years later, offered Israel an effective peace with all the Arab States in return for the Israeli withdrawal from all the territories still occupied since 1967.[20] Total peace in exchange for total withdrawal: the formula would have been attractive in other times, but George W. Bush took no serious interest in it.

In the autumn of 2002, Barack Obama opposed the very principle of an invasion of Iraq, which, according to him, could only strengthen the enemies of the United States. At the time, this lucidity isolated him within the Democratic Party, but served his victorious presidential campaign in 2008. This popular dynamic pushed for a disengagement from the Middle East by a withdrawal of troops as much as by a reduction in energy dependence. In June 2009, the President gave a historic speech in Cairo on reconciliation between 'America and Islam'. Rather than invoking the Arab world, Obama preferred to address the 'more than a billion followers' of a religion whose shared values with the United States he emphasized. Muslims and Americans were urged

[19] From 2003 to 2005, the Saudi branch of Al-Qaeda carried out a campaign of bloody attacks in Arabia.
[20] In addition to the Syrian Golan Heights, these were the Palestinian territories of East Jerusalem, the West Bank, and the Gaza Strip.

to fight together against the 'violent extremism' of Al-Qaeda. While describing the American–Israeli relationship as 'unshakable', Obama deemed the plight of the Palestinians to be 'intolerable' and their aspiration to statehood 'legitimate'. A half-century after the Suez crisis, the popularity of the United States was once again at its zenith in the Arab Middle East, reminding us that anti-Americanism was no more of a Pavlovian reflex there than it was anywhere else, being nourished by resentment towards specific concrete policies.

Obama also began his mandate by holding his hand out to Iran, while supporting European mediation on the nuclear issue. But the re-election of Ahmadinejad in June 2009 following a contest marred by fraud provoked an unprecedented wave of protest in the Islamic Republic. This was the 'green movement', which involved hundreds of thousands of demonstrators throughout the country and was harshly repressed by the police and the Revolutionary Guards. Advanced technology also enabled the regime to curb the cell phones and social networks that now acted as an echo chamber of protests around the world. Obama kept a low profile, breaking away from the 'regime change' policy of his predecessor. In September, the revelation of the construction site for a new uranium enrichment facility led to a coordinated response between Obama and his European peers; the following months saw a tightening of sanctions endorsed by the UN. Washington remained convinced that Iran was indeed seeking to acquire the capabilities for embarking on a military programme that it had not yet actually initiated.

Netanyahu regained the leadership of the Israeli government in March 2009, ten years after having lost it. The 'global war on terror', the crushing of the second intifada, and the takeover of Gaza by Hamas had exacerbated his rejection of the two-state solution. If he pretended to give in to Obama on this point, it was in order to issue an unprecedented demand, for Palestinian recognition of the Jewish character of the State of Israel, a requirement absent from the peace treaties signed with Egypt in 1979 and Jordan in 1994. Still under pressure from Washington, in November 2009, Netanyahu announced a 'freeze' on colonization for a period of ten months, but excluding East Jerusalem and the 'natural' development of existing settlements. Having successfully evaded any meaningful concession, in 2010 the Israeli Prime Minister exploited the Republican momentum in Congress, as he had in 1996, against a backdrop of aggressive campaigns led by Christian Zionists against Obama. The balance of power was reversed between the two leaders: the American President, despite his enthusiasm at the UN for a Palestinian state, shamelessly vetoed the admission of Palestine.[21]

Obama had more success in refocusing the fight on terrorism by directing it against Al-Qaeda alone. In Iraq, the resulting truce with the nationalist guerrillas made it possible to recruit anti-jihadist militias in Sunni circles. In the tribal areas of the Afghan border, as well as in Yemen, American drones inflicted severe losses on Al-Qaeda cadres. In May 2011, Bin Laden was killed in a US helicopter raid in Pakistan. Obama declared that 'justice has been done', a decade after the attacks in New York and Washington. The American President confirmed the imminent withdrawal of his forces from Iraq, determined as he was to end the parenthesis of this disastrous conflict. But he thereby conferred exorbitant power on Prime Minister Nouri al-Maliki, whose Shiite sectarianism turned into remorseless hostility towards the Sunni minority. The militias that had been so effective against Al-Qaeda were disbanded. The local jihadists regained their confidence and their leader, Abu Bakr al-Baghdadi, refused to pledge allegiance to Bin Laden's successor. An 'Islamic State in Iraq' took shape clandestinely along the Syrian border. Veterans of Saddam rubbed shoulders with veterans of Zarqawi, each bringing their own experience of terror as a weapon of war.[22]

The return of the Nahda

Since 1990, the Arab peoples have represented the blind spot in the American Middle East. The 'stone revolution' in the West Bank and Gaza resulted merely in the frustrations of a peace reduced to a process, before the second intifada exhausted popular momentum in the escalation of armed factions. In Iraq, the United States abandoned the insurgent people to the ferocity of Saddam in 1991, and rid them of this barbarity in 2003 only to hand them over to the tyranny of the militias. In addition, the

---

[21] In November 2012, Palestine obtained only the modest status of non-member observer state at the UN.

[22] A manual very popular among Iraqi jihadists at the time was called *The Management of Savagery*.

destruction and exodus caused by the regime change in Baghdad served as powerful foils for the Arab dictatorships. Their propaganda raised the spectre of the chaos that would inevitably follow the end of their reign. The various despots, who had already used the 'global war on terror' to intensify their repression, now designated their opponents, including even the most patriotic ones, as mere agents of a subversion hatched in Washington. The Bush administration had succeeded in tarnishing the very principle of a democratic transition by associating it with foreign occupation and the anarchy of the militias. Obama's Cairo speech helped to loosen things up somewhat, but it was the in-depth evolution of Arab societies that led to lasting upheaval in the Middle East.

The expression 'democratic uprising' is preferable to that of 'Arab Spring', for it was less a season of blossoming freedom than the continuation of the long struggle of the Arab peoples for their self-determination. This struggle, which began with the Nahda of the nineteenth century, suffered two historic defeats: the imposition of mandates from 1920 to 1948, followed by the hijacking of national independences until 1969 by dictatorships still in place. The dictatorships in Egypt, Yemen, and Libya were tempted by the dynastic model already established in 2000 in Syria, with the transmission of absolute power from Hafez to Bashar al-Assad. But the new Arab generation, born at the end of the previous century, shared neither the exaltation of the 'saviours of the nation' from the time of their grandparents, nor the Islamizing moralism of the period after the 'oil shock' with which their parents had often been imbued. The demographic transition which Europe had taken two centuries to bring about was accomplished in forty years in the Arab world. It led to the emergence of a better educated, more critical generation of young people who had grown up in families of two or three siblings.

It was these young adults, both men and women, often parents themselves, who took to the streets with the slogan 'The people want to overthrow the regime'.[23] The wave of protests started in Tunisia at the very end of 2010 and forced the dictator Ben Ali, after twenty-three years in power, to flee to Arabia. The Tunisian revolution was aided by the vitality of the trade union and associative movements, the army's refusal

[23] The Palestinian variant of this slogan was 'The people want an end to the division' between the PLO's West Bank and Hamas's Gaza Strip.

to repress protest, and the tradition of a century and a half of constitutionalism, which would rally the parties around the establishment of a new Republic, even if it meant fighting tooth and nail over its terms for the next three years. The Arab dictatorships of the Middle East could exploit the way they had fragmented civil society, mainly by sectarianism, and they could rely on veritable praetorian guards. They also played on the dominant position of the Islamists within the opposition and on the fear, even the rejection, that the latter sometimes aroused inside the country as well as abroad. Finally, they drew on an unprecedented level of oil prices, the income from which they monopolized by capturing it at source or transferring it from abroad.[24]

The Egyptian uprising against Mubarak, whose non-violent dimension echoed the anti-British 'revolution' of 1919, led to a coup d'état. Admittedly, the despot was overthrown in February 2011, after ruling for three decades, but it was a military junta that assumed power, and it made a pact with the Muslim Brotherhood to stifle the popular movement. Immediately afterwards, in Libya, the uprising in Benghazi led to a split within the army and to a polarization between loyalist Tripolitania and insurgent Cyrenaica.[25] A similar split occurred the following month within the Yemeni army, between supporters and opponents of Ali Abdullah Saleh, who had been in power for thirty-two years,[26] after weeks of peaceful demonstrations that were harshly repressed. In Bahrain, popular protest demanded a constitution, but did not question the reign of a Sunni dynasty over a predominantly Shiite emirate. The sectarianism of Iranian propaganda, however, served as a pretext for military intervention by Saudi Arabia and the United Arab Emirates, which stifled protest. In Saudi Arabia itself, the authorities spent $100 billion to drown out the slightest hint of dissent. This was not simply because Riyadh and Abu Dhabi were afraid of the foreign threat

---

[24] Russia and Iran invested part of their oil revenue in Syria, while Arabia and the United Arab Emirates did the same in Egypt.

[25] The rebels rallied around the flag of national independence, the flag of the monarchy overthrown in 1969 by Gaddafi, just as the Syrian revolutionaries the following month brandished the flag of their own independence, which the Ba'ath had replaced with its own in 1963.

[26] Saleh, President of North Yemen since 1978, became the head of state of a unified Yemen in 1990, still with Sanaa as its capital.

from Iran. The two great fundraisers of the Arab counter-revolution also feared a breakthrough by the Muslim Brotherhood, encouraged by Turkey and Qatar. Once again, the sectarian prism proves to be misleading, since Qatar was just as Wahhabi as Saudi Arabia and its support for the Muslim Brotherhood was just as political as that of Riyadh for the Salafists.

The Syrian Revolution

While the world celebrated the illusion of an 'Arab Spring', the peoples were the victims, as early as March 2011, of a military putsch in Egypt, a successful counter-revolution in Bahrain, and two civil wars, overtly in Libya and covertly in Yemen. It was in this degraded context that peaceful demonstrations began in Syria, where Assad immediately ordered the liquidation of these supposed 'terrorists'. He was supported in this ultra-repressive option by Russia and by Iran, where the 'green movement' had been quickly crushed two years earlier. Syrian dissidents organized themselves into federated local coordination with a programme of democratic transition. This horizontal structure, with strong popular roots, allowed them to resist a repression that was nonetheless fierce. Local self-defence groups, bolstered by more and more deserters, rallied to the banner of a Free Syrian Army (FSA). But this FSA, with its headquarters in Turkey, had neither a chain of command nor supply structures. Moreover, Obama, whose support in Libya, within the framework of NATO, enabled the insurgents to seize Tripoli in August 2011, had no desire to embark on a new campaign. Netanyahu, once he was assured that the Assad regime was maintaining calm on the Golan Heights, also requested the United States to hold back. In addition, Erdoğan's project for a 'security zone' south of his border in Syria, on the model of the one established in 1991 in Iraq, was rejected by Washington. The flow of refugees to Turkey, which had been stemmed twenty years earlier by the provision of sanctuary, now continued with even more intensity than the parallel flows to Lebanon and Jordan.

Assad embarked on a military escalation in which the unconditional support of Russia and Iran guaranteed him the monopoly of airpower, heavy artillery, and armoured vehicles. Hezbollah also supported loyalist forces in urban fighting, before engaging directly to make up for their shortcomings. Systematic destruction aimed to expel populations that were deemed 'rebellious' and punished as such. The massacres of Sunni civilians fuelled a spiral of sectarian 'retaliations'[27] which allowed the regime to pose as a 'defender' of minorities. The revolutionary camp was handicapped by Obama's refusal to grant it the international legitimacy that he had conferred, in March 2011, on the Libyan opposition. This lack of diplomatic recognition was coupled with limited support for the supposed central structure of the FSA. The United States also vetoed any delivery by its allies of surface-to-air missiles to the guerrillas. Each insurgent group therefore developed its own arms network, in a process of fragmentation and one-upmanship aggravated by the rivalry between, on the one hand, Turkey and Qatar and, on the other, Saudi Arabia and the United Arab Emirates.

In Egypt, the military junta let the Muslim Brotherhood win the legislative elections at the end of 2011, while retaining executive power in its own hands. The various components of the anti-Mubarak uprising failed to coalesce into a third way between the generals and the Islamists. This polarization culminated in the June 2012 presidential election, won with 51.7% of the vote by the Muslim Brotherhood candidate, Mohamed Morsi. The latter thought he could remove the obstacle created by the military by dismissing the highest-ranking officers and by appointing the very self-effacing General Abdel Fattah el-Sisi to defence. But the new minister patiently paved the way for the army's reconquest of power, taking advantage of Morsi's sectarian and muddled policy. Waves of anti-Islamist demonstrations, protected and encouraged by the military, led in July 2013 to the overthrow of Morsi by Sisi. As in February 2011, an authentic popular uprising was hijacked by a classic coup, pending the rite of unanimous plebiscites.[28] It was the end of a two-and-a-half-year interlude of protest, henceforth associated with riots, instability, and Islamist intolerance. This was a striking echo of the sequence which, from 1952 to 1954, led from the overthrow of the monarchy to the seizure of power by Nasser. Saudi Arabia and the United Arab Emirates rewarded

---

[27] This murderous dynamic recalls that of the Lebanese conflict in January 1976 (see above, p. 286).
[28] In May 2014, Sisi, appointed marshal in the interim, was 'elected' President with 97% of the votes.

the putschists with the immediate allocation of $20 billion to Egypt. Turkey and Qatar, deeply committed to the Muslim Brotherhood, were forced to acquiesce in the new situation.

Obama's error

In July 2012, the Syrian revolutionaries, despite a very unfavourable balance of power, succeeded in seizing the suburbs of Damascus and the eastern part of Aleppo. The Assad regime compromised by ceding the largely Kurdish areas of the northeast to the PKK Peshmerga, trans-ferred from Turkey as part of a ceasefire between the Kurdish guerrillas and Ankara. As for Obama, he refused to provide the Syrian opposition with the instruments of victory. He limited himself to warning the Assad regime that the use of chemical weapons would constitute a 'red line', tacitly accepting bombardments with conventional shells and barrel bombs.[29] The conflict therefore continued to stagnate and its human toll to increase, while Assad saw the killings and expulsions as a chance to 'sanitize' the nation. Obama's priority was a resumption of negotiations on the Iranian nuclear issue, from which he hoped for a lasting peace in the Middle East. This was why he gave Putin such a relatively free rein, allowing him to wage a mock 'Cold War' in Syria at the lowest cost.

In June 2013, the election of the reformer Hassan Rouhani as President of the Islamic Republic encouraged Obama's hopes on the Iranian front. In July, the Sisi putsch sealed the failure of the revolutionary option in the most populous of Arab countries, confirming Netanyahu in his preference for a restoration of dictatorial order on Israel's borders. In August, the Assad regime thought it could break the insurgent front around Damascus by bombarding the rebel-held suburbs with sarin gas.[30] It was the same calculation which, a quarter of a century earlier, had led Saddam to gas the Kurdish town of Halabja. This time, the military manoeuvre

---

[29] Stuffed with TNT and with metal shot, these 'barrels' were dropped by aircraft at low altitude.

[30] About 1,400 people, the vast majority of them civilians, were killed in these strikes, which mixed conventional and chemical payloads (the latter caused 1,000 deaths).

was cut short by a sudden burst of activity in the revolutionary camp, convinced that Obama would punish the crossing of his own 'red line'. But, after having planned joint raids with France, the American President decided to favour dialogue with Putin.[31] An agreement to dismantle the Syrian regime's chemical arsenal was concluded under the aegis of the United States and Russia. If only to ensure the implementation of this agreement, Assad was back at the centre of the stage.[32]

The importance of this reversal was capital. Although it was part of a long line of American denial of the rights of Arab peoples, this time it represented a real break, because a public engagement by the United States had proved to be meaningless. This devaluation of Washington's voice was accompanied by the collapse of the credibility of the UN, paralysed in Syria by Russian and Chinese vetoes. The systematic violation of international law, particularly in its humanitarian aspect, was becoming a norm that the horror in Syria was rendering commonplace in the Middle East. Moscow's questioning of the very reality of Damascus's chemical carnage fuelled a modern wave of denial of these crimes. Worse still, the jihadists drew on this scandal to justify their absolute condemnation of the international system, to which they claimed to be the only virtuous alternative. Their 'Islamic State in Iraq and Syria', proclaimed a few months earlier, and referred to by its Arabic acronym Daesh, stepped up its recruitment in Europe, in the name of the so-called 'defence' of Muslims who were, it alleged, under attack everywhere.

The anti-Assad guerrillas launched their 'second revolution' in January 2014, this time against Daesh, expelled from Aleppo and northwestern Syria. However, the regime stepped up its attacks against the areas thus cleared of the jihadist threat. The PKK, whose Syrian branch had established autonomy in what it called Rojava,[33] observed a de facto

---

[31] Specific strikes were envisaged to show Assad that, after the most heinous of his war crimes, he could no longer count on impunity. This was quite different from NATO's air campaign in Libya in 2011, and even more from the American invasion of Iraq in 2003.
[32] The Syrian dictator would retain, in violation of this agreement, a chemical capability, with regular bombardments of insurgent areas with sarin gas as well as chlorine.
[33] *Rojava* means 'west' (of Kurdistan) in Kurdish and corresponds to the northeast of Syria (see above, p. 258).

truce with Daesh and let Assad's services operate in its area. In June, Baghdadi switched to the Iraqi side of the border and launched a lightning offensive against Mosul. The army fell apart, yielding the city to the jihadists and opening the road to Baghdad. Najaf's most revered ayatollah called for 'popular mobilization' within Shiite militias that stemmed the advance of Daesh. In July, Baghdadi proclaimed himself 'caliph' from his base in Mosul and invented a prophetic ancestry to justify such claims. His supporters now threatened the Kurdish regions of Syria and Iraq, while attacking the Yazidi minority, whose women were reduced to slavery.

It was only in August 2014, a good two months after the rout of Mosul, that Obama ordered the first strikes against Daesh in Iraq, extended to Syria the following month, to defend the Kurdish enclave there. The reluctance of the American President to embark on a new military engagement in the Middle East cannot on its own explain this cruel discrepancy, from which Daesh drew the greatest advantage. Just as he failed to grasp the seriousness of abandoning his 'red line' in Syria, Obama was slow to take stock of the threat from Daesh, which, unlike Al-Qaeda, would strike Europe rather than the United States.[34] Faced with jihadist guerrillas whose mobility was their main asset, he favoured a long-term campaign, whose air strikes were supported on the ground, in Iraq, by the army and the Shiite militias and, in Syria, by the Kurdish forces. He thus allowed Daesh to pose as a champion of a Sunnism besieged on all sides, which facilitated its recruitment and financing. Obama organized his anti-Daesh coalition of seventy countries[35] in the service of American power, as Bush Sr and Bush Jr had done in 1990 and 2003 respectively. But it would take three long years for this coalition to reconquer Mosul, which had fallen to Daesh in a few days. In the meantime, France, Belgium, the United Kingdom, Germany, and Sweden, among others, were hit by a terrorist campaign aimed at European countries.

---

[34] Daesh's first attack in Europe was perpetrated in May 2014 against the Jewish Museum in Brussels.

[35] Only France and the United Kingdom made a significant contribution to this coalition, placed under sole American command.

The Putin moment

The conclusion of a multilateral agreement on Iranian nuclear power in July 2015[36] confirmed Obama in his Middle Eastern strategy. But this agreement was endorsed in Tehran by President Rouhani alone, elected two years earlier, while Khamenei, who since 1989 had drawn on his theocratic legitimacy as a 'Guide', persevered in his diatribes against the United States. As for the Revolutionary Guards, already deeply involved in the Syrian conflict, they consolidated their presence in Iraq through the militias of 'popular mobilization', and in the name of the fight against Daesh. The two traditional pillars of US policy in the region, Israel and Saudi Arabia, were also strongly opposed to the deal. Netanyahu led a virulent campaign in the United States, and even appeared before both houses of Congress in a vain attempt to counter the White House. As for King Salman of Saudi Arabia, he let his son Mohammed, the youngest defence minister in the world,[37] rail against the agreement. Mohammed bin Salman and Mohamed bin Zayed,[38] the crown prince of the United Arab Emirates, launched a major intervention in Yemen in March 2015. They accused Iran of turning this country into a satellite state through the Houthis, a guerrilla group from the far north of the country and allied with former President Saleh.[39] At the very moment of the signing of the Vienna agreement, the Saudi air force and its local allies regained control of the port of Aden, where the Yemeni government, recognized by the international community, had begun to relocate.

In September 2015, Obama's virtuous wager on a regional dynamic of appeasement was further thwarted by the direct intervention of Russia in the Syrian conflict. Putin was encouraged in this escalation by Iran;

[36] The agreement was signed in Vienna by Iran, the United States, Russia, China, and the European Union.

[37] Mohammed bin Salman took over the defence portfolio in January 2015, at the age of twenty-nine.

[38] Their closeness means that they are often associated with the two abbreviations MBS and MBZ.

[39] Under pressure from Saudi Arabia, Saleh was obliged to hand over power to his Vice-President, Add Rabbu Mansour Hadi, in 2012. But he then made a pact with the Houthis, allowing them to seize Sanaa in 2014, and then to occupy the rest of the country.

the Iranians were worried about the fragility of the Assad regime in the face of a guerrilla offensive, this time massively supported by Turkey. But, even without having read Mahan, the Russian President could gauge how greatly his country's self-assertion in the Middle East would serve its power around the world. He also announced his commitment to Syria in a keynote speech at the UN, where he celebrated the sovereignty of regimes identified with states. This was the Russian version of the 'global war on terror'; the label 'terrorist' authorized, as with Bush, the repression of opponents of all persuasions. The Kremlin, which already had a maritime base in Syria, set up an air base in Latakia, with extraterritorial status. The Russian air force could focus its strikes on anti-Assad insurgents, leaving the US-led coalition to deal with Daesh in the east of the country. The war in Syria was thus led by Putin at a very reasonable cost, with the bulk of the military losses being outsourced to 'private' mercenary companies.[40]

Turkey, isolated in the face of the Russian counter-offensive in Syria, also felt threatened by the anti-jihadist alliance forged by the United States with the PKK. In addition, an attempted putsch killed more than 200 people in July 2016, shaking the very foundations of Turkish power. Erdoğan, supported in the ordeal by Putin, decided from now on to collaborate with him in Syria. Turkey abandoned the insurgents of Aleppo to the assault of Assad's forces and the pro-Iranian militias, supported by the Russian air force.[41] A tripartite process was set up between Moscow, Ankara, and Tehran in order to neutralize, one after the other, the redoubts still held by the opposition. These successive surrenders led to the transfer of survivors to the Idlib pocket, up against the Turkish border, in the northwest of the country. The Russian military oversaw this restoration of the Assad regime in the name of a so-called 'reconciliation' among Syrians. Netanyahu, meanwhile, relied on Putin to curb the Iranian presence on Israel's northern border. European diplomats turned to Moscow in the hope of influencing the Syrian

[40] The United States has already resorted to this type of mercenary force during its 2003–2011 occupation of Iraq, but with a presence on the ground of tens of thousands of regular combatants.

[41] There is a striking parallel here with the abandonment, in 1921, of the Syrian nationalists by Mustafa Kemal, in return for recognition by France of post-Ottoman power in Turkey (see above, pp. 243 and 258).

crisis. Putin was received throughout the Middle East with a pomp once reserved for American dignitaries. He was now the strong man in the region, and not Obama, who left the White House to Donald Trump in January 2017.

Trump the liquidator

The demolition of multilateralism, a process to which the new head of state devoted his constant endeavours, was accompanied by an internalization on the part of his administration of the fundamentals of American policy in the Middle East. Support for Israel was not so important in itself; rather, it was a way of maintaining, within the United States, the support of Christian Zionists for the Republican President. The basis of the pact with Saudi Arabia was no longer the importing of its oil, but its role as guarantor of prices, the United States having become the world's largest producer. Trump was convinced that Iran could act as a foil, bringing Israel and Saudi Arabia closer together under his aegis. In May 2017, he visited these two countries one after the other. In June, he allowed Arabia, the United Arab Emirates, and Egypt to impose the blockade of Qatar, which was required to break with Iran and the Muslim Brotherhood. In December, Trump solemnly acknowledged Jerusalem as the capital of Israel. He thus celebrated in his own way the centenary of the Balfour Declaration, which did not mention the term 'Arab' any more than he did, since freedom of worship for Palestinians already amounted to the denial of their national rights. In May 2018, Trump denounced the Iran nuclear deal and moved his embassy in Israel from Tel Aviv to Jerusalem. The ceremony was blessed by two American pastors who were unconditional supporters of the President, as well as being Christian Zionists.

Trump celebrated the reconquest of Mosul in July 2017 as a resounding victory over Daesh, while pro-Iranian militias gained a foothold in this historically Sunni city. It took another two years of military operations for the last jihadist bastion to finally be liquidated, this time in Syria. Trump decided to withdraw American troops from Syria without any guarantee for his Kurdish partners, abandoned to an offensive by Turkey. The crisis was settled directly between Ankara and Moscow, while the Assad regime strengthened its hand in Kurdish areas, even if American disengagement was ultimately only partial. Obama had already proved in 2013 that the word of the United States was no longer worth much in the Middle East, and in 2019 Trump demonstrated that the United States was even ready to abandon its comrades there overnight. The solidity of Putin's support for his allies was all the more appreciated in the region, where the Revolutionary Guards continued to strengthen the web of influence of the Islamic Republic. The Pentagon discovered very belatedly that the American bases in Iraq, besieged on all sides, were now intent solely on ensuring their own defence against the provocations of Iran.

Trump stuck to his 'maximum pressure' line against the Islamic Republic. This system of American sanctions was extended to any company that continued to trade with Iran, so that the United States could crack down on European competition. The effectiveness of such sanctions on the Tehran regime was more debatable, especially since they served as an alibi for the failures of the Iranian government and strengthened a form of patriotic solidarity around it. In the same spirit, the protest movements of January 2018 and of November 2019 in Iran, movements that were harshly repressed, suffered from the very clumsy encouragement of Washington. It would take more to dissuade Trump from persevering with his strategy. In January 2020, at the White House, alongside a radiant Netanyahu, he unveiled a 'peace plan' which validated the annexation by Israel of a good part of the West Bank. A rump state of Palestine would emerge out of enclaves linked by a complex system of tunnels. Arabs and Europeans were called upon to finance this 'deal of the century' at zero cost to the American taxpayer. The PLO categorically rejected this plan, which no Arab regime dared to support in public; no steps were taken to even set it in motion. Powerless to wage war or guarantee peace, Trump signed the death certificate of the American Middle East. He was content to be the 'witness' to the treaty signed in September between Israel and the United Arab Emirates,[42] a strategic rapprochement which owes much more to the disengagement of the United States than to their mediation.

[42] Mohamed bin Zayed, the strongman of the United Arab Emirates, did not even travel to Washington for the occasion. The other 'Abraham Accord', signed the same day between Israel and Bahrain, was much less ambitious.

The end of hegemony

Russia would, however, be quite incapable of occupying the dominant position that America had enjoyed. It was able to batter Syria and share its spoils with Iran and Turkey, but the reconstruction of this devastated country was beyond its administrative and financial strength. Putin could shine out in a Middle East of predators and despots, surpassing them all in brutality, cynicism, and violence. All this was merely a negative resource in a region already overwhelmed by these problems. The Russian President believed only in regimes, whose formal sovereignty he contrasted with the right of peoples to self-determination. He even obtained a de facto mandate on Syria from a UN that was as lax as the League of Nations had been with France. The Assad regime, shaken by the settling of scores in its upper echelons, was, however, merely a shadow of its former self; it was exhausting itself fighting the threat – an existential threat, in its own view – of a mass return of refugees.[43] These refugees would return only if a minimum of rights were guaranteed to them, which the Syrian dictatorship categorically refused to grant them. Russia was thus trapped by the very fragility of the despot on whom it had wagered everything, a despot who owed it his survival, but whom Russia could not force to make the slightest concession.

No Arab country has seen the restoration of the status quo that prevailed before the revolutionary wave of 2011. Everywhere, colossal budgets, themselves predicated on an oil revenue that will inevitably come to an end, have been engulfed in conflicts that still drag on. Sisi now leads Egypt in a dictatorship even more repressive than that of Mubarak, and has organized his stay in power at least until 2030. But he has failed to quell the jihadist insurgency rampant in the still strategic Sinai peninsula. As for Khalifa Haftar,[44] a former comrade of Gaddafi, whose militia, in Cyrenaica, is active right up by the Egyptian border, he portrays himself as the Libyan equivalent of Sisi. This is why, in May 2014 and April 2019, he launched two civil wars to seize Tripoli, with the

---

[43] The conflict had forced more than half of the Syrian population from their homes, with 6.6 million refugees abroad and a comparable number internally displaced.
[44] Exiled to the United States from 1984 to 2011, Haftar baptized his militia the 'Libyan National Army' and was proclaimed 'marshal' in 2016.

support of the United Arab Emirates, Egypt, Russia, and Saudi Arabia. But however much he described his enemies as 'terrorists', it was they, and not he, who managed, in December 2016, to reduce the jihadist stronghold that Daesh had established in Sirte. In addition, Haftar's appetite for exclusive power stirred up a motley but effective coalition of Libyan forces against him, a coalition to which Turkey successfully gave its support in January 2020. In Yemen, the campaign unleashed in March 2015 by Saudi Arabia and the United Arab Emirates was devastating for the local population, but it did not give the petro-monarchies any decisive victory. Abu Dhabi gradually withdrew its forces from July 2019, relying henceforth on the separatists of South Yemen and on the supporters of the ousted dictator Saleh,[45] which weakened the Saudi hand all the more.

These various military stalemates, against a backdrop of American disengagement, were not to China's advantage either: this country's unquenchable thirst for oil currently takes the place of any Middle Eastern policy. Beijing is seeking to diversify its oil suppliers, as well as the countries it is targeting with its massive investment policy, against a backdrop of support for all the regimes in power, regardless of the contradictions that set them apart. This explains how Saudi Arabia and the United Arab Emirates, on the one hand, and Iran, on the other hand, maintain a privileged partnership with Beijing. The various despots, whether republicans or monarchs, appreciate this benevolent show of power, and in return prohibit any criticism of the fate of Muslims in western China. But these are merely mutual good practices between dictatorships, without any vision of the future of the region beyond the indefinite renewal of the status quo. No more than Putin can Xi Jinping replace Trump as the Middle Eastern hegemon, despite the global standoff between China and the United States.

The bankruptcy of the Arab regimes of the Middle East and their clientelist dependence on external sponsors stem from the uncompleted process of national construction, intimately linked to the dictatorial hijacking of postcolonial independence. The Saudi regime, the only

---

[45] Saleh was eliminated by the Houthis in December 2017, causing his supporters, led by his nephew and former head of the presidential guard, to move over into the orbit of the United Arab Emirates.

regime left outside the Ottoman grip as well as colonial subjection, is now seeking to regenerate itself under the rule of Mohammed bin Salman,[46] turning into a dictatorial model in synch with the regional norm. The immense resources of Saudi Arabia allow it to lavishly finance this enterprise, which is hardly 'reformist'. The other Arab despots do not have this latitude, faced as they are with the immense challenge of continuing to provide basic services to an only apparently somnolent population. In October 2019, Lebanon and Iraq were shaken by a wave of explicitly 'revolutionary' protest against a regime whose sectarianism fuelled corruption. These two movements set patriotism and non-violence against the arbitrariness of the militias and the stranglehold of Iran. The holy cities of Najaf and Karbala again became poles of resistance of Arab Shiism to Persian desires for domination.

The Middle East does not need a new hegemon, but rather an order that will finally be based on the aspirations of its peoples. The end of the Ottoman Empire, instead of taking such aspirations into account, led to their quelling by the French and British Mandates; these were themselves followed by independence movements that were hijacked by military juntas. The 'strategic depth' Erdoğan dreamed of on his southern border has shrunk to meagre 'safe zones' in Syrian territory, where mercenaries are recruited to serve as cannon fodder in Turkey's campaigns in Libya and the Caucasus. This military activism on the part of Ankara cannot, however, compensate for the damage to the population resulting from authoritarian regression and the economic slump. As for the Islamic Republic, its Arab adventures, however much they may have been crowned with success, have been bitterly criticized by Iranian protesters since the external successes of the regime represent defeats for a society in need of a state. The imperial nostalgia that underlies the Middle Eastern ambitions of Turkey and Iran is encouraging in turn a rapprochement between the United Arab Emirates and Israel. This nascent alliance, significantly, links an Arab state without a people[47] to a state founded on the dispossession of an Arab people.

---

[46] He became crown prince in June 2017, and eclipsed the power of his father, King Salman, who was in declining health.

[47] Only 10% of the population of the United Arab Emirates are nationals of the country.

For it is indeed a state of war against peoples, a war waged by regional predators outside their borders, and by local dictatorships inside these same borders, which characterizes the Middle East today. It is illusory to believe that regional stability can be based on such a state of open or hidden war. The breakdown of the Egyptian–Syrian–Iraqi triangle, which has structured the Middle East for so many centuries, has triggered a sequence of constantly renewed crises. Syria is in thrall to the appetites of its occupying powers; Egypt has collapsed under its own weight and appears to be lagging behind the petro-monarchies; while in Iraq the patriotic younger generation is paying a heavy price for Iranian expansionism. The inevitable depletion of revenue – economic revenue linked to oil, strategic revenue derived from 'anti-terrorism' – nevertheless condemns the counter-revolutionary project to failure. Only the popular reappropriation of nation-building will be able to haul the Middle East out of this impasse and allow the immense resources of its women and men to flourish at long last.

It will then be time to write a new page in the history of the Middle East.

Chronology

2 August 1990	Iraq invades Kuwait, annexed on the 8th.
17 January 1991	Start of 'Desert Storm'.
28 February 1991	Ceasefire between the United States and Iraq.
30 October 1991	Opening of the Madrid peace conference.
13 July 1992	Yitzhak Rabin, Prime Minister of Israel.
13 September 1993	'Oslo Accords' signed at the White House.
1 July 1994	Yasser Arafat returns to Gaza.
4 November 1995	Rabin assassinated in Tel Aviv.
29 May 1996	Binyamin Netanyahu, Prime Minister of Israel.
6 July 1999	Ehud Barak, Prime Minister of Israel.
26 March 2000	Failure of the Clinton–Assad summit in Geneva.
23 May 2000	Israeli withdrawal from southern Lebanon.
29 September 2000	Beginning of the 'Al-Aqsa intifada'.
6 February 2001	Ariel Sharon, Prime Minister of Israel.
11 September 2001	Al-Qaeda attacks in New York and Washington.
28 March 2002	Arab Peace Initiative in Beirut.
29 March 2002	Israeli reoccupation of the West Bank.
20 March 2003	Invasion of Iraq by the United States.
9 April 2003	Saddam Hussein's regime falls.
11 November 2004	Death of Arafat in Paris.
27 April 2005	Withdrawal of Syrian troops from Lebanon.
12 September 2005	End of Israel's unilateral withdrawal from Gaza.
20 May 2006	Nouri al-Maliki, Prime Minister of Iraq.
12 July 2006	Beginning of the 'thirty-three-day war' between Israel and Hezbollah.
30 December 2006	Execution of Saddam Hussein in Baghdad.
14 June 2007	Takeover of the Gaza Strip by Hamas.
31 March 2009	Netanyahu again Prime Minister of Israel.
4 June 2009	Speech by Barack Obama at Cairo University.
13 June 2009	'Green movement' of protest in Iran.
14 January 2011	Tunisian President Ben Ali flees to Saudi Arabia.
25 January 2011	Mass protests begin in Egypt.
11 February 2011	Anti-Mubarak putsch in Cairo.
16 February 2011	Beginning of the anti-Gaddafi uprising in Benghazi.

14 March 2011	Intervention of Saudi Arabia and the United Arab Emirates in Bahrain.
15 March 2011	Anti-Assad protests begin in Syria.
20 August 2011	Capture of Tripoli by Libyan revolutionaries.
17 June 2012	Mohamed Morsi elected President of Egypt.
9 April 2013	Proclamation of the 'Islamic State of Iraq and Syria' (Daesh).
14 June 2013	Hassan Rouhani elected President of Iran.
3 July 2013	Putsch in Egypt by General Abdel Fattah el-Sisi.
14 August 2013	Repression of Islamist gatherings in Cairo.
21 August 2013	Chemical bombardment of suburbs of Damascus.
16 May 2014	Beginning in Benghazi of the second Libyan civil war.
10 June 2014	Beginning of Daesh's lightning offensive in Iraq.
8 August 2014	First strikes in Iraq by the anti-Daesh coalition.
26 March 2015	Intervention by Saudi Arabia and the United Arab Emirates in Yemen.
14 July 2015	International Iran nuclear deal.
30 September 2015	Direct Russian engagement in Syria.
8 December 2016	Reconquest of Sirte, a stronghold of Daesh in Libya.
22 December 2016	Fall of the last insurgent neighbourhoods of Aleppo.
5 June 2017	Blockade of Qatar led by Saudi Arabia.
21 June 2017	Mohammed bin Salman, crown prince of Saudi Arabia.
9 July 2017	Mosul officially 'liberated' from Daesh.
8 May 2018	US withdrawal from the Iran nuclear deal.
14 May 2018	Transfer to Jerusalem of the American embassy in Israel.
23 March 2019	Fall of the last stronghold of Daesh in Syria.
4 April 2019	Relaunch of the civil war in Libya by Haftar.
1 October 2019	Start of anti-government protests in Iraq.
9 October 2019	Turkish offensive in northeastern Syria.
17 October 2019	Beginning of a 'revolutionary' protest in Lebanon.
16 January 2020	Turkish intervention in Libya in support of the Tripoli government.

28 January 2020	Trump–Netanyahu 'peace plan'.
4 August 2020	Catastrophic explosion in the port of Beirut.
15 September 2020	Peace treaty between Israel and the United Arab Emirates.

Further reading

Achcar, Gilbert, *The people want: a radical exploration of the Arab Uprising*, translated by G. M. Goshgarian (London: Saqi, 2013).

Arjomand, Said Amir, *After Khomeini: Iran under his successors* (New York: Oxford University Press, 2010).

Baczko, Adam, Gilles Dorronsoro, and Arthur Quesnay, *Civil war in Syria: mobilization and competing social orders* (Cambridge: Cambridge University Press, 2017).

Bonnefoy, Laurent, *Yemen and the world: beyond insecurity*, translated by Cynthia Schoch (New York: Oxford University Press, 2019).

Filiu, Jean-Pierre, *From deep state to Islamic State: the Arab counter-revolution and its jihadi legacy* (London: Hurst and New York: Oxford University Press, 2015).

Kienle, Eberhard, *Egypt: a fragile power* (London: Routledge, 2021).

Lacroix, Stéphane, *Awakening Islam: the politics of religious dissent in contemporary Saudi Arabia* (Cambridge, MA: Harvard University Press, 2011).

Louër, Laurence, *Sunnis and Shi'a: a political history*, translated by Ethan Rundell (Princeton, NJ: Princeton University Press, 2022).

Shlaim, Avi, *The iron wall: Israel and the Arab world*, second edition (New York: W. W. Norton & Company, 2014).

Vignal, Leila, *War-torn: the unmaking of Syria, 2011–2021* (London: Hurst, 2021).

Conclusion
The cradle of crises

The Russian invasion of Ukraine in February 2022 is a paradoxical illustration of the persistence of the centrality of the Middle East in international relations. It was in this region that the countdown to the worst conflict in Europe since the Second World War began. The American retreat of August 2013 after the chemical bombing of Damascus clearly convinced Putin that Western reactions would be equally moderate in the face of the Russian annexation of Crimea which he ordered six months later. Such a show of strength, far from being a one-off, marked the beginning of the Kremlin's war of attrition against a Ukraine deemed both too independent and too liberal. In September 2015, in Syria, Russia had moved from substantial but indirect engagement to a large-scale military campaign. The offensive techniques that Moscow tested and then made commonplace in the Syrian theatre have since demonstrated their destructive reach in Ukraine, terrorizing the population there and driving it into exodus. This is the case with the bombings of hospitals, schools, and public infrastructure, but also with the delusive 'humanitarian corridors' where civilians are trapped to put added pressure on the local resistance. The parallel has also been regularly drawn between the devastating siege of Aleppo in 2016 and that of Mariupol six years later, with, in both cases, the methodical destruction of a bastion of the resistance, finally forced to capitulate on a field of ruins.

Many decision-makers and strategists have ended up relegating the Middle East to the margins of major geopolitical issues, without measuring the symbolic dimension inherent in the balance of forces, and the power that results from it. By choosing to provide the Syrian opposition with the means to survive, but never to win, Obama did not understand that he was offering Putin the opportunity to carry out, in the heart of the Middle East, the simulacrum of a 'Cold War' by proxy. By lending unconditional support to the Assad regime, the Kremlin conquered a choice position with all the Arab dictators, even those most

349

linked to the United States, since the 'dropping' of Mubarak by Obama had caused such anxiety for all of these despots. In any case, the Russian President did not have to force himself to act this way, since he shared and continues to share with the tyrant of Damascus the same conspiratorial culture, derived from the training they both had in the opaque world of the intelligence services. The 'people' are allowed to exist in their eyes only in the slogans of propaganda, and when these people manage to organize themselves and dare to form an opposition, then they should be crushed by reducing them to an infamous 'conspiracy' on the part of foreigners. If we add to this the status of heir enjoyed by the two presidents, one appointed by the ailing Yeltsin, the other by his father Hafez al-Assad, the complementarity between 'Vladimir Assad' and 'Bashar Putin' should have sparked debate long before the Ukrainian crisis.

We saw, in the previous chapter, that Russia is methodically using Syria, and more generally the Middle East, to consolidate the restoration of the status of global power enjoyed by the USSR. The aim is nothing less than to defeat the 'new world order' that the United States has instituted and managed, for its own benefit, since 1991 from the Middle East. But Obama set his geopolitical sights on the Pacific Ocean, with a view to confrontation with China, and he did not take Putin's Middle Eastern aims seriously, aims which his successor Trump then tried to appease rather than to fight. It is true that Netanyahu, very close to the Republican President, leaned towards cooperation with Putin, in his eyes the only bulwark against Iran establishing a lasting presence on the northern border of Israel. It mattered little that this breakthrough by Tehran and its henchmen took place within the framework of a collaboration with Moscow in the service of the Assad regime. The bottom line for Netanyahu and Trump was to limit the damage of this Russian policy rather than to contain it at the source. The United States was also kind enough to assume most of the burden of the fight against Daesh, allowing the Russian air force to concentrate its strikes against a Syrian opposition much less well equipped than the jihadists. This shows clearly that Russia, in its bid to relaunch its expansionism in Europe from the Middle East, has in this region benefited as much from the commitment of the United States in support of Israel or against Daesh as from its disengagement.

As for this American disengagement from the Middle East, it is less military than political, diplomatic, and symbolic. Contrary to popular cliché, the 'American Middle East' did not die, after three decades, in the humiliating withdrawal from Afghanistan in August 2021, when the United States was forced to cohabit in Kabul for two weeks with its sworn enemies the Taliban. It was in January 2020 that the American construction of a world hegemony based on control of the Middle East wavered, never to recover. We have seen that this was when Trump and Netanyahu announced, from the White House, a 'deal of the century' meant to settle definitively the Palestinian question on the basis of a rump state, demilitarized and deprived of territorial continuity. However, the feeble 'Palestinian Authority' had only to categorically refuse this diktat and the 'deal of the century' collapsed, revealing the fragility of the entire American system in the region. It is significant that the agreement signed the following month in Qatar between the United States and the Taliban focused on the modalities of the American withdrawal from Afghanistan, and not on the means of restraining a triumphant insurgency. Washington's inability to impose, manage, and consolidate a peace process in the Middle East signalled the abdication of its status as the dominant power in the region long before the humiliation of Kabul.

The founding act of this post-American Middle East also took place in September 2020, i.e. almost a year before the fall of Kabul, when the 'Abraham Accords' were concluded. An optical illusion largely fuelled by Trump's propaganda saw these 'Abraham Accords' as the fulfilment of the Israeli–Palestinian 'deal of the century', whereas the fiasco of the latter was exactly what led to the conclusion of the former. The underlying logic of the 'Abraham Accords' aimed to dissociate Arab–Israeli normalization from the handling of the Palestinian question, opening the way to strategic cooperation between Israel and the United Arab Emirates, now bound together by a 'hot peace', unlike the 'cold peace' concluded by Israel with Egypt in 1979 and then Jordan in 1994. The United States was merely the modest 'witness' of this multifaceted alliance between Tel Aviv and Abu Dhabi, an alliance that, as the Ukrainian crisis would demonstrate, was anything but aligned with Washington. Israel and the United Arab Emirates refused to endorse American sanctions against the Kremlin, Dubai becoming the privileged sanctuary of Russian oligarchs registered on the various Western 'blacklists'.

This same Ukrainian crisis, which has seen Russia mobilizing on the European scene the instruments of its power forged in the Middle East, now acts as an indicator of the disorder that has been worsened by the failure of the American project for the region. There is indeed no vacuum here, but on the contrary an overflow of power, or rather of powers in the plural, because neither Russia nor China is in a position to assume the structuring ambition of an American hegemony that fell victim to its own militarization – a militarization which had become an end in itself, before brutally receding. The Kremlin has proved, through its failure to sponsor a political transition in Syria, that its military activism, largely facilitated by the United States and Israel, is not driven by any vision other than that of preserving the dictatorial status quo at all costs. It is the same static vision that underlies the economic activism of China, whose investments in all the camps of the Middle East are based on the perpetuation of regimes that are nevertheless opposed to each other in the long term. The inability of Moscow and Beijing to implement a dynamic of peace – for Russia in a Syria that has been bled dry, for China between its various partners – echoes the collapse of the 'deal of the century' so dear to Trump. To replace the vanished hegemon would require an additional dimension of power, political, diplomatic, and symbolic, a dimension that neither Russia nor China seems able to deploy in the Middle East.

It is therefore the regional predators who occupy centre stage today, in complex relationships that defy all automatic reflexes and involve the specific dynamics of the preservation and projection of the power of each party. The prophesied clash between the axis born of the 'Abraham Accords', on the one hand, and Turkey and Iran, on the other, did not happen – far from it, since Ankara spectacularly reconciled itself with the United Arab Emirates and then with Saudi Arabia, whatever the flatterers of the three regimes concerned might say. On the contrary, it is between Turkey and Iran that tensions are rising, against the backdrop of President Erdoğan's growing interventionism against Kurdish separatism, not only in Syria but also in northern Iraq. As for the United Arab Emirates, it has put an end to its direct engagement in Yemen, leaving Saudi Arabia to seek a way out which – given the balance of power on the ground – will at least require Tehran to moderate its local allies. The Ukrainian crisis has also confirmed the importance for Riyadh of its partnership with Moscow in the management of oil prices, even if such a strategic partnership publicly upsets Washington.

The conflicts that are described as insoluble in the Middle East at the beginning of the third millennium are therefore neither more nor less so than those mentioned throughout this book, ever since the foundation of the Eastern Roman Empire. In the spirit of secularism which is being observed here, a secularism that desacralizes not only religious discourse but also political and nationalist narratives, one needs to rigorously distinguish competing propaganda from actual practices. We have seen, for example, how the Byzantine Empire and Sassanid Persia, despite the state monotheism claimed by each of their sovereigns, cohabited harmoniously for some two centuries before tearing each other apart until they both had to yield to the power coming from Arabia. We have also seen how the supposed 'golden age' of Christianity and Islam was in fact riddled with bloody repressions and internal feuds which, under the guise of doctrinal quarrels, largely involved struggles over power; how a caliphate rivalling that of Baghdad was able to establish itself in Cairo and how the aberration of this coexistence of two 'Commanders of the Faithful' favoured the cycle of the Crusades; and how these Crusades, sometimes exalted as a 'clash of civilizations', were a relatively minor confrontation in a Middle East where Christian and Muslim kinglets frequently collaborated, before the devastation of the Mongol invasions sowed ruin for all in the region.

This primacy of politics in the tormented history of the Middle East acquired a new dimension at the beginning of the sixteenth century, with the Ottoman Empire taking control of most of this area apart from a Persia henceforth united around a state Shiism, itself the object of complex negotiations between the Safavid shah and the clerical hierarchy. And even within this framework, filled with the tumult of the 'religious wars' of Europe at that time, the border drawn in 1639 between the Ottomans and the Safavids did not correspond, as we have seen, to any denominational, ethnic, or linguistic delimitation; indeed, the two holiest cities of Shiism were even in Ottoman territory. This border has nevertheless continued in broad outline until today, despite the terrible conflict between Iraq and Iran from 1980 to 1988. If one adds to this the fact that a large part of the Shiite population of contemporary southern Iraq only left Sunnism and converted at the end of the nineteenth century, certain fashionable generalizations appear singularly fragile, beyond the essentialist bias that they arbitrarily legitimize. And it is the

Shiite strongholds of Baghdad, Basra, and Karbala that today animate the fiercest resistance to Iranian expansionism in Iraq, invalidating any analysis in terms of sectarian identity alone.

The geopolitical overview and the sectarian prism which nevertheless provide the framework for most current commentaries thus struggle to account for the dynamics which structure the Middle East at a deeper level. To better understand them, we need to adopt the perspective of peoples and their right to self-determination. This right emerged in the region as an echo of Greek independence, won in 1829 against the Ottoman Empire; in this conflict, the Ottomans lost twice over, since the Egypt of Muhammad Ali turned against them and seized the Levant. The model of enlightened despotism which then imposed itself from Cairo combined state construction, authoritarian modernization, and nationalist self-assertion. It was the beginning of the long cycle of the Arab Renaissance, the Nahda, albeit a top-down Nahda, driven by the determination of a strong power – a Nahda which yielded, half a century later, to the British occupation of Egypt. The continuation of the Arab Renaissance was nevertheless ensured by a bottom-up Nahda whose cultural effervescence extended from Alexandria to Aleppo, from Beirut to Baghdad. This emancipatory movement combined strictly 'nationalist' aspirations, invoking the rights of the Arab people irrespective of sect, with language that we would today describe as 'Islamist', demanding restitution to the Arabs of the caliphate usurped by the Ottomans. These two currents engaged in harmonious dialogue within this Nahda, which, at the very moment when the European powers were playing the 'minority' card, was forging the keys to a coexistence which contrasted with the 'balkanization' of the European part of Ottoman territory.

However much the forces of this Nahda, led by Sharif Hussein of Mecca, gave their support in 1916 to France and Great Britain, this brotherhood of arms was betrayed by the establishment of the 'mandates' of these two European powers on territories promised to the Arab allies. The crushing by the French army, in 1920, of the Arab kingdom (a consti-tutional kingdom, after all) ruled by the son of Hussein in Damascus marked the failure of the 'nationalist' dimension of this Nahda, before Hussein's expulsion from Mecca and Medina five years later marked the defeat of its 'Islamist' component, to the benefit of Wahhabi fundamen-talism and the future Saudi Arabia. It was against the background of this twofold failure that the half-century cycle of Arab independences began in 1922 with the end of the British protectorate over Egypt – a cycle that came to a close in 1971, with the admission to the UN of the United Arab Emirates, Qatar, Bahrain, and Oman. But this virtuous cycle was thwarted by the two decades of hijacking of Arab independences, from 1949 to 1969, when putsches overthrew the nationalist and pluralist elites that had fashioned independence in favour of supposedly 'progressive' military juntas.

This perspective shows that the famous 'Arab Spring' of 2011, far from being a seasonal eruption, was part of a long history of struggle by the Arab peoples for self-determination, frustrated initially by the colonial powers and then by militarized dictatorships. This dialectic sheds light on the fact that a dynamic of protest across the whole Arab world does not in the slightest diminish the deeply nationalist character of each of the protests concerned. But a counter-revolutionary wave would mobilize to liquidate popular demands in the name of a return to a mythical status quo. The crisis of the Arab regimes is so serious, however, that nowhere has the status quo prevailing before 2011 been restored. Sisi's Egypt has five times more political prisoners than under Mubarak, while Sisi's Libyan emulator has vainly unleashed two civil wars without ever managing to seize Tripoli. The massive involvement of Saudi Arabia and the United Arab Emirates in Yemen may be the major cause of an unprecedented humanitarian crisis, but the protégés of the petro-monarchies have had to abandon the attempt to retake Sanaa from Tehran's allies. As for Syria, the tyrant Assad continues to reign there, but on a wasteland, half of whose population has been either displaced within the country or expelled outside its borders. In many respects, the Syrian people, who had won their independence against the mandate granted to France by the League of Nations, must now submit to the 'mandate' granted de facto by the UN to Russia. The flag of Assad's opponents, indeed, is the same as the flag of their nationalist elders in their resistance against the French Mandate.

The leitmotif of the rights of peoples is thus much more useful in shedding light on current events and prospects in the Middle East than discourses on the inevitability of religious conflicts and on the 'stability' that dictatorships allegedly ensure. Authoritarian regimes, far from appeasing regional contradictions, bring these to a climax by constantly repressing popular aspirations to a finally authentic self-determination. And if there is any inevitability in the Middle East, it lies not in this or that falsified version of a formidable history, but in the international consensus which, actively or by default, leads to endorsing a persistent denial of the rights of peoples in the region. The emancipatory forces, already facing an extreme degree of repression by the regimes in power, also have to face indifference at best, complacency in favour of dictator-ships at worst. The disastrous American invasion of Iraq, which replaced Saddam Hussein's terror machine in 2003 with the extreme violence wielded by sectarian militias, contributed a great deal to this deadly impasse.

However, history and the individual stories within it continue, and this openness of a history that is always in the making is in itself a source of hope. This is why our dive into the past millennium and a half of Middle Eastern history has endeavoured, by bringing out the logics of the possible at a given period and by re-establishing certain factual sequences that are too little known, to defuse the kind of hate speech that is frozen and essentialist in its approach to the region. This intellectual adventure has been undertaken at a time when all authoritarian regimes, without exception, are trying to impose state propaganda, and where history is called upon only to justify the whims of the moment. The jihadist monster, with its sinister parody of the 'caliphate', worked in exactly the same way, nourishing its globalized communication with the conscious or unconscious generalizations of some of the Western media. Despite these dire constraints, scholars, thinkers, and civil society activists are working tenaciously across the Middle East to restore to the history of these peoples and this region all its nobility and all its authenticity. It is in resonance with their work and with their hopes that this book has been written as a contribution to the necessary and collective debate on the past, and therefore the destiny, of this Middle East, a region that is so central, so rich, and, let us dare to say it, so filled with hope.

If you have followed me this far, let me end on this note. A note of history and a note of hope.

Index

Abbas, Mahmoud, PLO leader 325
Abbas II, Shah (1642–1666) 160
Abbas the Great, shah (1588–1629)
 158–60
Abbas Helmy Pasha I (1848–1854) 191
Abbasid dynasty
 al-Abbas, Abu 147
 administration 56
 attack on Byzantines 72–3
 attacks on 74–5
 attempts to establish code 65
 Buyids and 90–2
 caliphs assassinated 100
 context of civil wars 76–7
 Crusaders and 99
 divine right of Shiism 64
 elites and dissidents 110–11
 ends Umayyad dynasty 52–3
 Fatimids and 109
 grateful to Ottomans 166
 Hulagu Khan ends 123–4
 leaves Baghdad for Samarra 77
 loses Syria 84–5
 loss of power 81
 Mahdi prophecies and 82
 minor and major jihad 63
 repression of Imams 67–9
 in Samarra 70, 93
 Seljuk defence of 93–4
 state religion and 147
 Sunnism and 59–61, 109, 123
 supplant Umayyad 5
 suppress messianic uprising 74
Abd al-Ilah, crown prince 260
Abdelkader El Djezaïri, emir
 capitulates to France 195

 protector in Damascus 189–90
 resists France 186
Abduh, Muhammad 217–18
Abdul Hamid II, sultan (1876–1909)
 absolutism/'Hamidian' 218–20
 Armenians and 202, 220–2, 239
 assassination attempt 222
 brings about constitution 214
 conversion plans for Shiites 221
 deposed and exiled 227
 ends Tanzimat 217
 outcomes of reign 222–3
 Sunni Islam and 219–20
 Tanzimat era 229
 Young Turks 226
Abdulaziz, sultan (1861–1876) 214
Abdullah I, king (1921–1946) 260
 given Transjordan 244
 partition of Palestine 262
Abdullah, king (2005–2015) 327
Abdulmejid I, Sultan (1839–1861)
 211–14
Abraha (general), Arabian campaign of
 25
Abraham (Old Testament)
 the Black Stone in Mecca 74
 Muhammad and 49
Abraham Accords 351
Abu al-Abbas as-Saffah, caliph (750–754)
 53
Abu Bakr, Caliph (632–634) 35, 37
Abu Muslim, Abbasid revolution and
 52–3
Abu Sufyan, Umayyad leader 35, 36, 40
Abu Talib (Muhammad's uncle) 33, 34
accommodation, principle of 15

Acre
  Crusader conquest of 98
  Frederick II and 119
  Mamluk capture 128
Adams, John 182–3
Aden, Britain occupies 195, 200
al-Adid, caliph (1160–1167) 102–3
al-Adil I 'Saphadin', sultan (1200–1218)
    117–18
al-Afghani, Jamal al-Din 216
Afghanistan
  Bin Laden and 318–20
  Persia sieges Herat 186
  Russia versus Britain 194
  Soviet invasion of 300–2
  US withdrawal from 351
Agha Mohammad Qajar, shah (1789–
    1797) 172
Ahmad, Shihab al-Din, sultan (1461) 139
Ahmad Shah Qajar (1909–1925) 224–5
Ahmadinejad, Mahmoud
  Erdoğan and 326
  messianic ideology 324
  re-election of 328
Ahmed Riza, bey 226
Ahmed Shah Qajar (1909–1925) 250
Al-Ahram/The Pyramids newspaper 217
Ain Jalut, battle of 125
Alamut, Sabbah's fortress 98
Alawites
  Assad and 283
  Ba'ath Party and 304
  French 'state' of 252, 253
  Hafez al-Assad and 292
  origins of 89–90
  post-First World War 243
  Taymiyyah and 130
Albania, Ottoman Empire and 138, 212
Aleppo
  ancient city 5
  Byzantine attack on 84
  Caliph Sulayman and 51
  communal riots 212
  Crusaders and 99
  effect of Crusades 110

Hanano District 257
minority Shiism 101
Mongols sack 124
Ottoman rule 148–9, 161–2, 242
post-First World War 243
Russian bombing of 349
Timur attacks 134
Yaqut and Ibn Khallikan 123
Zengid rule of 104
Alevi Islam 152
Alexandria 4, 14
Algeria
  French occupation of 184, 186, 200,
    201
  Jewish population 197
  Justinian conquers 23
  Ottoman Empire and 157
  treaty with Washington 182
Ali al-Hadi al-Askari, imam (835–868) 67
  Fatima and 81
  Legitimist Shiism 67
Ali ibn Abi Talib, caliph (656–661) 35
  Caliphate and Discord 40–1
  the Great Discord 59
  Harun al-Rashid's burial 57
  refuses oath to Abu Bakr 37
Ali ibn Musa al-Reza, imam (799–818)
    67
Allenby, General Edmund 239
  High Commissioner in Cairo 245
  Occupied Enemy Territory
    Administration 241–2
Alliance Israélite Universelle (AIU) 189,
    197
Alp Arslan, sultan (1063–1072) 93–4
Amalric of Jerusalem (1163–1174) 102,
    103
al-Amin, caliph (809–813) 57–8
Amin, Qasim, The Liberation of Women
    218
Anatolia
  becomes Ottoman 138
  Timur in 134
  Toynbee's 'Western question' 202–3
Anthony, Saint 15–16

Antioch
  969 Byzantine siege 84
  attacked by Khosrow I 23
  Crusader state 97–8
  destruction of 24
  epidemic of Third Crusade 106
  Nur ad-Din 101
  patriarchate of 14
  restored to Byzantines 102
Apocalypse in Islam (Filiu) 1
Aq Qoyunlu/White Sheep 133
Aqaba
  Battle of 239
  First Gulf War and 295
Arab Congress of Paris 231
Arab democratic uprisings 7, 329–32
  bloodlands of 8
Arab League
  'Abdullah plan' 327
  excludes Egypt 288
  PLO as member of 285
  in Tunis 299
Arab Liberation Movement
  al-Shishakli and 270
Arab Nahda/Renaissance 354
  circulation of writings 217–18
  in Egypt 209–10
  failure of elites 303
  feminists 8
  hijacks independences 276
  imperialists' betrayal of 249
  Islamism 218
  khassa/elite and *amma*/masses 230
  meaning of 207
  millet/community 213, 219, 229–30
  Muhammad Ali's Egypt 210
  nationalism and 218
  watan/homeland 217, 230
  Young Turks and 230–2
Arab Revolt (1916) 237–9
  Battle of Aqaba 239
  King Hussein and 247
Arab worlds
  Balfour Declaration and 244
  'golden age' ideal 41–2

  independence movements 271–3
  with Iraq against Iran 296–7
  Mamluks and 142
  mukhabarat 272
  nationalism 184, 236
  Palestine and 254–6
  pluralism 265
  poets 30
  pre-Islamic kingdoms 28–33
Arabian peninsula
  Abraha's campaign in 25
  Felix: Yemen and Himyarites 28
  invades Syria 5
  Muslim conquest of 37–8
  nomads and settled people 31
  Ptolemy on Arabia Deserta 28
  role of sheikhs 31
  Wahhabi dissidence 201
Arabic language
  Baghdad sultanates and 142
  common language of elites 92
  flourishing of 76
  Ibn al-Nadim's 'Repertory' of 92
Arafat, Yasser
  al-Assad and 286–7
  death of 325
  elected president 316
  exile of 299–30
  Nasser and PLO 278
  Oslo Accords 315
  peace talks with Barak 317–18
  PLO and 280–1
  Reagan sees as Soviet pawn 293
  Saudi finance and 284–5
  survives Tunis bomb 299
Arcadius, emperor (383–408) 12, 20–1
Armenia/Armenians
  Abdul Hamid II and 202
  border arbitration 245
  Cappadocia and 73
  Crusaders and 97, 97n
  emigrants in Persia 159
  genocide of 239–41
  Greater Armenia negotiation 257
  'Little' and 'Great' 105

Armenia/Armenians (*cont.*)
  massacre of 228
  Ottoman integration 137
  Ottoman massacres 220–2, 227, 231
  Rome and Persia partition 20
  Russia and 185, 246
  Syrian Druze revolt and 252
  Turkish denial of genocide 246
  Young Turks and 226
Armenian Church 18, 163
Ashkelon, Crusades and 102, 107
Asia Minor, 'theme' political areas 71
assabiyya, meaning of 53–4
al-Assad, Bashar
  civil war and 332–3
  communities of Syria 253
  exhausted regime 341
  Hanano District in Aleppo 257
  inherits presidency 317
  Lebanon and 324–5
  uses sarin gas 334–5
al-Assad, Hafez
  Alawites and 283
  Arafat and 286–7
  boycott of UN 285
  death of 317
  with Khomeini against Saddam 292
  PFLP and 281
  PLO and 294
  rectifying mistakes 282
  Soviet friendship and 293, 294
  US peace efforts 286
Assassins
  Baybar eliminates from Syria 127–8
  extremism of 143
  long shadow of 109–10
Assyrians
  Armenian genocide and 241
  in Ottoman Empire 239
  rights guaranteed 245
al-Atassi, Hashim, president (1936–1939)
  253
Atatürk, Mustafa Kemal
  amnesty for genocide 241
  'Ataturk Protection Law' 273

Battle of Dardanelles 237
  becomes Turkey's leader 245–6
  death of 253
  fights in Tobruk 200
  Kurds in Syria and 257
  trades Aleppo for Antioch 243
  Young Turks 227
Australia, Gallipoli and 236–7
Austria, peace with Ottomans and 165
Avars 11
Aybak, Izz al-Din, sultan (1254–1257)
  122
Ayyubid dynasty
  after Saladin 115, 117–19
  Jerusalem pact with Crusaders 123
  Mongol invasion and 120
  Saladin 103–5
  stability of 141
  Sunni Islam and 108
  Turanshah succeeds Salih 121–2
Azerbaijan
  Mongol expansion and 120
  Ottoman Empire and 152, 167
  Timur in 134
  unrest in 224
Al-Azhar mosque, Cairo 82, 83, 86
  Coptic cleric at 245
  of Hussein 82
  'Lighthouse of Islam' 109
  Muhammad Abduh and 217–18
  theological legitimization 92
al-Aziz, Caliph (975–996) 86
Azzam, Abdullah Yusuf
  'global jihad' 301–2

Ba'ath Party
  in Iraq 303
  Iraq–Syria gap 283
  religious diversity 283
  in Syria 303
Bábism and the Báb (Ali Mohammed)
  215
Baghdad
  1347–1350 plague 131
  Abbasids and 69, 77, 85

Arab Revolt and 238
Arabs and elites 142
Ayyubid Sunni sultanate 108
Buyids and 81, 90–2, 91
'City of Salvation' 55
Crusaders and 99
end of caliphate 123–5, 128
founding of 5
House of Wisdom 58
massacre of Shiite population 158
population of 4
rivalry with Cairo 3
Safavids hold 174
Seljuk dethroned 115
Sunni madrasa established 94
Timur attacks 134, 135
Baghdad Pact 274
al-Baghdadi, Abu Bakr
declares 'Islamic State' 329
millenarian sects 110
takes Mosul 336
Bahais, Persian campaign against 250
Bahrain
Al-Khalifa rivalry with Al-Thani 195
fear of Muslim Brotherhood 331–2
independence of 275
Iran and 288
Saudi Wahhabism 208
al-Bakr, Ahmed Hasan
Ba'athist Party 282–3
dismissed by Saddam 291
Sunnism of 283
Baldwin of Boulogne, King of Jerusalem
(1100–1118) 97
Balfour (Arthur) Declaration 239
Arab boycott of institutions 244
Balkan wars, Ottoman Empire and
227–8
Balochistan 193
al-Banna, Hassan 264–5
Baradaeus, Bishop of Edessa 18–19
Barak, Ehud 317–18
Barbaross, Hayreddin 153
Barbary War 181–3
Barjawan, tutor 86–7

Barmakid family, *Thousand and One Nights* 56–7
Baybars, sultan (1260–1277) 150
administration of 126–7
advises Qutuz 125
eliminates Syrian assassins 127–8
leads Mamluks 121, 122
seizes throne 125–7
Bayezid, Şehzade 152, 156
Bayezid I the Thunderbolt, bey (1389–1402) 132, 135
Bayezid II, sultan (1481–1512)
Mamluks and 140
overthrown by Selim 148
Bedouins
Italy confines to camps 255
murder of al-Hakim and 88
oratorical contests 30
in Palestine 197
on pilgrimage route 222–3
Saudi *Ikhwan* 248
Begin, Menachem
Camp David accords 287–8
fall of the Shah 293
formation of Israel 263
invasion of Lebanon 293
Ben Ali, Zine El Abidine 330
Ben-Gurion, David
anti-fascism in Second World War
258–9
founding of Israel 262, 263
Berbers, Isma'ili missionaries 82
Bernadotte, Folke 262
Bilad al-Sham
Aleppo 161–2
Cairo and 142
Christian population 162
Crusades and 110
Fatimids and Byzantines 94
Maronites in 105
Ottoman Empire 201
refuge for Isma'ilis 107
Bin Laden, Osama
Afghanistan and 318–20
Al-Qaeda terrorism 318–20

Bin Laden, Osama (*cont.*)
  Assassins and 109–10
  Iraqi branch and 322
  killed by US operation 329
  against Russia in Afghanistan 302
  see also Al-Qaeda
Birnbaum, Nathan 198
Bismarck, Otto von 193–4
Black Sea, demilitarization of 188
Black September group 281, 282
Blum, Léon 253
bombards, Mahmud I and 167
Bonaparte, Louis-Napoleon, Prince
      Imperial 187–8
Bonaparte, Napoleon, in Egypt 180–1
  in Egypt 201
Bonneval, Comte de, bombards and 167
Bosnia
  annexed by Austria-Hungary 226
  becomes Ottoman 138
  revolts against Ottomans 212
Bossuet, Jacques-Bénigne 118
Bourgeois Gentleman, The (Molière) 165
al-Boustani, Boutrus 230
Britain
  1854 alliance with France 188
  African imperialism 202
  Balfour Declaration 239, 244
  battle of El-Alamein 259
  consulate in Aleppo 161
  controls Egypt 200
  Crimean War 187–8
  disengages east of Suez 275
  division of Ottoman Empire 6
  Egypt and 6, 192, 209, 217, 258, 265,
      355
  founding of Israel and 261
  Gallipoli 236–7
  gives Egypt independence 244–5
  imperialism in Africa 194–6
  India and 191
  Iraq no-fly zone 312
  Iraq War and 321
  Jewish people and 163–4, 187, 254–6
  massacre of Egyptian police 270

  Muslim Policy 255
  Occupied Enemy Territory
      Administration 241–2
  occupies Persia 193
  post-war Iran 273
  represses Arab strike in Palestine
      255–6
  Reuter's Persian deal 215–16
  Russia and 185–6, 186, 192–4, 215
  Shah Abbas and 158
  in Sudan 194–5
  supports Greece 184
  Sykes–Picot Agreement 239, 243
  Triple Entente 236
  see also First World War; Second World
      War
al-Bukhari, Muhammad ibn Isma'il 59
Bulgaria
  Balkan Wars 227–8
  siege of Constantinople 73
  Tsarist Russia and 193
Busaids/al-Said, House of 169
Bush, George H.W.
  'Desert Storm' Gulf War 309–14
  Madrid peace talks 314
Bush, George W.
  election of 318
  'war on terror' 319–20
  weakens Saudi relations 327
al-Bustani, Butrus 217
Buyid dynasty
  Abbasids and 90–2
  in Baghdad 81
  Toghrul expels 93

Cable News Network (CNN) 311
Cairo
  Al-Azhar mosque 82, 83, 86, 92
  end of caliphate 128
  founding of 5
  as megacity 4
  population 85, 264
  al-Qahira established 81
  rivalry with Baghdad 3
Canada, Gallipoli and 236–7

Cantacuzene, John 131
Cappadocia, Armenia and 73
Carter, James (Jimmy)
   Camp David accords 287–8
   hopes for peace 309
   hostage crisis 293
Catherine II the Great, Empress (1762–
   1796) 166
Caucasus region
   Muslims leave 228
   Russian colonization of 186, 193, 200
Cem, brother of Bayezid II 140
Chalcedon, patriarchate of 14
Chaldiran, battle of 148, 150
Chardin, Jean 160
Charlemagne, emperor (768–814) 72–3
Charles V, Holy Roman emperor (1519–
   1556) 153
Charles XII, King of Sweden (1697–1718)
   166
Chechnya, resists Russia 186
chemical weapons
   Obama's 'red line' for Syria 334–5
   Saddam uses on Kurds 298, 299
   Yemen 278
China
   international role of 352
   Iran and 324
   oil and 342
   Silk Road 3
   UN Security Council and 335
Chirac, Jacques 324–5
Christian populations
   1860s massacres 189–90
   in Bilad al-Sham 162
   cohabitation in Middle East 228–30
   favouritism in Syria 212
   fragmentation of communities 213–14
   Islam tolerance of 174
   massacres in Damascus 213
   massacres in Lebanon 213
   in Ottoman Empire 188–9, 213
   in Persia 159, 160, 185
Christianity
   accommodation principle 15

al-Hakim discriminates against 87
Arianism heresy 12
autonomous churches 105–6
Byzantium and 2
Council of Nicea 11
destruction of Holy Sepulchre 87
discrimination against 76
divisions within 42
emperor at Constantinople 14–16
filioque controversy 95
Hagia Sophia basilica 23–4
heresies and break-aways 17–18, 21,
   38–9
internal conflicts 353
'Latin' Jerusalem 97
Miaphysitism 17
monastacism and ascetics 15–16, 24
Nestorianism 17
Nicaean council 14
patriarchates 14–15
'People of the Book' 38–9
plurality in Syria 90
within rise of Islam 47–8
in Yemen 31
see also Crusades; Holy Roman
   Empire; Roman Empire, Eastern/
   Byzantium; Roman Empire,
   West
Churchill, Winston, Khartoum and 195
Cilicia
   Armenian genocide 240
   Crusaders and 97
   granted to France 245
   'Little Armenia' 105
Circassians
   against Druze 252
   resist Russia 186
class, Arab elites 264–6
Clinton, William (Bill)
   division of Hebron 317
   handling of peace process 326–7
   missile strike on Al-Qaeda 319
   Netanyahu and 316
   peace talks 315–18
Cold War, Middle East and 7

colonialism/imperialism
  bankrupts Middle East 191–2
  betrayal of the Nahda 249
  eve of First World War 200–1
  historiography of 180
  Kurdish resistance 257
  Napoleon in Egypt 180–1
  Suez crisis 274
  unites Sunnis and Shias 244
  the Western question 201–3
  Wilson and self-determination 242–3
Committee of Union and Progress
    (CUP) 140, 226–7
Conrad III (1138–1152) 101
Constantine XI, emperor (1449–1453) 137
Constantine the Great (306–337) 11
Constantinople
  1204 capture by Crusaders 117
  becomes Istanbul 246
  Bulgarian siege of 73
  Byzantine dominance 11
  Crusades and 8
  establishes empire 11–14
  fall of 137–9
  Hagia Sophia 23, 137
  looks to Europe 9
  Ottoman capture of 3, 137–9
  siege of 27
  Topkapi palace 138
  Umayyad sieges of 71
  see also Ottoman Empire; Roman
      Empire, Eastern/Byzantium
Coptic Church
  Justinian and 24
  opposed to Constantinople 18
  other Churches and 70
  persecution of 27
  proto-national Church 41
  Second Crusade and 105–6
  University of Al-Azhar 245
Coptic language 50
Crémieux, Adolphe 197
Crete, Ottoman pursuit of 164–5
Crimea
  Russian occupation of 166

Tatars flee to Anatolia 188
Crimean War
  origins and outcome 187–8
  peace conditions of 188
  Treaty of Paris 213
Crusades 3
  First
    intolerance softens 99–100
    Jerusalem as goal 95–7
    occupation of Levant 97–101
    Zengi takes Edessa 100
  Second
    failure of 101–3
    proposal of 100–1
  Third 106–7
    Ayybids and 115–16
  Fourth 116–17
  Fifth 118–19
  Sixth 119
  Seventh
    battle of Al Mansurah 122
    Salih and Mamluks 121
  Eighth 128
  Baybars seizes fortresses 128
  Byzantine Empire and 8
  counter-Crusades 110
  fatal for Fatimids 6
  as Frankish colonialism 110
  historical perspective of 353
  Latin states 121, 128
  outcomes of 128–9
  'Shepherd's Crusade' 122
Ctesiphon 4
  features of 21
  Safavids and 174
  see also Persia
Cyprus, Ottoman Empire and 157
Cyril, patriarch of Alexandria 17

Dabiq, battle of 148–9
Daesh/'Islamic State'
  al-Baghdadi 329
  Syrian civil war and 335–6
  takes Mosul 336
  US and fight against 350

Damascus
  1347–1350 plague 131
  ancient city 5
  capital for Saladin 108
  centre of power 42
  Druze revolt 252
  effect of Crusades 110
  Fakhr al-Din II 162–3
  Fatimids and 83
  France occupies 257
  Hejaz railway 199
  massacre of Christians 189–90
  Ottoman Empire 161
  post-First World War 243
  Second Crusade siege 101
Dara, Persian victory at 26
ad-Darazi, Muhammad bin Ismail
    Nashtakin 88
Dashnak/Armenian Revolutionary
    Federation 221, 226
da'wa, meaning of 53–4
Dawla, meaning of 53
al-Dawla, Adud, grand emir (949–983)
  91
al-Dawla, Mu'izz, emir of Iraq (945–967)
  91
al-Dawla, Sa'ad, emir of Aleppo
  (967–991) 84–5
al-Dawla, Sayf, emir (945–967) 84, 91
Dayan, Moshe 279
de Gaulle, General Charles 259–60
de Lesseps, Ferdinand 191
democracy
  2011 uprisings 330–2, 355
  persistent denial of 9–10
  self-determination principle 9, 242
dhimmi/protection 70
Dioscorus, patriarch of Alexandria 18
Disraeli, Benjamin 193
Djalili, Hussein, governor of Mosul 174
Djemal, Ahmed, Pasha (1914–1918) 228
  allies with Germany 236, 237
  Armenian genocide and 240
Dodecanese Islands 245
Druze
  as a 'British plot' 202
  cohabitation in Lebanon 230
  emir Fakhr al-Din II 162–3
  French 'state' of 252, 253
  Hafez Assad as Alawite 283
  massacre of Maronites 189–90
  origins of 88–90
  post-First World War 243

East India Company, sepoy revolt and
  192
Ebussuud Efendi 156
Edessa
  944 siege 73
  fall in 1144 106
  Khosrow's attempt on 23
  Persian victory 26
  Second Crusade 101
  theological school 21
  Zengi reconquers 100
Egypt
  1347–1350 plague 131
  2011 uprising 7
  army 209
  assassination of Sadat 293
  attacks Israel with Syria 283–4
  Baybars establishes Mamluks 125–7
  blockade of Qatar 339
  Britain controls 200, 217, 258, 265, 355
  as British base 202
  British imperialism 6
  British massacre of police 270
  in Byzantine domain 11
  centre of stability 141–2
  Cold War and 7
  'Cold War' with Saudis 309
  Coptic Church 70
  Coptic language 18
  Crusades oust Fatimids 6
  dealing with Wahhabism 208–9
  democratic uprising 330
  demographics of 264
  Description de l'Égypte 181
  Eastern Roman Empire 13–14

Egypt (*cont.*)
    eschatological anxiety 100
    excluded from Arab League 288
    Fatimid dynasty 67, 81–4, 107–8
    Fifth Crusade 118–19
    France controls 6, 9
    Free Officers 270–1
    gold mines 14
    Islamization of 70
    Kafur and Fatimids 82
    Kissinger peace efforts 285–6
    lags behind 343
    London grants independence 244–5
    long nineteenth century 231
    Mamluks 132–3
    marginalization of 176
    Morsi wins election 333
    Mubarak and 293, 331
    Muhammad Ali Pasha 183–5, 209–10,
        354
    Muslim Brotherhood 264–6, 270, 331,
        333–4
    Muslim conquest of 38
    Napoleon in 180–1, 201
    Nasser's rivalry with Faisal 277–9
    Nizari dissent 107
    Nur ad-Din and 102–3
    Ottoman control 169–71, 174
    patriarch of Alexandria 18
    Phocas and 26
    railway 191
    reaction against migrants 192
    repels Mongols 124–5
    Revolutionary Command Council
        271
    Sassanid occupation 41
    Sinai and Israel 279
    Sisi and 333, 334, 341, 355
    Six-Day War 279–80
    slave trade 132–3
    Suez Canal and 6, 191–2, 196, 274
    sultanate with Syria 6
    Sunnism 276
    supplies Mecca and Medina 170
    Syria and 211–12

    trade with Europe 170
    troops in Yemen 280
    Umayyad rule in 47
    United Arab Republic 275–6, 277
    viziers' power 94
    Waft Party 265
Eisenhower, Dwight D.
    CIA in Iran 273–4
    end of colonialism 309
    Suez crisis 274–5
El-Alamein, battle of 259
Enver (Isma'il) Pasha (1914–1918) 227,
    228
Ephesus, Council of (431) 17
Erdoğan, Recep Tayyip
    cooperation with neighbours 326
    Putin's support 338
Eshkol, Lévy 279
Europe
    1347–1350 plague 131
    appeal from Ottoman Armenians 221
    barbarians from 13
    Jewish pogroms 197
    pushes back Ottomans 165–6
    rivalries in Ottoman Empire 6
    Sèvres Treaty 245–6
    source of barbarians 11

Faisal I, King of Iraq (1921–1933)
    Arab Revolt 238, 239
    enthroned in Iraq 243–4
    First World War release from
        Ottomans 242
Faisal II, King of Iraq (1939–1958) 275
Faisal Al Saud, king (1964–1975)
    Fatah Party and 278
    oil embargo on US 284
    PLO and 284–5
    rivalry with Nasser 277–9
Fakhr al-Din II 162–3
al-Farabi, Abu Nasr, philosopher 76,
    91–2
Farouk I, king (1936–1952) 260
    murder of Banna and 265
    overthrown 270

Fatah Party
  Arafat and 278
  challenged by PFLP 281
Fath Ali Shah Qajar (1797–1834) 172, 185
Fatima bin Muhammad 81
Fatimid dynasty
  Abbasids and 109
  Assassin terrorism 98–9, 100
  Bilad al-Sham 94
  Buyid rivalry with 91
  conquers Egypt 5
  end of caliphate 107–8
  establishes link to Fatima 147
  expansionism 82
  expels Jerusalem's Christians 96–7
  First Crusaders and 100
  Al-Hakim 86–8
  Isma'ilis and 81–4, 98–9, 100, 109
  jihad against Byzantines 85
  loses power to viziers 94
  loses Sicily 95
  Nur ad-Din and 102–3
  Seljuks and 98–9
Filiu, Jean-Pierre
  Apocalypse in Islam 1
  Gaza, a history 2
  Le Miroir de Damas 2
First World War
  Dardanelles battle 237
  Gallipoli 236–7
  Middle East bloodlands 8
  Moudros armistice 242
  Ottoman allies with Germany 236
  Otttoman losses 242
  Paris Peace Conference 242
  Triple Entente 236
Florence, Fakhr al-Din II and 162
France
  1854 alliance with Britain 188
  aids Saddam against Iran 296
  Algeria and 186, 201
  Blum government 253
  colonialism 200, 252–3
  consulate in Aleppo 161
  declines Iraq War 321

Description de l'Égypte 181
  division of Ottoman Empire 6
  Egypt and 6, 9, 180–1, 210
  Fourth Crusade against Byzantium
    116–17
  granted Cilicia 245
  imperialism in Africa 195
  Iraq no-fly zone 312
  Lebanon and 243, 295
  in Morocco 199
  Ottoman pact 165
  protects Catholics 238
  Revolution 207
  supports Greece 184
  Sykes–Picot Agreement 239, 243
  Syria and 243, 265, 324–5, 355
  Triple Entente 236
  truce with Suleiman 153
Francis of Assisi, Saint, Fifth Crusade
  and 118
François I, king (1515–1547) 153
Frederick I Barbarossa, Holy Roman
  Emperor (1155–1190) 106
Frederick II, Holy Roman Emperor
  (1220–1250)
  Fifth Crusade and 118–19
  outcome of Crusades and 128–9
  Sixth Crusade 119
Free Syrian Army (FSA) 332–3
Fuad I, king (1922–1936)
  Egyptian independence and 245
Fuad Pasha, Mehmed 189–90

Gaddafi, Muammar 271–2
  'Jamahiriya'/massocracy 288
Gallipoli, battle of, Armenian genocide
  and 240
Gandhi, Mohandas K. (the Mahatma)
  244
Gaza
  captured by Persia 27
  monastic community 16
  Second Crusade 102
  uprisings 7
  see also Israel; Palestinians

Gaza, a history (Filiu) 2
Gemayal, Bashir 293–4
Genghis Khan (1206–1227) 120
Genoa, Ottoman Empire and 137, 156
Georgia, Mongol expansion and 120, 134
Germany
  Congress of Berlin 199
  declines Iraq War 321
  financial imperialism 201
  First World War Ottoman alliance
    236–7
  Middle East railways 199–200
  see also First World War; Hitler, Adolf;
    Second World War
Ghassanid family
  Byzantine relations 29–30
  fragmentation of 34
Al-Ghazali, Sufism and 94
Ghazan Khan (1295–1304) 129
Gnosticism, Mesopotamia and 69
Godfrey of Bouillon, ruler of Jerusalem
  (1099–1100) 97
Gökalp, Ziya, head of CUP 227
gold mines in Egypt 14
Gold of Paris, The (at-Tahtawi) 210
Gorbachev, Mikhail
  Madrid peace talks 314
  Reagan and 298
Gordon, Major-General Charles G.,
  Khartoum and 194–5
Greece
  Balkan Wars 227–8
  emigrants to Egypt 192
  granted Izmir 245
  Greeks exiled from Turkey 228, 246
  nationalist insurrection 184
Greek language, Umayyads and 50
Greek Orthodox Church 163
Guide for the Perplexed, A (Maimonides)
  106
Gulf Emirates, aid Saddam's war 296
Gulf War: 'Desert Storm' (1990–1991)
  Bush Sr launches 309–12
  'new order' and aftermath 312–14
Gulf War, Iran–Iraq (1980–1988) 291–3

  ceasefire 298–9
  Kurdish Peshmurga and 295–8
  Saddam declares ceasefire 296
Gulf War: occupation of Iraq *see* Iraq
  War (2003–2011)

Haftar, Khalifa 341–2
Hagia Sophia, True Cross relic and 27
al-Hakim bi-Amr Allah, caliph
  (996–1021) 86–8, 89, 92
al-Hallaj, al-Husayn ibn Mansur 62–3
Hamas
  attacks on 316–17
  'axis of resistance' 325
  formation of 300
  pressures PLO 317
  repression of 315
  takes Gaza Strip 325–6
Hanafism 60, 173
Hanano, Ibrahim 257
Hanifa, Abu
  death of 65
  founding work of Sunnis 60
  Timur and 135
Hariri, Rafic 324–5
Al-Harith/Arethas 29
Harun al-Rashid, caliph (786–809) 56–7
  Charlemagne and 72
  death of 73
  orders Imam Musa's death 67
Hasan al-Askari, Imam (868–874) 67–8,
  89
Hasan al-Basri, ascetic 62
Hasan ibn Ali, caliph, second imam (661)
  46, 48
Hashemites
  Arab Revolt and 237
  Ibn Saud and 248
  Muhammad and 34
Hashim ibn Abd Manaf, Quraysh leader
  32–3
Hattin, battle of 128
Ibn Hawqal, geographer 92
Hejaz region
  Arab Revolt and 237–8

caravan cities 30
  geography of 28
  pagan deities 31–2
  political and religious division 42
  railway 201
  Saudi assault on 208
Helena, mother of Constantine
  sacred relics and 11, 26
Heraclius, emperor (610–641)
  Mazdean desecrations 27
  replaces Phocas 26
  returns relics to Jerusalem 36
Herat, siege of 186, 193
Herzl, Theodor 198
  The State of the Jews 198
Herzogovina 226
Hezbollah
  'axis of resistance' 325
  Hariri and 'Cedar Revolution' 325
  Israeli withdrawal 317
  Khamenei as guide 299
  suicide attacks 294–5
  Syria and Iran establish 294
  Syrian civil war and 333
Al-Hirah, Mesopotamia
  Lakhmid dynasty and 28–30
  Mondhir attacks 30
Hisham, Caliph (724–743) 51–2
Hitler, Adolf 255
Holy Roman Empire
  creation of 95
  Fifth Crusade and Kamil 119
  'Latin' Jerusalem 97
Honorius, Emperor (rule 393–423) 12
House of Wisdom (*Beit al–Hikma*) 58
Hulagu Khan (1256–1265) 136
  takes Baghdad 123–4
  withdraws from Syria 125
Hungary
  battle of Mohács 165
  uprising 274
al-Husayn, Abu, collection of hadith 59
Hussein bin Ali, king (1916–1924) 247–8
Husayn ibn Ali, second imam (661–670)
  67

Hussein, King of Jordan (1952–1999)
  PLO and 281
  Rabin and 315
  renounces West Bank claim 300
Hussein, shah (1694–1722) 160
Hussein, Muhammad Ahmad, Mufti 259
Hussein, Sharif, Governor of Mecca
  237–9
Hussein ibn Ali, third imam (670–680)
  48, 67
  the Great Discord 59
al-Husseini, Mohammad Amin, mufti
  (1921–1948) 254, 255

Ibadis of Oman 168
Ibn al-Nadim, Repertory of Arabic
  literature 92
Ibn Battuta, chronicler 131
Ibn Buya, Ahmad, grand emir (945–967)
  75
Ibn Hanbal, Ahmad
  fundamentalists and 130
  Al-Muhasibi and 62
  Musnad hadith collection 61
Ibn-Ishaq, Hunayn, physician 58
Ibn Khaldun 115
  group/preaching/power 82, 93, 151,
  248
  on social structure 53–4
  Timur and 134–5
  transposing 304
ibn Khalid, al-Fadl 57
ibn Khalid, Ja'far 57
ibn Khalid, Yahya 57
Ibn Khallikan, biographical dictionary
  123
Ibn Killis, vizier 86
Ibn al-Muqaffa 69
Ibn Nusayr, Alawites and 89
Ibn Saud, Abdelaziz, king (1932–1953)
  247–9
Ibn Saud, Muhammad 169
Ibn Sina/Avicenna
  Maimonides and 106
  philosophy 91–2

Ibn Taymiyyah
  against Alawites 292
  attacks Sufism 130
  jihad against 'bad Muslims' 169
  jihad against infidels 129–30
Ibn Zubayr, caliph (683–692) 48–9
Ibrahim Pasha, Egyptian general 187
  administration of 210
  attacks Syria 184
Ibrahim Pasha, grand vizier (1523–1536)
    170
Idriss, king (1951–1969) 271
Ilkhanid dynasty 129, 133
Illyria, Justinian conquers 23
Imru al-Qays, Lakhmid leader 29
Inal al-Alai', sultan (1453–1461) 139
India
  Britain's 'Muslim policy' 255
  British imperialism in 195
  British view of Suez Canal and 191
  First World War action in Iraq 237
  land routes to 3–4
  sepoy revolt and 192
  Suez Canal as route to 196
  Timur in 134
  Victoria as empress of 193
Innocent III, Pope 116–17
Inönü, Ismet
  Anti-USSR 272–3
  succeeds Atatürk 253
Iran, Islamic Republic of
  Afghan refugees 301
  chemical weapons against 297–8
  cult of martyrs 297
  Erdoğan and 326
  fight against Daesh 337
  Gulf War with Iraq 291–3, 295–9
  hostage crisis 290
  Iraq and 'axis of resistance' 323–6
  Islamic revolution 7, 225, 289–91
  nuclear programme 324, 337, 339
  protest against Ahmadinejad 328
  Putin and 327
  Rouhani's election 334
  Shiite particularism 304–5

Syrian civil war and 333
Tehran population 4
Trump and 339
Turkey and 352
using Kurds in war 296–7
see also Persia/Iran
Iraq
  1963 coup 277
  1991 uprising 7
  Abbasids 6, 74–5
  anti-USSR 273
  Arab Revolt and 238
  Ba'ath Party 277–8, 283, 321
  dividing line of 174
  First World War and 242
  'greater Syrian' idea 265
  Gulf War 'Desert Storm' 309–14
  Gulf War with Iran 291–3, 295–9
  independence from Britain 249
  Indian War in First World War 237
  Iran supports Kurds in 288
  League of Arab States 260
  long nineteenth century 231
  mainly Shiite 276
  Mongol control 125
  nationalizes oil 283
  Ottoman Empire and 6, 174
  Party of National Brotherhood 265
  post-First World War uprising 243
  post-Saddam government 322–3
  protests in 343
  railways 202
  Saddam's personality 297
  Safavid Iraq line endures 158–9
  Sunni–Shia rivalry 329
  Syrian settlers 50
  Timur attacks 134–5
  Umayyad rule in 47
  US bases in 339
  younger generation 343
  Zanj uprising in 70–1
Iraq War (2003–2011)
  disaster of 356
  enables jihadists 322
  Shia versus Sunni 322–3

US occupation of 320–3
'weapons of mass destruction' 320
Isfahan, battles of 134, 148
Islam
    Alevi esoteric dogma 152
    amnesty to Shiites 46
    assabiyya, *da'wa*, and *mulk* 53–4
    Ba'ath diversity 283
    ban on divine representation 72
    branches of 90
    Chinese Muslims 342
    cohabitation of sects 230
    concept of *takfir* 129
    context of civil wars 76–7
    conversion to 47
    counter-Crusades 110
    Dawla/state 53–4
    dhimmi/protection 70
    Eastern Roman Empire resists 3
    era of one caliph 75–7
    factions 47–9
    fear of discord 166–7
    fiqh/law 65
    first dynasty of 3
    first two caliphs 37–9
    five pillars of 36
    fundamentalists and 130
    furu/branches 65
    the Great Discord 40–1, 54, 59
    hajj 74, 208
    the Hidden Imam 89
    homogenized Qur'an 50
    Ibn Khaldun on social structure 53–4
    ijtihad 65
    ilm/science 65
    infidels 129–31
    intellectual libertines 69
    internal conflicts 9, 353
    Iraq's Sunnis versus Iran's Shiites 291–3
    jihad 36, 129–30
    Khomeini's revolution 289–91
    mawali/non-Arab converts 52–3, 55
    messianists 81–2
    millenarian sects 110
    Muhammad and 33–7

Mutazilism 58, 61–2
Nur ad-Din and 101–2
Obama's 'American and Islam' address
    327–8
Omar and Qur'an version 39–40
Ottoman population 213
'People of the Book' 38–9, 86
prohibits apostasy 37–8
Al-Qadisiyyah 292
Qur'an as created 92
Qur'an revealed 34
rapid spread of 3, 41–2
as religion and state 64–6
sharia interpretations 65–6
social practices and 284
Sunni versus Shia 304–5, 353–4
Syria and branches of 89–90
and Syrian Christians 213
title of 'caliph' 166
tolerance/non-tolerance 174–5
Turkey's Sunni state 246
Turkmen military jihad 141
ulama/scholars 64–5, 156
united against colonialism 244
usul/foundations 65
varieties of 109
see also Isma'ili Islam; Mohammad the
    Prophet; Qur'an; Shia Islam; Sufi
    Islam; Sunni Islam
Islamic jurisprudence
    fiqh 60–1
    Malikism 60–1
    mazhah/legal schools 59–60
    al-Muqaffa and sharia 69
    Shafiism 61
'Islamic State' *see* Daesh/'Islamic State'
Islamist movement, Yassin founds 316
Isma'il I, shah (1501–1524) 148–9
    Hidden Imam claims 147–8, 150–1
Isma'il ibn Ja'far, imam (702–762) 67
Ismail Pasha of Egypt (1863–1879) 191–2
Isma'ili Islam
    Assassins and 127–8
    Crusaders and 99
    decline of Fatimids and 107–8

Isma'ili Islam (*cont.*)
  ecumenism 86
  establishes Fatimid caliphate 81–4
  establishes link to Fatima 147
  Al-Hakim and 87
  Mahadi of Salamieh 74
  missionaries 82
  politics of extremism 143
  Sunni teachings and 83
  in Syria 89
  terrorism and 109–10
Israel
  1990s peace talks 314–18
  Abraham Accords 351
  assists Iran against Iraq 293
  Balfour Declaration 239
  Camp David Accords 287–8
  Cold War and 7
  division of Hebron 317
  effect on Arab world 272
  Erdoğan and 326
  first intifada 299–300
  founding of 261–4
  Golan Heights 283–4, 286
  Hezbollah attacks 295
  Ibn Khaldun and 304
  invades Lebanon 293–5
  Jewish immigration right 263–4
  joint Egypt–Syria attack 283–4
  Kissinger peace efforts 285–6
  Likud Party 287
  nuclear power 293
  Obama and 328–9
  Oslo Accords 315
  'Palestinian question' 7
  Rabin peace negotiations 315–16
  Reza's Iran and 282, 289
  Sadat's Egypt and 282
  Saddam's demands on 310
  settlements 328–9
  shifting relations and 302–3
  Sinai 274–5, 279, 283–4, 286
  Six-Day War 279–80
  Syrian civil war and 332
  treaty with UAE 340
Trump and 339, 340
two-state solution 326
United Arab Emirates and 343, 351
uprisings in 7
US policy pillar 309
West Bank and Gaza 279, 288, 315, 320
withdraws from Lebanon 317
Istanbul
  change from Constantinople 138
  as megacity 4
  population 264
Italy
  confines Bedouins 255
  granted Dodecanese 245
  invades Libya 200, 201, 258
  Mediterranean coast and 6

Ja'far al-Sadiq, sixth imam
  Abbasid revolution and 53
  accepts Abbasid Caliphate 67
Jahez (Abu Uthman amr ibn Bahr al-Kinani al-Basri), writer 76
Jalal al-Din Mangburni, Sha (1220–1231) 120
Jalayrids in Baghdad 133
janissaries
  overthrow Selim III 211
  revolt of 167
  uprising 175
Japan, Meiji era 222
Jefferson, Thomas 182–3
Jerome of Stridon
  hagiography of Hilarion 16
  monastery of 16
Jerusalem
  Al-Aqsa mosque 97
  Ayyubids' pact with Crusaders 123
  Christians in 187
  destruction of temple 33
  Dome of the Rock 49, 50
  First Crusade 95–7
  Frederick II and 119
  Gulf War of Iraq–Iran 295
  Holy Sepulchre 87, 95

Jewish messianism and 164
Justinian's monasteries 24
Kingdom of 97–101
local Christians expelled 96–7
Mamluks capture Acre 128
massacre of Jews and Muslims 96
Muhammad and 36
Noble Sanctuary site 316, 317
Ottoman administration 196–7
Saladin and 103, 104, 109
second (Al-Aqsa) intifada 317
Second Crusade 102
Seljuks and 94
Temple Mount 50
Third Crusade 106, 107
Trump and 339
Jesus of Nazareth
in Islam 34–5
Mandylion fabric and 73
Jewish people
Al-Hakim discriminates against 87
Balfour Declaration 239
ban on divine representation 72
birth of Zionism 196–9
demographics of Palestine 197
destruction of temple 33
discrimination against 76
driven from Iberia to Levant 163–4
expelled from Mecca 35
Heraclius imposes baptism on 27
Holocaust 261
Israel and 304
Jewish state in Palestine 254–6
Justinian's code and 24
leave Hitler's Germany 255
Lehi 262
Maimonides and 106
in Medina 31
Muhammad and prophets 35
in Ottoman Empire 137, 188–9, 213, 229
'People of the Book' 38–9
in Persia 159, 160
pogroms 197
right to Israel immigration 263–4

rights in Europe 213
Temple Mount 50
tolerance towards 174
US post-Second World war considerations 261
Zionism 239
jihad
Azzam and 'global jihad' 301–2
against 'bad Muslims' 169
codification of 63
Iraq War and 322–3
major and minor 63
John Damascene 72
John Paul II, pope 118
John the Baptist 48, 50
Jordan/Transjordan
'Arab Paetrea' 28
Arab Revolt and 239
emirate 244
immigrants from 313
Madrid peace talks 314
Muslim Brotherhood and 276
partitioned Palestine and 262
shifting relations with Israel 302
Six-Day War 279
Junayd al-Baghdadi 62
Justin II, emperor (565–578) 29–30
Justinian, Code of 65
Justinian I, emperor (527–565)
Ghassanid family and 29–30
Khosrow I and 22–5
laws of 23
occupies part of West 96
plague of 24–5
westward expansion 22–3

Kabir, Amir (Mirza Taghi Khan) 215
Kafur, Abdul al-Misk 82
Kamil, sultan (1218–1238) 118
al-Kawakibi, Abd al-Rahman 218
al-Kazim, Musa, imam 147
Kemal, Mustafa see Atatürk, Mustafa Kemal
Kenya, US embassy attack 319
Khalid, king (1975–1982) 286–7

al-Khalifa family 195
Khamenei, Ali, ayatollah 295, 298
  'axis of resistance' 323–4
  succeeds Khomeini 299
al-Kharaki, sheikh 150–1
Kharijites
  the Great Discord 40–1
  in Oman 168
Khomeini, Ruhollah, ayatollah
  death of 299
  Islamic Revolution 225, 289–91
  repressing Kurds 295
  Saddam's hostility towards 291–3
  war with Iraq 323
Khorasan
  Mongol expansion and 120
  Timurids in 136
Khosrow I, Shah (512–14)
  death of 25
  reorganizes empire 23
Khosrow II, Shah (590/591–628)
  death of 27
  executes Lakmid ruler 34
  rule of 25–8
Khoushqadam, Sayf ad-Din, sultan
    (1461–1467) 139
Khublai Khan 123
Khurasani, Akhund, Ayatollah 224, 225
Khwarazm 128
  Baghdad and 115–16
  Jalal al-Din and Mongols 120
al-Khwarizmi, mathematician 58
Kissinger, Henry 285–7
Kitbuqa, General 125
Kizilbachs 147, 151
  shock troops 158
Kléber, General Jean-Baptiste 181
Knights Hospitaller 101
Knights Templar 101
Komnenoi dynasty
  Crusades and 96
  emergence of 95
Komnenos, Alexios I, emperor (1081–
    1118) 96
Köprülü, Ahmed 164–5

Kurd Ali, Muhammad, historian 230
Kurdistan Workers' Party (PKK)
  Saddam uses 297
  in Syria 334, 335
  in Turkey 326, 338
Kurds 7
  Armenian genocide and 240
  autonomy proposed 245
  city of Mahabad 258
  dissidence and repression 228, 257–8
  driven out of Iran 296
  Druze revolt and 252
  Gökalp of CUP 227
  identity and 108
  nationalist separatism 256–8
  Ottoman Empire and 219
  peshmerga 258
  Peshmerga in First Gulf War 295–8
  Post-'Desert Storm' uprising 312
  Saddam's chemical attack on 298,
    299
  Saladin and 102, 103
  Syria cedes 334
  Trump withdraws support 339
  Turkey represses 246
  uprising in Iraq 288
  with US in Iraq War 321
  used in Gulf War 296–7
  Yazidis and 323
Kuwait
  attracts immigrants 284
  Britain and 195–6, 200
  independence of 275, 276
  Iraq invades 7, 310
  restored sovereignty 313

Laden, Osama bin see Bin Laden, Osama
Lakhmid dynasty
  Christianity and 29
  Al-Hirah 28–30
Al-Lat, Al-Uzza, and Al-Manat
  daughters of Allah 34
  as pagan deities 31
Lausanne, Treaty of 257
League of Arab States 260

League of Nations
  mandates over Middle East 243, 257
  Wilson and 242
Lebanese National Movement 286
Lebanon
  1975 civil war 286–7
  anti-colonial pressure 259–60
  al-Bustani's writings 217
  'Cedar Revolution' 324–5
  Christians and 325
  cohabitation of groups 229–30
  Druze and Maronite conflict 189–90
  effect of Six-Day War 280
  Fakhr al-Din II and Beirut 162
  French mandate 243
  French sectarianism 252–3
  Greater 243
  Hezbollah 294
  Israel invades 293–5
  Israel withdraws from 317
  Madrid peace talks 314
  Maronites 104–5
  protests in 343
  sectarianism of 304
  Vichy France and 258
Lemkin, Raphael 241
Leo I, emperor (457–474) 14
Leo III, emperor (717–741) 72
Leo V, emperor (813–820) 73
Levant
  becomes 'Middle East' 196
  emigrants to Egypt 192
Liberation of Women, The (Amin) 218
Libya
  Barbary War 182–3
  civil war 341–2
  Erdoğan's revenge 200
  Gaddafi comes to power 271–2
  Italy invades 200, 201, 231, 255, 258
  'Jamahiriya'/massocracy 288
  King Idriss 271
  NATO and 332
  split after uprising 331
Lombards 11
Louis VII, king (1131–1180) 101

Louis IX, Saint (1226–1270)
  outcome of Crusades 129
  Seventh Crusade 121–2
Louis XI, king (1461–1483) 122
Louis XIII, king (1610–1643)
  as protector of Catholics 163, 187
Louis XIV, king (1643–1715)
  protects Catholics 163
  support for Venice 165
Louis-Philippe, king (1930–1848) 184, 185

Macedonia 226
Maghreb, Fatimids in 81, 82
Mahadi of Salamieh 74
Mahan, Admiral Alfred 196, 309
Mahdi, return of
  Ahmandinejad and 324
  Isma'ili claims 81–2, 147
Mahmud I Ghazi, sultan (1730–1754) 167
Mahmud II, sultan (1808–1839)
  military reform 211
  reconciles with Russia 184
Maimonides, Moses, Rabbi 106
  A Guide for the Perplexed 106
Majlesi, Mohammad-Baqer, sheikh 160
al-Malaki, Nouri 329
Malatya reconquest 73
al-Malik, Abd, caliph (685–705) 49–50,
  52, 55
Malik Ibn Anas, Muwatta 60
Malik-Shah I, sultan (1072–1092) 93–4
Malta, emigrants to Egypt 192
Mamluks 6
  abandon Syria to Timur 134
  accession of 115
  al-Salih and 121
  assassinate Turanshah 122
  Baybars seizes throne 125–7
  grip in Egypt and Syria 132–3
  against Lebanese Shiites 130
  massacre of 209
  Muhammad Ali massacres 183
  Ottoman overthrow of 148–50
  power struggles 176
  Qutuz becomes sultan 122

Mamluks (*cont.*)
    relations with Ottomans 139–41
    stability of 142–3
    Timur drives out of Syria 134
    vassals of Ottomans 169–71
    victory over Mongols 125
    Western imperialism and 201–2
Al-Ma'mun, caliph (813–833) 57–8, 70
Manaf (goddess) 33
Al-Mansur, caliph (754–775)
    Abu Hanifa and 60
    Baghdad caliphate 54–6
    cracks down on intellectuals 69
    four pillars of power 66
Al Mansurah, battle of 122
al-Maqdisi, geographer 92
Marcian, emperor (450–457) 17
Maron, John 104–5
Maronites
    Lebanese civil war 286
    Louis XIII and 163
    massacres by Druze 189–90
    Ottoman peace 162
    post-First World War 243
    Saladin and 104–5
    Second Word War and 260
Marwan I, caliph (684–685) 49
Marwan II, caliph (744–750) 52–3
Mashal, Khaled 316
al-Masudi, Abu al-Husan Ali ibn
        al-Husayn, historian 76
Maurice, General 25–6
mawali/non-Arab converts 52–3, 55–6
Al-Mawardi, theologian 92
Mazdaism *see* Zoroastrianism
McMahon, Henry 237–9
Mecca
    692 siege of 49
    Arabia Deserta 28
    the Black Stone 74
    expulsion of Jews 35
    Fatimids and 83
    Kaaba 32
    before Muhammad 30–3
    Muhammad and 35–6

Ottomans and 152, 167–9
    pagan *hajj* 32
    pilgrimage route 222–3
    seized by Ibn Saud 248
    sultan refrains from *hajj* 175
    supplied from Egypt 170
    truce with Muhammad 63
    Wahhabi control of *hajj* 208
Medina
    Arab Revolt and 238
    Arabia Deserta 28
    Christianity in 31
    civil war in 42
    Fatimids and 83
    mosques 50
    Muhammad and 35, 37
    Ottomans and 152, 167
    supplied from Egypt 170
    Umayyads shift away 46
Mehmed I, sultan (1403–1413) 136
Mehmed II, sultan (1444–1446 and
        1451–1481)
    Ottoman conquest of Byzantium
        136–9
    relations with Mamluks 139–40
Mehmed IV, sultan (1648–1687) 164–6
Mehmed V, sultan (1909–1918) 227
Menderes, Adnan 272
Menou, General Jacques-François 181
Mesopotamia
    Muslim conquest of 38
    Ottoman Empire and 201
    in Persian domain 11
    Sassanid Persia in 19–22
    Selim I occupies 148
    Tigris and Euphrates Rivers 4–5
Miaphysite Church 18–19
    Ghassanid family and 29
    Islam and 38–9
    persecution of 27, 33
    renewed pressure on 41, 42
Middle East
    1990s peace talks 314–18
    agreed dividing lines 173–4
    cohabitation of peoples 228–32

complex sequences of 115
concept of 9–10
denial of self-determination 9–10
East–West splits 12
effect of US disengagement 341–4
elite classes 264–6
French sectarianism 252–3
geography of 3–5, 8–9
global hegemony and 309
historical perspective 353–6
imperial invention of 194–6
khassa/elite and *amma*/masses 77
medieval 'holy wars' and 110–11
one caliphate 75–7
Ottomans in Mediterranean 156–7
Pax Americana period 285–7
poles of Egypt, Syria, and Iraq 4–5
population of 4
religious justification of conflict 42
religious mosaic of 1
rural population of 264
self-determination principle 239
Sèvres Treaty 245–6
shifting alliances and conflicts 302–5
stereotype of 'Oriental despot' 160
Trump's disengagement from 339–40
US disengagement from 349–52
water 4–5
the Western question 201–3
migration, Zionism and 231
Mihna, Mutazilism and 58
Miroir de Damas, Le (Filiu) 2
Mohács, battle of 165
Mohammad Ali Shah Qajar (1907–1909)
  224
Mohammad Shah Qajar (1834–1848)
  185–6
Mohammed bin Salman, crown prince
  337, 343
Molière, *The Bourgeois Gentleman* 165
Mondhir/Alamoundaros 29–30
money, bimetallic 50
Möngke Khan 136
  disappearance of 124
  sends Hulagu to Middle East 123

Mongol Empire
  Baghdad 6
  bloodlands of 8
  empire diminishes 136
  ends Abbasid rule 123–4
  Genghis Khan and 120
  Ilkhanid kingdom 129
  invasions of 3
  joins with Heraclius 27
  Mamluks against 142–3
  plague pandemic 4n
  population drop and 4
  religious toleration 120
  Shiism of 143
  Timurids in Khorasan 136
  Timur's expansion 134–6
monotheistic religions, mosaic of history
  1–2
Montenegro 227–8
Montesquieu, *Persian Letters* (Chardin)
  160
Morocco
  France in 199, 200
  peripheral position of 247
  treaty with Washington 182
Morsi, Mohamed 333
Mossadegh, Muhammad
  anti-British protest 273
  nationalizes oil 274
Mosul
  Nadir Shah attacks 174
  Saladin captures 109
  Zengid rule of 104
Mount Lebanon *see* Lebanon
Mozaffar ad-Din Shah Qajar (1896–1907)
  Abdul Hamid and 221–2
  constitution and 223–4
Mu'awiya I, caliph (661–680)
  amnesty to Shiites 46
  the Great Discord 40–1, 59
Mu'awiya II, caliph (683–684) 49
Mubarak, Hosni 245
  Obama and 350
  overthrown 331
  succeeds Sadat 293

Muhammad Ali Pasha, Wali (1805–1848)
  administration of 183–5
  dealing with the Sauds 208–9
  death of 191
  reign of 209–10
Muhammad al-Baqir, imam (712–733) 67
Muhammad-Hasan al-Najafi, ayatollah
  173
Muhammad ibn Ali al-Jawad, imam
  (819–835) 67
Muhammad Reza Pahlavi, shah
  (1941–1979)
  leaves Iran 290
  relations in Middle East 288–9
  replaces father 258
  return after Mossadegh ousted 274
  Stalin and 273
Muhammad the Prophet
  Arab nationalism 217
  biography of 33, 33n
  collection of sayings 68–9, 68n
  Dome of the Rock and 49
  establishing links to 147
  the hadith 59–60
  Hijra 34–5
  life and campaigns 33–7
  Qur'an revealed to 34
  the Sunna and 59
  truce with Meccans 63
  Wahhabi destroy mausoleum 208
al-Muhasibi, al-Harith 62
Mu'izz al-Dawla see Ibn Buya, Ahmad,
  grand emir
al-Muïzz, caliph (953–975) 82
mulk, meaning 53–4
Munich Olympics, 1972, Black
  September 282
Murad I, bey (1362–1389) 132, 135
Murad II, sultan (1421–1444 and
  1446–1451) 136–7
Murad III, sultan (1574–1595) 157
Murad IV, sultan (1623–1640) 157
Murad V, sultan (1876) 214
Musa ibn-Ja'far al-Kazim, imam
  (765–799) 67

Musa Ibn-Nusayr 51
Musaylima (god) 34
Muscat seizes Zanzibar 169
Muslim Brotherhood
  Erdoğan's AK Party and 326
  foundation of 264–6
  pro-Saddam 310
  repressed in UAR 276
  rule with military in Egypt 331
  shifting alliances 303
  spread of 284
  structure 265
  in Syria 292
Al-Mustansir (1226–1242) 123
Al-Musta'sim, caliph (1242–1258)
  Hulagu Khan and 123–4
al-Mutanabbi, poet 84
Al-Muta'sim, caliph (833–842) 61–2
al-Mutawakkil, caliph (847–861) 62
al-Mutawakkil III, caliph (1508–1516)
  149–50
Mutazilism
  attempt to impose 64
  Hanbal and 61–2
  suppression of 58
al-Muttalib, Abd 33
Muwatta (Malik Ibn Anas) 60–1
Muzaffarids in Shiraz 133

Nabataen kingdom 28
Nadir Shah (1736–1747)
  attacks Mosul 174
  ends Safavid dynasty 171–2
Naguib, Muhammad 270–1
Nahavand, battle of 38
Napoleon III, Emperor (1852–1870)
  Franco-British alliance 188
  sends troops to Syria 190
  Suez Canal and 191
Naser al-Din Qajar Shah (1848–1896)
  215–17
Nasir, caliph (1180–1225) 123
Nasser, Gamal Abdel
  becomes president 271
  conflict with Israel 278–9

overthrow of Farouk and 270
rivalry with Faisal 277–9, 280
shifting fronts 302–3
Suez crisis 274
UAR and 275–6
Nathan, Rabbi of Gaza 164
nation-states, identity and 108
nationalism, militarized 276–7
Nestorian Church
Abbasids and 69
at Al-Hirah 29
Islam and 38–9
Mongols and 120
Nestorius and spread of 17, 18, 19
persecution of 33
renewed pressure on 41, 42
Sassanid refuge 21–2
Netanyahu, Benyamin
1999 defeat of 317
anti-US campaign 337
background 316
rise to power 315–16
Syrian civil war and 332
Trump and 339, 340, 350, 351
Netherlands
consulate in Aleppo 161
tulips to Ottoman Empire 167
New Zealand, Gallipoli and 236–7
Nicaea, Council of (325) 11
filioque controversy and 95
Nicaea, Council of (787)
iconoclasm and 72
Nicaea, Fourth Crusade and 117
Nicholas I, tsar (1825–1855) 188
Nikephoros I, emperor (802–811) 72–3
Nile River 4–5
Nixon, Richard 285–7
nomadic people, in Ottoman Empire
229
see also Bedouins
Normans: conquest of Sicily 95
North Africa plague 1347–1350 131
North Atlantic Treaty Organization
(NATO), Turkey and 272, 326
Norway, Oslo Accords and 315

Nouri, Fazlullah, Ayatollah 224
nuclear power, Iran and 324. 337, 339
Nur ad-Din the Zengid, emir
(1146–1174)
death of 108
hegemony and conflict 111
leniency towards Armenians 105
religion and 101–2
Saladin and 103–4
Second Crusade and 101–3
Syria and 109
Turkish identity 108
Nuwas, Abu 69

Obama, Barack
Cairo speech 327–9, 330
drops Mubarak 350
Iran nuclear deal 337
Israel and 328–9
Libya and 332
Putin and 349
'red line' about chemical weapons
334–5
strikes against Daesh 336
Syrian civil war and 333
oil
1973 crisis 304
1973 embargo 284
Assad blocks Libya pipeline 295
China and 342
Iran and 273, 288
Iraq nationalizes 283
Saudi price drop 298
US values 260–1
Oljeytu Khan (1304–1316) 133
Oman
British imperialism and 195
independence of 275
Iran and 288
Kharijites and 168
Portuguese in 168
Al-Said/Busaids 169
Wahhabism 167, 208
Omar Ibn Abd al-Aziz, caliph (717–720)
51

Omar Ibn al-Khattab, caliph (634–644)
   35
  death of 39
  Islamic triumphs of 38
Orhan Gazi, bey (1324–1362) 131
Orthodox Churches
  attacks by Fourth Crusaders 116–17
  iconoclasm and 72, 73
  Ottoman integration 137
  in Palestine 187
  Russian protection of 238
  Syriac/Jacobite 18–19
Osman, caliph (644–656) 39–40
Osman I Gazi, bey (1280–1299) 130–1
Osman II, sultan (1618–1622) 157
Ostrogoths 11
Ottoman Empire
  Abdulmejid's emancipation edict 213
  administrators and army 154–6
  adopts Hanafism 60
  after Suleiman I 156–8
  Aleppo and 161–2
  alliance with Germany 236
  Armenians and 220–2, 227, 231,
    239–41
  Balkan Wars ousts 227–8
  bans Christian/Jewish discrimination
    188
  becomes Turkey 245–7
  capture of Constantinople 3
  Committee of Union and Progress
    (CUP) 226–7, 240
  compared to Safavids 151
  conscripting Christians 219, 227, 229
  consolidation of 9
  constitution and 214, 218, 226
  Crimean Tatars to Anatolia 188
  custody of Mecca and Medina 152,
    167–9, 175
  dealing with Wahhabism 208–9
  demographics of religions 213
  diplomatic and military setbacks
    164–6
  disappearance of 9
  diverse population of 226

  division agreed with Safavids 173–4
  domination of Middle East 174
  drives Greeks into exile 228
  Eastern question 213
  edict of Gülhane 212
  Edirne as capital 132
  effect of Sèvres Treaty 245–7
  ethnic and sectarian diversity 174
  European rivalries and 6
  France in Egypt 180–1
  Franco-British division of 6
  Germany and 199
  Greek independence 354
  Hamidian absolutism 218–20
  Hejaz railway 201
  Iraq 6
  janissaries 132, 155–6, 175
  Kosovo victory 132
  law of fratricide 138
  legitimacy as caliphs 211
  lose Occupied Enemy Territory
    Administrations 242–5
  versus Mamluks 139–41
  mutes Western imperialism 201
  in North Africa 200
  pact with France 165
  revolts against 213
  Russia expels Muslims to 194
  Russia occupies Crimea 166
  state Sunnism 173, 229
  status of Holy Places 254
  Syria and 212
  takes Constantinople 137–9
  Tanzimat 207, 211–14, 217, 219, 228–9
  Timur's battles against 135–6
  title of 'caliph' 166
  Treaty of Küçük Kaynarca 166
  truce with France 153
  Tsar Nicholas I calls 'sick man' 188
  Tulip Era 166–7
  Turkmen and 140–1
  turns towards Europe 142
  violence against Christians 228–9
  war with Russia 219
  wide control 353

Young Turk revolution 225–8, 230–1
see also Roman Empire, Eastern/
  Byzantium; Turkey

Pachomius 16
pagan beliefs before Muhammad 31
Pahlavi language, Umayyads and 50
Pakistan
  Afghan refugees 301
  Iran and 324
Palestine
  1936 Arab general strike 255–6
  anti-fascism 258–9
  Arab Revolt and 238–9
  Balfour Declaration 239, 244
  birth of Zionism 196–9
  British mandate over 254–6
  celebration of Young Turks 230–1
  Christian pilgrimages to 95
  Church of the Nativity 187
  demographics of 197, 198
  disappearance of 263
  French conquest of 181
  'greater Syrian' idea 265
  Irgun 261, 262
  'Islamic Congress' 255
  Lehi group 259
  partition of 261–2
  protection of religious groups 187
  riots in Jerusalem 243
  Sixth Crusade 119
  Supreme Muslim Council 254
  UN proclaims state of 300
  US considerations 261
  Western question 202
  Zionist movement 256
Palestine Liberation Organization
    (PLO)
  death of Arafat 325
  excluded from Madrid talks 314
  Faisal and 284–5
  first intifada 299–300
  isolation of 281
  Lebanese civil war and 286–7
  membership in Arab League 285

Nasser establishes 278
  not in Camp David process 287–8
  Oslo Accords 315
  pressure from Hamas 317
  sets up in Jordan 280–1
  Trump and 340
Palestinian Authority 320, 351
  agreement 315
  Arafat elected president 316
Palestinians
  abandonment of 264
  Arab support for 265
  Arafat and the PLO 278
  Catastrophe's effect on area 272
  first intifada 299–300, 314
  Hamas formed 300
  immigrants from 313
  Oslo Accords 315
  partition areas 263
  repression of Hamas 315
  Saddam's demands for 310
  second intifada 317, 320, 329
  shifting relations and 302–3
  Six-Day War and 279–80
  Trump and 339, 340
  West Bank uprisings 7
pan-Arabism
  Arab socialism 265–6
  Islamism compared to 284
  loses appeal 280
Pashtuns 194
Paula (abbess) 16
'People of the Book' 86
Peres, Shimon
  shares leadership with Shamir 299
  succeeds Rabin 316
Persia, Church of 21
Persia/Iran (before 1979)
  629 peace concessions 27
  Abbas the Great 158–60
  Abdul Hamid and Mozaffar 221–2
  Afghan siege of Isfahan 160
  anti-USSR 273
  Arabized 54
  Armenian population in 159

Persia/Iran (before 1979) (*cont.*)
  ayatollahs 172–3, 250–1
  British and Russian influence 201
  British occupation 193
  Buyids and 91
  compared to Ottomans 151
  Constitution of the Islamic Republic
      225
  constitutionalism 223–5
  controls Iraq 5
  Ctesiphon 19
  dividing line of 174
  dominance of 11
  end of Ilkhanids 133
  end of Savafids 171–2
  First World War neutrality 249–50
  forming Shiism 171–2
  holy sites within 171
  imposes Shiism 151
  Isfahan 173, 175
  Isma'ili missionaries 94
  Khosrow I and Justinian 22–5
  under Khosrow II 25–8
  long nineteenth century 231
  long rule of Naser al-Din 215–17
  long Sassanid rule 41–2
  mawali/converted 55
  Mesopotamia 19–22, 38
  military power of Abbas 158
  modernization reforms 250–1
  Mongol expansion and 120, 125
  Mongol Shiism and Sunnism 133
  nationalizes oil 274
  Pahlavi language 20
  palace revolt 25–6
  partnership with Israel 282
  peace with Romans 21–2
  plunder of Ctesiphon 39
  Qajars 174
  receives holy relics 26
  religious dissidence 151–2
  repelling Murad IV 158–9
  repression of Kurds 257
  Reuter and infrastructure 215–16
  Russian attacks on 185
  Safavid Iraq line endures 158–9
  Sassanids and 13, 48
  sieges Herat 186
  state Shiism 147–8, 353
  Syriac language in 21
  Timur's campaign in 134
  ulamas against tobacco 216–17
  women's veils 251
  Zand dynasty 172
  Zoroastrianism and 3
  see also Iran, Islamic Republic of
Phalangists
  Gemayal and Israel 293–4
  Lebanese civil war 286
Philippe II (Auguste), king (1179–1223)
  Third Crusade 106
Phocas, General 26
plagues
  1347–1350 131
  impact of Black Death 136
  sixth-century population drop 4
  Justinian's 24–5
Poland: peace with Ottomans 165
Popular Front for the Liberation of
      Palestine (PFLP) 285, 300
  hijacks Western planes 281
  repression of 315
Portugal
  Persian Gulf and 6
  Shah Abbas and 158
  Yemen and Oman jihads against 168
Powell, Colin 320
Ptolemy the geographer 28
Putin, Vladimir
  Iran and 327
  Obama and 334
  strong man of Middle East 339
  Syrian civil war and 334, 337–8

qadi/religious judges
  Abu Hanifa's work and 60
  Al-Mansur and 66
Al-Qadir, caliph (991–1031)
  'Epistle' interprets Sunnism 92
  long reign 92

Al-Qadisiyyah 292
Al-Qaeda
  Assassins and 109–10
  Bin Laden's global wars 318–20
  global jihad 302
  Iraqi branch and 322
  Pushtuns and 194
  US kills Bin Laden 329
Al-Qa'im, caliph (1031–1075) 92
Qaitbay, sultan (1468–1496) 139–41
Qaitbay, An-Nasir Muhammad ibn,
  sultan (1496–1498) 140
Qajar dynasty
  British and Russian influence 201
  Naser al-Din 215–17
  rise of 174
  rule in Persia 172
  Russian attack and 185
Qansuh al-Ghuri, sultan (1501–1516) 140,
  149
Qara Qoyunlu/Black Sheep 133
Qardahi, Christine 230
Qarmatians 74
Qasim, Abd al-Karim 275–6
Qatar
  independence of 275
  Muslim Brotherhood and 332
  Saudi Wahhabism 208
  Al-Thani rivalry with Al-Khalifa 195
Qudama ibn Ja'far al-Katib al-Baghdadi,
  philologist 76
Al-Quds see Jerusalem
Qur'an
  debates over 65
  'falsification' accusations 68–9
  the hadith 59–60
  Mutazilism and 58
  the Sunna 58
Quraysh tribe
  control Mecca 31–2
  Muhammad and 36
Qutuz, Saif ad-Din, sultan (1259–1260)
  122
  assassinated by Baybars 125–6
  victory over Mongols 125

Rabia of Basra, Sufi poetess 8, 62
Rabin, Yitzhak
  assassination of 315–16
  chief of staff to Eshkol 279
  Oslo Accords 315
  US peace talks 314–15
al-Radi bi'llah, caliph (934–940) 74
al-Rahman, Abd 53
railways
  Germany 199–200
  Hejez 201
Reagan, Ronald
  anti-USSR 298
  Lebanon and 309
Reuter, Paul, Baron von 215–16
Reza Shah Pahlavi (1925–1941)
  Britain replaces with son 258
  coup against Ahmed Shah 250
  partnership with Israel 282
Richard I 'Lionheart', king (1189–1199)
  106–7
Roman Catholic Church
  Crusade against Byzantium 116–17
  French protection of Catholics 238
  Louis XIII's protection of 187
  Maronites and 105
  missionaries 163
  Ottoman Catholics 213
  quarrels with Eastern Churches 163
Roman Empire, Eastern/Byzantium
  1347–1350 plague 131
  Akroinon victory 71–2
  Barbarossa takes Plovdiv and Edirne
    106
  Bilad al-Sham 94
  break-away churches 17–19
  Christianity's orientation 2
  civil war leads to Ottomans 131
  construction of 11–14
  control of Syria and Egypt 5
  Crusades and 8
  distinguished from 'Franks' 96
  division agreed with Sassanids
    173–4
  East–West differences 12–13

Roman Empire, Eastern/Byzantium (*cont.*)
  'exit from Arabia' 41–2
  fall of 136–9
  founding of 2
  Fourth Crusade against 116–17
  Khosrow and 25–8
  Lakhmids and 29–30
  'Macedonian dynasty' 73
  metropolis of Christianity 95
  Muslim progress and 38–9
  peace with Persia 21–2
  push into Syria 84–5
  'reconquesting' Syria 81
  resists Islam 3
  Seljuks and 95, 102
  shocked by Crusaders 99
  slave trade 132–3
  Theodosius II banishes pagans 15
  Umayyad sieges of Constantinople 71
  see also Constantinople; Istanbul;
     Ottoman Empire; Turkey
Roman Empire, West
  barbarian invasions 13
  compared to East 12–13
  creation of Holy Roman Empire 95
  distinguished from Byzantines 96
  see also Holy Roman Empire
Rome, ancient
  destroys Jewish temple 33
  invasions and sacks of 2
  patriarchate of 14–15
Roosevelt, Franklin D. 309
  champions rights 259
  Middle East oil and 260–1
Rothschild, Edmond de 197
Rouhani, Hassan
  election of 334
  nuclear power agreement 337
Rum, sultanate of
  Mongols and 120, 125
  sacked by Crusaders 115
Russia/USSR
  Bolshevik take-over 239
  Britain and 186, 192–4, 215
  Cold War Middle East 7

colonial expansion 200
colonizes Caucasus 193
Crimean War 187–8
end of USSR 314
expels Muslims 194
Gorbachev and Reagan 298
Hitler's invasion of 258
Hungarian uprising 274
invades Afghanistan 300–2
invasion of Ukraine 349
Iran and 324
limits of Middle East position 341
Muslims leave Caucasus 228
occupies Crimea 166
oligarchs in Dubai 351
Orthodox Christians 187–8, 238
Ottoman Empire and 211, 214, 219
pact with Turkey 246
Persian constitutionalism and 223–5
pogroms 197
Putin and Iran 327
Six-Day War and 280
Soviet collapse 313
Stalin and Iran 273
supports Greece 184
supports Iraq against Iran 296
Syrian civil war and 333, 337–8,
  349–50
Triple Entente 236
UN Security Council and 335
US Middle East policy and 285–7
withdraws from Afghanistan 309

Sabbah, Hassan-i
  'Assassins' terrorism 98–9
  death of 100
  millenarian sects 110
  seizes Alamut 94
Sabbatai Zevi 164
Sadat, Anwar
  assassination of 293
  Camp David Accords 287
  expels Soviet advisers 282
  rectifying mistakes 282
  Reza Shah and 289

Saddam Hussein 356
  chemical weapons 297–8, 298, 299
  deals with uprisings 312–13
  deputy to al-Bakr 283
  'Desert Storm' Gulf War 309–12
  executes al-Sadr 291
  fall of 320
  first Gulf War 291–3
  Muslim Brotherhood and 303
  personality cult of 297
  supports Syrian Muslim Brotherhood
    292
  toppled 321
al-Sadr, Baqir, ayatollah 291, 322
al-Sadr, Muqtada 322
Safavid dynasty
  Abbas the Great 158–60
  consolidation of 9, 150–2
  division agreed with Ottomans 173–4
  end of 171–2, 174
  ethnic and sectarian diversity 174
  historical perspective of 353
  intercessors of Mahdi 151
  Isma'il I establishes 147–8
  Kizilbachs and 158
  substitutes for hajj 175
  Suleiman turns against 152
  Turkmen and 147
Sahnun, Maliki school and 60
Al-Said/Busaids 169
Sa'id Pasha, Muhammad (1854–1863) 191
Saladin (Yusuf bin Ayyub Salah al-Din)
    (1174–1193) 115
  consolidates power 103–4
  counter-Crusade 104–5
  death of 107
  divides domain for heirs 117
  hegemony and conflict 111
  Kurdish identity 108
  leniency towards Armenians 105
  makes Damascus capital 108
  outcome of Crusades and 128
  religious asceticism and 103
  Syrian bloc and 109
  takes Jerusalem 104

  uncle Shirkuh and 102–3
Salafists 313
Saleh, Ali Abdullah 331, 342
Salih Ismail, sultan (1237–1245) 120–1
Salman al-Saud, king (2015–) 337
Samarra, Abbasid capital 61–2, 77
Saphadin see al-Adil I 'Saphadin', sultan
    (1200–1218)
Sarkis, Élias 286
Sassanid dynasty
  conquest of Yemen 25
  context of civil wars 76
  Ctesiphon and palace 21
  division agreed with Byzantium 173–4
  Khosrow I 22–5
  under Khosrow II 25–8
  long period of rule 41–2
  in Mesopotamia 19–22
  Omar defeats 38, 39
  Shapur II 19–20
  territory of 13
  Zoroastrianism and 3
Saudi Arabia
  1973 oil crisis 284, 304
  aids Saddam's war 296
  attracts immigrants 284
  Bin Laden and 318, 319
  cause of Afghanistan 301
  'Cold War' with Egypt 309
  'Desert Storm' Gulf War and 310–11,
    313
  as dictatorial model 343
  drops oil prices 298
  Egypt and 303
  fear of Muslim Brotherhood 331–2
  George W. Bush and 327
  Ibn Saud and 247–9
  Khalid succeeds Faisal 286–7
  League of Arab States 260
  Muslim Brotherhood and 276
  Nasser's rivalry with Faisal 277–9
  not dominant 5n
  pact with US 309
  population of Riyadh 4
  Roosevelt and oil 260–1

Saudi Arabia (*cont.*)
  Trump and 339
  Wahhabism 167, 208, 231, 304, 354
  Yemen and 342, 352
Sayf ad-Din 101
Second World War
  Afrikakorps versus Allies 259
  events in Middle East 258–61
  Hitler invades Russia 258
  Hitler seizes power 255
  Italian fascists in Libya 255
  Turkey as pro-Germany 253
  Yalta summit 260
Selim I, sultan (1512–1520)
  acquires Medina and Mecca 150
  Egypt and 169
  fights Isma'il 148–9, 173
  legacy of 152
  overthrows family 148
Selim II, sultan (1566–1574)
  domination of the Mediterranean
    155–7
  succession battle with Bayezid 152
Selim III, aultan (1789–1807) 209, 211
Seljuks
  adopt Hanafism 60
  First Crusade and 99
  Mongols and 120, 130
  restoration of 93–4
  Second Crusade 101–2
  Turkish identity and 108
Serbia
  Balkan Wars 227–8
  Ottoman victory 132, 138
  Tsarist Russia and 193
Severus, patriarch of Antioch 18
Sèvres, Treaty of 245–6, 257–8
Al-Shafi'i, Muhammad ibn Idris 61
Shah Mosque, Isfahan 159
Shajar al-Durr, Sultana 8
  de facto rule of 122
  ensures Turanshah's succession 121
Shamil, imam (1834–1859)
  capitulates to France 195
  resists Russia 186

Shamir, Yitzhak
  beginning of intifada 299–300
  excludes PLO from talks 314
Sharon, Ariel 318
  equates Arafat with Bin Laden 320
  fall of the shah 293
  invasion of Lebanon 293
  visits Noble Sanctuary 317
Sherley, Robert 158
Shia Islam
  Abbasid dynasty and 52–8
  Abbasid insurrection 53–4
  ayatollahs 172–3
  Bábism and 215
  Buyids and 75, 91–2
  declared official Iran religion 147–8
  divine right 64
  effect of Iraq war 323–4
  emergence of Sunnism 59–62
  fosters slave revolt 70–1
  Hamid's conversion plans for 220,
    221–2
  Hidden Imam/Mahdi 67–9, 89, 143,
    151–2, 160, 172–3, 291
  imposed on Iran 151
  Iranian ayatollahs 299
  Isma'ilism 67
  Khomeini's revolution 289–91
  Legitimist 67
  messianism 66–9, 74, 124
  notion of imams 66
  origins of 40–1
  Ottoman massacre in Baghdad
    158–9
  Persian constitutionalism and 224
  political quiet 143
  Saddam and 312–13
  Sayf al-Dawla and Syria 84
  as state religion 147
  Sudanese Mahdist leader 194–5
  with Sunnis against Crusaders 99
  in Syria 89
  the twelve imams 68–9
  Twelver dogma 172
  Wahhabi assaults on 208

Zaydites 168
Shiraz, Safavids take 148
Shirazi, Hasan, ayatollah 216, 225
Shirkuh, Second Crusade 102–3
al-Shishakli, General Adib
  fall of 275
  Syrian coup and 270
Sicily
  Fatimids in 81
  Norman conquest 95
Sidon
  fall of 99–100
  Kitbuqa devastates 125
silk trade route
  Aleppo 161
  Middle East as centre 3
Simeon the stylite, Saint 16
Sinan, Mimar 154
el-Sisi, Abdel Fattah
  overthrow of Morsi 333
  repression of 341
Sitt al-Mulk 86
Six-Day War 279–80
slavery
  alliance of self–emancipated 77
  Mamluk trade 121, 132–3
  Zanj uprising 70–1
Social Democrat Hunchakian Party
  221
Society for the Advancement of
  Kurdistan 256
South Yemen 275, 342
Spain
  Al-Andalus 51, 56, 81
  Iraq War and 321
Stalin, Joseph
  Jewish militants in Palestine 261
  support for Israel 265
  troops in Iran 273
State of the Jews, The (Herzl) 198
Sudan
  Britain controls 200
  British crushes insurrection 194–5
Suez Canal
  Britain continues protection 244

building of 191–2
Sufi Islam
  Baktashis 167
  Buyids and 94
  diversity within 167
  fight for Turkmen 141
  Halvertis 167
  Kurds and 256
  Mevlevis 167
  muhasaba 62
  Nasiirand 123
  Nazchabandis 167
  not reined in 172
  Nur ad-Din and 101
  pioneers of 62–3
  prohibited in Turkey 246
  Taymiyyah's attack on 130
Sulayman, caliph (715–17) 51
Suleiman I the Magnificent, sultan
  (1520–1566)
  administration of Egypt 170
  death of 156
  elimination of son 156
  long reign of 152, 153–4
Suleiman II, sultan (1687–1691) 165
Sunni Islam
  Ayyubids and 108
  Buyids and 75, 91
  collected sayings 68
  effect of Iraq war 323–4
  Egypt and 83–4
  emergence of 59–62
  fear of discord 166–7
  founders and prison 65
  four schools of 54, 65
  Hanbali rite 61–2, 88, 92, 169
  Hanifism 60
  Iraqi Ba'athists and 283
  Isma'ili teachings and 83
  last Abbaids and 123, 124
  madrasa in Baghdad 94
  Malikism 60–1
  Ottoman Empire 229
  period of dominance 143
  in Persia 172

Sunni Islam (*cont.*)
  recommendations for women 65
  Seljuk restoration and 93
  Shafiism 61
  with Shias against Crusaders 99
  in Syria 89
  tension under Al-Hakim 87–8
  Yemen and 168
Sykes–Picot Agreement 6, 239, 243
Syria
  1963 coup 277
  2011 uprising 7
  anti-colonial pressure 259–60
  Armenians marched to 240
  attacks Israel with Egypt 283–4
  Ba'ath Party 277–8, 283, 304
  Byzantine rule 11, 84–5
  Christian and Muslim relations 212
  Christian plurality 89
  civil war 332–3, 337–8
  Cold War and 7
  coups in 271
  Crusaders and 99
  Daesh 335–6
  the Druze in 89
  Erdoğan and 326
  First Crusade and 99–100
  First World War sufferings 242
  form of government 47
  France and 181, 243, 265, 355
  French sectarianism 252–3
  'greater Syrian' idea 265
  Kissinger peace efforts 285–6
  Kurds in 257
  long nineteenth century 231
  loses Alexandretta 253
  Madrid peace talks 314
  Mamluks 132–3
  minorities of Islam 243
  Mongols invasion and 125
  Muslim Brotherhood 292
  Nur ad-Din and 109
  under Ottomans 174
  Petra 28
  power games 110–11

  railways 202
  refugees from 332, 341
  rivalries over 5–6
  Russian support 337–8, 349–50
  Saladin and 103–4
  Sassanid occupation 41
  Second Crusade 102–3
  Selim I attacks 148–9
  settlers in rebellious areas 50
  shifting relations 302–3
  al-Shishakli coup 270
  sides with Iran 292, 295–6
  Six-Day War 279–80
  Social Nationalist Party 265
  sultanate with Egypt 6
  Timur attacks 134–5
  Trump withdraws from 339
  Turkey and 332, 338
  UAR and 275–7
  Umayyad control 46–54
  uses chemical weapons 334–5
  Vichy France and 258
  Wahhabism 208
  see also Aleppo; Bilad al-Sham;
    Damascus
Syriac Church 41, 163
Syriac language 21

al-Tabari, Muhammad ibn Jarir, historian
  76
Tabuk, Muhammad and 36–7
Tahmasp I, shah (1524–1576) 150
at-Tahtawi, Rifa'a, *The Gold of Paris*
  210
Takla, Bishara and Sami Takla, *Al-Ahram/
  The Pyramids* 217
Talaat (Mehmed) Pasha (1917–1918) 228
  Armenian genocide 240
  assassination of 241
Talib Abd Manaf, Abu (Muhammad's
  uncle) 33, 34
Tanzania, US embassy attack 319
Tatars, Crimean 166
terrorism
  9/11 attacks 319

the Assassins and 109–10
Black September group 281, 282
Bush's 'war on terror' 319–20
campaign in Europe 336
PFLP hijacks Western planes 281
Tewfik Pasha I, Mohamad (1879–1892) 192
Al-Thani family 195
Theodosius I, emperor (379–395) 12
Theodosius II, emperor (402–450)
  banishes pagans 15
  Nestorian heresy and 17
  Yazdegerd and 21
Theophilus, emperor (829–842) 73
Thousand and One Nights 56–7
Tiberius II Constantine, emperor
  (578–582) 30
Timur the Lame/Tamerlane, Emir
  (1370–1405)
  aggressive expansion of 134–6
  death of 136
  against Ottomans 135–6
  Sunni Islam of 133
tobacco in Persia 216
Toghrul, Sultan (1037–1063) 93
Toynbee, Arnold 202–3
Trebizond, Ottoman seizure of 138
Tripoli
  Crusader state 98
  Fatimid port 85
Truman, Harry S. 309
  Palestine and 261
  Turkey and 272
Trump, Donald
  Israel and 350
  Middle East disengagement 339–40,
    350
Tulunids, Copts and 70
Tuman bay, Al-Ashraf, sultan (1516–1517)
  149
Tunisia
  Arab League headquarters 288
  constitution 207
  democratic uprising 330–1
  Fatimids and 5, 81
  first constitution 214

France 200
  Justinian conquers 23
  Ottoman Empire and 157
  peasants' revolt 214
Turanshah, Al-Malik al-Muazzam, Sultan
  (1249–1250)
  assassination of 122
  death of 122
  Seventh Crusade and 121–3
Turkestan, Russia seizes 193, 200
Turkey
  ambitions of 343
  Ankara's population 4
  anti-USSR 272–3
  Crusades fragment identity 108
  demographics 264
  end of Seljuks 130
  Erdoğan's Libyan revenge 200
  Erdoğan's new approach 326
  Greeks expelled from Izmir 246
  Haftar and 342
  Iran and 352
  joins NATO 272
  Kurdish separatism 246, 256–8
  military hierarchy in 303
  minorities 246
  Muslim Brotherhood and 332
  NATO membership 313, 326
  from Ottoman Empire 245–7
  pact with USSR 246
  PKK and 338
  pro-Germany 253
  safe zones on border 343
  secularist reforms 246–7
  Seljuks in Anatolia 93–4
  Sunni state 246
  Syrian border security zone 332
  Syrian civil war and 338
  UAE and 352
  see also Ottoman Empire
Turkmen
  Aq Qoyunlu/White Sheep 133
  Kizilbachs and 158
  Qara Qoyunlu/Black Sheep 133
  Safavids and 150

Turkmen (*cont.*)
  White Sheep and Black Sheep 141,
    147–8
Tusan Pasha, Ahmed 208
al-Tusi, Nasir al-Din, scientist 123
Tutush, ruler of Damascus (1078–1095)
  94
Tzimiskes, John I, emperor (969–976)
  85, 96

Ukraine
  Mariupol and Aleppo 349
  Russian invasion of 349, 351–2
ulama/scholars 64–5
Umayyad dynasty
  Abbasid revolution and 52–3
  coexistence of 109
  context of civil wars 76–7
  conversion to Islam 36
  in Córdoba 81
  empire of 46–54
  era of 42–54
  expansion of 5
  the Great Discord 40–1
  Hashim and 33
  languages of 50
  legacy of 54
  Muslim battles 35
  Osman and nepotism 39–40
United Arab Emirates
  Abraham Accords 351
  attracts immigrants 284
  blockade of Qatar 339
  Britain occupies 200
  independence of 275
  Iran's nuclear programme 324
  Israel and 343
  'Pirate Coast' 195
  treaty with Israel 340
  Yemen and 342, 352
United Arab Republic 275–6
United Nations
  collapse in credibility 335
  League of Arab States and 260
  Nasser and 279

Palestinian partition plan 261–2
PLO and 285
Syria boycotts 285
United States
  9/11 attacks 109
  1973 oil embargo 284
  aids Saddam against Iran 296
  Arab Revolt and 238–9
  Barbary War 181–3
  Clinton and peace process 326–7
  Cold War Middle East 7
  'Desert Storm' Gulf War 309–12
  devalued voice 335
  disengagement from Middle East 342,
    349–52
  Eisenhower and Iran 273–4
  El-Alamein 259
  enters First World War 238–9
  Iran hostage crisis 290, 293
  Iran nuclear deal 337
  Iran's Islamic Revolution and 225
  Iraq no-fly zone 312
  Iraq War 356
  Israel policy 304, 309
  Israel's attack on Lebanon 295
  kills Bin Laden 329
  neo-conservative prejudices 320
  'new world order' 7
  Obama's 'American and Islam' address
    327–9
  Pax Americana period 285–7
  peace talks 314–18
  post-war anti-colonialist posture
    260–1
  Reagan and Gorbachev 293, 298
  Russia in Afghanistan 301–2
  Saudi pact 309
  Six-Day War and 280
  strikes against Daesh 336
  Suez crisis 274
  Syrian use of chemical weapons 334–5,
    349
  takes Hawaii 196
  Trump's disengagement 339–40, 350
  withdrawal from Afghanistan 351

Al-Urwa al-withqa/The Firmest Bond
   review 217
Uthman *see* Osman
Uzun Hasan, White Sheep Turkman
   141

Vandals sack Rome 13
Venice
   Crete 164–5
   Fourth Crusade against Byzantium
      116–17
   Ottoman rule 138, 156, 165
Victoria, Queen (1837–1901) 193
Visigoths sack Rome 13
viziers, evolution of role 56, 56n
Volney, Comte de 170
Voltaire, on Kamil 118

al-Wahhab, Muhammad ibn Abd 169
Wahhabi Islam 354
   Afghanistan and 301
   in Arabia 183, 201
   criticism of 230
   Ibn Saud and 248–9
   jihad against infidels 129–30, 169
   origins in Hanbalism 62
   Saudi Arabia and 208, 231, 276
   spread of 284
   Sunni and Saudi pact 167
Walid I, caliph (705–717) 50–1
al-Walid, Khalid ibn 37–8
waqf 66
Washington, George 182
water, ancient sources of 4–5
Wilhelm II, emperor (1888–1918)
   tour of Middle East 199–200
   Zionist movement and 198
Wilson, Woodrow
   loss of League of Nations 242
   self-determination principle 239
women
   Amin's *Liberation of Women* 218
   Armenian genocide and 241–2
   free female Muslims 76
   of Middle East 8

rights of 230
Shia/Sunni inheritance 68n
Sunni guidelines for 65
Turkish suffrage 247

Xi Jinping 342

Yaqut, geographer 123
Yassin, Ahmed 316
Yazdegerd, Shah 20–1
Yazid I, caliph (680–683)
   ceremony of allegiance to 46
   Ibn Zubayr and 48–9
   massacres Hussein and family 48
Yazid II, caliph (720–724) 51
Yazidis
   Baghdadi attacks 336
   Iraq War and 323
Yemen
   2011 uprising 7
   Christians in 31, 47
   Egypt and 303
   Houthis and 337
   humanitarian crisis 355
   immigrants from 313–14
   Italy and 200
   Nasser's army in 278
   Ottoman control 167–9
   Portuguese in 168
   Sassanid conquest of 25
   Saudis and 337, 342, 352
   UAE withdraws from 352
   Wahhabism 208
   Zaydites 74, 167–8
Young Turks 226–8
   Arab Nahda and 230–2
Yunus, Pasha, grand vizier 154

al-Zahawi, Jamil Sidqi, poet and
   philosopher 230
Zain al-Abidin, Ibn al-Hussein, imam
   (680–712) 67
Zand dynasty 172
zandaqah 69, 69n
Zangwill, Israel 198

Zanj
  govern southern Iraq 77
  uprising 70–1
Zanzibar
  British imperialism and 195
  Muscat seizes 169
al-Zarqawi, Abu Musab 322
Zayd ibn Ali Imam (714–740) 66, 168
Zaydan, Jurji 217
Zaydites 74
Zaynab bint Ali
  mosque 83
  patron saint of Cairo 83, 83n
Zengi (Imad al-Din), general 100, 101

Zionism
  Balfour Declaration and 239
  birth of 196–9
  founding of Israel 261–4
  immigration pressure 231
  Palestine and 254
Zoroastrianism 292
  Ahura Mazda 20
  Heraclius and desecrations 27
  Islam sees as idolatrous 39
  origins and ideas of 20
  Persian state religion 3
  sacred book Avesta of 20
  Takht-e Soleyman 39